THE WAVES OF TIME

LONG-TERM CHANGE AND INTERNATIONAL RELATIONS

K R DARK

Continuum
London and New York

Continuum, The Tower Building, 11 York Road, London, SE1 7NX
370 Lexington Avenue, New York, NY 10017-6550

First published 1998. Reprinted in paperback 2000

British Library Cataloguing-in-Publication Data
A catalogue record of this book is available from the British Library.

ISBN 1-85567-402-5 (hardback)
0-8264-4762-7 (paperback)

Library of Congress Cataloging-in-Publication Data
(to follow)

Typeset by YHT Ltd, London
Printed and bound in Great Britain by Creative Print and Design Wales, Ebbw Vale

Contents

This book is dedicated
to my Aunt
Amelia Joan Bartlett

Introduction

Since the – largely unexpected – end of the Cold War and the collapse of the Soviet Union, scholars of International Relations have usually seen the study of change as at the core of their concerns.[1] The new significance attached to this topic,[2] which had long been somewhat neglected, has focused attention on those few earlier studies which attempted to understand change and has prompted much new work in this area.[3]

The centrality of understanding how and why changes occur in world politics has also been highlighted by ongoing worldwide processes, such as 'globalization', and by the rapid formation of new states in many parts of Eastern Europe and elsewhere. It is clear both that such changes are of fundamental importance to understanding contemporary world politics, and that their explanation depends – by definition – on theories of change.[4] Likewise, conflicts and wars resulting from long-standing historical divisions, identities and hostilities – as in the former Yugoslavia in the 1990s – have emphasized the role of the past in shaping the present world of international politics. It has become impossible to claim, with any credibility, that the study of the past – even the 'distant' past – is irrelevant to the analysis of modern world politics.

This new interest in the analysis of change has encompassed both 'established' and younger scholars, producing sufficient new work that the study of 'global change' has recently been defined as a distinct sub-discipline within the academic study of world politics.[5] It has, in turn, led to an awareness that the study of global political change requires the analyst to adopt a much longer time-scale than has hitherto been common: to see change over millennia, rather than decades.

So the analysis of change in International Relations has become increasingly synonymous with the study of 'long-term change'. This too has had important consequences for the nature of the study of world politics, because it has necessitated an engagement with new sources of information of types unfamiliar in the analysis of contemporary politics. For example, if medieval and pre-medieval evidence is to be employed, archaeological as well as textual sources may need to be addressed, even when questions of political change are the principal area of interest. It also potentially opens the discipline to a wide range of new theoretical approaches from those subjects where analysing change has long been the central concern.

Adopting a much greater time-depth, and employing a range of sources previously unused in the discipline, an increasing number of studies have attempted to examine how and why large-scale political change occurs.[6] These have both sought their own solutions to this question, and examined some of the answers suggested by other disciplines, especially sociology and economics.[7]

However, not all studies of change (not even those using long time-scales of analysis) agree on the relative significance of long- and short-term modes of analysis. These studies can, therefore, be broadly divided between those which seek to explain change entirely in terms of sequences of short-term events and those which seek to locate contemporary changes in much longer-term frameworks.

This book looks primarily at the second of these perspectives, the long-term approach to change, but seeks to integrate this with the first more closely than has previously been attempted. In so doing, it is, of course, in keeping with the general trend in the discipline – as already mentioned – toward much longer time-scales of analysis.[8]

The 'historical horizon' – once set at AD 1500, 1648, or even 1945 – marking the limits of the temporal scope of International Relations has all but disappeared in most current discussions of change. This is not to say, of course, that all scholars of International Relations have realigned their academic attention so as to focus on issues of change, or on the long-term, nor that they should. However, this is a notable trend in contemporary work in the mainstream of the discipline, with deep-seated implications for the nature of the study of world politics as a whole.

The first chapter, therefore, attempts to introduce these developments by outlining the most important theories of long-term change in International Relations.[9] This is, so far as I am aware, the only published overview of this material as a whole. The second chapter will review, in a similar way, some potentially relevant approaches to the analysis of long-term change deriving from other – arguably related – disciplines. Again, this is the first time such a review has been published. These chapters enable us to recognize that there are similarities between theoretical approaches (relating to this issue) within International Relations and a wide range of cognate fields of academic inquiry. They lead to a discussion, in the third chapter, of the strengths and weaknesses of these 'interdisciplinary' approaches. Such an outline also – as we shall see – prompts discussion of the appropriate epistemology for the analysis of long-term change, and of International Relations in general. So the second part of the third chapter will set out a new epistemology enabling the integration of apparently contrasting perspectives.

Using this new epistemological framework, in the fourth chapter I shall propose a new theory of long-term change, drawing extensively from the theoretical material outlined in the preceding chapters and introducing new concepts and approaches. In the last three chapters, this theory will be used (in a preliminary fashion) to analyse data from both pre-modern and modern contexts. This will serve both to evaluate the credibility of the theory itself, and to apply this new theory to the question of the emergence and large-scale dynamics of contemporary world politics.

In discussing long-term perspectives, however, one must give due regard to shorter-term approaches where these address issues across long time-scales. This highlights the way in which short-term and long-term approaches to the analysis of change may be seen as complementary alternatives, not incompatible opposites.

It must be stressed that, in focusing on the long-term, this book is not written to suggest that short-term analyses of change are invalid or flawed, nor that other forms of thematic study are worthless. Instead, they are seen here as incomplete accounts (as are all accounts) of change, to which a long-term perspective can add a greater understanding of the way in which change takes place and of its character and potential consequences.

The limitations of the reviews that are attempted in the first two chapters must also be noted at the outset. Clearly, a single chapter on either of these subjects is incapable of providing a complete catalogue, or a fully rounded discussion, of all such approaches. Theories are necessarily simplified by précis in such a context. Two chapters cannot, therefore, set out the full depth and richness of each approach, but simply offer an introduction to previous work on the subject. These chapters should, then, be read in that context.

All these approaches could be, and in many cases have been, discussed in whole books focusing on one theory alone. Instead of trying to undertake such a futile task as to give full accounts of these perspectives in a few paragraphs, I shall simply discuss a broad sample of existing approaches in sufficient detail to illustrate and introduce the range of theoretical perspectives employed, and to highlight differences between them. Fuller accounts are, of course, available in the references cited, to which I refer the reader who wishes to understand more fully any specific approach mentioned here. If, at first, such a review seems a surprising way to begin a book presenting new research, it will become clear that it is essential in order to understand later chapters, especially as these draw extensively on theoretical concepts unfamiliar, perhaps, to many analysts of International Relations.

In order to present as concisely as possible the range of current perspectives on long-term change found in International Relations theory, I have divided them into 'schools'. These are based on the presence or absence of shared theoretical characteristics such as 'state-centricity'.

All that is meant by schools is 'groups of scholars sharing common approaches', rather than implying any perceived theoretical unity or common cause. All of these exhibit a high degree of diversity, which can of course be only partly 'captured' in a brief overview. The 'schools' are then further grouped under broad conventional headings based on their underlying principles and units of analysis.[10]

It is clear that the divisions between these schools and paradigms are often less clear-cut than it is possible to indicate briefly. Nevertheless, I hope that this review represents each viewpoint (and the range of approaches overall) fairly, even if complete 'scholarly objectivity' is considered logically impossible.

This book as a whole is intended to serve four distinct purposes, forming themes throughout the work. First, it may provide an introduction to the study of long-term change – and to some extent of change in general – in International Relations. Second, it is intended to introduce into the debate a range of new theoretical material from other disciplines. Its third purpose is to set out and conduct a preliminary application of a new theory of change, and the fourth is to offer a new provisional interpretation of large-scale world political development from the earliest governed societies to the present. It is these last two purposes which form the basis and the rationale for this book. By presenting new research, this work is intended as a contribution to theoretical and other debates on the analysis of long-term change.

However, there are some issues of definition which must be addressed at the outset. Any study of long-term political change immediately begs the question of what is meant by the terms 'long-term' and 'political change'. By the former, I mean change seen on a long time-scale, that of millennia, rather than the scale of decades and centuries. There are several equally valid ways to conduct 'long-term analysis' in International Relations, and many topics which one might choose to examine with these. One might, for instance, write a long-term narrative history of world politics, or conduct a comparative study using long-term data. Both approaches have been employed to some effect. Alternatively, as here, attention may be focused on examining the underlying processes (by which I mean 'modes of change') existing in both the past and the present.

In discussions of global history in general, the existence of such processes – as more than simply sequences of events – has been generally accepted in scholarly debate. A clear example is the process of 'urbanization'. This may be discussed with reference to many different times and places and be seen to produce very different sequences of events, but it is still identifiable as a general process ('mode of change') operating on a global scale rather than simply the sum of heterogenous sequences of events.

In this book the focus is also on large-scale political change. By 'political change' I mean the origin, growth, decline, cessation or reorganization of political systems, structures and units at any level of analysis from the intra-state group to the global system. I also mean the generation, modification or cessation of those events and processes which cause these changes. When referring to 'large-scale political change' I do not mean change which is necessarily especially geographically extensive. Instead I refer to that which is 'fundamental', in that it affects the very character of polities and of international relationships. Examples of such change are the transition from non-state to state societies, and the emergence and collapse of international systems.

Consequently, a long-term study of the processes of large-scale political change, as discussed here, is a long-term perspective on the underlying processes of fundamental change of this sort. It will be argued that such processes of change are most clearly visible in a long-term view, while they are usually imperceptible in short-term studies.

In order to approach questions of this historical scale in a theoretically-informed manner, the debate will encompass perspectives from many disciplines. The analysis and examples given use data from many historical periods and regions of the world. I owe an ability to use this approach to two factors. First, the opportunity to discuss aspects of this work with specialists in several fields – philosophers, historians, sociologists, archaeologists, anthropologists, economists, geographers and biologists, as well as political scientists. Secondly, without professional training as an archaeologist and historian, alongside other formal training in anthropology, sociological and biological theory and mathematics, prior to working professionally in International Relations, I doubt if I would ever have been willing to undertake such a wide-ranging study.

In this book I shall draw both directly and indirectly on all these aspects of what may be a unique background for a scholar of International Relations. My gratitude to many colleagues, ranging across several academic fields, must therefore be especially noted especially Anthea Harris, who read and commented on the whole text. These have all assisted this work, whether by their teaching, informal discussions, provision of published and unpublished material, or encouragement, over more than a decade. In alphabetical order, they include: Professors J. Bell, L. Binford, M. Casson, I. Clark, D. Dumville, A. Giddens, I. Hodder, E. James, E. Jones, A. Lowe, M. McGwire, P. Rahtz, C. Renfrew, S. Strange, P. Taylor, S. Van der Leeuw, E. Zubrow; Drs C. Balim, G. Edwards, C. Hope, J. McGlade, J. Muke and C. Wyatt; and Messrs J. Forsyth and P. Towle. I am also grateful to my colleagues while a fellow of Clare Hall, University of Cambridge, and all my colleagues and students at the University of Reading. It has been invaluable to be able to use the libraries of Cambridge, Oxford, London and Reading Universities and of the Royal Institute of International Affairs in London.

Special thanks are also due to Abigail Buckle, Mark Zacher, Barry Jones and Jack Spence, for generously providing both help and much encouragement at various times while I was writing this book, as well as in relation to other aspects of my work. As ever, my greatest gratitude is of course to my wife and family for their assistance and encouragement throughout this research. None of the above should, however, be held responsible in any way for either the views, or any errors, contained in this book.

Notes

1   For an excellent discussion of attempts to cope with that change in International Relations theory: Kegley, C. W., 1994, 'How did the Cold War die? Principles for an autopsy', *Mershon International Studies Review* 38.1, 11-41. See also: Cox, M., 1994, 'Rethinking the end of the Cold War', *Review of International Studies* 20, 187-200; Hopf, T., 1993, 'Getting the end of the Cold War wrong', *International Security* 18, 202-15; Allan, P. and Goldmann, K. (eds), 1992, *The End of the Cold War: Evaluating Theories of International Relations*, Dordrecht; Mastanduno, M., Lake, D. A. and Ikenberry, G. J., 1989, 'Toward a realist theory of state action', *International Studies Quarterly* 33, 457-74; Collins R. and Waller, D., 1992, 'What theories predicted the state breakdowns and the revolutions of the Soviet bloc?', *Research in Social Movements, Conflicts and Change* 14, 31-47.

2   For example: Rosenau, J. N., 1992, 'Governance, order and change in world politics', in J. N. Rosenau and E-O. Czempiel (eds), *Governance Without Government: Order and Change in World Politics*, 1-29; Richardson, J., 1994, 'History strikes back: the state of International Relations theory', *Australian Journal of Political Science* 29.1, 179-84; Harris, A. L., 1996, 'Long term perspectives in International Relations theory, the United States and the end of the Cold War', *Contemporary Political Studies* 1, 13-20; Czempiel E.-O. and Rosenau J. N. (eds), 1989, *Global Changes and Theoretical Challenges*, Lexington Books, Lexington, MA; Ruggie, J. G., 1997, *International Transformations*.

3   Little, R., 1994, 'International Relations and large-scale historical change', in A. J. R. Groom and M. Light (eds), *Contemporary International Relations: A Guide to Theory*, 9-26. For an interesting case study: Ray J. L., 1989, 'The abolition of slavery and the end of international war' *International Organization* 43, 405-440

4   For a recent critical review of globalization: Jones, R. J. B., 1995, *Globalization and Interdependence in the International Political Economy*

5   Dark, K. R., 1996, 'Defining global change', in B. Holden, (ed.), *The Ethical Dimensions of Global Change*, 8-19

6   Even in the title of, perhaps, its most famous contemporary textbook: Kegley, C. W. and Wittkopf, E. R., 1995, *World Politics: Trend and Transformation*, 5th edn., New York. Although even relatively 'conservative' sub-disciplines, such as international history, have shared this new interest: Lynn, J.A., 1996, 'The evolution of army style in the modern West 800-2000', *The International History Review* 18.3, 505-545; Brands H.W., 1992, 'Fractal history, or Clio and the chaotics', *Diplomatic History*, 495-510

7   Little, R., 1994, 'International Relations and large-scale historical change', in A. J. R. Groom and M. Light (eds), *Contemporary International Relations: A Guide to Theory*, 9-26. Not all such studies have derived their theory wholly from these sources: Walker, R. B. J., 1989, 'History and structure in the theory of international relations', *Millennium* 18.2, 163-83; Kratochwil, F., 1986, 'Of systems, boundaries and territoriality: an enquiry into the formation of the state system', *World Politics* 39.1, 27-52

8   Kegley, C. W. and Wittkopf, E. R., 1995, *World Politics. Trend and Transformation*, 5th edn., New York, 4-5, 35-8 and 104-6. See also Little, R., 1994, 'International Relations and large-scale historical change', in A. J. R. Groom

and M. Light (eds), *Contemporary International Relations: A Guide to Theory*, 9-26. Although not all such studies adopt a long-term view: Hammond G. and Shaw B.P., 1995, 'Conflict, the rise of nations, and the decay of states: the transformation of the international system?', *Journal of Conflict Studies* 15.1, 5-29

9   In this book I shall use the term 'International Relations' to refer to the analysis of world politics, and the terms 'world politics', 'international politics', and 'international relations' synonymously to refer to global politics. By this latter term I mean the politics of human communities worldwide whether examined in local, regional or larger geographical scope. Thus these variations in terminology should not, here, be read to indicate changes in emphasis. Likewise, by 'theory' I mean only a body of concepts forming a framework of analysis.

10 For their approach to International Relations theory, see, for example: Viotti, P. R. and Kauppi, M. V., 1993, *International Relations Theory. Realism, Pluralism and Globalism*, 2nd. edn., New York; Brown, C., 1997, *Understanding Intenational Relations*; Little, R. and Smith, M. (eds), *Perspectives on World Politics: A Reader*.

1

Beyond the horizon: theories of long-term change in International Relations

Introduction

There have long been scholars in International Relations who saw the importance of analysing change, including long-term change.[1] This point was, for example, made on theoretical grounds in volumes edited by Buzan, Jones and Holsti.[2] But it was probably the changes of the late 1980s and early 1990s – as already mentioned – which made this form of analysis seem a disciplinary imperative.[3] It must, however, be stressed that this represented a dramatic 'return of history' to a discipline which had become somewhat 'de-historicized' in the course of the twentieth century.[4] There had been created a 'historical horizon' at AD 1500 beyond which few scholars dared venture. A question which earlier scholars highlighted, and which remains fundamental to any study of world political change, are the issues of both the temporalities of study and the various ways in which 'change' can be defined and described.

Types of change and of modes of analysis

A definition of the term 'political change' has already been given, but before discussing International Relations' theoretical perspectives on the analysis of long-term change, it may be worth examining some more general points regarding the ways in which change can be analysed.

Change can be analysed in terms of 'events' (temporally discrete happenings), structures (frameworks of action), or processes (modes or types of change).[5] It can be analysed in a comparative synchronic ('same time') or diachronic ('through time') fashion, or in terms of diachronic continuities and discontinuities.[6] Some scholars have sought to differentiate between 'transformation' and 'change' in qualitative terms, but here no such definition will be employed.

The use of 'history' has likewise been an area of debate. History can be taken to refer either to the past (that is, all time prior to the present) or, more specifically, to the reconstruction of the past through its written remains. History in the former sense can be used as analogy, framework or theme; it can be event, structure or process. Processes and structures can be 'historically specific' (existing at a specific time) or 'transhistorical' (existing across different periods of time).

Scales of analysis also play a crucial role in deciding how analysis will take place. Such scales can be temporal, geographical or in terms of more conventional International Relations theorists' 'levels of analysis'.[7] Decisions regarding each of these questions will provide the bases for contrasting approaches to the understanding of change in International Relations.

Similarly, classic problems of International Relations theory still apply to this, as to other areas of study. Most of all, there is the question of the unit of study, whether one focuses (for example) on the state, the individual or the global system. Alternatively, as here, one might try to integrate all of these by relating the study of one to the others.

Leaver has pointed out[8] that it is sometimes hard to draw clear lines between contrasting paradigms of International Relations; but it is generally supposed that one can classify International Relations theory into several broad categories. These are often defined as the Realist, Pluralist and Structuralist (also sometimes called Globalist) paradigms.[9]

This conventional framework for subdividing International Relations theory has obvious shortcomings, given the diversity of approaches represented within these over-arching paradigmatic groupings. But it provides a structure for discussing existing perspectives on long-term change in International Relations theory which can be used in this chapter. This must, of course, be prefaced also by the note that it might be possible to place a theory or theorist in one of two or more of the paradigms discussed, simply by giving more or less importance to specific aspects of their work. To these paradigms must, however, be added what may be broadly defined as a postmodernist paradigm.

International Relations theory and long-term change

International Relations theorists have been most concerned with long-term analyses as means of discussing the emergence and decline of states and international systems in the global arena, and in the study of war-origins. Similarly, long-term approaches have been employed to examine nationalism, economic growth and decline, the formation of national identity and the role of the environment.

International Relations has also had to explore the possibilities of long-term analysis while engaged in theoretical debate, involving the competition between a range of, often seemingly mutually exclusive, viewpoints.[10] These paradigms offer contrasting views on the understanding of world politics and carry with them differing views of long-term political change.

In view of the importance of Realism in the history of International Relations theory, I shall begin by discussing Realist approaches to the analysis of long-term change.[11] Perspectives encompassed within the Pluralist, Structuralist (or Globalist) and post-modernist paradigms will then be examined.

The inclusion of several distinct Realist theories here is a testimony to the deep-seated theoretical differences between classical Realism and other Realist analyses, and to the richness of the Realist tradition of International Relations theory. While classical Realism all but denied change, except in historical-particularist terms, neo-Realism and structural Realism encompass several scholars who have attempted a Realist approach to long-term change. Thus, their work has produced a rich Realist tradition of writing about change, and especially long-term change.[12]

Realism and long-term change

The classical Realist school of International Relations analysis as found in the work of Carr or Morgenthau, emphasizes that change occurs in international systems which are state-centric and anarchical.[13] By the anarchical system, Realists mean that there is no 'world government' overseeing the actions of states.[14] In classical Realist analyses, the state is seen as the primary actor in this anarchical system, and the international system is viewed as no more than a composite of states, and institutions designed to serve their needs.[15] According to classical Realist theories of change, the international system exhibits the same characteristics with regard to change in each period of its existence, at least since the Treaty of Westphalia in 1648.

The principal characteristics of the international system in the classical Realist view are that states compete and each state tries to maximize its advantages in relation to others.[16] This is said to be true of all periods in history, and a range of allegedly transhistorical mechanisms (such as 'the balance of power'), which are supposed to assist this, have been identified.[17] Change, therefore, occurs as the result of competition deriving from the self-interests of states, which conflict and converge in a variety of configurations. These configurations are seen by classical Realists as both historically specific and without general patterning. Yet classical Realism sees the basis of change (the conflict and coincidence of interests between states) as itself unchanging.[18] Without world government, and while there are nation-states, in the Realist view this continual process of inter-state competition will continue unchanged. So in classical Realism there is change only in the details of which states gain pre-eminence and which fail to achieve their aims.[19]

Today, classical Realism has many critics, but neo-Realism and structural Realism remain widespread approaches to International Relations.[20] Neo-Realism is the combination of a Realist stance with structuralist elements.[21] Waltz argued that the principal change in the international system over several centuries was a shift to bipolarity after World War II, and stressed 'unit-level' processes.[22] To Waltz, the 'units' in question are states 'whose, interactions form the structure of international political systems', and which are, in his opinion, functionally identical. Like classical Realists, Waltz is greatly interested in the capabilities of states, which he acknowledges are unequal, and sees the relationships between them (the Realist 'balance of power') in terms of the distribution of capabilities. Waltz's views have been both very influential and controversial in International Relations theory, but here, it is important to recognize that Waltz introduced a greater diachronic dimension, although hardly a theory of long-term change, into Realist analysis.

Recently, Waltz has reiterated his view that long-term change for the neo-Realist is essentially a question of the rise and fall of 'great powers': the dominant states with the inter-state system. As he writes, 'for more than three hundred years the drama of modern history has turned on the rise and fall of great powers'.[23]

Waltz's neo-Realism is arguably less concerned with change than that of two other contemporary scholars working within a Realist framework of analysis: Gilpin and Modelski. Both can be classified as 'structural Realists' rather than neo-Realists, but both are firmly within the state-centric tradition to which Waltz also belongs.

In Gilpin's opinion, the international system contains 'elements of in-stability', whether it is multipolar or bipolar, and Gilpin sees the system as liable to fluctuation due to small variations in context, a view akin to non-linear dynamics based theories of change in mathematics.[24] Gilpin does not, however, derive his theory from non-linear dynamics but from the applica-tion of structural Realism to long-term history and long-term economic history.[25]

Gilpin's view, like that of Waltz, is based on Realist theory; and like Waltz, Gilpin seeks an accommodation with structural theory.[26] Gilpin is, however, far more willing than is Waltz to envisage change within the international system which goes beyond the rise and fall of 'great powers'. For instance, he sees a key cause of change being that states 'attempt to change the international system if the expected benefits exceed the expected costs': the Realist concept of 'self-interest' in action.

Alongside his use of elements of Realist theory, Gilpin's basis for analys-ing change incorporates 'rational choice theory', which stresses optimization and market factors in explaining change. These combine conveniently with his Realist view in estimating the 'cost–benefit' analysis of state-actors in their manoeuvres in international political competition.

To Gilpin, the international system is stable so long as 'nobody rocks the boat'; and no-one is inclined to do so if the benefits to be gained are less than the expected costs. The system is, however, liable to change as the economic costs of stability rise faster than can be maintained. This, Gilpin argues, destabilizes the system, so that, because of destabilization, the system will change. Despite the importance placed on economics in his model, Gilpin

considers that political factors lie behind change, employing political explanation rather than adopting a materialist view. A principal aspect of this
political analysis is the importance which he places on war as a causal factor
in global political change. These political factors must also be seen in the
context of the economic dimensions of Gilpin's model.

Gilpin uses economics to build a diachronic framework, or structure, for
the rise and fall of states. This he envisages as cyclical, extending throughout
the 2400-year span of Western history analysed by him. Gilpin sees the result
of economic and political changes in terms of a cycle of expansion,
equilibrium, confrontation and decline. In this view, economic factors mean
that 'the growth of every society . . . [by which Gilpin means 'state'] follows
' . . . an S-shaped curve'.

In this pattern of the rise and fall of 'great powers', Gilpin sees as a constant
the emergence and collapse of hegemonies based on the pre-eminence of a
single state. In this way, Gilpin produces a long-term structural Realist
theory which accounts not only for inter-state competition but also for the
emergence and disappearance of state actors and their relative importance at
any given period in history. Gilpin's view is, therefore, similar in many
respects to that of the Structuralist theorists, in that he stresses both
economic factors and the role of hegemony in long-term political change,
but he stands separate from Structuralist theorists in his emphasis on the state
and in the role which he assigns to both war and inter-state competition.

Close to Structuralist analysis also, but again within the structural Realist
tradition, is Modelski's theory of long-term political change.[27] Modelski also
takes a view which combines economic and political factors and is state-
centric. Like Gilpin, Modelski accepts a Realist notion of hegemony and
places great importance on war as a key means of change in international
politics.

Modelski's view is that international politics is essentially cyclical.[28]
Modelski has not usually adopted such a long time-scale for his studies as that
used by Gilpin, although he has been extending his studies to earlier periods
of history in an ongoing research programme.[29] In what may be described as
its 'classic' form, Modelski's analysis depends on the study of the period since
AD 1500. This date was seen by him as representing the origin of the modern
international system.

In Modelski's interpretation, during the period since 1500 there have
been four stages of international political history, in each of which one state
has been dominant. The transitions between these stages have been marked
by major wars, after which the principal victor has been able to reshape the
international system to the victor's advantage. The basis for these cycles is
the difficulties faced by a hegemon when confronted with new competitors
and unbearable costs in maintaining its own position in the system. Thus,
states rise and fall from pre-eminence, as in Gilpin's view, on both political
and economic grounds, and according to Realist concepts of inter-state
competition and the search for dominance.

Recently, both Modelski and Gilpin have been exploring ways of relating 'long cycle' and economic approaches through the application of evolutionary theory.[30] This has led Modelski to suggest that world politics and the world economy have 'co-evolved', and to adopt a much longer time-scale of analysis.

Alternatively, one might see the 'power transition' theorists of war-origins as state-centric analysts of long-term change, albeit with reference to limited, although important, questions of the causes of war.[31] The work of the leading exponent of this approach, Organski, will serve to exemplify 'power transition' theory.[32] Organski argues that 'great-power' wars are most likely to occur at phases of change between the relative 'power' (seen in Realist terms) of states. To support this view Organski and others adopting this perspective draw upon comparative historical studies, looking for patterns confirming or refuting their theory.

'Power transition theory' must be separated from the sociologically-based 'power cycle theory' proposed by Doran. Doran's theory suggests that states and inter-state systems are driven into patterns of rise and decline by economic factors, which change relative capabilities between states within a system, and so prompt differing forms of action. As such, Doran's view stands distinct from those of Organski, Modelski and Gilpin, but is still within the Realist paradigm.

Another state-centric view, if it may be so classified, which addresses the question of long-term political change in an explicit fashion, is that employed by Cox.[33] While sometimes described as Realist, Cox's view of Realism is so modified by Marxist and other elements as to make it, in my opinion, at most only partly Realist in character. It may be useful, however, to introduce it in this section for two reasons. First, it clearly represents an alternative way of linking economics to a state-based approach to that employed by Gilpin and Doran. Secondly, it illustrates the difficulties of defining even the boundaries of Realism and Structuralism, seemingly fundamentally different in basis.

Cox divided the analysis of the international system into a series of sets: production, the form of the state, and structures of 'world order', but arguably made his Realist orientation clear by stressing that 'states undoubtedly act with a certain autonomy'. Cox's approach was hardly that of a conventional Realist, however, as he argued that the definition between states and markets is illusory. However, Cox has placed his own work fully in the Structuralist paradigm and this aspect of his studies is discussed further below – clearly illustrating the fluidity of these conventional divisions.

Most recently, and very firmly within the structural Realist approach, Buzan and Little have developed a major research programme on the long-term analysis of the inter-state system.[34] This applies a straightforwardly structural Realist perspective to both state and non-state societies, emphasizing both the role of external factors in causing change and the centrality of the 'structural differentiation of units'. This latter point is based on the view that the international system and its units are mutually constituted; as the structure of its units changes, so does the international system.

This programme might be seen as building upon the work published by these scholars and Charles Jones, in their book *The Logic of Anarchy*[35], which sought to free Realism from many of the potential criticisms of neo-Realism. This work itself might be claimed to be one of the most theoretically sophisticated studies of long-term political change within the Realist tradition, combining as it does detailed theoretical discussions with empirical analyses. Here change features as a major component of a structural Realist study, and the temporal span of analysis stretches far beyond that employed by Modelski, Doran or Waltz. In their analysis Buzan, Jones and Little hoped to add three factors to structural Realist understandings of change. These factors comprise: the disaggregation of 'power' into its components, as they see these; the incorporation of the concept of functional differentiation referred to above; and the acknowledgment of a greater role for 'interaction capacity'. The last was defined as interaction between external factors (such as technological diffusion) and political units. To these they add the concept that the international system long comprised separate sub-systems which only coalesced into a single whole with the expansion of Europe. They then attempt to integrate these views with a world historical perspective on the development of the inter-state system.[36]

This attempt to reformulate neo-Realism to encompass change has, perhaps, been among the most successful, but it is not the only attempt to examine change in a Realist framework following the end of the Cold War, and its impact on Realist theory.[37] An extensive Realist literature has developed on the end of the Cold War and the emerging international system, perhaps in part due to the widely perceived failure of Realist scholars to anticipate either the Cold War's end or the collapse of the USSR.[38] While some Realists felt it necessary to address the shortcomings of Realism and the relationship between Realist theory and 'historical reality' (in Schroeder's terms)[39], many felt that this was unnecessary. They have argued that Realism still offers adequate explanations of change in international politics based on short-term factors and Realist theory alone.

Mearsheimer, for instance, has argued that these events can be adequately explained in what might be described as 'unreconstructed' classical Realist logics of inter-state competition and shifts in polarity, accompanying the rise and fall of 'great powers' in inter-state competition.[40] Alternatively, Layne has proposed that a neo-Realist framework still fits the current international system, and that differential economic, technological and military growth and international anarchy explain the rise of 'great powers', which by their emergence then impact upon the structure of the international system.[41] Neither feels it necessary to take a long-term perspective to explain the end of the Cold War or the subsequent changes in international politics. This serves to remind us that not all Realists have become convinced of the value of longer-term perspectives or of the need to revise Realist theory to give more centrality to change. It also shows that the 'three traditions' of Realism still remain active today.[42]

Although it can be debated whether the 'English School' of International Relations theory may correctly be classified as 'Realist', this is another state-centric approach to world politics. Despite the call for its 'closure' at the start of the 1980s,[43] this school has produced a literature on long-term change in the 1990s. Especially notable is the important book by Adam Watson *The Evolution of International Society*.[44] Set clearly within the 'English School' tradition of 'soft', almost Pluralistic, state-centricity this work examines the operation of inter-state systems over thousands of years, tracing patterns of change back to the earliest European inter-state system in ancient Mesopotamia. Watson's method of analysing this material is to apply standard 'English School' theoretical concepts (such as 'International Society') to pre-modern state systems and to concentrate on the way in which inter-state systems were organized in the past. In this fashion, Watson produces a long-term comparative history of the international system, which relates closely to 'English School' approaches to contemporary international politics.

Interestingly, other 'English School' theorists, during the same period, have noted strong links between their conceptual basis and that of neo-liberals in the USA.[45] This tends to highlight the way in which the 'English School', despite containing such well-known theorists of 'power politics', 'anarchy' and the state-centric approach as Bull and Wight, can also be seen to relate to Pluralism.[46]

An alternative 'Realist' approach, which places very great importance on non-state factors, is the 'civilizational' Realism of Samuel Huntington.[47] Huntington argues that the post-Cold War period will see the prominence of cultural and religious cleavages in world politics. These, he suggests, will form the basis for new patterns of conflict which will be merely the latest chapter in an age-old 'clash of civilizations'. Huntington's approach is relevant here, because he not only takes a long-term view but believes that structural context of state action can emerge over extremely long time-spans. Huntington's model is, therefore, one of continuity and structure but with these factors employed within a Realist tradition of analysis. So, he too may be seen as representing the less 'statist' side of Realist theory and yet fully within the tradition of Realism, which sees an essentially unchanging set of systemic constraints limiting state behaviour and deriving from system-level factors.

Also on the borders of Pluralism and Realism is Spruyt's theory of 'Institutional Selection'.[48] This is a stage-centric approach, but one which sees the state as operating in a structural context which also contains important institutional actors. These will be 'selected' by evolutionary processes and surviving institutions will play an important part in the formation of new international systems. Like many Pluralists, he believes that the state may be in decline as a type of political organization. However, his approach is focused on historicizing the state and the issue of sovereignty. This approach might be compared with Cederman's analysis of states and nations as complex adaptive ecological systems, within a context of formal modelling.[49] This too uses some Realist elements, but encompasses many non-state actors.

Pluralism and long-term change

Pluralism, and in contemporary International Relations theory this has generally meant 'neo-liberalism', has tended to place much more explicit importance on theories of change. Pluralists have also been interested in the study of long-term change. This is unsurprising, because theorists working in this school have tended to use theories of change to support core concepts of their theory of international politics in general. Many neo-liberal theories, such as interdependence, regime theory, the triumph of free-market economics and democracy and the decline of the nation-state, are based on historical interpretations.[50] All of these rest on an analysis of change on different grounds to those used by Realist scholars. Pluralists, in general, have been far more willing to consider the possibility that the rate of change and the basic parameters of international politics might also change over time.

In some cases very explicit long-term generalizations have underlain neo-liberal theory, for example in 'Democratic Peace' theory.[51] So, Pluralism – and especially neo-liberalism – is already very closely allied to specific views of long-term change.

It is not unexpected, then, that we can identify some characteristically Pluralist perspectives on the long-term in International Relations theory. First and foremost in the neo-liberal understanding of long-term political change must be considered the theory of progress.[52] Neo-liberals vary over whether progress is seen as a constant or discontinuous process, and over whether progress exists in reality or only potentially, but agree that progress is a diachronic process.

This emphasis on progress has taken the form of an explicit or implicit theory of global development, in which history is seen as moving toward the triumph of liberal values and democracy. This view is exemplified by Fukuyama's notion of an 'end to history'. This 'end' – represented by the 'triumph of liberal democracy' – presumes a highly directional mode of change throughout human history.[53] However, not all neo-liberal scholars take such a unidirectional view of political development.

Similar views of long-term change lie behind Pluralist interpretations of the changing role of international institutions.[54] The view that institutions are becoming ever more important in international affairs also rests upon long-term historical perspectives, although these are seldom explicitly set out.

In general, Pluralists, and especially neo-liberals, have seen change as closely connected to economic factors such as the growth of economic integration, transnational linkages and interdependencies, and the emergence of 'regimes'.[55] Interdependence and Regime theories have been used to understand how change comes about in contemporary international economic relations. Krasner has suggested, for example, that 'disasters' or 'crises' prompt changes leading to the formation of new international 'regimes' (voluntary agreements or conventions) to alleviate resulting problems. These are then maintained until further, insuperable, problems occur. Regime theory can also, of course, be applied to changes in non-economic activities, or even to intra-state co-operation.

Economic perspectives on change have, therefore, played a large role in neo-liberal theories of international politics. However, neo-liberals have been more willing than Realists to assign a key causal role to cognitive factors in producing change in international politics. This approach is widely found in Pluralist studies of change, for example in the work of Ernst Haas.[56] It is exemplified by the neo-liberal view that importance has to be given to the role of changing 'epistemic communities' – communities of knowledge – in promoting political change. This view, associated with the work of Peter Haas,[57] assigns to cognitive factors a causal role unlike that which would be envisaged by Realist scholars. It places the focus on perception and communication rather than on economics or military technology.

Perhaps the best-known Pluralist study of change, however, is that of James Rosenau, set out in his book *Turbulence in World Politics*.[58] The explanation of change in international politics, Rosenau argues, is that there is a clear linkage between small-scale (micro-level) action and large-scale (macro-level) change. Drawing on the concepts of 'complexity theory' in mathematics and physics, he takes the analogy of weather systems to compare with international political systems. This provides him with the term 'turbulence' to describe the unusual levels of both complexity and dynamism found in contemporary world politics. These perspectives enable him to suggest that international politics exhibit both 'evolutionary' (gradual) changes and 'breakpoint' (more sudden) changes. He also argues that some forms of transhistorical generalizations about the nature of global political change are possible.

Attaching importance to changes in the analytical skills of individuals and to their allegiances, Rosenau centres his analysis on the individualistic level. This approach then permits the linkage of multiple levels of analysis, including, but not centred on, the state.

Rosenau has elaborated his views into a wide-ranging theory of change, incorporating ancillary concepts such as 'cascading interdependence', based on fast-changing patterns of interaction among both political entities and resources. These give him the conceptual tools for analysing change without reference to the confines of state-centricity or reliance upon economic factors alone. Rosenau's work is one of the most sophisticated analyses of change yet to come from the Pluralist tradition. It exhibits both theoretical sophistication and an elegant ability to encompass differing form and tempos of change within the same theoretical framework.

John Lewis Gaddis, from his standpoint as an international historian, has adopted a somewhat similar approach to the analysis of change. Both he and Rosenau make use of recent advances in the mathematical theory of complexity, and conceptual changes with evolutionary biology.[59] In a series of important recent writings about the analysis of change and the end of the Cold War, Gaddis has noted that evolutionary biologists, mathematicians, and physicists share many of the same theoretical perspectives as historians in their analysis of change. He stresses the role of narrative and contingency in these, and calls for the rejection of the outdated views of both science and history held by some International Relations theorists.[60]

Gaddis draws attention to what he describes (by analogy with geology) as 'tectonics', by which he means underlying factors and change as based on underlying 'processes that lie outside our normal range of perception'.[61] These processes result from the combination of varying factors and operate over long time-spans, being hard to reverse once set in motion. Gaddis combines this understanding of underlying historical processes with a cyclical approach to change. Unlike Modelski, however, Gaddis claims that, as cycles might themselves be modified as a result of changes taking place, they can only be thought of in a generalized and almost impressionistic fashion.

Rosenau and Gaddis provide us with a very clear outline of what one might describe as a Pluralist theory of long-term change. The work of these scholars shares sufficient common ground that, despite their differing viewpoints, it may serve as a contrast with that of Realists such as Gilpin, Buzan, Little, Modelski and Doran.

However, Pluralism and neo-liberalism are not synonymous, even if neo-liberalism is today the dominant Pluralist perspective, and a wide diversity of perspectives is encompassed within this paradigm also.[62] The 'world society' approach of John Burton also employs a Pluralist paradigm to analyse international affairs.[63] 'World society' approaches tend to build from the definition of patterns of interaction and employ these to define the global system as a whole.[64] Change is addressed by historical analysis, charting the development of patterns of interaction in a historical–particularist or evolutionary fashion.

There are many similarities between 'world society' perspectives on change and those of the neo-liberals. Proponents of this view, like Haas and Rosenau, have endeavoured to adopt an individualistic approach, in their case one more explicitly incorporating the analysis of 'human needs', which are characterized through an explicit 'needs theory'.[65] This search for the satisfaction of needs relates closely to the individualistic outlook of 'world society' analysts. To quote Burton: 'the individual must be the unit of analysis, because it is human needs that ultimately have to be catered for in the interest of public policy at all levels'.[66]

While the concentration on the individualistic level of analysis is perhaps the most striking similarity between 'world society' theory and neo-liberalism, these features are not the only similarities between neo-liberal and 'world society' approaches to change. For example, 'world society' theorists assign a lesser role to conflict in producing change than would Realists, and stress the role of political co-operation. However, the diversity of approaches adopted by such analysts must be emphasized: compare for instance the work of Zurn and Lipschutz with that of Schmidt, Breitmeier and Janicke and Weidner.[67] 'World society' theory has been actively developed in recent years by scholars such as Siegelberg, Luhmann and List. The approach adopted by these scholars differs in detail, from Luhmann's 'systems theory' perspective to List's emphasis on the individual and inter-action as bases of analysis.

These are, however, not the only Pluralists working outside mainstream neo-liberalism. For example, Cerny's *The Changing Architecture of Politics*.[68] attempts to examine the issue of change from a structurationist perspective, and on a transnational global scale reminiscent of that which might otherwise be found mostly among Structuralist analysts, disaggregating the state in a Pluralist manner and stressing the ways in which the character of states is changing in the contemporary international situation.

Cerny has much in common with other Pluralist analysts: the emphasis on individualistic agency, the lack of a unitary model of the state, and an interpretation of current global changes emphasizing the fundamental trans-formation of the state structure. Yet he places far greater importance on the state as a unit of analysis than many Pluralists might choose to afford it, and he assigns a key role to 'structuration' in the explanation of political change. In these respects Cerny's work is especially interesting because it bridges sociological and International Relations theory and stands at the borders of Structuralism, Realism and Pluralism, if firmly on the Pluralist side.

In addition to such scholars there are also theorists for whom long-term perspectives seem to offer the opportunity to revise the theoretical basis of International Relations in general. Currently a major research programme within the Pluralist paradigm has been undertaken by Yale Ferguson, examining long-term historical information using Pluralist concepts.[69] This promises to provide a Pluralist version of world political history, as supplied for Realism by Buzan and Little and for the 'English School' by Watson.

To date, Ferguson's views have been most clearly set out in *Polities*, co-written with Richard Mansbach. This outlines both a neo-liberal theoretical foundation for long-term analysis in International Relations, and examines a series of case-studies, from ancient Mesopotamia to medieval Italy and beyond. Much of the theoretical basis reflects conventional neo-liberal concerns, for example in discounting a state/non-state analytical divide. Viewing the division of world politics into discrete 'levels of analysis' as counter-productive, and rejecting an over-emphasis on the state as a unit of study, the authors call for a multicultural and long-term perspective on world politics. Ferguson and Mansbach's book, therefore, makes much more direct use of neo-liberal theory than does Cerny's work, but uses a long-term perspective to suggest ways in which International Relations theory as a whole may be modified in the context of long-term studies.

There are, therefore, several distinctive characteristics which are shared by Pluralist analysts of change, and especially of long-term change, and are not found so strongly represented in the Realist paradigm, but again there is a diversity of approaches within this tradition. There is, however, another paradigm in International Relations theory for which long-term change has always been a central part of its core theoretical concerns: Structuralism.

Structuralist approaches to long-term change

The Structuralist paradigm is not a single unified approach. Nor is it easily definable in terms of shared aims or research agendas in the ways in which one might classify both Realism and Pluralism.[70] Instead, it is a group of perspectives which adopt a global scale of analysis first and foremost, and share the view that structures, or frameworks of action, play a part in shaping global politics.[71] These include Marxist and non-Marxist perspectives, and theories of change based on economic and on other grounds.

By far the most widely employed Structuralist approach is World-Systems Analysis, first developed by Immanuel Wallerstein.[72] World-Systems Analysis is closely linked to, and derived from, Marxist theories of long-term change, but Wallerstein stresses that his is not a Marxist approach, and by no means all world-systems analysts would characterize themselves as Marxists. Nevertheless, Wallerstein places central importance on the coincidence of economic and political factors in bringing about the emergence and decline of 'world-systems': patterns of interaction and exploitation with both a geographical and a temporal existence. These form zones – the core, semi-periphery and periphery – which shape political and economic relations and are based on unequal economic contacts. Wallerstein relates the development of such patterns to the functioning of the capitalist international economic system and sees them as closely related to Kondratieff long-waves of economic growth and decline.[73] To him, world-systems are primarily economic patterns and caused by economic factors, but they also have political dimensions and act as causal factors in determining long-term political change.

The world-system of today represents only the expansion, by 'structural transformation', of other similar economic zones into core–periphery relationships of a single world-system. Other world-systems existed in the past, with the globe only being 'incorporated' into a single system as the result of imperialism. Before these world-systems existed, international interactions centred on 'world empires', which were in some sense forerunners of 'world-systems'.

Wallerstein's work is also more closely related to geopolitical studies than are most theories of long-term change employed in International Relations, and Wallerstein tends to view the repeated pattern of core–periphery relationships, which he discerns in the global economy, as continually reproduced over time. To transform this one would require the transformation of the capitalist system.

Wallerstein's work has been built upon by many other scholars and is the subject of ongoing research programmes in both Europe and the USA. Recently, exponents of this theoretical school have suggested a far longer period over which core–periphery patterns of relationship can be recognized. Attempts have been made to demonstrate the existence of world-systems relationships in the prehistoric, Classical and medieval economies of Europe, the Mediterranean and Asia.[74]

This revision of Wallerstein's perspective has produced one of the most important recent books on long-term change in International Relations, and arguably one of the most theoretically developed versions of world-systems analysis in general: Frank and Gills' edited volume *The World System. Five Hundred Years or Five Thousand?*[75] In this work the editors bring together a series of studies which suggest that the World-System approach can be applied to the whole history of sedentary societies. Their perspective suggests a single world system (without the hyphen, to separate it from 'world-systems') has existed continuously for at least 5000 years. They suggest that this world system can be analysed using 'World-Systems Analysis' concepts such as 'core–periphery relations' and 'hegemony', and by assigning importance to the impact of economic cycles in bringing about change in world politics. This is a very interesting attempt, by scholars within the discipline, to apply International Relations theory on a long timescale. Unsurprisingly, not all world-systems analysts agree with Frank and Gills' perspective. This has prompted a debate among world-systems analysts over the merits of this version of the theory, with which Wallerstein himself disagrees.[76]

An alternative Structuralist perspective, discussed in the same volume, which has recently come to the fore in current debate on long-term change in International Relations, is Wilkinson's 'civilizational approach'.[77] This is an attempt to revive the study of 'civilizations' in the long term, an approach neglected until recently in International Relations theory despite its long history in political scholarship.[78]

By 'civilization' Wilkinson means a collection of politically interacting cities, without any assignment of cultural value-judgements.[79] These patterns of interaction produce networks of contacts, resulting in systems which exhibit core–periphery relationships. The economic links of such networks are referred to by Wilkinson as *oikumenes*, and form the basis of the pattern of political relationships. As such, Wilkinson's views are close to, but distinct from, those of scholars working within this new long-term variant of world-systems analysis. Their incorporation within the same volume asserts the increasingly close relationship between these two perspectives.

Other scholars aim to expand upon Wallerstein's work, while remaining closely allied with it. This is the perspective of Christopher Chase-Dunn, who has emphasized the economic basis of Wallerstein's approach and adopted a more explicitly Marxist formulation of World-Systems Analysis.[80]

Unlike Wallerstein, however, Chase-Dunn affords much more attention to world history before c AD 1500. This is exemplified in his important recent book (jointly-authored with Thomas Hall) *Rise and Demise*. While published as a work of sociology, it is effectively a work of long-term International Relations.

Chase-Dunn and Hall apply world-systems concepts to data encompassing approximately 12,000 years of political history. Drawing far more extensively on archaeological and anthropological information than has been usual in World-Systems Analysis in International Relations, they attempt to expand this theory to encompass 'chiefdoms' and 'very small world systems'. They also try to bring together other recent work into a single revised account of the emergence of the modern world-system. Notably, they reject the necessity of core:periphery relations as the defining feature of world-systems and aim to encompass a much wider diversity of societies and variety of processes within this form of explanation.

World-Systems Analysis is not, however, the only form of Structuralism. Nor is it the only non-Marxist approach to change to come from this paradigm but the majority of work on change by Structuralist scholars has been Marxist in origin. This is exemplified by the work of Rosenberg and Halliday.[81]

Halliday has adopted a straightforward 'historical materialist'[82] approach to the analysis of change, deriving his conceptual basis from Marxist scholarship, which he restates as a basis for the analysis of world politics. Halliday's approach is explicitly historical, and emphasizes the totality of human history. It concentrates on the socio-economic context of world politics, in a framework giving causal primacy to economic factors. It sees the role of class-analysis and conflict, including revolution, as at the core of explanations of change, and locates the process of change in the working of (perhaps unperceived) economic factors.

Rosenberg's theory of the long-term is also closely in accordance with Marxist theories of history.[83] It is, again, explicitly historical and materialist, emphasizing classical Marxist concepts such as 'class' and a socio-economic mode of analysis, but adds to this a more sociological perspective than that found in many Marxist works. To Rosenberg, social structures have a determining effect on the operation of international systems and these are to be explained in terms of the Marxist 'theory of value', the explanation of world politics in terms of social and economic relations and an acknowledgement of the temporal contingency of political forms.

Other scholars working within a Marxist or neo-Marxist tradition have chosen, instead of Marx's writing, to place special importance on the works of either Gramsci or Lenin in explaining long-term change. Yet other Structuralist scholars employ a mixture of Marxist and non-Marxist approaches. For example, Galtung has analysed imperialism using both Marxist and non-Marxist perspectives in an attempt to explain long-term patterns of core–periphery relations without employing a world-systems framework of analysis.[84]

Perhaps the best known of those working in the Gramscian tradition is Cox.[85] He has placed great importance on the operation of transnational social and economic factors and the role of transnational interest-groups. These groups can be seen as comprising a 'historical bloc' exercising 'hegemony' in the Gramscian sense to structure international politics in their favour. Change comes about when interests change or social or economic factors force realignments.

There has also been attention to long-term world political change as long-term social change. This is exemplified by Jan Aart Scholte's book *International Relations of Social Change*.[86] Scholte uses aspects of Marxist theory, especially Critical Theory, but attempts to take a systemic view of a global society. Using a multi-disciplinary framework of analysis, Scholte draws on theory from sociology, economics, history, anthropology, geography and literary criticism, in addition to political science.

Scholte sees change as transnational in character and deriving from the interplay of both material and non-material factors: it is neither wholly determined nor entirely unstructured. As neither a materialist nor determinist view, this cannot be described as Marxist, even if it contains some Marxist elements. However, it is clearly within the Structuralist paradigm.

If Scholte's work serves to demonstrate the diversity of approaches to long-term change within this paradigm, and the willingness of Structuralist theorists to employ a multi-disciplinary approach to studying change, this is true also. This is true also of the Structuralist school of long-term analysts of war-origins which has developed in International Relations. Two examples will suffice to illustrate this approach: the studies by Eckhardt and by Cioffi-Revilla.

Eckhardt[87] undertook a life-long study of the relationship of 'civilizations, wars and empires' encompassing the whole period of the existence of state-societies globally. In this, a form of quantitative Structuralism was applied to historical data to examine potential correlations between forms of political organization and war. The primary theoretical contribution of this work is, perhaps, the historical scope and attention to detail of his analyses.

Cioffi-Revilla[88] has incorporated archaeological and anthropological data much more fully into his analysis of war-origins, using somewhat similar methods. The project with which he is associated, 'The Long Range Analysis of War Project', represents a sophisticated application of this method to a wide range of data, building on Eckhardt's work.

Other Structuralist scholars have taken an equally long-term view. An interesting example of such a study is that by Blachman and Puchala,[89] which analysed the Cold War in the context of 'bipolar' inter-imperial struggles from the Ancient World to the, then, present. This required the examination of millennia of political history to produce an intriguing pattern of possibly recurrent conflict on an international scale, based on a structural analysis of world politics.

Nor are Eckhardt, Cioffi-Revilla and other Structuralist students of war-origins the only scholars to favour a quantitative Structuralist approach to long-term change in international politics. A distinct sub-discipline of 'trend analysis' has tried to apply the examination and extrapolation of long-term trends, whether social, economic, military or ecological, to the study of international relations.[90] Perhaps the most widely known 'trend analysis' of this sort has been that undertaken by the Meadows and their colleagues.[91]

Examples of 'trend analysis' have included the 'global models' promoted by the WOMP project.[92] These have taken a global perspective in the formulation of dynamical computer or mathematical models and simulations of world political (and other) changes, sometimes over long time-spans. An interesting example of this approach is provided by Barry Hughes' book *International Futures*,[93] where (as in many such studies) demographic growth is assigned a key causal role. Most such studies have, in turn, relied upon either trend projection, such as that of the Meadows' 'limits of growth' project, or systems theories of change.

Trend projections have generally run into the problems of estimating the relative significance of trends and the likelihood of their continuation.[94] It must be stressed that, although included here under Structuralism, trend-analysis has been used by Pluralists and Realists also, and these studies have shared these common problems. Recently experimental attempts have been made to 'calibrate' trend-projection by encompassing cultural factors and the historical analysis of the origins both of trends and the societies which are affected by them. Such factors may, it is argued, enable some degree of estimation to be made of which trends are liable to persist and which are likely to fade out.[95]

Less well-known forms of Structuralism adopt yet different perspectives. For example, there is the work of Mowat, on the borders of history, theology and international politics, who takes a transhistorical comparative historical view of international politics on a geographically broad scale.[96] This is in contrast to the Marxist and materialist works already mentioned, placing importance on individuals, beliefs, and values as strongly as would most neo-liberals, and yet seeing change as distinct both from the inter-state system and from economic factors. Employing a multi-disciplinary view-point and attempting to integrate interpretations of religious, political, cultural and economic factors, his work is at once Structuralist and non-materialist in character, showing that the simple correlation of Structuralism and either materialism or Marxism is invalid. Consequently, Structuralism, like both Realism and Pluralism, has a rich and varied literature on long-term change exhibiting both a wide diversity of approaches and contrasting methodologies. These range from theories derived from literary criticism to those of physics. The wealth of theoretical discussion of long-term change in all of these paradigms and the mainstream context of most of this material within the discipline, show the centrality of long-term analysis to the core debates of International Relations theory. The importance attached to theories of the long-term in validating all of these paradigms conclusively demonstrate that the analysis of long-term change must lie at the very core of International Relations, whether one chooses to work within a Realist, a Pluralist or a Structuralist paradigm.

There is, of course, one perspective from which long-term change is theoretically irrelevant, and perhaps would be claimed to be an impossible area of study: the post-modernist paradigm. This has become a highly visible, if small, part of contemporary work on International Relations theory.

Post-modernism

Post-modernism in International Relations theory is part of a much broader interdisciplinary movement of the same name. It is very difficult to define, both in International Relations theory and more generally, because it is an essential part of the post-modernist paradigm to remain unbounded and 'open', and to retain a wide diversity within this general framework.[97] Post-modernism eschews a research programme of its own, or usually even self-definition as a unitary school. In practice, the main intention of post-modernist scholars has been to provide a critique on the analysis of international politics rather than to attempt to understand world politics as such.

Particular targets of post-modernist critique are the use of 'essentialist' and 'foundationalist' premises: those attributing a universal or unchanging character to the subject of analysis. In a post-modernist view, positivistic method, claims of objectivity or limited subjectivity are rejected. Concepts of rational argumentation, and especially the rational or scientific validation of hypotheses, are also seen as fundamentally flawed.

Instead, post-modernists have stressed extreme subjectivity, non-rational approaches, diversity, and views which challenge currently held opinions on these grounds. In this sense, post-modernists have often been keen to stress their links with Critical Theory (especially in the common interest in 'emancipation') and philosophical concepts supposedly supporting a relativistic epistemology, such as Social Constructivism.[98] The one theoretical position post-modernists characteristically share, which might define their viewpoint as distinctive, is this basis in a relativist epistemology.

The practice of post-modernism provides a clearer view of its shared characteristics than perhaps its rhetoric of diversity and incomparability would lead one to expect. This enables the recognition of some common theoretical characteristics among post-modernist scholars, as Brown has recently observed, of which two are especially important at this point in this review.[99]

The first is the denial that there is an external reality which can be accessed through reason, and this includes an external historical reality. Belief in a historical reality is essential to any form of long-term study, so this opposes post-modernist relativism and long-term analysis at the outset.

The second is the theory that all knowledge is entirely subjective and contextual, so that all historical interpretations are no more than 'personal opinions', which require only contemporary social or political explanation. In post-modernist epistemologies, therefore, historical interpretations cannot be verified (or assigned any relative probability) on rational grounds. Consequently, all historical reconstructions are incapable of refutation, verification or ranking in terms of relative likelihood.[100] That is, the post-modernist theory of change views change as continuously occurring but sees history or even the contemporary world as unknowable by reference to either data-collection or logical reasoning. Any attempt to trace the development of a historical entity, such as a state, is liable to claims that it is 'essentialist' in that it ascribes the diachronic regularity of continued existence to that entity. Post-modernism also – at least in theory – tends to deny historical comparison, in that it envisages every situation in the present and past as in all respects unique.

Unlike the other paradigms reviewed above, post-modernism does not have any need for a theory of long-term change. In theory at least, post-modernism bases itself on epistemological philosophy rather than on history. In theoretical writings, post-modernist authors often deny the ability of those in the present to understand the past even partially, and stress that any account of the past is entirely a construct of the present, as if a work of historical fiction. It is not a partial representation of the past for the purposes of the present, but merely a construct of the present.

However, in practice this does not mean that post-modernist scholars – including those in International Relations – have had no place for historical studies. Ironically, one of the most characteristic post-modernist analytical strategies has been to examine history through the concept of 'genealogy'. The concept of 'genealogy' in post-modernist theory is close to an extreme version of 'historical particularism': all that happens in history must be seen as unique, and incomparable. Thus, the past cannot be compared with the present, nor can we seek general explanations, origins or 'ends'. But genealogy also goes beyond this in asserting that there is no single 'history' at all, rather there is a multitude of interrelated histories, which are the context within which rival forms of knowledge compete for dominance. For example, in a recent paper, Walker supposes that 'stories' about 'beginnings and endings' are no more than ways of legitimating present positions, rather than representing history as it actually was.[101]

If International Relations can in general be characterized as a combination of history and theory, in post-modernist theory it is a wholly theoretical exercise. Thus, it may not be unfair to see post-modernist theory (although often not practice) as representing an anti-historical tendency within International Relations.[102] But this does not mean that post-modernist approaches contain nothing of value for the analyst of long-term change.

Conclusion to the review of International Relations theory approaches

From this review, it is clear that International Relations theory contains a wide range of theoretical positions on the way in which long-term change may be analysed. There is also wide variation over the advantages of attempting such an analysis.

However, it has become clear that long-term historical studies are too important for Realists, Pluralists, or Structuralists to ignore or belittle. It is also clear that conducting these studies brings the International Relations scholar into unfamiliar territory. Unfamiliar in one respect because of the temporal and geographical scope of the materials involved; unfamiliar in another, because by looking at pre-modern periods there is need to rely upon unfamiliar source materials.[103] Archaeological and ethnographic records supply us with information about the majority of human history and these types of data remain crucial sources of information about the past until some surprisingly late periods.

For instance in Europe, archaeological evidence remains a key means of political and social reconstruction until the twelfth century, and later in some areas.[104] In the Pacific Islands this 'historical horizon' is often in the eighteenth century or later, and even then the available sources are frequently 'Contact Period' ethnographies rather than indigenous histories.[105]

Yet the potential wealth of these sources for informing International Relations is only now being appreciated, as scholars working in the Realist, Pluralist and Structuralist paradigms begin to investigate them. It is unsurprising, therefore, that scholars of International Relations have looked to other disciplines for assistance in interpreting these materials. For example, Richard Little and Barry Buzan have turned to history and historical sociology to assist in building a long-term structural Realist theory of change. The theoretical problems of coping with large-scale change have also prompted exploration of other disciplines, James Rosenau, for instance, examining theories from mathematics and biology.[106]

In the next chapter, I shall outline some of the theoretical perspectives developed in fields which have, in their recent history, had a longer period of addressing the analysis of long-term change as at the centre of their disciplinary concerns. These include subjects previously discussed in this context and also some new material which may be relevant.

Notes

1   Brewin, C., 1992, 'Research in a global context: a discussion of Toynbee's legacy', *Review of International Studies* 18.2, 115–30.

2   Buzan, B. and Jones, R. J. B. (eds), 1981, *Change and the Study of International Relations*; Holsti, O. R., Siverson, R. M. and George, A. L. (eds), 1980, *Change in the International System* Boulder, CO.

3   Forming the basis for contributions such as: Lundestad, G. (ed.), 1994, *The Fall of Great Powers*, Oslo and Oxford.

4   Knutsen, T. L., 1992, *A History of International Relations Theory.*

5   Rosenau, J. N., 1995, 'Signals, signposts and symptoms: interpreting change and anomalies in world politics', *European Journal of International Relations*, 1.1, 113–22.

6   This terminology is well established in a range of disciplines directly concerned with change, including anthropology, archaeology and philology. For example, see Renfrew, C. and Bahn, P., 1996, *Archaeology. Theories Methods and Practice*, 2nd edn.

7   This has generated an extensive scholarly literature. For example see: Singer, J. D., 1961, 'the level-of-analysis problem in International Relations', in K. Knorr and S. Verba (eds), *The International System: Theoretical Essays*, Princeton, NJ; Moul, W.D., 1973, 'The level of analysis problem revisited', *The Canadian Journal of Political Science* 61.6, 494–513; Yurdusev, A. N., 1993, 'Level of analysis and unit of analysis: a case for distinction', *Millennium* 22.1, 77–88; Buzan, B., 1995, 'The level of analysis problem in International Relations reconsidered', in K. Booth and S. Smith (eds), *International Relations Theory Today*, 198–216; Onuf, N., 1995, 'Levels', *European Journal of International Relations* 1.1, 35–58.

8   Leaver, R., 1994, 'International political economy and the changing world order: evolution or involution?', in R. Stubbs and G. D. Underhill (eds), *Political Economy and the Changing Global Order*, 130–41.

9   Although note the comments of Smith on this issue: Smith, S., 1995, 'The self-images of a discipline: a genealogy of International Relations theory', in K. Booth and S. Smith, *International Relations Theory Today*, 1–37.

10   Powell, R., 1994, 'Anarchy in International Relations Theory: the neorealist–neoliberal debate', *International Organization* 48.2, 313–44; Baldwin, D. (ed.), 1993, *Neorealism and Neoliberalism: The Contemporary Debate*; Keohane, R. (ed)., 1986, *Neo-Realism and Its Critics*, New York; Linklater, A., 1990, *Beyond Realism and Marxism: Critical Theory and International Relations*; Burchill, S. and Linklater, A. *et al.*, 1996, *Theories of International Relations.*

11   For a recent account of the current state of Realism: Buzan, B., 1996, 'The timeless wisdom of Realism', in S. Smith, K. Booth and M. Zalewski (eds), *International Theory: Positivism and Beyond*, 47–65.

12   On Realism's difficulties with 'change': Walker, R. B. J., 1987, 'Realism, change and International Political Theory', *International Studies Quarterly* 31.1, 65–86; Kratochwil, F. V., 1993, 'The embarrassment of changes: neo-Realism as the science of realpolitik without politics', *Review of International Studies* 19.1, 63–80; Wohlforth, W. C., 1995, 'Realism and the end of the Cold War', *International Security* 19, 91–129; Kegley, C., 1993, 'The neoidealist moment in international studies? Realist myths and new international realities', *Inter-*

national Studies Quarterly, 131–46; Hall, R. B. and Kratochwil, F. V., 1993, 'Medieval tales: neorealist "science" and the abuse of history', *International Organization* 47.3, 479–500; Lebow, R. N., 1994, 'The long peace, the end of the Cold War, and the failure of realism', *International Organization* 48.2, 249–77. See also: Ruggie, J. G., 1983, 'Continuity and transformation in the world polity: toward a Neorealist synthesis', *World Politics* 35.2, 261–85 and Allan, P. and Goldmann, K. (eds), 1992, *The End of The Cold War: Evaluating Theories of International Relations*, Dordrecht. Frankel, B. (ed.), 1996, *Realism: Restatements and Renewal*; Cox, R. W., 1997, *The New Realism*.

13   Classically: Bull, H., 1977 *The Anarchical Society: A Study of Order in World Politics*, New York. See also: Jervis, R., 1978, 'Cooperation under the security dilemma', *World Politics* 30, 167–214; Grieco, J. M., 1988, 'Anarchy and the limits of cooperation: a Realist critique of the newest liberal internationalism, *International Organization*42.3, 485–507. For a discussion of the same issue from a non-Realist perspective: Young, O., 1978, 'Anarchy and social choice: reflections on the international polity', *World Politics* 30, 241–63. See also: Milner, H., 1991, 'The assumption of anarchy in International Relations theory: a critique', *Review of International Studies* 17.1, 67–86.

14   Bull, H., 1977 *The Anarchical Society: A Study of Order in World Politics*, New York; Powell, R., 1994, 'Anarchy in international relations theory: the neorealist–neoliberal debate', *International Organization* 48.2, 313–44.

15   Wight, M., 1977, *Systems of States*. For a recent review of Realism: Griffiths, M., 1992, *Realism, Idealism and International Relations: a reinterpretation*. See also: Brown, S., 1984, 'The world polity and the nation-state system', *International Journal* 39, 509–28.

16   Viotti, P. R. and Kauppi, M. V., 1993, *International Relations Theory. Realism, Pluralism and Globalism*, 2nd edn, New York, 59–61.

17   For a recent discussion: Sheehan, M., 1996, *The Balance of Power*. See also: Patomaki, H., 1991, 'Concepts of "action", "structure", and "power" in Critical Social Realism: a positive and reconstructive critique', *Journal for the Theory of Social Behaviour* 21.2, 221–50.

18   See Layne, C., 1994, 'Kant or cant: the myth of democratic peace', *International Security* 19, 10–11.

19   Doran, C. and Parsons, W., 1980, 'War and the cycle of relative power', *American Political Science Review* 74, 947–65.

20   Linklater, A., 1995, 'Neo-Realism in theory and practice', in K. Booth and S. Smith (eds), *International Relations Theory Today*, 241–62; Garnett, J. C., 1992, 'States, state-centric perspectives and interdependence', in J. Baylis and N. Rengger (eds), *Dilemmas of World Politics*, 61–84.

21   Waltz, K. N., 1959, *Man, the State and War*, New York; Waltz, K. N., 1979, *Theory of International Politics*, Reading, Mass.

22   For summaries of the principal critiques of Realism: Viotti, P. R. and Kauppi, M. V., 1993, *International Relations Theory. Realism, Pluralism and Globalism*, 2nd edn, New York, 61–6; Dougherty, J. E. and Pfaltzgraff, R. C., 1996, *Contending Theories of International Relations*, 4th edn, New York.

23   Waltz, K. N., 1993, 'The emerging structure of international politics', *International Security* 18.2, 44–79.

24   Gilpin, R., 1981, *War and Change in World Politics*.

25   Gilpin, R., 1987, *The Political Economy of International Relations*, Princeton, NJ.

26   This point, and the following account of Gilpin's views, are based on his *War and Change in World Politics*. See also: Gilpin, R., 1994, 'The cycle of great powers: has it finally been broken?', in G. Lundestad (ed.), *The Fall of Great Powers*, Oslo, 313–30. More recently, Gilpin has endeavoured to combine his views with evolutionary perspectives: Gilpin, R., 1996, 'Economic evolution of national systems', *International Studies Quarterly* 40, 411–31.

27   Modelski, G., 1987, *Long Cycles in World Politics*, London and Seattle.

28   Modelski, G., 1987, *Long Cycles in World Politics*, London and Seattle; Modelski, G., 1962, 'Comparative international systems', *World Politics* 14, 662–674; Modelski, G., 1978, 'Long cycles of global politics and the nation state', *Comparative Studies in Society and History* 20, 214–38; Modelski, G. and Thompson, W., 1988, *Seapower in Global Politics 1494–1994*, London. For developments on this theme: Modelski, G. (ed.), 1987, *Exploring Long Cycles*, Boulder, Colo.

29   Modelski has also adopted an evolutionary approach: Modelski, G., 1996, 'Evolutionary paradigm for global politics', *International Studies Quarterly* 40, 321–42; Modelski, G. and Thompson, W. R., 1996, *Leading Sectors and World Powers: The Co-evolution of Global Economics and Politics*, Columbia, Calif.

30   Both scholars' work on this is presented, along with other evolutionary studies of world politics and economics, in *International Studies Quarterly* 40, 1996: see notes 26 and 29 in this Chapter.

31   Organski, A. F. K. and Kugler, J., 1980, *The War Ledger*, Chicago. See also: Levy, J. S., 1985, 'Theories of general war', *World Politics* 37.3, 344–74; Woosang, K., 1992, 'Power transitions and great power war from Westphalia to Waterloo', *World Politics* 45, 153–72.

32   Organski, A. F. K., 1968, *World Politics*, 2nd edn, New York, chapter 12, esp. 357–9; Organski, A. F. K. and Kugler, J., 1980, *The War Ledger*, Chicago.

33   Cox, R. W., 1987, *Production, Power and World Order*, New York. For Cox as a Realist: Olson, W. C. and Groom, A. J. R., 1991, *International Relations Then and Now*, 279–80. For the development of Cox's theoretical views: Cox, R. W. and Sinclair, T. J., 1996, *Approaches to World Order*.

34   Personal communication at BISA Conference on long–term change (London, 1995). See also: Buzan, B., 1993, 'From international system to international society: Structural and Regime Theory meet the English School', *International Organization* 47.3, 327–52; Little, R., 1995, 'Neorealism and the English School: a methodological, ontological and theoretical reassessment', *European Journal of International Relations* 1.1, 9–34.

35   Buzan, B., Jones, C. A. and Little, R., 1993, *The Logic of Anarchy*, New York.

36   Buzan, B. and Little, R., 1994, 'The idea of international system: theory meets history', *International Political Science Review* 15.3, 23–56; Little, R., 1994, 'International Relations and large-scale historical change', in A. J. R. Groom and M. Light (eds), *Contemporary International Relations: A Guide to Theory*, 9–26.

37   For a defensive discussion from a Realist perspective: Little, R., 1995, 'International Relations and the triumph of capitalism', in K. Booth and S. Smith (eds), *International Relations Theory Today*, 62–89.

38 Deudney, D. and Ikenberry, G. J., 1991, 'Soviet reform and the end of the Cold War: explaining large-scale historical change', *Review of International Studies* 17.3, 225–50; Kegley, C. W., 1994, 'How did the Cold War die: principles for an autopsy', *Mershon International Studies Review* 38.1, 11–42; Kratochwil, F. V., 1993, 'The embarrassment of changes: neo-Realism as the science of realpolitik without politics', *Review of International Studies* 19.1, 63–80; Lebow, R. N., 1994, 'The long peace, the end of the Cold War, and the failure of realism', *International Organization* 48.2, 249–77; Wohlforth, W. C., 1995, 'Realism and the end of the Cold War', *International Security* 19, 91–129; Koslowski, R. and Kratochwil, F. V., 1994, 'Understanding change in international politics: the Soviet empire's demise and the international system', *International Organization* 48.2, 215–47; Pipes, R., 1995, 'Misinterpreting the end of the Cold War', *Foreign Affairs* 74.1, 154–60; Ray, J. L. and Russett, B., 1996, 'The future as arbiter of theoretical controversies: predictions, expectations and the end of the Cold War', *British Journal of Political Science* 26, 441–70.

39 Schroeder, P., 1994, 'Historical reality *vs* neo-Realist theory', *International Security* 19.1, 108–48. For examples of other post-Cold War attempts to combine Realism with an awareness of change: Doran, C. F., 1991, *Systems in Crisis*; Foss, N. J., 1994, 'Realism and evolutionary economics', *Journal of Social and Evolutionary Systems* 17.1, 21–40; Kupchan, C. A., 1994, *The Vulnerability of Empire*, Ithaca and London.

40 Mearsheimer, J., 1990, 'Back to the future: instability in Europe after the Cold War', *International Security* 15.1, 5–56.

41 Layne, C., 1993, 'The unipolar illusion: why new great powers will rise', *International Security* 17.4, 3–51.

42 For a recent collection of papers illustrating the continuing vigour of Realism: Brown, M. E. *et al.* (eds), 1995, *The Perils of Anarchy*, Cambridge, Mass.

43 Jones, R. E., 1981, 'The English School of International Relations: a suitable case for closure', *Review of International Studies* 7.1, 1–13.

44 Watson, A., 1992, *The Evolution of International Society*. See also: Watson, A., 1987, 'Hedly Bull, state systems, and International Studies', *Review of International Studies* 13, 147–53; Watson, A., 1990, 'Systems of states', *Review of International Studies* 16, 99–110.

45 Hurrell, A., 1993, 'International society and the study of regimes: a reflective approach', in V. Rittberger (ed.), *Regime Theory and International Relations*, 49–72; Evans, T. and Wilson, P., 1992, 'Regime theory and the English School of International Relations: a comparison', *Millennium* 21.3, 329–51. See also Waever, O., 1992, 'International society – theoretical promises unfulfilled?', *Cooperation and Conflict* 27, 97–128.

46 For examples of the work of the 'English School': Wight, M., 1978, *Power Politics*; Bull, H., 1977, *The Anarchical Society*. On this 'school' see: Grader, S., 1981, 'The English School of International Relations: evidence and evaluation', *Review of International Studies* 14.1, 29–44; James, A., 1993, 'System or society?', *Review of International Studies* 19.3, 269–88; Wilson, P., 1989, 'The English School of International Relations: a reply to Sheila Grader', *Review of International Studies* 15.1, 49–58.

47 Huntington, S. P., 1993, 'The clash of civilizations', *Foreign Affairs* 72, 22–49.

Huntington, P. R., 1996, *The Clash of Civilizations and the Remaking of World Order*, New York.

48   Spruyt, H., 1994, 'Institutional selection in international relations: state anarchy as order', *International Organization* 48.4, 527–57. See also Spruyt, H., 1994, *The Sovereign State and its Competitors*, Princeton.

49   Cederman, L-E., 1995, 'Competing identities: an ecological model of nationality formation', *European Journal of International Relations* 1.3, 331–65.

50   Viotti, P. R. and Kauppi, M. V., 1993, *International Relations Theory. Realism, Pluralism and Globalism*, 2nd edn, New York, 228–448; Zacher, M. W. and Matthew, R. A., 1995. 'Liberal international theory: common threads, divergent strands', in C. Kegley (ed.), *Controversies in International Relations Theory*, 107–150; Zacher, M. W., 1992, 'The decaying pillars of the Westphalian temple: implications for international order and governance', in J. N. Rosenau and E-O. Czempiel (eds), *Governance Without Government: Order and Change in World Politics*, 58–101; Doyle, M., 1986, 'Liberalism and world politics', *American Political Science Review* 80, 1151–62.

51   Doyle, M. W., 1995, 'Liberalism and world politics revisited', in C. Kegley (ed), *Controversies in International Relations Theory*, 83–106.

52   On 'progress' in International Relations see: Adler, B. and Crawford, B. (eds), 1991, *Progress in Post-War International Relations*.

53   Fukuyama, F., 1993, *The End of History and the Last Man*, London and New York.

54   For example: Spiro, P. J., 1995, 'New global communities: non-governmental organisations in international decision-making institutions', in B. Roberts (ed.), *Order and Disorder after the Cold War*, Cambridge, Mass., 251–62.

55   See: Kratochwil, F. and Mansfield, E. D. (eds), 1994, *International Organisation. A Reader*, New York; Rittberger, V. (ed.), 1993, *Regime Theory and International Relations*: Krasner, S. D. (ed.), 1983) *International Regimes*, Ithaca; Levy, M. A., Young, O. R. and Zurn, M., 1995, 'The study of International Relations', *European Journal of International Relations* 1.3, 267–330.

56   Haas, E. B., 1990, 'Reason and change in international affairs: justifying a hypothesis', *Journal of International Affairs*, 209–40; Haas, E. B., 1990, *When Knowledge is Power: Three Models of Change in International Organization*, Berkeley, Calif.

57   Haas, P. M., 1989, 'Do regimes matter: epistemic communities and Mediterranean pollution control', *International Organization* 43, 377–404; Haas, P. M., 1992, 'Epistemic communities and international policy coordination', *International Organization* 46, 1–35.

58   Rosenau, J. N., 1990, *Turbulence in World Politics: a Theory of Change and Continuity*, Princeton. See also: Rosenau, J. N., 1989, 'The state in an era of cascading politics: wavering concept, widening competence, withering Collosus or weathering change?', in J. A. Caporaso (ed.), *The Elusive State*, Newbury Park, Calif., 17–48; Rosenau, J. N., 1995, 'Governance in the twenty-first century', *Global Governance* 1.1, 13–43. See also Rosenau, J. N., 1986, 'Before cooperation: hegemons, regimes and habit-driven actors in world politics', *International Organization* 40, 879–94.

59   Gaddis, J. L., 1992, *The United States and the End of the Cold War*, esp. 186–92. Although Gaddis is a historian, his work is placed in this chapter because it has formed part of mainstream debate in International Relations theory. See also:

Gaddis, J. L., 1987, 'Expanding the data base: historians, political scientists and the enrichment of security studies', *International Security* 12, 3–21.

60   Gaddis, J. L., 1996, 'History, science and the study of international relations', in N. Woods (ed.), *Explaining International Relations Since 1945*, 32–48.

61   Gaddis, J. L., 1992, *The United States and the End of the Cold War*, 155–67.

62   See Kegley C. (ed.), 1995, *Controversies in International Relations Theory*, New York.

63   Burton, J. W. 1972, *World Society*.

64   Burton, J. W., 1965, *International Relations: A General Theory*. For a clear summary of Burton's contribution and related work, see: Olson, W. C. and Groom, A. J. R., 1991, *International Relations Then and Now*, 204–16.

65   Burton, J. W. (ed.), 1990, *Conflict: Human Needs Theory*. See also: Doyal, L. and Gough, I., 1991, *A Theory of Human Needs*: Braybrooke, D., 1987, *Meeting Needs*, Princeton, NJ.

66   Burton, J. W., 1983, 'The individual as the unit of explanation in International Relations', *International Studies Newsletter* 10, 14–17; Burton, J. W., 1983, *Dear Survivors*, 216.

67   Golte, J. W., 1995, (World Society Research Group), *In Search of World Society*, University of Frankfurt.

68   Cerny, P. G., 1990, *The Changing Architecture of Politics, Structure, Agency and the Future of the State*, Newbury Park, Calif. See also: Cerny, P. G. (ed.), 1993, *Finance and World Politics: Markets, Regimes and States in the Post-Hegemonic Era*.

69   Ferguson, personal communication at BISA Conference 1994. Ferguson's project is currently ongoing, however, see: Ferguson, Y. H. and Mansbach, R. W., 1996, *Polities: Authority, Identities and Change*, Columbia, Calif.; Ferguson, Y.H. and Mansbach, R. W., 1996, 'Political space and Westphalian states in a world of "polities": beyond inside/outside', *Global Governance* 2.2, 261–87.

70   Kegley C. (ed.), 1995, *Controversies in International Relations Theory*, New York. For some key differences: Viotti, P. R. and Kauppi, M. V., 1993, *International Relations Theory. Realism, Pluralism and Globalism*, 2nd edn, New York, 449–531.

71   For some notable examples: Bergesen, A., 1980, 'From utilitarianism to globology: the shift from the individual to the world as a whole as the primordial unit of analysis', in A. Bergesen (ed.), *Studies of the Modern World System*, New York, 231–77; Thompson, W. R., 1986, 'Polarity, the long cycle and global power warfare', *Journal of Conflict Resolution* 30.4, 587–615; Boswell, T. and Sweat, M., 1991, 'Hegemony, long waves, and major wars: a time series analysis of systemic dynamics', *International Studies Quarterly* 35, 123–49; Goldstein, J. S., 1988, *Long Cycles: Prosperity and War in the Modern Age*, London and New Haven, Conn.; Goldstein, J. S., 1991, 'The possibility of cycles in international relations', *International Studies Quarterly* 35, 477–80. Note also Thompson's work within this perspective: Thompson, W. R. (ed.), 1983, *Contending Approaches to World System Analysis*, Beverley Hills, Calif.; Thompson, W. R., 1988, *On Global War: Historical–Structural Approaches to World Politics*, Columbia, Calif.; Rasler, K. and Thompson, W. R., 1991, *Global War and State-Making Processes*; Thompson, W. R., 1992, 'Dehio, long cycles and the geohistorical context of structural transition', *World Politics* 45,

127–52; Gills, B. and Palan, R. (eds), 1994, *Transcending the State–Global Divide: A Neostructuralist Agenda in International Relations*, Boulder, Colo.

72   Wallerstein, I., 1974–88, *The Modern World System*, 3 vols, New York; Wallerstein, I., 1979, *The Capitalist World Economy*; Wallerstein, I., 1983, *Historical Capitalism*; Wallerstein, I., 1984, *The Politics of the World Economy*; Wallerstein, I., 1991, *Geopolitics and Geoculture*; Wallerstein, I., 1991, *Capitalist Civilization*, Binghampton, NY; Wallerstein, I., 1992, *The Time Space of World-Systems Analysis*, Binghampton, NY; Wallerstein, I., 1996, 'The interstate structure of the modern world-system', in S. Smith, K. Booth and M. Zalewski (eds), *International Theory: Positivism and Beyond*, 87–107. See also: Arrighi, G., Hopkins, T. K. and Wallerstein, I., 1989, *Antisystemic Movements*, London and New York; Gourevitch, P., 1978, 'The international system and regime formation: a critical review of Anderson and Wallerstein', *Comparative Politics* 10.3, 119–38; Hollist, W. L. and Rosenau, J. N., 1981, 'World systems debates', Special Issue of *International Studies Quarterly* 25.1, 5–17; Zolberg, A. R., 1981, 'Origins of the modern world-system: a missing link', *World Politics* 33.2, 253–81; Hopkins, T. K. and Wallerstein, I. (eds), 1980, *Processes of the World System*, Beverley Hills, Calif.; Bergesen, A. (ed.), 1983, *Crises in the World System*, Beverley Hills, Calif.; Bergesen, A. (ed.), 1980, *Studies of the World System*, New York; Goldfrank, W. L. (ed.), 1979, *The World System of Capitalism: Past and Present*, Beverley Hills, Calif.; King, A. D. (ed.), 1991, *Culture, Globalization and the World System*, Binghampton, NY; Wallerstein, I., 1991, *Unthinking Social Science: The Limits of Nineteenth-Century Paradigms*.

73   For a discussion of the relationship between economic cycles and the international economy from this perspective: Hopkins, T. K., and Wallerstein, I., 1979, 'Cyclical rhythms and secular trends of the capitalist world economy', *Review* 2, 483–500; Mandel, E. and Wallerstein, I. (eds), 1992, *New Findings in Long Waves Research*, New York. For an interesting application of this approach to the history of imperialism: Bergesen, A. and Schoenberg, R., 1980, 'Long waves of colonial expansion and contraction, 1415–1969', in Bergesen, A. (ed.), *Studies of the Modern World System*, New York, 231–77. For a bibliography of related publications to 1979, see: Barr, K., 1979, 'Long waves: a selective annotated bibliography', *Review* 2.4, 675–718. See also: Berry, B. J. L., 1991, *Long-wave Rhythms in Economic Development and Political Behavior*, Baltimore, Md; Hall, P., 1988, 'The intellectual history of long waves', in M. Young and T. Schuller (eds), *The Rhythms of Society*, 37–52. See also: Rosecrance, R. N., 1986, 'Long cycle theory and International Relations', *International Organization* 41.2, 283–302; Beck, N., 1991, 'The illusion of cycles in international relations', *International Studies Quarterly* 35.4, 455–76; Thompson, W. and Vescera, L., 1992, 'Growth waves, systemic openness, and protectionism', *International Organization* 46.2, 493–532.

74   Champion, T. C., 1989, *Centre and Periphery*; Rowlands, M., Larsen, M. and Kristiansen, K. (eds), 1987, *Centre and Periphery in the Ancient World*. See also Woolf, G., 1990, 'World-systems analysis and the Roman Empire', *Journal of Roman Archaeology* 3, 44–58.

75   Frank, A. G. and Gills, B. K. (eds), 1993, *The World System: Five Hundred Years or Five Thousand?* See also: Frank, A. G., 1990, 'A theoretical introduction to 5000 years of world system history', *Review* 13.2, 155–248; Frank, A. G., 1991, 'A plea for world system history', *Journal of World History* 2, 1–28; Frank,

A. G., 1993, 'The Bronze-age world system and its cycles', *Current Anthropology* 34.4, 383–430.

76 Wallerstein, I., 1993, 'World system versus world-systems. A critique', in A. G. Frank and B. K. Gills (eds), *The World System. Five Hundred Years or Five Thousand?* 292–6.

77 Wilkinson, D., 1992, 'Cities, civilizations and oikumenes I', *Comparative Civilizations Review* 27, 51–87; Wilkinson, D., 1993, 'Cities, civilizations and oikumenes II', *Comparative Civilizations Review* 28, 41–72. On the relationship between 'civilizations' and world-systems, Sanderson, S. K. (ed.), 1995, *Civilizations and World-Systems: Two Approaches to the Study of World-Historical Change*, Walnut Creek, Calif.

78 Wilkinson, D., 1987, 'Central civilization', *Comparative Civilizations Review* 22, 31–59.

79 Wilkinson, D., 1993, 'Civilizations, cores, world economies, and oikumenes', in A. G. Frank and B. K. Gills (eds), *The World System. Five Hundred Years or Five Thousand?* 221–246.

80 Chase-Dunn, C. and Rubinson, R., 1977, 'Toward a structural perspective on the world system', *Politics and Society* 7.4, 453–76; Chase-Dunn, C., 1981, 'Interstate system and Capitalist world-economy: one logic or two?', *International Studies Quarterly* 25.1, 19–42; Chase-Dunn, C., 1990, *Global Formation, Structures of the World Economy*, Cambridge, Mass.; Chase-Dunn, C., 1992, 'The comparative study of world-systems', *Review* 15.3, 313–33; Chase-Dunn, C., 1993, 'Comparing world-systems: concepts and working hypotheses', *Social Forces* 71.4, 851–86; Chase-Dunn, C., 1994, 'The historical evolution of world-systems', *Sociological Enquiry* 64.3, 257–80; Chase-Dunn, C. and Hall, T. D. (eds), 1991, *Core/Periphery Relations in PreCapitalist Worlds*, Boulder, Colo. Chase-Dunn, C. and Hall, T. D., 1997, *Rise and Demise*, Boulder, Colo.

81 But note that there are other historical materialist analysts of change, for example: Bromley, S., 1994, *Rethinking Middle East Politics*; Smith, H., 1996, 'The silence of the academics: international social theory, historical materialism and political values', *Review of International Studies* 22.2, 191–212; Smith, H., 1994, 'Marxism and International Relations theory', in A. J. R. Groom and M. Light (eds), *Contemporary International Relations: A Guide to Theory*, 142–55.

82 Halliday, F., 1994, *Rethinking International Relations*.

83 Rosenberg, J., 1994, *The Empire of Civil Society*. See also, Rosenberg, J., 1994, 'The international imagination: International Relations theory and classic social analysis', *Millennium* 23, 85–108.

84 Galtung, J., 1971, 'A structural theory of imperialism', *Journal of Peace Research* 8, 81–191.

85 Cox, R., 1983, 'Gramsci, hegemony and International Relations: an essay in method', *Millennium* 12.2, 165–75; Cox, R. W., 1987, *Production, Power and World Order*, New York; Cox, R. W., 1986, 'Social forces states and world orders: beyond International Relations theory', in R. D. Keohane (ed.), *Neorealism and its Critics*, New York, 204–54; Cox, R. W. and Sinclair, T. J., 1996, *Approaches to World Order*.

86 Scholte, J. A., 1993, *International Relations of Social Change*; Scholte, J. A., 1993,

'From power politics to social change: an alternative focus for International Studies', *Review of International Studies* 19.1, 3–22.

87 Eckhardt, W., 1992, *Civilizations, Empires and Wars*.

88 Cioffi-Revilla, C. 1991, 'The long-range analysis of war', *Journal of Interdisciplinary History*, 21, 603–29; Cioffi-Revilla, C. and Lai, D., 1995, 'War and Politics in Ancient China, 2700 BC to 722 BC', *Journal of Conflict Resolution*, 39, 467–94.

89 Blachman, M. J. and Puchala, D. J., 1991, 'When empires meet. The long peace in long-term perspective', in C. W. Kegley (ed.), *The Long Post-War Peace*, New York, 177–201.

90 An interesting discussion of both the approach and its pitfalls is provided by: United Nations Development Programme/World Future Studies Federation, 1986, *Reclaiming the Future*.

91 Meadows, D. H., Meadows, D. L. and Randers, J., 1992, *Beyond the Limits*; Brown, L. R. *et al*, 1994, *Vital Signs*.

92 Falk, R., 1978, 'The world order models project and its critics', *International Organization*, 31, 531–45; Falk, R., 1987, *The Promise of World Order*; Falk, R., 1995, *On Humane Governance. Towards A New Global Politics: The WOMP Report of the Global Civilization Project*.

93 Hughes, B., 1993, *International Futures*, Boulder, Colo.

94 Dark, K. R. with Harris, A. L., 1996, *The New World and the New World Order*, Ch. 3.

95 Dark, K. R. with Harris, A. L., 1996, *The New World and the New World Order*, Ch. 3.

96 Mowat, R. C., 1991, *Decline and Renewal*.

97 For a sample of the perspectives involved: Docherty, T. (ed.), 1993, *Postmodernism. A Reader*; Lechte, J. (ed.), 1994, *Fifty Key Contemporary Thinkers. From Structuralism to Postmodernism*, 95–119 and 231–51. In a more critical context: Rosenau, P. M., 1992, *Post-Modernism and the Social Sciences*, Princeton.

98 Rengger, N. J., 1995, *Political Theory, Modernity and Postmodernity*; Rengger, N. J., 1996, 'Clio's cave and the claims of "substantive social theory" in world politics', *Review of International Studies* 22, 213–31; Vasquez, J. A., 1995, 'The post-positivist debate: restructuring scientific enquiry and international relations theory after enlightenments fall', in K. Booth and S. Smith, *International Relations Theory Today*, 217–40; Lapid, Y., 1989, 'The Third Debate: on the prospects of international theory in a post-positivist era', *International Studies Quarterly* 33, 235–54; Devetak, R., 1996, 'Critical Theory' (pp. 145–178) and 'Postmodernism' (pp. 179–209), both in Burchill, S. and Linklater, A. *et al*, *Theories of International Relations*.

99 Brown C., 1996, 'International Relations Theory and International Distributive Justice', *Politics* 16.1, 1–8.

100 For a 'post-modern' view of the cognate debate in historical theory (historiography): Jenkins, K., 1995, *On 'What is History?'*

101 Walker, R. B. J., 1995, 'International Relations and the concept of the political', in K. Booth and S. Smith, *International Relations Theory Today*, 306–27. See also the same author's: 1993, *Inside/Outside: International Relations as Political Theory*.

102 By this I mean that post-modernists are unlike all other International Relations

theorists in that their approach does not depend *in theory* on a view of historical change. In practice, almost all post-modernist writers make reference to historical assumptions or interpretations, such as the view that 'medieval perceptions were different from those of contemporary actors'.

103 Dark, K. R., forthcoming, 'Problems and possibilities in the long-term analysis of International Relations', (BISA Long-Term Change Conference Paper 1995)

104 *Ibid.*

105 Wolf, E. R., 1982, *Europe and the People Without History*, Berkeley and Los Angeles.

106 Little, R., 1994, 'International Relations and large-scale historical change', in A. J. R. Groom and M. Light (eds), *Contemporary International Relations: A Guide to Theory*, 9–26; Rosenau, J., 1990, *Turbulence in World Politics: A Theory of Change and Continuity*, Princeton.

2

How times change: the interdisciplinary context

The range of theoretical perspectives on long-term change developed in International Relations can be complemented and expanded with reference to those derived from other disciplines. Here, I shall discuss the theories of change, with special reference to approaches capable of application to the analysis of long-term change, in several disciplines: sociology, geography, history, archaeology, anthropology, economics, biology and mathematics.

It could be argued that all of these are related to International Relations. Whether or not that is the case, by the nature of their subject matter one might expect them all to have to address questions of long-term change, or to produce approaches potentially relevant to this study.

The 'hard sciences' are included here not because I wish to align International Relations theory with these disciplines, but simply because of their interest in the explanation of change and evolution in complex systems, which might potentially be likened to the subject matter of International Relations.[1] It must be stressed that this is not to suggest that we should *a priori* assume that human and natural systems are at all similar, but that it seems equally sensible not to assume *a priori* that they are necessarily fundamentally dissimilar in all respects.[2]

In many, but not all, cases the disciplines discussed here have also already been examined by other scholars, with the hope of providing an indication as to how International Relations may address the issue of long-term change.[3] However, there is no published review of how these theories of change may assist International Relations. Consequently, this survey may be worth while both as an overview, setting the interdisciplinary context of previous International Relations studies of change, and as an introduction to a range of new material upon which I shall draw, in part, later in this book.

Sociological approaches

Sociology has been concerned with change since its origins.[4] Comte expressed concern with dynamics and the search for laws underlying change.[5] Durkheim, a century later, still saw change (which he conceived in terms of evolution) as central to his concerns, and much twentieth century sociology employed Marxist theory to approach the study of change.[6]

The principal alternative theory of social change was for long that of 'social evolution'.[7] Since the time of Spencer, sociology has used concepts of Darwinian evolution as a basis for interpreting changes in human social groups and their organization. A key focus of this research was the view that progress toward increased complexity (seen in terms of increased differentiation of functions) was discernible throughout human history.

Two important exceptions to the general tendency to treat social change in terms of either evolution or Marxist historical materialism are the approaches adopted by Sorokin and Pareto. In Sorokin's view change was patterned and its study should aim to recognize this.[8] Sorokin considered human history from the seventh century BC until the early twentieth century AD, employing a global scale of analysis to identify systems and integrating both non-material and material culture. According to his view there are only a few basic types of system, which recur through time, and change is a product of oscillation between these basic systems. The reasons for change are to be found within systems themselves and human actors play an insignificant role in bringing about these changes. Consequently, change must be seen as intrinsic to all systems, and long-term change is a cyclical repetition of a few basic systemic types.

Pareto took a psychological view of change, seeing this as resulting from élite psychology and its relationship to the psychology of those governed by the ruling élite.[9] Using concepts of equilibrium to account for the maintenance of systems, he saw change resulting from a loss of equilibrium. The key factor enabling equilibrium to exist at all was the circulation of élites of differing types, these types having been defined in psychological terms.

Both Sorokin and Pareto represent anti-materialist tendencies which are still strongly represented in sociological theories of change. Although the work of these scholars is no longer credited by most modern sociologists, they help us to identify two distinct trends in the sociological study of change. These are the cultural psychological approach and Marxist dialectical materialism.[10]

In the same way as the conflict between competing groups to secure control is central to Pareto's view, more recently 'conflict theories' of change have been employed in sociology. This approach is especially associated with American scholars of the 1950s and with the work of Dahrendorf.[11] To Dahrendorf, for instance, the outcome of conflict is change, although other conflict theorists see a wider range of possibilities.

Dahrendorf saw both change and conflict as intrinsic to society. In his view societies are based on coercion and change is derived from class conflict. In turn, these conflicts derive from what he describes as 'life chances': the probability of satisfying interests and needs. Change is, therefore, a result of internal factors and the pursuit of interests and needs.

Another key figure in conflict theory is Raymond Aron, who sought to use dialectical analysis to understand change. Aron drew from this the interpretation that inter-group conflict and international tension were general characteristics of human societies.[12] In his view, contradictions cause conflict and conflict brings about change.

Among the most widely debated twentieth-century sociological theories of change is that developed by Parsons, whose work developed the evolutionary tradition within sociology.[13] Taking a structural view of society, Parsons argued that societies are systems comprised of individuals seeking maximizing strategies. Using evolutionary concepts and anthropological functionalism, he employed the concept of 'equilibrium' to explain system maintenance, and 'differentiation' (involving reorganization and adaptation), to explain change over time.

Parsons used some aspects of systems theory, such as the inter-relationship of change in sub-systems, but the key to his view of change is that it is evolutionary. Parsons attempted to recognize cultural and evolutionary universals, incorporating both external and internal sources of change in his approach.

While 'Parsonian functionalism' is no longer widely employed in sociology, it has produced derivative studies, such as that of Smelser.[14] Perhaps the most sophisticated attempt to combine an evolutionary perspective and sociological theory in the study of long-term change is, however, Stephan Sanderson's book *Social Transformations*.[15]

In this work, Sanderson adopts an evolutionary approach to very long-term change, drawing on the work of both anthropologists and, to a much lesser extent, archaeologists for supplementary perspectives. Sanderson's explanatory basis for evolution is materialistic and he draws on both world-systems and Marxist theories. However, he also uses historical sociology based on both materialist and non-materialist approaches. Sanderson's work is by far the most wide-ranging and interdisciplinary perspective yet adopted by evolutionary sociologists.

Not all social analyses of change have, however, been based on these grounds. A key critic of evolutionary and Marxist approaches in sociology has been Anthony Giddens. It is Giddens' theory of 'structuration' that is probably the most widely employed sociological theory of change in use today.[16]

Giddens' theory of structuration most clearly set out in his book, *The Constitution of Society*.[17] It is a theory of practice which combines much of what many would claim they intuitively know about the nature of social action with the clarification gained from an interdisciplinary academic framework drawing on history, geography, anthropology and other disciplines in addition to social theory.

Structuration is founded on the view that there are 'frameworks of action' which constrain our freedom of action but which also enable us to act in the first place: what Giddens calls 'the duality of structure'. Within these 'codes of action' social life is played out, but the individual in society is no passive pawn to wider processes of change: the individual both initiates change and participates in it. Consequently, rather than emphasizing the determinism of materialist or ecological perspectives, structuration places greater importance upon both decision-making and the knowledgeability of actors. It stresses that structures themselves can be transformed by action.

At the heart of Giddens' view is the approach that the individual is a 'conscious strategic actor', making decisions on the basis of experience and knowledge. 'Social reproduction' – the reproducing of structure diachronically – results, therefore, from the repetition of structures in action.

Yet the role of the individual can serve to transform the structures, and so bring about change in the underlying logic or basis of society itself. Structures, therefore, not only both enable action and constrain it, but exist in a reflexive relationship with the participants in those structures.

The emergence of structure, 'structuration', arises from the interaction between individuals and the structures within which they live, and between individuals themselves, transforming rather than reproducing the structures. Consequently, while structures can be reproduced – in order to continue existing social systems – they can also be transformed, bringing about new social frameworks. Such a perspective encompasses both the human and the natural world, so it can include 'structures' such as geographical situation and resources. Structuration enables the 're-centring' of the individual, and aims to establish a framework for discussing individual action in relation to its social, economic and environmental contexts.

Another aspects of Giddens' work which is of special interest here is his recognition of the importance of unexpected consequences of action. Giddens stresses the partial, and possibly distorted, view of every human being who has been, or is, a participant in action. Consequently, changes can come about both intentionally and unintentionally in the course of both individual action and the reproduction and transformation of structure, in a situation of partial perception.

Giddens' theory has, in turn, been criticized by Margaret Archer, who favours instead an theory of 'morphogenesis'.[18] Archer's theory of change has recently been set out in detail in her book *Realist Social Theory: The Morphogenetic Approach*,[19] which offers a drastically different and original perspective on theories of change. She rejects explanations based on collectivism and individualism, and opposes theories which conflate structure and agency (such as 'structuration theory') with those, such as her own, based on emergence and morphogenesis.

In Archer's view, the role played by time in bringing about change has been dramatically underestimated. She suggests that a cyclical process of structural conditioning, social interaction and structural elaboration means structure and agency operate on different time-scales, with neither necessarily precedent to the other. Time, then, plays an active role in differentiating phases of this cycle, and not a passive part as a dimension in which change occurs.

At the core of Archer's approach is morphogenetic theory itself. This she derives from Walter Buckley,[20] who defined it as 'processes which tend to elaborate or change a system's given form, structure or state'. Archer opposes this to 'morphostasis' which is defined as processes preserving systemic form. This clearly relates her work both to systems theory and to biological theories of change, whence the concept of morphogenesis ultimately derives.

In addition to the work of Archer and Giddens, Bourdieu has also contributed to the study of the part played by individualistic action in bringing about change.[21] Central to Bourdieu's approach is his concept of *habitus*. This term is used to refer to structures which are both strategy-generating and enable actors to cope with unforeseen situations. These structures are capable of generating commonalities of action, and are transmitted through enculturation.

The conceptual basis of Bourdieu's theory is elaborated by his attempt to link *habitus* to materialism. This has led him to assign a causal significance to material factors which is absent from Archer's and Giddens' work.

Between them these scholars have provided contemporary sociological theory with a rich literature on the theory of change, although this has not all been explicitly linked to the long-term. Other more directly long-term studies have also been carried out, however, in the paradigm of 'historical sociology', which has become an important sub-discipline within the field.[22]

In contrast to the theories so far discussed, the studies of historical sociologists are usually based on empirical studies. Among them, perhaps the most widely cited analyses have been the work of Michael Mann, Charles Tilly and Theda Skocpol.

In Mann's long-term history of 'social power',[23] his approach, like that of Tilly in the same school of analysis, was to use long-term narrative, thematically tracing the diachronic development of institutions and relationships. Such histories have formed the basis for classifications and explanations based on sociological rather than historical categories and questions.

Tilly has adopted a more materialist perspective than has Mann, who sees 'social power' as having both non-material and material aspects.[24] In Tilly's work a broadly Marxist viewpoint is combined with those derived from other sources. Rather than appearing classically Marxist, Tilly's view can be seen as related to both a Weberian and a structural perspective, stressing options which could have been chosen and integrating organizational and economic perspectives.

Skocpol has discussed the history of revolution and of the state.[25] Taking a comparative institutionalist approach to historical sociology, her theory is opposed to both Marxist and formal theorists of revolution. Like Tilly in this respect, she adopts a structural approach and locates change in transnational factors rather than in domestic politics and society alone.

Other historical sociologists have not agreed with a structural paradigm, preferring instead a historical particularist view. A clear example is Barrington Moore's attempt to understand the 'social origins of dictatorship and democracy', although pausing to search for generalization more often than might most historical particularist historians.[26] In his case the aim was to identify 'paths of modernity', and so the need to stress both contrasts and similarities is found throughout his work, with a strong emphasis on the former.

Others working in this paradigm, such as John Hall, have taken a cognitive or social approach. Hall, in his well-known study of 'the rise of the West', chose to stress such factors, centring his discussion on the role of religion and social organization, and to incorporate these with political factors.[27] Hall also gave some credence to theories of social evolution and of progress, and less attention to economic factors than the other scholars so far discussed.

Interesting also is the work of Carneiro and Taagepera, as it illustrates the close relationship between some scholars of historical sociology and those working in anthropology.[28] Carneiro developed a theory of the origin of the state based partly on social factors, but also on environmental context, especially the pressures of occupying a physically circumscribed area. In this way Carneiro's work forges a clear link between sociological analysis and environmental determinism, a viewpoint which has historically been much more important in anthropological theories of long-term change than in sociology.

A somewhat similar approach to that of Carneiro is that of Rein Taagepera, who in an important series of studies investigated the relationship between size and duration of empires. Identifying a step-like pattern in the growth of empire size, he has drawn attention to the increasing size of empires over approximately the last 5000 years.

Also interesting among recent work by historical sociologists is Giovanni Arrighi's *The Long Twentieth Century*.[29] Arrighi adopts a theoretical position similar to that of some Structuralist scholars in International Relations. Combining a Marxist perspective and world-systems theory, he fuses these with Braudelian Annaliste historiography. This he employs to trace the relationship between the accumulation of capital, hegemony and the development of states over a 700-year timescale.

Alternatively, some sociologists have placed importance on human biology rather than on economics or environmental factors, adapting socio-biological and evolutionary approaches, as found in the work of the founder of 'sociobiology', Edward Wilson.[30] In this view human behaviour is the outcome of evolutionary factors, such as 'selection', producing inborn (and so intrinsic) human instincts and propensities to specific forms of action. Change can, therefore, be explained both in terms of such behaviours and in terms of the application of evolutionary and ecological theory to human groups.

An interesting recent sociological theory of long-term change related to this approach is that proposed by Tim Megarry. This study also has the interest here of attempting to examine evidence from the distant past in a sociological, and specifically – in part – socio-biological, context.

Megarry's views are most clearly expressed in his *Society in Prehistory*.[31] In that work, Megarry adopts a perspective which attempts to combine socio-biological and evolutionary theories with cognitive and social approaches. In his view, people inherit some characteristics from evolutionary adaptation but these are to be seen alongside cultural factors, rather than overriding them. In Megarry's opinion, similarities can be recognized between human societies (and arguably how they respond to and initiate change) relating closely to shared problems and challenges rather than to underlying nature alone.

An alternative – now generally neglected – among sociological theories of change is the view that change may be explained by cognitive factors. A clear example of these studies is found in the work of McClelland.[32] McClelland argued that 'entrepreneurial personality types' cause change. Taking a Freudian approach to the origin of such characteristics, he claims that this is a universal in time and space, although achievement-orientation of this sort is facilitated by some cultures rather than others.

However, more attention has usually been given to the oft-quoted Weber theory of change, embedded in his analysis of the origins of capitalism.[33] Weber's theory is also based on a cognitive view of causation. According to Weber, religious beliefs (in this case Calvinism) lead to social and economic values, in turn leading to specific types of economic activity and so to socio-economic change.

This theory has been modified by the work of later scholars, but remains a major contribution to sociological approaches to the study of change. Critical studies of Weber's theory have questioned both its generality and the specific case of the role of Calvinism in promoting economic change. For example, Stokes has noted that Calvinism in South Africa produced different economic behaviour to Calvinism in Europe, suggesting that the causal relationship is more complex than Weber supposed.[34]

The diversity of theoretical approaches to the analysis of long-term change, and of change in general, in sociology attests the vitality of research on this issue. It also suggests the centrality which it is perceived to hold for the majority of sociologists. There are also, of course, sociologists who deny that the study of change, and of long-term change, is either significant or worthwhile.

Geographical approaches

Recently, geographers have shown much interest in the study of change.[35] This discipline long contained scholars who examined change in terms of environmental determinism or 'possibilism' (what could be possible in specific contexts). This co-existed with another long-standing school of economic explanation, currently visible in the treatment of the collapse of Soviet dominance in eastern Europe and the subsequent economic transition from centrally-planned economies. These 'transition studies' have almost entirely used a materialist framework of analysis, correlating economic and other forms of change, and seeing economic factors as causal.[36]

Not all geographers favouring materialist, or specifically Marxist, theories of change have applied this specifically to the transition in eastern Europe. Marxism, in various forms, has been a widespread form of explanation in geography. For example, Harvey has used a historical materialist approach to examine how economic change has led to 'postmodernity' in Western societies. 'Postmodernity' is defined in his study as both a post-industrial socio-economic situation and an 'attitude'.[37] Harvey stresses the importance of economic process rather than structure, but other geographers prefer a structural approach, as for example by drawing attention to the work of Sayer.[38] This contrast between materialist and structural approaches has (alongside calls for a more 'people-centred' geography) been the basis for an 'agency–structure' debate analogous to that in International Relations, and including discussion of concepts relating to structure derived from sociology.[39]

Sociology has made other important contributions to geographical approaches to change, such as Urry's use of Weberian theory.[40] Geography also has its post-modernists (in the more usual sense of this term), such as Dear and Soja.[41] The latter, for example, stresses the view that hypotheses cannot be validated, and so a plurality of alternative hypotheses is always preferable.

Recently, too, political geography has been transformed by the rediscovery of the analysis of long-term political change, especially as a result of the work of Peter Taylor.[42] Taylor, and others, have been employing world-systems approaches. Taking a long-term perspective on contemporary geopolitics, they use data from historical and cartographic sources for the period since AD 1500.

In his own studies, Taylor has combined the approaches of Wallerstein with those of 'long-cycle' theorists, to examine the global economy of the last 500 years in terms of both diachronic change and spatial patterning. To these, Taylor adds the work of theorists of imperialism and of nationalism, to provide a multi-scalar study of global geopolitical change over almost 500 years.

Taylor's approach has formed the basis for the emergence of a school of 'world-systems analysis' in geography. For example, one may note the work of Johnston on the rise and decline of state organization, and that of Agnew.[43] Generally, however, geographers working in this paradigm have been unwilling to break with the concept that Wallerstein's modern world system begins in the sixteenth century, and so take their analyses back no further.

Other geographers have adopted a different perspective on the analysis of change. Guelke has advocated an 'idealism' based on his understanding of Collingwood's cognitive approach to history.[44] Alternatively, Cohen, for instance, has adopted a more explicitly systemic view, combining this with earlier geographical concepts of 'shatterbelts' (peripheral zones of instability) and the theory of 'gateway' states and regions (strategically-located small but highly-developed units).[45]

Others again have examined the relationship between geography and time itself. They have stressed that time periods involved in contact between areas may give a more accurate depiction of spatial relations than mere distances. Time and space themselves bear a close relationship to technologies of communication, whether by the sending of information between locations or by travel. Important here is the major contribution to geographical studies of change made by Hägerstrand.[46]

His theory of 'time–space geography' has made a wide interdisciplinary impact on studies of change and geographical location. It rests upon a definition of geographical space in terms of communication or travelling times, rather than 'Euclidean' physical territorial extent. Situating events in this 'time–space' matrix produces a different understanding of their location to that gained by simply placing them in absolute physical space.

Hägerstrand's work has been built upon by many scholars, notably Pred. Pred has combined cognitive, structural and processual aspects, utilizing both structuration theory and time–space geography, to study change. He argues that change is contingent (historically specific), but relates this to its geographical context.

The most widespread context in which geographers have analysed change is, however, perhaps in the study of 'development theory'. Unlike any of these other approaches, this has become a whole sub-discipline of geography primarily focused on issues of change. This sub-discipline is made up of scholars – not always professional geographers by training – who attempt to analyse change in order more usefully to understand contemporary global social and economic issues.[47]

Like International Relations theory, 'development theory' contains a 'structuralist' (and 'neo-structuralist') school, interested in issues such as core–periphery relationships, and schools favouring liberal or Marxist (including 'post-Marxist') economic theories of change. Organizational approaches are also employed, as in the work of Perkins and Syrquin, who use empirical data to observe regularities in the relationship between state size and the speed of economic diversification.[48] In a recent review of the range of perspectives in this sub-discipline, even the title of which is contested (Booth himself prefers 'social development'), Booth noted the existence of these and two other major viewpoints: 'actor-orientated' approaches and post-modernism. The latter has had a more significant impact in the recent history of 'development studies' than in International Relations theory.[49]

Actor-orientated approaches, such as those of Hebinck and Long,[50] have taken a reflexive view of individualistic action and situational constraints (such as environment and economic structures) and have considered the range of options open to individual actors and the diversity of contexts within which they are located. These approaches locate change in 'individual choice', but stress the context of such choices.

Responses to post-modernism in 'development studies' have been varied, and the approach which post-modernists scholars in this field have tended to adopt is close to that of 'social constructivism'. 'Development studies' have a form of post-modernist analysis which permits some degree of discussion of change, albeit in terms of the construction of historical reality rather than its existence.

Consequently, it is clear that, like sociology, geography contains a range of more or less competing paradigms and theories of change. These include those which directly address, or can clearly be related to, questions of long-term change. It may be surprising, perhaps, to find that geographers have such a restricted range of approaches to change, given their subject matter. However, we shall see that to some extent this is also the case in, arguably, one of the subjects most likely to examine long-term change: History.

History

History has two theories of change of its own which have been very widely discussed in an interdisciplinary context. The first is Marxism, which is, of course, in origin a historical theory. Unsurprisingly, therefore, there is a very extensive Marxist literature on the issue of change and on the theory of history (historiography) in general. Here again it is, of course, only possible to outline the range of those perspectives encompassed.[51]

Marxist views of history can be divided into four forms: Classical, Gramscian, Structural, and Critical. In Classical Marxism primacy in determining change is assigned to underlying economic factors, and the pattern of diachronic change is seen as teleological, passing through stages to its eventual culmination. In Gramscian Marxist historiography more of a role is allowed for cognitive factors and interaction, with emphasis placed on hegemony, understood here as uncontested ideological dominance.

Structural Marxists (as in anthropology) move even further from an economic understanding of change, seeing cognitive factors and the control of information as playing a major part in bringing about and shaping changes. Critical Theorists instead challenge the purpose and methodology of historical research as such. Critical Theory questions the reason behind the production of historical studies and tries to identify the uses they serve to those producing them. It attempts to discover the effects which specific approaches or interpretations have on wider society. In these respects, Critical Theory in historiography is, of course, similar to Critical Theory in International Relations.

Although the Marxist tradition of historiography has been frequently debated, most historiographical debate has taken place outside of a Marxist framework. Here, the work of two philosophers of history – R. G. Collingwood and Karl Popper – deserves special note, given its centrality to subsequent historiographical debate.

In his classic *The Idea of History*,[52] Collingwood set out a theory of explaining long-term change (including political change) based on an empathetic approach. In this, understanding is acquired by attempting to reproduce those cognitive processes which led to a specific action. This he intended to be used alongside a 'question and answer' method of analysis, so as to produce historical studies which while similar to the 'work of the novelist' were 'meant to be true'.

Collingwood's views are easily misunderstood as a call for either relativism or a totally empathetic mode of study. Instead, Collingwood favoured a view of history grounded in an appreciation of the relationship between historical method and source-materials having an existence independent to that of the observer.

In contrast to many philosophers of history, it is possible to correct any misconceptions regarding Collingwood's outlook by comparing his theoretical work to his own practical studies of the past. In addition to being a professional philosopher, Collingwood was one of the leading archaeologists and historians of Roman Britain of his generation.[53] There, he showed a particular interest in the use of deductive logical argument, and especially hypothesis-testing by experimentation, to evaluate alternative models. These included an emphasis unusual for his time on cognitive and social aspects of the Roman period.

Collingwood's practical application of his perspective displays both his attempts to 'question' available written and material sources by generating and testing hypotheses, and his aim of incorporating human intentionality in his studies. This approach, however, explicitly rejected generalizing and universalizing theories, and with them the concept of historical cycles, forging a clear link between his perspective and that of Popper.

Popper, well-known of course for his theory of refutation, was essentially concerned with epistemology in the study of the past.[54] However, in his work *The Poverty of Historicism*, he offers a wide-ranging critique of universalizing and generalizing approaches to historical change.[55] Popper's view, like that of Collingwood, was to see change as resulting from individual intentionality rather than from laws of universal applicability.

Both Collingwood and Popper agree that hypothesis-testing is possible and that the search for universal historical laws ('historicism') must be rejected, so that any approach based on them, whether Marxist or non-Marxist in character, is invalid. As a consequence of the work of these two scholars, few if any modern historians favour what are perceived to be 'historicist' theories, such as those once advanced by Toynbee and Spengler, which attempt to formulate diachronic laws.

The other group of historiographers whose theory of the long-term is probably most widely discussed among non-historians today is the 'Annaliste school'.[56] Although diverse, their approach is well-illustrated by the work of the most famous 'Annaliste', Fernand Braudel, and exemplified in his book, *Civilization and Capitalism 15th-18th Century*.[57]

Braudel's studies have emphasized the significance of analysing change on many, but related, scales of time and space. These range from the event (*événement*) through the medium term (*moyen durée*) to the long term (*longue durée*) comprising centuries, or even millennia. Braudel emphasized that processes operating on all of these time-scales are potentially interrelated but that separate types of process may operate on different chronological, or spatial, scales.

At different scales different types of explanation may be most effective, but this is not simply the basis for a resort to economic or environmental determinism. Cognitive factors (*Mentalitiés*) are seen as operating across all scales, and – while rejecting environmental determinism – ecological contexts and the interplay of social and economic factors are seen as important in bringing about change.

Annaliste scholars have been at the forefront of historiographical thinking about long-term change for a generation or more, and the school has developed a distinctive character. Such an approach has obvious relevance to the questions considered here. It suggests that the integration of multiple scales in time and space is important in analysing change, and that the processes operating within the remarks which they provide are also able to be analysed in this way. In Annaliste analyses this integration is achieved without making the assumption, common to many other schools of analysis, that the same processes are to be found at all scales of analysis. Nor is it assumed that each process necessarily operates on only one scale.

Annalistes have not worked in a vacuum, ignorant or scornful of the other approaches mentioned here. They have, for example, adopted the concept of economic cycles such as Kondratieff waves. Braudel, for example, has advanced a proposition, based on Annaliste analysis, that such cycles existed prior to the Industrial Revolution.

Many would group Annaliste theory with 'structural history'. The latter has recently been the subject of an excellent review by Christopher Lloyd in his book *The Structures of History*.[58] Lloyd identifies the capacity for existence of a non-materialist structural history which is independent of the Annaliste tradition yet supersedes Marxist historiography. In Lloyd's 'structurist history', as he refers to it, agency is given a much more central role than in most Marxist versions and importance attached to cognitive factors. But Lloyd still retains a key role for 'relatively autonomous' structures. Combining this with an epistemological discussion which highlights the limitations of relativistic perspectives, Lloyd suggests a multi-scalar approach. This places causal emphasis on structural contexts and incorporates a non-Marxist debate over 'social hierarchies' as organizing bases for past societies. Lloyd's view can thus perhaps be seen to represent the most closely argued recent statement of the 'structural' position in historiography, outside the Annaliste school.

Among professional historians, however, the most widespread theoretical approach is not that of Annaliste theorists or of other structural historians, but the historical particularist approach. This is the theory that history is comprised only of sequences of heterogeneous events comprehensible as narrative. Such sequences may be chronologically or thematically organized. they may be focused on political events, social narratives or economic actions, but they are based on the same theoretical concepts. These concepts were established, at least in the English-speaking world, by the philosophical studies of Collingwood and Popper referred to above.

Historical particularism is based on the view that there are no processes or structures operating in history. It claims that historical generalizations or cross-cultural regularities do not exist. Such approaches would be grouped with the belief in historical laws (such as historical materialism) as 'historicism' or even 'metahistory' by historical particularists.

The principal opposition to historical particularism was for long the Marxist school. This in itself may perhaps have dissuaded non-Marxist historians from approaching questions of long-term regularity and change. These questions have, therefore, been closely connected with discussions of Marxist approaches, such as the much-criticized work of Anderson on the borders of history and historical sociology.[59] It was part of the debate over the 'scientific' and regularizing outlook of the short-lived behaviouralist 'new history' school,[60] and these factors have rendered any such approach apparently peripheral or dubious when seen from the perspective of mainstream historical research. Historians have, therefore, been extremely reluctant to examine other theories of long-term change, although a small 'world-systems' school exists within the discipline. Some scholars, such as Paul Kennedy,[61] have incorporated historical particularist and materialist perspectives to produce a historical theory of change in which the narration of heterogeneous sequences of events can be combined with explanations posed principally in economic terms.

Kennedy's *The Rise and Fall of the Great Powers*[62] is a clear example of this. Kennedy's book attempts to trace in a narrative manner a sequence of recurrent rise and fall among major states since the sixteenth century. There is, he argues, a close relationship between the economic growth and decline of 'great powers', states holding a pre-eminent position among contemporaries, and political roles. The linkage, for Kennedy, is recognizable as the costs of pre-eminence combined with a correlation between economic and military superiority which links economic factors with politics.

Kennedy's approach has been the subject of much, generally unfavourable, comment by historians. Interestingly, although it was written as a work of history and not of political science, to the International Relations theorist Kennedy's approach might seem a clear example of 'structural Realism'.

However, Kennedy is keen to point out in his book that he is a historian, not a scholar of International Relations.[63] It can, therefore, be seen as an exemplar of the attempt by some historians to combine both historical particularist and materialist paradigms of historiography in the study of long-term change.

There are, of course, exceptions to the generalization that historiography has been dominated by historical particularist and materialist approaches. One such is post-modern historiography.[64] The origin of this approach has been associated primarily with the work of Rorty and White.[65] It has produced, as one would expect, a wide diversity of studies centred on the concept that historical studies are a form of narrative fiction. This, it is claimed, tells us more about the context of its production than about the periods which it seeks to investigate. The post-modern historiographical theory can be summed up as 'history is construct'; that is what we call 'knowledge of the past' is no more than a representation of the present. Here we have historiographers who oppose the existence of a knowable past, and for that matter a knowable present: historians opposed to the knowability of history.

The remaining exception to the pervasiveness of historical particularism in historiography has been the work of the so-called 'World Historians'. This perspective is not centred on an epistemological position. It represents an attitude to the geographical and chronological scope of history and to the range of issues which history can be taken as encompassing. To World Historians, history can be examined on a worldwide or at least continental scale and over very long time-spans.

Interestingly, although they have been keen to encompass unfamiliar topics – such as the spread of disease – in historical analysis, the work of World Historians has tended to avoid theoretical debates about methodology and causation. Thus, it contributes surprisingly little to the theoretical discussion here.

It must be stressed that, although World History has been popular with historical sociologists and scholars of International Relations, it still exists on the scholarly and professional limits of mainstream historiography. The reasons for this are unclear; it may be because of its uneasy relationships with both historical particularism and Marxist historiography. Alternatively, there may be a suspicion that any broad study must be less rigorous than one tightly focused on specific events. In consequence, even the most acclaimed World Historian, William McNeill,[66] is seen by some, to quote a recent work, as 'a liminal figure ... whose work is not yet regarded as quite respectable among the majority of his fellow historians'.[67] McNeill's studies of broad historical themes, however, exemplify the grand sweep of this approach, its potential contribution, and the close relationship between its themes and the work of both sociologists and anthropologists.

This situation may be gradually changing as, despite its somewhat marginal position, World History remains a popular approach with a sizeable group of scholars internationally, and is perhaps becoming more acceptable to mainstream historians. It is, however, yet to achieve the prominence inside history which it has recently been afforded in International Relations theory, and to a lesser extent by historical sociologists.

However, the degree to which historians have themselves been aware of theoretical paradigms in use in other subjects should not be underestimated. Perhaps the clearest illustration of this is Peter Burke's book *History and Social Theory*,[68] in which he draws on theoretical discussions in sociology and anthropology as well as historiography. In taking this approach, he points to the distinctive strengths of historiographical theory. These he sees as including, for example, the ability to integrate 'micro-histories' of individualistic action with large-scale accounts of historical change.

Burke alerts us to the way in which historical case-studies can highlight the contingency of seemingly general theories, such as 'economic laws', but also to how historians can themselves employ sociological and anthropological concepts. To Burke, a synthesis of history and social theory (by which he understands sociological and anthropological theory) is required to enrich the discipline. This must not, however, lose sight of the theoretical strengths which it already has.

Burke devotes a whole chapter of his work to theories of change, including those of social evolution, structuration and historical sociology. The lack of specifically historical theories of change – other than structural history and Marxism is, however, noticeable.

Thus, in history, we see another discipline where long-term studies are given a central role, and in which there are a series of contrasting theoretical approaches to their analysis. The most surprising aspect of history, in this respect, is the relative lack of theoretical discussion of long-term change (even among World Historians) compared to what would perhaps be expected by non-historians.

Anthropological approaches

Anthropologists have long been interested in change, but has also developed few of its own theoretical approaches to it. Early anthropological approaches were divided between evolutionary, functionalist and Marxist schools.[69]

During the twentieth century, anthropological theory was dominated first by functionalism, and then by structuralisme, while later structuralisme too was abandoned. Functionalism held that all human culture (a term which anthropologists use very widely to describe all aspects of human political, social, artistic and economic activity) is explicable by reference to its function. Structuralisme was the belief that all perception, and so all action, was shaped by the cognitive structures of the mind, which structuralistes sometimes argued had emerged from physical evolution.[70]

This too is today rejected by anthropologists, who favour approaches derived from other disciplines. These include materialist, socio-biological, ecological, evolutionary or post-modernist theories, and an approach similar to that of historical sociology. Of these, the evolutionary, ecological and materialist approaches are probably those most widely in use.

The evolutionary approach in anthropology has, perhaps, been most closely associated with Leslie White and Elman Service.[71] To Service the development of civilization could be classified into stages, from the hunter-gatherer band through the tribe and chiefdom to the state.

Although much criticized, evolutionary approaches have remained a major part of anthropological theory. For example, this way of studying long-term transformations is probably the most widely employed in contemporary American anthropology.[72] It is, however, often combined with other theories, as in the work of Boyd and Richerson, who employ both evolutionary theory and socio-biological concepts.[73]

A recent example which illustrates the sophistication of current anthropological evolutionary approaches to long-term political change is the book *The Evolution of Political Systems*.[74] This consists of a series of studies by scholars, both anthropologists and archaeologists (no disciplinary division exists between these subjects in the USA, whereas they are distinct in Europe and elsewhere), on the question of long-term political dynamics. The perspectives encompassed in this work include demographic, ecological, economic and technological viewpoints. Some of these use cyclical approaches to change, while others emphasize non-cyclical views. Among the contributors there are also those who employ cognitive factors or analyses of decision-making, while others emphasize the study of competition as the basis of explaining changes. There is a wide diversity of approach within this single major volume, but the papers are united by the fact that they all adopt key evolutionary concepts (such as adaptation) as part of their theories of change.

Materialist anthropology has been perhaps less prominent than materialist history or sociology. In this area, the work of French anthropologists has been particularly visible, especially that of Althusser and Godelier.[75] These scholars noted that the ethnographic data with which they worked could not be explained in materialist terms alone, and modified their approach to encompass a greater role for cognitive factors. So, for instance, Godelier observed that economic activities in Melanesia were undertaken as a result of cognitive factors and within a structure resulting from the beliefs and values of those involved. Modifying Marxist theory in this way, anthropologists produced a distinctive approach, the 'structural Marxist' school, which has been widely employed in other disciplines. The best-known materialist approach to anthropology to be employed in the English-speaking world is probably that of Marvin Harris, who links materialism and ecological theory.[76]

These evolutionary and Marxist views were long opposed in anthropology by scholars adopting a historical particularist mode of explanation, known in anthropology as 'culture history'. Scholars working in this school often favoured explanations based on the 'diffusion' of characteristics over time between populations, as a result of contact.

While culture historical approaches are no longer generally employed by anthropologists, a very different theory of long-term change from that of both most Marxists and evolutionary theorists, has recently been developed by Jonathan Friedman. Friedman is an eminent Marxist anthropologist, whose early work related closely to theoretical studies in 'functional process-ual' archaeology.[77]

In his book *Cultural Identity and Global Process*[78] his theory of anthropology is applied to long-term data. Here Friedman adopts an eclectic view, drawing on approaches from sociology, history, archaeology and other disciplines, including both world-systems analysis and aspects of post-modernism. He combines these with a structural Marxist framework of analysis, to produce a distinctive perspective on long-term change. Fried-man's view explicitly links the two aspects he studies, identity and the processes of change, incorporating both cyclical and non-cyclical inter-pretations to address questions similar to those examined by Frank and Gills in International Relations theory.

Whereas Friedman's work represents a new development, ecological approaches have a long history in anthropological theory, being incorp-orated into functionalist, Marxist and evolutionary analyses. Recent work in this area may be exemplified by the studies presented in Moran's *The Ecosystem Approach in Anthropology*.[79] Building on the work of scholars such as Rappaport, Chagnon, Irons, Vayda, Orlove and others, the contributors also adopt an eclectic view, drawing on biology, geography, archaeology and, of course, anthropological theory. For example, in what is perhaps the most explicit theory of change in that volume, Lees and Bates have proposed an 'event-centred' and evolutionary ecological perspective.[80]

A cognitive approach has been adopted by scholars such as Goody and Gellner.[81] This examines cognitive factors in long-term historical context. Setting them in social and economic context, it reflexively relates inter-pretations of changing beliefs, perceptions and values to changes in information-processing (especially literacy), education and the structure of knowledge.

There is, of course, also a post-modernist wing of anthropological theory. This shares such close theoretical similarities with interdisciplinary post-modernism (as discussed in the previous chapter) that further discussion of this approach is not needed here.

Finally, there are scholars who adopt a historical approach close to that of historical sociologists. These employ historical particularism or structural history to examine long-term patterns of change. Examples of this approach are the oft-quoted books on the rise of English individualism and the 'Contact Period' of European colonization, by Alan MacFarlane (*The Origins of English Individualism*[82]) and Eric Wolf (*Europe and the People Without History*[83].).

Anthropological theory has, therefore, tended to approach change through the application of general theories such as evolution and Marxism. It shows relatively little diversity of theoretical approaches compared, for instance, to sociology. A lack of theoretical diversity is, however, certainly not a charge which one might level at the next subject of this survey: archaeology.

Archaeological approaches

Archaeologists might reasonably be expected by political scientists to have developed theories of long-term political change, considering the time-scales involved in their subject matter. Since the nineteenth century, at latest, archaeology has been explicitly identified with the study of long-term change. Archaeologists themselves have felt able to reconstruct political, social and economic organization from their sources since at least the 1930s. Moreover, archaeology has enabled the identification of a large number of previously unknown past societies, including several large-scale states, such as the Hittite empire.[84] So archaeology is an obvious source for theories of analysis of long-term change.

Unsurprisingly, then, faced with studying (inter alia) the rise and fall across millennia of both states and broader international communities, archaeologists have been at the interdisciplinary forefront of theoretical studies of long-term change. This is a realization which seems inexplicably to have passed many political scientists by. It is especially hard to explain why this lack of attention came about, given the routine use of such data and theories by anthropologists, biologists and even many geographers. Presumably it derives from a perception of archaeology's irrelevance to the study of modern world politics. As we shall see, this may be a severe misperception.

Archaeology has produced a vast amount of theoretical work on change. This is probably partly because of the sheer numbers of archaeological theorists (compared to those of any other discipline mentioned in this book) who concentrate their efforts on this issue alone. Archaeological theorists both produce their own theoretical perspectives and draw extensively upon those of other disciplines, modifying them where this seems required.

Archaeologists have also long been very eclectic in their approach to those disciplines in which they seek theoretical perspectives. Currently these include anthropology, sociology, philosophy, history, biology, physics, mathematics, geography, linguistics and literary theory.

These characteristics combine to provide archaeology with an apparently bewildering array of theories of change, both 'indigenous' and 'imported'. However, despite this it is possible to recognize four paradigms into which almost all of the many schools of archaeological theory may conveniently be grouped.

Most archaeological theorists would voluntarily place themselves into one of these four major theoretical paradigms. The paradigms are: historical particularism (also called 'culture history' in archaeology), processualism, post-processualism (which is broadly equivalent to the post-modernist and post-structuralist movements of other disciplines) and, to a much lesser extent, Marxism. Most Marxist scholars in archaeology do not, however, see themselves specifically as 'Marxists', and prefer to label themselves 'pro-cessualists' or 'post-processualists'.[85]

The modern debate over long-term change began in archaeology as a result of the rise of 'processual' archaeological theory in the 1960s. Process-ual archaeology, which originated in the 'New Archaeology' movement, stresses the need for explaining change and for the study of long-term process, and seeks regularities between changes in differing societies and geographical areas.

In its earliest form (functional processualism) processualism was closely associated with behaviouralism. However, this association ceased as beha-viouralism became first isolated (as 'Behavioural Archaeology') and then effectively obsolete in the discipline, in the later 1970s and 1980s. After that time, a successor within the processualist tradition (cognitive processualism) emerged and is widely found today. Cognitive processualism includes a variety of perspectives, including a world-systems school, a structural approach related to Annaliste historiography, a morphogenetic perspective, an evolutionary approach, and an individualistic view somewhat reminis-cent of Giddensian structuration and conceptually related to it.

A clear and elegant expression of the cognitive–processualist approach is provided by Jim Bell's important recent discussion of archaeological theory, *Reconstructing Prehistory*.[86] Bell is not himself an archaeologist, but an epi-stemological philosopher, albeit one well versed in current archaeological (and anthropological) theory. In his analysis of theory and method, he explores similar and contrasting perspectives from archaeology, anthro-pology and philosophy, examining themes of wide general interest.

Despite its title, Bell's book is not tied simply to the study of prehistoric societies, but encompasses both pre-modern and modern data in the examples given. In conclusion, he supports a cognitive processual view of explanation, based on analysis at an individualistic level, and sees change as the outcome of decision-making. This, he argues, is compatible with both a Popperian philosophy of historical knowledge and a liberal democratic (International Relations theorists might say 'neo-liberal') viewpoint on contemporary society.

Bell's work, both in his recent book and more generally, forms part of an ongoing interdisciplinary dialogue – especially in the UK – between social theorists, anthropologists, mathematicians, philosophers and archaeological theorists. Even compared to International Relations theory, cognitive processual archaeology has a strikingly multi-disciplinary perspective, and stresses its general relevance to issues of social science and biological theory.

The cognitive processual approach has produced a number of theoretical perspectives of its own which directly relate to the study of long-term political change. To give two examples, both of which will be discussed in relation to International Relations theory later in this book, we may focus on the theories of 'peer-polity interaction' and 'scalar stress'. Both of these provide interesting perspectives on political change and complexity, and both address issues of relevance to world politics.

Peer-polity interaction (or 'PPI' as it is sometimes known) proposes that contacts between similar political units produce, over time, socio-political and cultural similarities between them.[87] These contacts may be between individuals, social groups or whole societies, but their effects are similar in that cultural convergence frequently occurs. This offers an alternative model of regional interaction to 'world-systems' perspectives, which are also found in archaeology. PPI sees inter-unit interaction as transnational, multi-level, reflexive, multi-channelled and contingent, rather than structured diachronically and unidirectional. It also sees this as primarily articulated through individuals, not social classes or political organization.

'Scalar stress' theory was set out by Gregory Johnson, working on the borders of anthropology and archaeology.[88] Johnson drew on much earlier work in anthropological studies of the relationship between demography and societal structure, to produce an empirically grounded theory of the relationship between the size of social groups and political organization.

Looking at a very large ethnographic dataset, Johnson pointed to a clear correlation between group-size and political structure. These differences were not, he showed, attributable to ecological or economic contexts; rather they derived from the way in which information was processed in those societies. Further research strengthened this evidence of a parallel between information-processing and the form of socio-political organization. In a classic paper, Johnson noted that larger and more organizationally complex groups also exhibited greater 'social stress'. This too was imposed by information-processing difficulties, and related to the effectiveness of the political structures involved.

Both of these approaches derive from archaeological theory, yet relate closely to problems at the core of political science. However, functional processualists, in particular, are keen to stress the 'scientific' character of archaeology and align it more firmly with the natural and physical sciences than with social science. This, to some extent, builds upon existing relationships between archaeology and the sciences (functional processual archaeologists would say 'the other sciences'), which are already close. The 'special relationship' which exists between archaeology and the laboratory sciences is partly a result of the large number of 'archaeological scientists'. These use biological, physical or mathematical modes of analysis in the study of primary archaeological sources. This has meant that the interdisciplinary environment exists whereby functional processualist archaeology has been able to employ mathematical and ecological theories in a much more extensive fashion than would be usual in a contemporary (post-behaviouralist) social science. Likewise archaeological theory has used new mathematical concepts (such as 'chaos theory') long before these have been widely employed in most other disciplines.

To give two notable examples: Renfrew, the leading British archaeological theorist, began to employ the (then new) mathematical 'catastrophe theory' to study the collapse of state-societies and to study the process of innovation, as early as the 1970s. At the very start of the 1980s, others – such as Whallon – used non-linear dynamics to study the emergence of social complexity, about a decade before this became 'popular' among social scientists.

Ecological and cultural evolutionary approaches have also been widely used in archaeology (for example in the work of Binford – arguably the originator of the 'new archaeology' – and Butzer). There are also a few functional processualists employing socio-biological approaches, as exemplified by the work of Shennan.

A distinctive, cognitive processual, ecological evolutionary perspective on change has also developed. An example of this is to be found in much of the work of Kent Flannery, one of the leading American archaeological theorists since the 1960s. His co-authored book (with Joyce Marcus) *The Cloud People*[89] is, for instance, often taken to characterize current evolutionary processualism in archaeology. In this and many earlier studies, Flannery has explored the evolution of complex societies, using both evolutionary theory and systemic approaches and combining these with ecological perspectives.[90]

Perhaps Flannery's most important theoretical contribution has however, been his theory of 'hypercoherence'. Flannery noted that some socio-economic sub-systems could become overly dependent upon the continued stability of other sub-systems, so that they became amenable to sudden dramatic change when this stability ceased. Very slight sub-systemic fluctuations could, then, produce system-wide changes, and often systemic collapse. The theory of hypercoherence was proposed nearly a decade before mathematical catastrophe theory confirmed his view that complex systems can exhibit such behaviour, for much the same reasons as he suggested.

Other archaeologists, in what they have provocatively termed the 'post-processual' school, have been strongly affected by post-modernist approaches and see their affinities as with literary or social science studies using Critical Theory, structuraliste, post-modernist or post-structuraliste theory. These archaeologists, like post-modernist scholars in other disciplines, have tended to stress the relativity of knowledge and the political content of interpretations of the distant past. This 'post-processual' school, and the fierce debate it initiated, dominated much archaeological theory in the 1980s and 1990s and has limited, but not halted, the development of processual theories since that time.

Alongside, and often within, these paradigms has existed a Marxist approach to archaeological explanation. This encompasses Classical Marxists, Structural Marxists, and Critical Theorists, but few Gramscians. Marxist theory in archaeology relates, therefore, to wider trends of Marxist analysis rather than presenting specifically archaeological Marxist theories of change.

Thus, archaeology has been perhaps the most vigorous of all disciplines in generating theoretical approaches to long-term change. From the viewpoint of the scholar of long-term change in international politics it has two key attractions. First, it contains a wealth of relevant theory of its own. Secondly, it acts as a 'collection point' for perspectives on long-term change, and related issues, in other disciplines. As such, it is curious that it has been until now almost completely ignored as a source of International Relations theory.

Before leaving this subject, however, an important contribution to one of the central debates regarding long-term political change must be noted. This is the – apparently conclusive – resolution of the long-standing controversy regarding the relative significance of external (exogenous) and internal (endogenous) causes of change in human societies. In the 1970s, building on work by another famous prehistorian, Grahame Clarke, Renfrew suggested that the – then conventional – explanation of most changes by reference to exogenous factors (notably 'diffusion') was erroneous. Instead, he proposed that the main alternative – that change usually derives from endogenous factors – was correct. As new archaeological data became available world-wide in the course of the 1960s, and new precision in chronology was given by new techniques such as radiocarbon dating, the material became available to evaluate both explanations on a global scale across many millennia. Renfrew himself undertook a literally worldwide study of change using this vast body of new evidence, examining the relative importance of endogenous and exogenous factors. The results of this were seemingly conclusive. 'Diffusionism' had envisaged change deriving from human migration or trade, and so occurring broadly in the same way over wide regions and sequentially in one area after the next. This was not borne out by the relative dating of changes in different areas, nor by the forms which these changes took. For example, similar changes could be shown to have occurred in related areas but at widely different times, although simultaneously in different but completely unconnected areas.

Colin Renfrew's study, published (in popular form) in his book *Before Civilization*,[91] is generally agreed by archaeologists today to have shown that the diffusionist model is no longer tenable. The sheer scale of this analysis has to be fully appreciated to understand why this result has been so conclusively accepted. In showing that change did not usually derive from such external factors, Renfrew drew on well-dated evidence encompassing thousands of years of human history, and a global scope of analysis, to support the 'independent invention' hypothesis as it is known. Archaeology – which has an especially vigorous critical tradition – has abandoned most other theoretical approaches set out in the 1960s. Despite this level of disciplinary critique, the view that change is usually endogenous in origin remains without serious challenge from any theoretical school in the subject.

Subsequent case-studies have also tended to offer strong support for such endogenous explanations. They have shown that changes previously ascribed to 'culture–contact' (such as migration) either pre-date their apparent causes, or took place without any preceding contacts which might have caused them. A notable case-study in this respect has been the general abandonment of exogenous explanations of the end of the Roman Empire. Recent work has made it increasingly clear that 'barbarian' migration only occurred *after* the Empire was in decline, and was not the cause of Imperial collapse. Thus, no archaeologist today would base an explanation of change on exogenous causes without first dismissing all possible endogenous causes.

This well-attested discovery, backed up by vast numbers of detailed observations, accrued over 20 years of worldwide archaeological study, has deep-running implications for all social and political sciences. If social and political change is usually endogenous, then this strongly suggests it is mostly internal factors which must be analysed if we are to build a general theory of change for International Relations. It is important to note, however, that the 'independent invention' hypothesis does not necessitate that *all* change is endogenous, merely that exogenous change is the exception rather than the rule. The wide range of case-studies so far examined in the course of this archaeological debate suggests, however, that such exceptions are somewhat rarer than might at first appear.

While archaeological theory has usually, in my view erroneously, been considered irrelevant to International Relations, economic approaches to analysing change have been widely employed by analysts of world politics.

Economic approaches

The analysis of change plays a central role in economics, and International Relations theorists have long drawn on economics for their theories of change. There are, of course, very many economic models of short-term change, but here it is the way in which economists approach the long-term which is of special interest. Interestingly this includes the use of cyclical approaches to change as a matter of course, in a way otherwise rare among non-scientific subjects.

There are five economic cycles in widespread usage, each of which is named after its inventor or its basis.[92] The 'Agricultural', or 'Cobweb', cycle is of varying length depending upon the type of economic activity involved, as it is founded in agricultural commodity price-fluctuations. The 'Inventory', or 'Kitchen', cycle is approximately four years long and is said to originate from changes in the stocks levels of companies. The 'Fixed

Investment', or 'Juglar', cycle is about nine years long, and originates from business expenditure. The 'Building', or 'Kuznets', cycle is eighteen years long and is related to booms in building activity.

It is, however, the 'Kondratieff' cycle which is of the greatest importance here, because it has the capacity to encompass long-term economic change.[93] It was developed from a study of prices and is not, in origin, an explanatory model. Lasting between 45 and 65 years, it envisaged a continual cycle of prosperity > recession > depression > recovery, and then back to prosperity.

There is debate among economists over whether these cycles, especially Kondratieff cycles, exist and, if so, whether they are completely independent or in some way related. There is also less clarity over the exact duration of the longer cycles, because of difficulties in measuring their length. Some scholars have suggested that, even if the Kondratieff cycle does not exist, there may well be a long economic cycle.

In their review of long-cycle theory in economics, Niemira and Klein outline alternative approaches to long-cycles in economic change, including Kondratieff cycles.[94] Three theoretical schools of economics studying long cycles are identified in their work: those of Schumpeter, Forrester, and Burns and Mitchell.

Schumpeter[95] saw cyclical change as encompassing the Kitchen, Juglar and Kondratieff cycles as a series of interlocked scales. He argued that innovations tend to occur in clusters and, therefore, that the process of innovation tends to cause uneven growth.

Schumpeter suggested that innovation itself shows a wave-like character. By using a broad definition of innovation, Schumpeter was able to argue that each wave was initiated by a flurry of innovation. To Schumpeter, therefore, innovation causes growth and, in consequence, innovation causes change.

Forrester[96] took another approach, while accepting the existence of the same cycles, he saw them as independent. The Kondratieff cycle, he supposed, was the result of over-investment causing fluctuation in the capital stock of a state.

Burns and Mitchell[97] viewed the long-cycle as a sequential pattern of industrial activity and then speculation, arguing that there was a cycle of cycles. This was envisaged as comprising a depression, followed by a dramatic increase in industrial activity (but not speculation), which – when a mild contraction in business followed – prompted incautiousness. So, a pattern of increasingly less industrial activity, and increasingly greater speculation, occurred after two or three cycles. Eventually, the speculative boom ends, with dire economic consequences, returning the cycle to its start point.

An alternative approach to long-term change in economics is that of Rostow,[98] building on the work of Schumpeter. In contrast to many long-cycle theorists, Rostow argues for a linear growth in the world economy, albeit one with a cyclical ('boom and bust') component. To do so, he uses conventional economic and historical methods to define stages of growth: traditional (pre-industrial), transitional or 'pre-conditions for take-off' (proto-industrial), 'take-off' (industrialization), 'drive to maturity', with, finally, 'search for quality' ('beyond consumption').

The basis for these in Rostow's view is a theory of production, using a somewhat wider range of variables than classical economics. In Rostow's view, when a sector of the world economy is established its usual course is then to 'slow down', for the rate of change to decrease. To Rostow, the latter is an empirical observation based on historical data.

Interestingly, Rostow has been keen to incorporate a long-cycle perspective into his theory of change. Consequently, not only are both approaches to some extent interconnected, but Rostow sees a relationship between the empirical trends he observes and those adduced in the Kondratieff model. Likewise, Schumpeter's theory, too, is credited by Rostow, and linked in his work to that of Kondratieff.

Interestingly, long-cycles have also been favoured by Marxist economists. Mandel,[99] for instance, has viewed them favourably, explaining them in Marxist terms as cycles of accumulation, in his recent book-length study of these patterns.

An alternative approach to economic change is suggested by recent efforts by economists to examine the religious, social and cultural contexts of economic activity. This is being actively explored by leading mainstream economists, such as Mark Casson.[100]

Another approach which economists have been exploring recently is the application of evolutionary theory to economic change (pioneered by Nelson and Winter) and exemplified in the work of Hodgson.[101] In subsequent studies, this has been further developed and combined with the mathematics of non-linearity and 'complexity'. Such an approach encompasses both work in which the mathematical basis of economic theory is retained – extreme applications such as that which Snooks has recently attempted.[102]

Also outside the mainstream of economic theory is the work of Paul Ormerod. In a provocative book, *The Death of Economics*,[103] Ormerod also draws on recent developments in mathematics. He suggests that as one of the ways in which economics can escape from the problems inherent in a mechanistic and law-like approach, is to employ a theory of change based on complexity studies in mathematics, and employ contextual approaches placing emphasis on non-economic factors. In this, Ormerod aims to revise the foundations of economic theory, discarding the 'rational actor' approach to human behaviour. While not a long-term study, Ormerod's book offers a framework of economic analysis which one can easily appreciate may be applied to long-term economic change.

Another perspective on economic change – especially 'growth' – has been to combine ecological, anthropological, sociological, historical and economic analyses in studying long-term change. The diversity of this approach is exemplified by the work of Karl Polanyi and Eric Jones. Polanyi[104] wrote extensively about early periods of economic history, developing an evolutionary model of three stages of economic growth (the reciprocal, redistributive and market economies) which could explain all the world's economic forms. Polanyi saw economic development as an evolutionary process, but one in which distinct stages were visible.

Jones,[105] who takes a very different approach, has argued that demographic change and economic growth have been closely linked throughout human history. In his view, population increase led to constant economic growth, even in pre-industrial societies. This forms the basis for his argument that the potential for increased intensity of production, forming the origins of the Industrial Revolution, is not a uniquely Western and late medieval (or early post-medieval) phenomenon. Jones argued that it has existed in many times and places during the existence of the state-system worldwide. Non-economic factors (especially political reasons) have, in his view, stopped this potential from being realized more widely. As such, Jones offers a long-term economic theory of change which integrates world historical, historical sociological and ecological approaches with economic analysis.

So, in economic theory we have another range of theories about long-term change, many of which are clearly related to concepts (such as long-cycle theory and world-systems analysis) widespread in International Relations theory. However, economic theories of change also relate closely to another valuable source for thinking about change: mathematics.

Mathematical approaches

Mathematics forms the basis for theories of change in physics and has its own theory of change. Some mathematicians (such as Zeeman) have suggested that this can be applied to human societies.[106] The approaches to change in mathematics which have usually been suggested as having special relevance to analysing change in human societies are: decision-analysis, network analysis, catastrophe theory, systems theory and the mathematics of complexity. These will be, therefore, the focus of attention in this brief review.

We may start by examining mathematical approaches to the analysis of how decisions are made, given the potential importance of decisions in bringing about political change.[107] This issue has been approached in two principal ways: by the analysis of the decision-making process itself, and by examining the range of possible decisions open to an individual (or organization) at any specific time. It might be claimed, for example, that in any situation a wide range of possible decisions are open to the individual, and that these might result in widely differing outcomes.

On one level this is true, but on another, decision-making can always be divided into a simple choice of 'yes' or 'no'. When employing a binary approach of this sort, one must, of course, make the allowance that 'no' includes thinking (or information-acquisition) time and postponement, in addition to straightforward rejection.

Contrasts of this sort can generate alternative theories of decision-making. These include approaches based on the probabilistic analysis of possible outcomes and the logical evaluation of sequences of decision-making. Some such decision-theories are well known to scholars of International Relations, such as game-theory and rational choice models.[108]

Network analysis,[109] which has been widely employed in sociology and anthropology, is also mathematical in basis. This is the formal expression of social relationships as sets of linkages. Such networks can represent static relationships, or moments in the course of more complex or dynamical relationships, or be used to analyse patterns existing in several different forms through time. As such, they constitute a potential mathematical approach to the analysis of change, although one less used in International Relations theory than elsewhere.

The analytical potential of this approach is, as in the case of formal decision-analysis, limited by its formalism and the incompleteness of the context which it is able to represent. However, it has the potential for enabling us to summarize complex relationships on many scales in time and space in a manipulable format. The understanding of social and political organization as networks can be combined with any of several mathematical theories of dynamics; these include systems theory, catastrophe theory and complexity theory.

Networks may be considered systems in the sense in which this term is used in the well-established fields of systems theory and complexity theory. Systems theory sees each part of the larger system as potentially related to the constituent smaller parts, referred to in systems terminology as sub-systems. Change is understood in terms of flows between the sub-systems. Those flows promoting change are referred to as 'positive feedback', and those promoting stability 'negative feedback'. In 'systemic' approaches much importance is usually placed on the part played by equilibrium, or systemic stability, and this has led to the classification and analysis of various forms which equilibrium might take in a dynamical system.

Systems theory may be divided into that which places importance on mathematical applications of the approach and that called 'systems-thinking'.[110] In the latter, systems concepts are used outside of a mathematical framework. Consequently, systems thinking illustrates the way in which mathematical concepts can pass from a formal (or mathematical) context into a social science or humanities context, without the need to transfer their mathematical foundations or to adopt a quantitative procedure for their application.

The systems theory concept of 'trajectory' (the pattern or sequence of changes undergone by a system through time) and the concept of sub-systemic interconnectedness together help link the systems approach to another mathematical view of change: catastrophe theory. This is a mathematical theory of sudden change which has been widely applied to human institutions and organizations.

Catastrophe theory[111] is based on the view that a gradual accumulation of seemingly minor factors can result in sudden negative transformations: the 'catastrophes' of the theory's title. By placing importance on the significance of minor factors in causing dramatic change, catastrophe theory has been a useful supplement to gradualist explanations of change.

The characteristic trajectory followed by catastrophic systems enables us to recognize this type of change even where mathematical analysis has not been undertaken. By providing a general mathematical basis for the analysis of sudden change, catastrophe theory has enabled systemic approaches to incorporate an understanding of how rapid transformations between one form (or 'state') of a system and another can occur. Like systems theory, catastrophe theory can be applied in a mathematical or a conceptual fashion.

Present applications of this approach have included the study of sudden change in innovation, complex system-dynamics and the examination of economic collapse. The potential of catastrophe theory has, however, to some extent been overshadowed by that of non-linear dynamics (especially 'chaos theory') in recent years. During this time the latter field has acquired a wide popularity both inside and outside the academic world.

The emergence of 'chaos theory', usually associated with the work of Lorenz and Prigogine,[112] must properly be seen as part of the wider growth of 'complexity theory' in mathematics.[113] They have both derived from the non-linear mathematics of fractal equations, which enable complex patterns and complex dynamics to be generated from relatively simple equations.[114]

The mathematics of non-linear systems has emphasized the importance of 'initial states' (the starting points of dynamical changes), the extreme sensitivity of systems undergoing change, and the potential of subtle and recurrent patterning (especially 'self-similarity': the reproduction of identical patterning on several scales). Such dynamics include those referred to as 'chaotic', which may be defined as 'phenomena which evolve in predictably unpredictable ways'.

Complexity theory[115] has tried to apply these and related mathematical concepts to model the formation and transformation of highly differentiated, but structured, systems. Complex systems in this sense exist at the limits of stable structures (like crystals) and 'chaotic' systems which have no stable form (such as heated gases).

The concept of complexity has been problematical for mathematicians, not least because there is no universally agreed definition of what a 'complex system' is in mathematical terms. A clear definition is, however, given by Anderson, who states that complex systems are those which are large and intricate and which generate behaviour which is not simply the sum of their parts. Langton and Packard – usually said to be the discoverers of 'complexity' in this sense – have argued that complex systems are also distinguished by a capacity to store and retrieve information. These are both aspects of complex systems which, along with other defining features of such systems, will be further discussed in Chapter 4.

Both non-linear dynamics in general, and especially complexity theory, share another feature which is of special interest here: the theory of self-organization. This suggests that complex systems can structure themselves 'automatically'. Seemingly the key relationship (according to Per Bak) is between scale and propensity for change. As an illustration of 'self-organization' he gives the example of a pile of beach sand, where the shape of the pile is a result of a series of avalanches of sand down its slopes, so that a stable form is reached through dynamical processes. This form can, of course, rapidly change if those processes recommence.

Complexity theory contains a wide diversity of perspectives on these problems. That of Gell-Mann[116] – one of the most famous 'complexity theorists' – relates complexity to conventional physics, while some would connect complexity and other aspects of non-linear dynamics more closely. Kauffman,[117] for example, has suggested the concept of 'antichaos', where non-linear systems show change converging around specific points, and so exhibit patterning.

Kauffman also suggests that when specific thresholds of interrelationship are reached, complex systems can dramatically transform their character to more complex forms ('phase transitions'). The conclusions Kauffman draws from this have been widely criticized, but although his interpretation of these seems untenable, these theoretical concepts enrich the mathematical discussion regarding the behaviour of complex systems. There seems no doubt that complexity theory will continue to generate stimulating concepts of this sort for some time yet.[118]

It is probably too early to assess the impact of complexity theory on mathematics and physics. However, the generation of theories about how 'complexity' forms, and what 'complexity' is, may be of theoretical value for social and political scientists.[119] Complexity studies have produced a 'growth industry' in mathematics at centres such as the Santa Fe Institute, where such approaches are being used to analyse a wide range of physical and natural questions and, to a lesser extent, applied to the study of human societies.

Together, these contrasting approaches to the mathematical analysis of networks and systems suggest that there is potentially a mathematical contribution to the discussion of perspectives on the analysis of long-term political change. They also show that such perspectives might be employed in a formal or a conceptual way, analogous with the distinction between systems theory and systems-thinking.

Biological approaches

Biology provides probably the most famous of 'scientific' perspectives on change, the theory of evolution. This is still the principal biological view of long-term change. Evolutionary theory has been greatly altered since the time of Darwin, and it seems that many of the preconceptions of scholars in the social sciences regarding it are frequently based on earlier perceptions of evolution than those employed by contemporary biologists.[120]

Biological evolutionary theory today, exemplified by the well-known work of Stephen Jay Gould,[121] recognizes that change can be continuous or discontinuous, progressive or regressive, directional or undirectional, rapid or gradual, multilinear or unilinear and contingent or structured. In animal studies concepts of intentionality and strategy have also been adopted by evolutionary theorists, while 'history' (in the sense of sequential narratives) has become an important aspect of evolutionary argument.

Evolution still relies upon concepts such as selection and adaptation, although these are not seen as universal explanations. Likewise, contextual factors still play a central role in understanding change, but these are combined with concepts of agency in animals, rather than being external determinants.

Systems approaches and non-linear dynamics have also played a role in biological approaches to change. Environmental factors, and demographics, alongside ecological theory are, of course, key parts of biological approaches to change, such as vegetation succession and population dynamics.[122]

The principal common characteristic of these views is that biologists tend to use the individual as the unit of analysis, and to take a processual view of change rather than one based on the analysis of events alone. By processual, I mean here that it is a perspective in which shared types of change (for instance, adaptation) are seen as common to many otherwise dissimilar transformations. Once identified, these processes are used as basic tools in the understanding of long-term change.

Thus, biology provides another potentially rich theoretical source for perspectives on long-term change of use to analysts of International Relations. Interestingly, it also offers the clearest instance of a single theory of change being dominant in an academic discipline throughout the twentieth century.

Conclusion

This array of differing approaches may seem at first both disparate and daunting. In the next chapter these approaches, and those set out in Chapter 1, will be critically evaluated. The existence of cross-disciplinary similarities between perspectives from International Relations and the other disciplines reviewed here will be assessed and it will be shown that so many similarities exist between these and the perspectives discussed in the preceding chapter that it is possible to identify and evaluate common interdisciplinary forms of analysis of long-term change.

Notes

1   As argued by: Rosenau, J. N., 1990, *Turbulence in World Politics: A Theory of Change and Continuity*, Princeton.

2   For recent discussions of the relationship between physical, natural and social sciences in the context of International Relations theory; Woods, N. 1996, 'The uses of theory in the study of International Relations', in N. Woods (ed.), 1996, *Explaining International Relations Since 1945*, New York, 9–31; Hollis, M and Smith, S., 1990 *Explaining and Understanding International Relations*.

3   For instance: Little, R., 1994, 'International Relations and large-scale historical change', in A. J. R. Groom and M. Light (eds), *Contemporary International Relations: A Guide to Theory*, 9–26.

4   Boudon, R., 1986, *Theories of Social Change*; Lauer, R. H., 1982, *Perspectives on Social Change*, 3rd edn, Boston, Mass.; Chirot, D., 1994, *How Societies Change*, Thousand Oaks, Calif.; Colomy, P. (ed.), 1992, *The Dynamics of Social Systems*. Hallinan, M. T., 1996, 'The Sociological Study of Social Change', *American Sociological Review* 62, 1–11.

5   Aron, R., 1968, *Main Currents in Sociological Thought 1*, New York, 73–143; Comte, A., 1858, *The Positive Philosophy*, New York.

6   Durkheim, E., 1933, *The Division of Labor in Society* Translated by G. Simpson, New York; Hinkle, R. C., 1976, 'Durkheim's evolutionary conception of social change', *The Sociological Quarterly* 17, 336–46.

7   Spencer, H., 1874, *The Study of Sociology*, New York.

8   Sorokin, P., 1957, *Social and Cultural Dynamics*, 2nd edn, Boston.

9   Pareto, V., 1916, *The Mind and Society*.

10 Callinicos, A., 1988, *Making History: Agency, Structure, and Change in Social Theory*, Ithaca, NY, and Cambridge.

11 Dahrendorf, R., 1959, *Class and Class Conflict in Industrial Society*, Stanford; Dahrendorf, R., 1979, *Life Chances*.

12 Aron, R., 1968, *Progress and Disillusion*, New York.

13 Parsons, T., 1966, *Societies: Evolutionary and Comparative Perspectives*, Englewood Cliffs, NJ; Parsons, T., 1951, *The Social System*, New York; Parsons, T., 1967, *Sociological Theory and Modern Society*, New York; Parsons, T., 1964, 'Evolutionary universals in society', *American Sociological Review* 29, 339–57; Parsons, T. and Smelser, N. J., 1956, *Economy and Society. A study in the Integration of Economic and Social Theory*; Parsons, T., 1977, *The Evolution of Societies*, Englewood Cliffs, NJ. See also Sanderson, S. 1991, *Social Evolutionism: A Critical History*.

14 Smelser, N. J., 1959, *Social Change in the Industrial Revolution*, Chicago; Smelser, N. J., 1968, *Essays in Sociological Explanation*, Englewood Cliffs, NJ.

15 Sanderson, S. K., 1995, *Social Transformations*, Cambridge, Mass. and Oxford.

16 Giddens, A., 1984, *The Constitution of Society*. For commentaries on Giddens' work: Cohen, I. J., 1989, *Structuration Theory. Anthony Giddens and the Constitution of Social Life*, London and New York; Bryant, C. G. A. and Jary, D. (eds), 1990, *Giddens' Theory of Structuration. A Critical Appreciation*, London and New York.

17 Giddens, A., 1984, *The Constitution of Society*.

18 First set out in Archer, M. S., 1988, *Culture and Agency*.

19   Archer, M. S., 1995, *Realist Social Theory: The Morphogenetic Approach.*

20   Buckley, W., 1987, *Sociology and Modern Systems Theory*, New Jersey; although
     Lockwood, D., 1964 'Social integration and system integration', in G. K.
     Zollschan and H. W. Hirsch (eds), *Explorations in Social Change*, Boston, Mass.;
     244–57 also plays a significant role in her sources.

21   Bourdieu, P., 1972, *Outlines of a Theory of Practice.*

22   Abrams, P., 1983, *Historical Sociology*, Ithaca; Smith, D., 1991, *The Rise of
     Historical Sociology*; Skocpol, T., 1984, 'Sociology's historical imagination', in
     T. Skocpol (ed.), *Vision and Method in Historical Sociology*, Cambridge and New
     York, 1–21; Skocpol, T. (ed.), 1984 *Vision and Method in Historical Sociology*;
     Sillitoe, A., 1996, *Key Issues in Historical and Comparative Sociology.*

23   Mann, M., 1986, *The Sources of Social Power. Vol. 1: A History of Power from the
     Beginning to* AD 1760; Mann, M., 1988, *States, War and Capitalism. Studies in
     Political Sociology*; Thomas, N., 1989, *Out of Time: History and Evolution in
     Anthropological Discourse*; Hastrup, K. (ed.), 1992, *Other Histories.*

24   For example, Tilly, C., 1984, *Big Structures, Large Processes, Huge Comparisons*,
     New York.

25   Skocpol, T., 1979, *States and Social Revolutions: A Comparative Analysis of
     France, Russia and China*; Skocpol, T., 1994, *Social Revolution in the Modern
     World.*

26   Moore, B., 1966, *Social Origins of Dictatorship and Democracy.*

27   Hall, J. A., 1985, *Powers and Liberties.* See also, Hall, J. A. (ed.), 1986, *States in
     History*; Hall, J. A., 1996, *International Orders. An Historical Sociology of State,
     Regime, Class and Nation.*

28   Carneiro, R. L., 1970, 'A theory of the origin of the state', *Science* 169,
     733–38; Carneiro, R. L., 1981, 'The chiefdom: precursor of the state', in G.
     D. Jones and R. R. Kautz (eds), *The Transition to Statehood in the New World*,
     37–9; Carneiro, R. L. 1987, 'Cross currents in the theory of state-formation',
     American Ethnologist 14, 756–70. Taagepera, R., 1968, 'Growth curves of
     empires', *General Systems* 13, 171–5; Taagepera, R., 1978, 'Size and duration
     of empires: systematics of size', *Social Science Research* 7, 108–27; Taagepera,
     R., 1978, 'Size and duration of empires: growth-decline curves, 3000 to 600
     BC', *Social Science Research* 7, 180–96.

29   Arrighi, G., 1994, *The Long Twentieth Century*, London and New York.

30   Wilson, E. O., 1975, *Sociobiology*, Cambridge, Mass.; Wilson, E. O., 1978, *On
     Human Nature*, Cambridge, Mass.

31   Megarry, T., 1995, *Society in Prehistory.* See also, Megarry, T. (ed.), 1996, *From
     the Caves to Capital*, New York.

32   McClelland, D. C., 1961, *The Achieving Society*, New York.

33   Collins, R., 1986, *Weberian Sociological Theory.*

34   Stokes, R. G., 1975, 'Afrikaner Calvinism and economic action: the Weber-
     ian thesis in South Africa', *American Journal of Sociology* 81, 62–81. See also:
     Eisenstadt, S. N. (ed.), 1968, *The Protestant Ethic and Modernization*, New
     York.

35   Bird, J., 1989, *The Changing Worlds of Geography*; Johnston, R. J. (ed.), 1993,
     The Challenge for Geography.

36   Amin, A. (ed.), 1994, *PostFordism: A Reader*; Thrift, N., 1989, 'New times and
     spaces? The perils of transition models', *Environment and Planning D: Society and
     Space* 7, 127–30. For an alternative Marxist approach: Duncan, J. and Ley, D.,

1982, 'Structural Marxism and human geography: a critical perspective', *Annals of the Association of American Geographers* 72, 30–59.

37   Harvey, D., 1982, *The Limits to Capital*; Harvey, D., 1984, 'On the history and present condition of geography: an historical materialist manifesto', *Professional Geographer* 36, 1–11; Harvey, D., 1989, *The Condition of Postmodernity: An Enquiry into the Origins of Cultural Change*.

38   Sayer, A., 1984, *Method in Social Science*.

39   Smith, S. J., 1981, 'Humanistic method in contemporary social geography', *Area* 13, 293–8; Smith, S. J., 1984, 'Practicing humanistic geography', *Annals of the Association of American Geographers* 74, 353–74; Cloke, P., Philo, C. and Sadler, D., 1991, *Approaching Human Geography*.

40   Urry, J., 1981, *The Anatomy of Capitalist Societies*.

41   Dear, J., 1988, 'The postmodern challenge: reconstructing human geography', *Transactions of the Institute of British Geographers* 13, 262–74; Soja, E. W., 1989, *Postmodern Geographies: The Reassertion of Space in Critical Theory*.

42   Taylor, P. J., 1989, *Political Geography*, 2nd edn; Taylor, P. J. (ed.), 1993, *Political Geography at the End of the Twentieth Century. A Global Analysis*; Taylor, P. J., 1994, 'The state as container: territoriality in the modern world', *Progress in Human Geography* 18, 151–62.

43   Johnston, R. J., 1993, 'The rise and decline of the corporate-welfare state: a comparative analysis in global context', in P. J. Taylor (ed.), *Political Geography at the End of the Twentieth Century*; Agnew, J. A. and Corbridge, S., 1989, 'The new geopolitics: the dynamics of geopolitical disorder', in R. J. Johnston and P. J. Taylor (eds), *A World in Crisis? Geographical Perspectives*, 266–88; Agnew, J., 1994, 'The territorial trap: the geographical assumptions of International Relations theory', *Review of International Political Economy* 1.1, 53–80.

44   Guelke, L., 1974, 'An idealist alternative in human geography', *Annals of the Association of American Geographers* 64, 193–202; Guelke, L., 1982, *Historical Understanding in Geography. An Idealist Approach*.

45   Cohen, S. B., 1994, 'Geopolitics in the new world era: a new perspective on an old discipline', in G. J. Demco and W. B. Wood (eds), *Reordering the World*, Boulder, Colo.; 15–48.

46   Hägerstrand, T., 1976, *Innovation as a Spatial Process*, Chicago; Thrift, N. and Pred, A., 1981, 'Time geography: a new beginning', *Progress in Human Geography* 5, 277–86; Pred, A., 1977, 'The choreography of existence: comments on Hägerstrand's time-geography', *Economic Geography* 53, 207–21; Pred, A., 1984, 'Place as historically contingent process: structuration and the time-geography of becoming places', *Annals of the Association of American Geographers* 74, 279–97; Pred, A., 1990, *Making Histories and Constructing Geographies*, Boulder, Colo.

47   Booth, D. (ed.), 1994, *Rethinking Social Development*.

48   Perkins, D. and Syrquin, M., 1989, 'Large countries: the influence of size', in H. Chenery and T. M. Srinivasan (eds), *Handbook of Development Economics*, vol. 2, Amsterdam, 1691–753

49   Moore, D. B. and Schmitz, G. G. (eds), 1994, *Debating Development Discourse: Institutional and Popular Perspectives*; Booth, D. (ed.), 1994, *Rethinking Social Development*.

50   Hebinck, P., 1990, *The Agrarian Structure in Kenya: State, Farmers and Commodity Relations*, Saarbrücken; Long, N. and Long, A. (eds), 1992, *Battlefields of*

Knowledge: The Interlocking of Theory and Practice in Social Research and Development.

51 Stanford, M., 1994, *A Companion to the Study of History.*

52 Collingwood, R. G., 1946, *The Idea of History.*

53 Co-author, for example, of: Collingwood, R. G. and Richmond, I. A., 1969, *The Archaeology of Roman Britain.*

54 Popper, K. R., 1963, *Conjectures and Refutations*; Popper, K. R., 1972, *Objective Knowledge: an Evolutionary Approach.* For a recent assessment of Popper's work: O'Hear, A. (ed.), 1995, *Karl Popper: Philosophy and Problems.*

55 Popper, K. R., 1961, *The Poverty of Historicism*, 3rd edn.

56 Skinner, Q. (ed.), 1985, *The Return of Grand Theory in the Human Sciences.*

57 Braudel, F., 1975, *The Mediterranean and the Mediterranean World in the Age of Philip II*, 2 vols; Braudel, F., 1981–4, *Civilization and Capitalism 15th-18th Century*, 3 vols.

58 Lloyd, C., 1993, *The Structures of History.*

59 Anderson, P., 1974, *Passages from Antiquity to Feudalism*; Anderson, P., 1974, *Lineages of the Absolutist State.*

60 Himmelfarb, G. G., 1987, *The New History and the Old*, Cambridge, Mass.

61 Kennedy's recent work has focused on 'trend analysis': Kennedy, P., 1993, *Preparing for the Twenty-first Century*, New York.

62 Kennedy, P., 1989, *The Rise and Fall of the Great Powers.* For comments see: Mann, M., Giddens, A. and Wallerstein, I., 1989, 'Comments on Paul Kennedy's *Rise and Fall of the Great Powers*', *British Journal of Sociology* 40.2, 328–40.

63 Kennedy, P., 1989, *The Rise and Fall of the Great Powers*, xxiii–xxiv.

64 For example: Young, R., 1990, *White Mythologies: Writing History and the West.* See also Joyce, P., 1991, 'History and Post-modernism', *Past and Present*, 133, 204–9; Kelly, C., 1991, 'History and post-modernism', *Past and Present*, 133, 209–13.

65 Jenkins, K., 1995, *On 'What is History?'*

66 McNeill, W. H., 1963, *The Rise of the West. A History of the Human Community*, Chicago; McNeill, W. H. 1974, *The Shape of European History*; McNeill, W. H., 1979, *Plagues and Peoples*, Harmondsworth; McNeill, W. H., 1984, *The Pursuit of Power*, Chicago; McNeill, W. H. 1986, *Mythistory and other Essays*, Chicago; McNeill, W. H., 1986, *Poly-Ethnicity and National Unity in World History*, Toronto; McNeill, W. H., 1990, 'The rise of the West after twenty-five years', *Journal of World History*, 1, 1–2; McNeill, W. H., 1991, *A World History*, Chicago; McNeill, W. H., 1993, *A History of the Human Community*, 4th edn, Englewood Cliffs, NJ; McNeill, W. H., 1992, *The Global Condition*, Princeton.

67 Mennell, S., 1989, 'Bringing the very long term back in', in J. Goudsblom, E. L. Jones and S. Mennell, *Human History and Social Process*, 1–10 (7).

68 Burke, P., 1992, *History and Social Theory.*

69 Keesing, R. M., 1990, *Cultural Anthropology*, 2nd edn; Harris, M., 1979, *Cultural Materialism*; Howard, M. C., 1993, *Contemporary Cultural Anthropology*, 4th edn, New York; Kuper, A., 1983, *Anthropology and Anthropologists*; Gardner, K. and Lewis, D., 1996, *Anthropology, Development and the Postmodern Challenge*; Hannerz, U., 1992, *Cultural Complexity: Studies in the Social Organization of Meaning*, New York; Harris, M., 1991, *Cultural Anthropology*,

3rd edn, New York. Barnard, A. and Spencer, J. (eds), 1996, *Encyclopedia of Social and Cultural Anthropology*.

70   Gellner, E., 1982, 'What is Structuralisme?', in C. Renfrew, M. Rowlands and B. Seagraves (eds), *Theory and Explanation in Archaeology*, 97–124.

71   White, L. A., 1949, *The Science of Culture*, New York; White, L. A., 1959, *The Evolution of Culture*, New York; Service, E., 1971, *Primitive Social Organization: An Evolutionary Perspective*, 2nd edn, New York; Cohen, R. and Service, E. (eds), 1978, *Signs of the State: The Anthropology of Political Evolution*, Philadelphia.

72   Fried, M., 1967, *The Evolution of Political Society*, New York; Haas, J., 1982, *The Evolution of the Prehistoric State*, New York.

73   Boyd, R. and Richerson, P. J., 1985, *Culture and the Evolutionary Process*, Chicago; Boyd, R. and Richerson, P. J., 1992, 'How microevolutionary processes give rise to history', in M. H. and D. V. Nitecki (eds), *History and Evolution*, New York, 179–209; Ingold, T., 1986, *Evolution and Social Life*.

74   Upham, S. (ed.), 1990, *The Evolution of Political Systems. Sociopolitics in Small-scale Sedentary Societies*. See also: Haas, J., 1982, *The Evolution of the Prehistoric State*.

75   Althusser, L., 1977, *For Marx*; Godelier, M., 1977, *Perspectives in Marxist Anthropology*.

76   Harris, M., 1994, 'Cultural materialism is alive and well and won't go away until something better comes along', in R. Borofsky (ed.), *Assessing Cultural Anthropology*, New York, 62–75.

77   Friedman, J., 1974, 'Marxism, structuralism and vulgar materialism', *Man* 9, 444–69; Friedman, J. and Rowlands, M.J., 1978, 'Notes towards an epigenetic model of the evolution of "civilization" ', in J. Friendman and M. J. Rowlands (eds), *The Evolution of Social Systems* 201–78.

78   Friedman, J., 1994, *Cultural Identity and Global Process*.

79   Moran, E. F. (ed.), 1990, *The Ecosystem Approach in Anthropology*, Ann Arbor, Mich.

80   Lees, S. H. and Bates, D. G., 1990, 'The ecology of cumulative change', in E. F. Moran (ed.), *The Ecosystem Approach in Anthropology*, 247–77.

81   For example: Goody, J., 1977, *The Domestication of the Savage Mind*; Gellner, E., 1983, *Nations and Nationalism*; Gellner, E., 1988, *Plough, Sword and Book*.

82   MacFarlane, A., 1978, *The Origins of English Individualism*.

83   Wolf, E. R., 1982, *Europe and the People Without History*, Berkeley Calif. and Los Angeles. Note, however that historical anthropology encompasses a wider range of approaches than simply those of MacFarlane and Wolf.

84   Gurney, D. R., 1990, *The Hittites*, revised 2nd edn.

85   Except where specific works are cited, the following account derives from: Dark, K. R., 1995, *Theoretical Archaeology*.

86   Bell, J. A., 1994, *Reconstructing Prehistory*, Philadelphia.

87   Renfrew, C. and Cherry, J. F. (eds), 1986, *Peer Polity Interaction and Sociopolitical Change*.

88   Johnson, G. A., 1978, 'Information sources and the development of decision-making organisations', in C. L. Redman *et al.* (eds), *Social Archaeology*, New York, 87–112; Johnson, G. A., 1982, 'Organizational structure and scalar stress', in C. Renfrew, M. Rowlands and B. A. Segraves (eds), *Theory and Explanation in Archaeology*, New York, 389–421.

89 Flannery, K. V. and Marcus, J. (eds), 1983, *The Cloud People: Divergent Evolution of the Zapotec and Mixtec Civilizations*, New York.

90 Flannery, K. V., 1968, 'Archaeological systems theory and early Meso-america', in B. Meggers (ed.), *Anthropological Archaeology in the Americas*, Washington, 67–87; Flannery, K. V., 1972, 'The cultural evolution of civilizations', *Annual Review of Ecology and Systematics* 3, 399–425.

91 Renfrew A. C., 1973, *Before Civilization*. See also, Renfrew, A. C., 1972, *The Emergence of Civilisation*.

92 Freeman, C. (ed.), 1984, *Long Waves in the World Economy*, London and Dover, NH; Reijnders, J. P. G., 1990, *Long Waves in Economic Development*; Solomou, S., 1987, *Phases of Economic Growth 1850–1973: Kondratieff Waves and Kuznets Swings*.

93 Berry, B. J. L., 1991, *Long-wave Rhythms in Economic Development and Political Behavior*, Baltimore; Freeman, C., Clark, J. A. and Soete, L., 1982, *Unemployment and Technical Innovation: A Study of Long Waves and Economic Development*.

94 Niemira, M. P. and Klein, P. A., 1994, *Financial and Economic Cycles*.

95 Schumpeter, J. A., 1935, 'The analysis of economic change', *Review of Economics and Statistics* 17.4, 2–10; Schumpeter, J. A., 1939, *Business Cycles*, New York.

96 Forrester, J. W., 1973, *World Dynamics*, 2nd edn, Cambridge, Mass.

97 Burns, A. F. and Mitchell, W. C., 1946, *Measuring Business Cycles*, New York.

98 Rostow, W. W., 1960, *The Process of Economic Growth*, 2nd edn, Oxford; Rostow, W. W., 1963, *The Economics of Take-off into Sustained Growth*, London; Rostow, W. W., 1971, *The Stages of Economic Growth: A Non-Communist Manifesto*, 2nd edn, Cambridge; Rostow, W. W., 1971, *Politics and the Stages of Growth*, Cambridge; Rostow, W. W., 1979, *Getting From Here to There*, London; Rostow, W. W., 1978, *The World Economy: History and Prospect*, London; Rostow, W. W., 1980, *Why the Poor Get Richer and the Rich Slow Down: Essays in the Marshallian Long Period*, London; Rostow, W. W., 1987, *Rich Countries and Poor Countries: Reflections on the Past, Lessons for the Future*, London and Boulder; Rostow, W. W., 1990, *Theorists of Economic Growth from David Hume to the Present: With a Perspective on the Next Century*, Oxford and New York.

99 Mandel, E., 1995, *Long Waves of Capitalist Development*, 2nd rev. edn.

100 For example, Casson, M., 1990, 'Entrepreneurial culture as a competitive advantage', *Research in Global Business Management* 1, 139–51; Casson, M., 1993, 'Cultural determinants of economic performance', *Journal of Comparative Economics* 17, 418–42.

101 Nelson, R. R. and Winter, S., 1982, *An Evolutionary Theory of Economic Change*. For some other examples, illustrating the diversity and strengths of this approach: Hodgson, G., 1996, 'An evolutionary theory of long-term economic growth', *International Studies Quarterly* 40, 391–410; Hodgson, G. M., 1991, 'Socio-political disruption and economic development', in G. M. Hodgson and F. Screpanti (eds), *Rethinking Economics: Markets, Technology and Evolutionary Economics*, 153–71; Hodgson, G. M., 1993, *Economics and Evolution: Bringing Life Back into Economics*; Moyr, J., 1990, 'Punctuated equilibria and technological progress', *American Economic Review* 80.2, 350–54; Moyr, J.,

1991, 'Evolutionary biology, technical change and economic history', *Bulletin of Economic Research* 43.2, 127–49; Anderson, P. W., Arrow, K. J. and Pines, D. (eds), 1988, *The Economy as an Evolving Complex System*, Reading, Mass.; Witt, U., 1993, *Evolutionary Economics*.

102 Killick, T. (ed.), 1995, *The Flexible Economy*; Snooks, G., 1996, *The Dynamic Society*.

103 Ormerod, P., 1994, *The Death of Economics*.

104 Polanyi, K., 1957, *The Great Transformation*, rev. edn, Boston; Polanyi, K., Arensburg, C. and Pearson, H. W., (eds), 1957, *Trade and Markets in the Early Empires*, Glenco, Ill.; Polanyi, K., 1963, 'Ports of trade in early societies', *Journal of Economic History* 23, 30–45.

105 Jones's approach is exemplified by: Jones, E. L., 1988, *Growth Recurring: Economic Change in World History*.

106 Zeeman, E. C., 1974, 'On the unstable behavior of stock exchanges', *Journal of Mathematical Economics* 1, 39–49; Loye, D. and Eisler, R., 1987, 'Chaos and transformation: implications of nonequilibrium theory for social science and society', *Behavioral Science* 32, 53–65; Foster, J., 1994, 'The impact of the self-organization approach on economic science: why economic theory and history need no longer be mutually exclusive domains', *Journal of Mathematical Computer Simulation* 39, 393–98; Foster, J., 1993, 'Economics and the self-organization approach: Alfred Marshall revisited?', *Economic Journal* 103, 975–91; Silverberg, G., Dosi, G. and Orsenigo, L., 1988, 'Innovation, diversity and diffusion: a self-organising model', *Economic Journal* 98, 1032–55; Allen, P. M., 1982, 'The genesis of structure in social systems', in A. C. Renfrew, M. J. Rowlands and B. A. Segraves (eds), *Theory and Explanation in Archaeology*, New York and London, 347–74.

107 For example, see: Moore, P. and Thomas, H., 1988, *The Anatomy of Decisions*, 2nd edn.

108 Zinnes, D. A. and Gillespie, J. V., 1976, *Mathematical Models in International Relations*, New York; Nicholson, M., 1989, *Formal Theories in International Relations*; Nicholson, M., 1996, *Causes and Consequences in International Relations: A Conceptual Study*, London and New York.

109 Knoke, D., 1990, *Political Networks*; Wellman, B. and Berkowitz, S. D. (eds), 1988, *Social Structures*; Thorelli, H. B., 1986, 'Networks: Between Markets and Hierarchies', *Strategic Management Journal* 7, 37–51.

110 Waddington, C. H., 1977, *Tools for Thought*; Checkland, P., 1981, *Systems Thinking, Systems Practice*.

111. Waddington, C. H., 1974, 'A catastrophe theory of evolution', *Annals of the New York Academy of Sciences*, 231; Zeeman, E. C., 1976, 'Catastrophe theory', *Scientific American* 234, 65–83.

112. Gleick, J., 1987, *Chaos: Making a New Science*, New York; Prigogine, I. and Stengers, I., 1986 *Order out of Chaos*, Toronto; Holden, A. V. (ed.), 1986, *Chaos*, Princeton.

113. Hofbauer, J. and Sigmund, K., 1988, *The Theory of Evolution and Dynamical Systems*, Cambridge; Khalil, E. L. and Boulding, K. E. (eds), 1996, *Evolution, Order and Complexity*, London; Weisbuch, G., 1990, *Complex Systems: An Introduction to Automata Networks*, Reading, Mass.; Berge, P., Pomeau, Y. and Vidal, C., 1984, *Order within Chaos: Towards a Deterministic Approach to Turbulence*, New York.

114. See note 113 for discussions of this property.
115. The following account is based on Coveney, P. and Highfield, R., 1995, *Frontiers of Complexity: The Search for Order in a Chaotic World*; Khalil, E. L. and Boulding, K. E. (eds), 1996, *Evolution, Order and Complexity*, London; Lewin, R., 1992, *Complexity: Life at the Edge of Chaos*, New York; Weisbuch, G., 1990, *Complex Systems: An Introduction to Automata Networks*, Reading, Mass.; Waldrop, H. M., 1992, *Complexity: the Emerging Science at the Edge of order and Chaos*, New York; Horgan, J., 1995, 'From Complexity to Perplexity', *Scientific American*, June, 74–9; Anderson, P. W., Arrow, K. J. and Pines, D., 1988, *The Economy as an Evolving Complex System*, Reading, Mass.
116. Gell-Mann, M., 1994, *The Quark and the Jaguar: Adventures in the Simple and the Complex*, New York.
117. Kauffman, S. A., 1988, 'The evolution of economic webs', in P. W. Anderson *et al* (eds), *The Economy as an Evolving Complex System*, Reading, Mass., 125–46; Kauffman, S. A., 1991. 'Antichaos and adaptation', *Scientific American*, August, 78–84; Kauffman, S. A., 1993, *The Origins of Order: Self-organization and Selection in Evolution*, Oxford and New York; Kauffman, S., 1995, *At Home in the Universe: The Search for Laws of Complexity*; Westhoff, F. H., Yarbrough, B. V. and Yarbrough, R. M., 1996, 'Complexity, organization, and Stuart Kauffman's *The Origins of Order*', *Journal of Economic Behaviour and Organization* 29, 1–25.
118. Mulgan, G., 1995, 'The simple truth about complexity', *Times Higher Education Supplement*, 22 December, 16.
119. For comparison, see: Kiel, L. D. and Elliot, E., (eds), 1995, *Chaos Theory in the Social Sciences*, Ann Arbor, Mich.
120. For a contemporary view from biology: Eldredge, N., 1985, *Unfinished Synthesis: Biological Hierarchies and Modern Evolutionary Thought*.
121. Gould, S. J. and Eldredge, N., 1977, 'Punctuated equilibria: the tempo and mode of evolution reconsidered', *Paleobiology* 3, 115–51; Gould, S. J., 1980, 'Is a new and general theory of evolution emerging?' *Paleobiology* 6, 119–30; Gould, S. J., 1982, 'Darwinism and the expansion of evolutionary theory', *Science* 216, 380–87; Gould, S. J., 1989, 'Punctuated equilibria in fact and theory', *Journal of Social and Biological Structures* 12, 241–50.
122. Bulmer, M., 1994, *Theoretical Evolutionary Ecology*, Sunderland, Mass.; Tuljapurkar, S., 1990, *Population Dynamics in Variable Environments*, New York; Morin, P., 1995, *Community Ecology*; Yodzis, P., 1989, *Introduction to Theoretical Ecology*, New York.

3

Making history: shared perspectives and shared problems in the study of long-term change

Introduction

It is immediately obvious from the previous two chapters that there are many interdisciplinary similarities in the way in which long-term change has been analysed. These similarities will form the basis for the critical examination of these approaches in this chapter.

Interdisciplinary similarities in the way change is analysed can first be classified in terms of two dimensions: the unit of analysis and the factors upon which explanatory importance is placed. In regard to the first of these dimensions one can see that there are four principal units of analysis:

1   the individual
2   the social group, be it the kin-group or 'social class'
3   the polity (state, chiefdom or whatever)
4   the network(s) of interactions between any or all of the former.

The second dimension gives us five categories:

1   politics
2   economics
3   social organisation, especially social structure
4   cognitive, including psychological, factors
5   ecological factors, including human demography.

These two dimensions may then be combined with a series of eight interdisciplinary modes of analysis of long-term change:

1   ecological
2   evolutionary
3   economic
4   cognitive
5   interactional (based on contacts or communication)
6   structural
7   historical particularist
8   mathematical/formal.

Between them, these two stages of classification not only account for *all* current International Relations theories of change, but *all* of those surveyed from other disciplines. In this chapter, I shall examine the strengths and weaknesses of each of these interdisciplinary modes of analysis and then consider if, and how, these strengths can be combined in building a new theory with which to analyse long-term change in world politics. In order to combine these approaches it will also be necessary to address more philosophical issues of epistemology, which will also enable a consideration of the post-modernist critique of long-term analysis.[1]

However, first it is necessary to examine where and why each of the existing approaches has its strengths and its weaknesses. This can, in part, be achieved by a critique of their logical basis, seeking inconsistencies, illogicality and 'circular argument'. But it can also be approached by examining the 'internal' critique of each approach produced by those scholars working within it. In some cases we shall see that this latter critique itself fatally undermines the logical basis of the perspective involved, a point previously overlooked.

One further critical approach will suffice to evaluate the relative merits of these alternative theories. This may be based on their ability to account for the global diversity of human cultures attested by sociology, anthropology, history and archaeology. As this diversity must be the outcome of – mostly pre-modern – changes, it may serve as a useful guide to the utility of each approach as a means of analysing long-term change.

Ecological approaches

These have the clear advantage that it is impossible to disengage world politics, whether today or in the past, from human biology.[2] As human biology inextricably links humanity (in both the past and the present) to the natural environment, it is reasonable to suppose that there is a biological context to politics both today and in the past.[3]

It is also clear, on general grounds, that biology places constraints on human behaviour. People are only 'so strong' or 'so tall', and this limits even the most basic human actions.[4] Environmental factors can also place constraints. Mountains may be too difficult to cross on foot to facilitate regular movement, or seas uncrossable given available technologies at specific historical times.[5] So biological and environmental factors certainly play some role in human activities. The question is: how large a role and when?

Attempts to link genetics directly to human behaviour have been inconclusive.[6] Although it is possible that there are some human genetic 'dispositions', these are unlikely to determine human behaviour so as to explain societal variability, because they are almost certainly shared by all humanity.[7]

One of the most important discoveries of modern human genetics has been that human social or cultural differences *cannot* be genetically explained. Rather, it has demonstrated the essential unity of humanity. This can, for example, counter pseudo-scientific notions of racism or sexism by showing that people of different sexes, and superficially different races, have very similar genetic makeups.[8]

If socio-biological theories were correct, given the genetic commonality of humanity we would expect to see common human responses to similar circumstances transhistorically and worldwide. Nor can evolutionary factors be used to explain variability in conjunction with such a view. The evolutionary formation of human biological characteristics would hardly permit any other possibility than similar reactions to shared external stimuli in like environments. However, this is not what we see in, for example, anthropological evidence of human cultural diversity.[9]

Of course, either cultural factors or complex dynamics might be claimed as mitigating socio-biological patterns, rendering such responses invisible. Yet this also suggests that either culture or contingency can override sociobiology, so rendering genetic factors of only limited significance after millennia of human cultural change and history. Consequently, there is no logical reason to adopt a socio-biological approach to the analysis of change, even without recourse to the possible moral difficulties of using such a perspective.

Theories relating political or socio-economic change to environmental changes also have problems. The principal difficulty here is one of correlation and causal linkage: to what extent do ecological and political changes coincide and how can these be related?

For instance, a recent survey of long-term data relating to this question has shown that there is no convincing evidence that states have ever fallen in conjunction with ecological changes.[10] This view has recently been supported by new biological data, which seems to demonstrate that the most celebrated claimed instance of ecologically triggered state-collapse (the Maya collapse) was not caused by environmental factors.[11]

One of the most detailed attempts to relate ecology to long-term political change is that developed by Baillie. Baillie, in a seminal series of publications, has drawn attention to the (somewhat counter-intuitive) possibility that volcanic activity may have global political impacts.[12] This is not only because of its immediate effects, but because it produces upper-atmosphere dust-clouds which spread globally to shield the earth from light. These inhibit photosynthesis and so plant growth. Baillie has convincingly shown that a cyclical pattern of volcanic eruptions correlates with global periods of historically-recorded famine. These also correlate with restricted plant-growth, visible in tree-ring studies. If one compares the reconstructible sequence of volcanic activity to periods of political change, however, it is clear that although there are a few correlations (as Baillie has pointed out), there are not very many.

Despite the clear causal mechanism which Baillie has demonstrated, there is no indisputable instance when this can be seen to have brought about major political change, such as state-collapse.[13] While not, therefore, a convincing explanation of long-term political change, Baillie's work is extremely valuable in reconstructing a recurrent pattern of environmental history with significant economic consequences.

The example of Baillie's work is used here because it is one of the most clearly argued and well-evidenced examples of such an ecological hypothesis. Other examples have seldom been based on such well-dated evidence or such close knowledge of the biological and physical sciences. The failure of such a well-argued case to convince clearly casts doubt on environmental explanations in general.

This not to say that famine, disease, sea-level and climate changes have not made a major impact on human societies and economies. It is clear that in some cases these impacts may have produced large-scale political responses.[14] The comparison of what are usually seen by International Relations scholars as the most important changes in European political history over the last two millennia, with changes in climate, rainfall, the spread of epidemics and sea-level changes provides no clear evidence, however, that there is a clear correlation with them. For instance, there are no major ecological changes in Europe attendant upon either the rise of the European empires or the emergence of the modern European inter-state system in the seventeenth century AD. Yet, according to most analysts, neither was politically insignificant.

So, while one must recognize that ecological factors provide an important context for politics, they cannot usually be used to explain large-scale political changes. Rather, they provide a setting within which political activity takes place, and with which that activity reflexively interacts.[15] Ecological factors present political decision-makers, and other members of human communities, with both problems and possibilities for communication (as illustrated by sea travel) and other forms of action. They can provide resources (such as timber for the construction of ships), but they also constitute among the greatest of constraints on those actions and resources.

The ecological context of international political change can, therefore, be seen as a 'platform' on which change occurs. By this, I do not mean that ecology constitutes a 'substructure' *determining* change, but that it forms a series of limitations and possibilities within which political change occurs. This is not a static relationship, as ecological processes themselves are dynamic. So the 'platform' constantly changes, and there is a reflexive relationship between human activity and its ecological context. This process of modification − whether of human behaviour or environmental contexts − is multi-directional.

It is in the extremely long term that we see this most clearly, whether we choose the example of the ending of the last Ice Age or the probability that there will be another.[16] Each has the potential to impact upon human societies, whether permitting colonization of the far north in the Mesolithic period, or potentially rendering geographical zones unhabitable in the latter case! In this sense, we must be reminded that the future might contain more dramatic ecological impacts than we have yet seen. But on the time-scales addressed in this book, there is no evidence that ecological factors are those driving world political change.

Evolutionary approaches

There have been many critical studies of 'social' or 'cultural' evolution, but this approach, too, contains some value.[17] It emphasizes the role of individuals as agents in change while seeing them as part of wider communities and incorporating the interplay of both conscious decision-making and uncontrolled circumstance. The stress on shared processes or types of change (adaptation, selection, etc.) may be a helpful contrast to entirely 'event-based' approaches, such as historical particularism. It also has the advantages of a well-developed theoretical base and clearly defined terminology.

These advantages have, however, to be set against some very important shortcomings. There are, for instance, serious difficulties with applying evolutionary terms such as 'trait' or 'selection' to human societies. The significance assigned to externals, such as environment, is also problematic, especially in view of the evidence, mentioned in the previous chapter, regarding the relative significance of endogenous versus exogenous factors in long-term change.

If one accepts the argument that change is more usually endogenous than exogenous in origin, then internal evolutionary processes must be stressed. This presents problems for the causal mechanisms envisaged by evolutionary theorists, which are almost always (at least partly) external.[18] As evolutionary theorists in biology have themselves noted, to overcome these problems, evolutionary explanations have to take a more agent-based approach, which arguably tends to undermine the 'evolutionary' component of the approach.[19]

However, the key endogenous means by which change takes place in evolution – adaptation – has a significant explanatory potential. Few scholars would claim that individuals and political units never 'adapt' to circumstances.[20] Consequently, this concept must be assigned some degree of validity, but again the problem lies in its use within an evolutionary framework of analysis. If we locate adaptation *within* the unit of analysis (in evolution usually 'the individual') but see causes as external, we are again forced to employ an exogenous causal basis of evolutionary change.

Evolutionary theories also present serious problems of rational validation. Evolution can be slow or sudden, continuous or discontinuous, regressive or progressive, contingent or general, and unilinear or multilinear. So, how can it be possible to recognize whether change is occurring in a specifically 'evolutionary' way?[21] It is recognizable only through the identification of specific 'evolutionary processes'. Apart from 'adaptation' (which is not compatible only with an evolutionary framework of analysis), it seems likely that it is impossible to apply these to human societies in a rigorous manner. This presents fundamental problems for the formulation of an evolutionary theory of political change, so far unresolved.

Consequently, evolutionary theory alone is unable to provide an adequate basis for the analysis of long-term change in International Relations. However, it can contribute some useful perspectives, perhaps especially those derived from the work of scholars examining 'punctuated equilibrium', such as that of Gould and Eldredge,[22] and the concept of 'adaptation' itself. Of interest also is the analysis of individuals and communities 'simultaneously' and the concept of shared processes of change potentially producing dissimilar events in different contexts.

Economic approaches

Once again, the forms of critique which have shown the shortcomings of both ecological and evolutionary approaches can be applied to economic approaches. The popularity of the economic approach among International Relations scholars renders such critiques of this approach of particular interest here. It suggests that many existing studies of change in International Relations have serious theoretical problems.

Economists, sociologists and anthropologists have long noted the diversity of political forms found in societies sharing the same modes of production and exchange. There also seems only a very partial correlation between large-scale political change and economic transformations.[23]

A fundamental historical critique of economic explanation can be based on this lack of correlation between economic and political change. This is seen in numerous examples of large-scale political change, including the rise of the Westphalian inter-state system, which did not correlate with major economic changes.[24] Nor did the Industrial Revolution itself bring about the fundamental transformation of this international political system, although it was arguably the most important economic change since the origins of farming! Problematical too is the difficulty in correlating the Renaissance and Reformation in Europe with any preceding economic transformation: these followed, rather than preceded, the religious and cultural changes.[25]

Anthropologists, especially those working in the structural Marxist school, have also presented this approach with serious challenges, on the basis of studying non-industrial societies. As Godelier and others have noted, there seems no doubt that economic activities in non-industrial communities can be the outcome of cognitive or social factors. Recent work in economics has shown the same characteristic: that social, cultural and ideological factors underlay economic change, rather than vice versa.[26] Material resources must, in any case, even in contemporary societies, be set alongside non-material aspects of 'power',[27] and can only be 'mobilized' through non-economic social and cultural contexts.[28]

If factors such as ideology, culture, social movements and political strategies can override and shape economics, then to what extent can we say that economic factors have 'caused' specific changes?[29] How can we tell that unobserved non-economic changes have not brought about both the political and the economic changes which we are examining? We must not *assume* that we have to give primacy to this variable.

It seems much more likely that economic factors routinely cause non-economic change. This is not to say that economic factors play no role in bringing about political change, but that currently a somewhat stronger case exists for the causation of economic change by non-economic factors than vice versa.[30]

There seems no reason to suppose that in the contemporary international system, with its decentralized transnational economic networks, economic change is likely to be more closely linked to political change than in the past. In the Middle Ages, for example, states and their economies were arguably far more closely associated.[31] So, the argument 'economics only causes change in complex (or industrialized) societies' can hardly be credible: if so, where is the evidence that this is in fact the case?[32]

That economics always takes place in a context – whether religious, social, ecological or cultural – and differences in these contexts produce different forms of the same type of economic system[33] – is not to claim that economic factors play no role whatsoever in large-scale political change. Economic factors present actors with potentials and constraints, they allow them access to some resources and deny access to others. So they must have a part in structuring the range of political options and possibilities. The question is rather – once again – one of, *to what extent* is this the case? That is, to what extent do economic factors 'matter' in explaining long-term change, especially if economies are as 'embedded' as recent studies suggest.

The concept of a 'platform' used to analyse ecological factors may also be useful here. This suggests that a reflexive relationship, within which multi-directional modification is often possible but need not always occur, more accurately depicts political and economic relations. This is to envisage an economic 'platform' analogous to that provided by the natural environment, where economic factors cannot determine either change or non-material aspects of life, but can present political actors with both resources and limitations.

Economic factors can themselves result from human–ecological relationships, as is shown by the case of agriculture. Ecological fluctuations can have, and have had, major economic impacts (the Irish potato famine is of course a well-known example) and economic factors can have major ecological impacts, as Global Warming and deforestation show. The two 'platforms' are, therefore, themselves in a reflexive relationship of possibilistic change.

They can be seen both providing a context for political change, but in neither case determining change.

The failure of large-scale economic change to prompt large-scale political change is clearly illustrated when one examines the relative chronology of large-scale political change and some key economic changes in Europe over the last two millennia: the end of the Roman imperial economy, the decline of feudal economic systems, the rise of proto-industrialization and the Industrial Revolution. One might also add economic globalization to the list.

None of these demonstrably caused a major political change. The first probably occurred some two centuries, at least, after the Western Roman Empire ended (with no equivalent change).[34] The second happened following the Reformation/Renaissance, as already mentioned. Proto-industrialization was a widespread, but not synchronous, change apparently unconnected with major political changes.[35] The case of the Industrial Revolution has also already been mentioned and it may be too early to assess the political impact, if any, of economic globalization.

As already discussed ecological transformations occur over similarly long (or longer) time-spans, but also seemingly without usually causing major political impacts. It seems more likely that both 'platforms' have their own dynamics which can operate reflexively. This model of the relationship between politics, economics and ecology will, therefore, be adopted as a working hypothesis here. Agency exists independently of both platforms, however, and can transform them. So it seems worthwhile to look also at agent-centred approaches.

Cognitive approaches

In discussing evolutionary theory, the potential value of examining the individual as a unit of study was mentioned. This is also at the core of the cognitive approach. Cognitive, and especially psychological, perspectives are widely used in International Relations to examine many other questions, so it might be hoped that they would be of assistance in approaching the issue of long-term change.

Cognitive analysis has the advantages of offering endogenous explanations of human cultural and political variability based on individual cognition, and of being potentially cross-culturally valid.[36] Much psychological work has been undertaken aimed at assessing the exact range of cross-cultural cognitive generalizations possible,[37] and there is no reason to suppose that human cognitive capabilities have altered during the whole period of *homo sapiens sapiens*.

However, none of the existing psychological explanations of change have received much support from scholars within their own fields.[38] Plainly no effective psychological explanation could be based on the assumption of

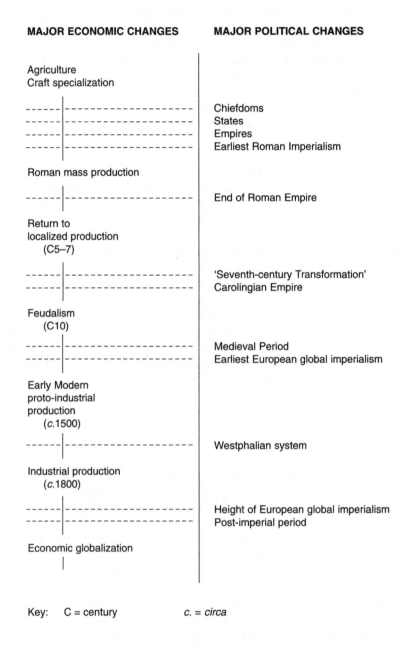

MAJOR ECONOMIC CHANGES   **MAJOR POLITICAL CHANGES**

Agriculture
Craft specialization

                                    Chiefdoms
                                    States
                                    Empires
                                    Earliest Roman Imperialism

Roman mass production

                                    End of Roman Empire

Return to
localized production
  (C5–7)

                                    'Seventh-century Transformation'
                                    Carolingian Empire

Feudalism
  (C10)

                                    Medieval Period
                                    Earliest European global imperialism

Early Modern
proto-industrial
production
  (c.1500)

                                    Westphalian system

Industrial production
  (c.1800)

                                    Height of European global imperialism
                                    Post-imperial period

Economic globalization

Key: C = century   c. = circa

Fig. 3.1   Table showing comparative relative chronologies of major economic changes and large-scale political changes in Europe. Clearly, major economic changes do not consistently precede major political changes. Instead, political change occurs within economic periods, with specific economies acting as 'platforms' for particular types of socio-political organisation.

specific universal responses to shared circumstances where identical stimuli would lead to agents enacting identical events. This cannot account for the known diversity of human societies, nor for the variety of human history.

Thus, although some universal psychological responses might exist in general terms, such commonalities are not sufficiently detailed to provide us with a general explanation of large-scale political change. Without a universalizing theory of this sort, anticipating specific common responses to shared situations, the psychological approach has the potential only to be a part of a wider theory of change.

An alternative cognitive approach is, of course, one based on the analysis of change in terms of individual agents, their beliefs and perceptions. This has several advantages over that based on psychological universals, while being potentially compatible with such psychological approaches. It places importance on the active role of individuals in 'making history', so according well with the results of anthropological, sociological, historical and anthropological studies of cultural diversity. It gives a central place to beliefs and perceptions, and to the role of cultural factors, again in accordance with the results of such studies.[39] Such a view also allows for links to be made with the advantages already noted in evolutionary theory, and permits endogenously-based explanation.

The principal problem faced by such approaches is of the extent to which 'free will', or independent agency, is possible. They also run the risk of emphasizing extreme subjectivity both in the actors involved and in the analyst. As already shown, human agents are not entirely without constraints; so perspectives assigning total free will to these agents are difficult to support. However, the work of post-modernist scholars alerts us to the need to question how it is possible to discern what is entirely subjective perception and what is not, and to cope with the diversity of the past.

The first of these problems has, in my view, been effectively answered by the work of Giddens and Archer. Their studies,[40] although in contrast to each other in many details, stress that it is possible to encompass a view of structured human action in which the structures themselves can be, and frequently are, transformed by agency. Consequently, the problem faced by 'constrained action' is simply overcome by the application of either a structurationist or a morphogenetic framework for the study of individualistic action.

The difficulties posed by human subjectivity are much more formidable. These will be discussed separately later in this chapter, as their resolution is important to several aspects of the approach adopted in this book. At this point, however, it may be worth noting that the acknowledgement of subjectivity, like the acknowledgement of structured action, need not necessitate the assumption that this invalidates an individualistic perspective. Nor does it require that the validation of historical hypotheses is impossible.[41]

The advantages of the individualistic–cognitive perspective are, therefore, such that it will be a major (but not the only) component of the approach used here.

Interactional approaches

These can also be divided into two main types: those based on studying patterns of contact (including warfare) and those based on communication. Despite this division, they have much in common. Each has the clear advantage that they account for the network of human relationships deriving from aggression, travel, trade and information-exchange. This is especially true if one sees the many types of non-material economic exchange as part of the latter category of activity. They also enable the analysis of what seems to be a universal characteristic of all human societies – communication.

Some interactional approaches – such as 'interdependence theory' and 'regime theory' – have been under debate in International Relations in recent years.[42] Perhaps the most interesting approach from outside International Relations is PPI, given its ability to encompass transnational, multi-level and inter-unit exchanges and relate these to processes of change and political activity.

Often, such approaches (as in the case of interdependence theory in International Relations) have been incorporated with a theory of change based on economics. Consequently, it may be difficult to separate those aspects based on interaction from those deriving from economic approaches. This is illustrated by World-Systems Analysis: perhaps the principal interdisciplinary alternative to using state-centric approaches to interaction.

State-centric models of interaction have the weakness that both the widespread recognition of transnational networks of interaction and the devastating critique of exogenous factors in causing change have effectively demolished any prospect of using interaction between states as an explanatory theory of long-term change. Because of their very character, state-centric theories of interaction cannot be revised to accommodate this critique. World-Systems Analysis too is flawed, by locating change in intrinsically exogenous systems and in its basis in economic relationships, as critiques of economic approaches apply equally to these patterns. Their repetition as structurally identical patterns in differing social, cultural, economic, and political situations seems largely unexplained by world-systems analysts except in historical particular or structural terms.

Communication-based approaches are, however, built on a generally-accepted universal human characteristic: inter-personal information-exchange. No known human society in the past or the present lacks this characteristic, even those of the Palaeolithic period. If we see cognitive approaches, including culture, as playing some role in political change, then it is reasonable to assign significance to the role of communication also. Here, as we shall see in more detail later, the work of those anthropologists and archaeologists studying the relationship between communication, information-processing, and societal scale is especially interesting.

Such studies, of course, fully encompass an awareness of human cultural variability, and no internal critique has yet undermined their arguments. Consequently, communication-based approaches (whether based on information-exchange or information-processing) may be assigned greater significance than has often been the case in International Relations.

Structural approaches

The structural approach also has several strengths, but serious weaknesses. Structural approaches can easily become deterministic or be founded on circular arguments. Claims of the independent existence of political and social structure, outside of the individuals concerned with its reproduction, present serious theoretical problems.

In its favour, we have already seen that cultural and political variability is explicable as structure. Giddens and Archer have provided valuable accounts of how agency and structure can coexist, producing a wide range of outcomes, without lapsing into structural determinism. The concept of structure itself is, in their work, both plausible and relatively unproblematic, therefore, compared to its usage in International Relations theory's more rigidly deterministic formulations. But this offers no causal explanation of change in itself. Thus, it is a sociological concept of structure (based on the work of Giddens and Archer) that may offer the most fruitful approach to this form of analysis, but, if so, it cannot in itself offer a new theory of long-term change.

Historiographical approaches to structural analysis have also generated much useful work, as Lloyd's book shows. Perhaps the most important aspect of this is that structural historians have been at the forefront of developing a multi-scalar approach to the analysis of long-term change. This offers the potential to resolve the 'level of analysis' problem in relation to long-term analysis, while also introducing a multi-scalar temporality. A multi-scalar approach of this sort can link the individual, social group, polity and the interactions between and among these units of analysis, and can relate these to events, structures and processes over long time-spans.

The rigid application of Braudelian temporality, however, may run the risk of formalizing historical relationships into its pre-designated temporal framework. It is also the case, as historians have observed, that historically based structural approaches also tend to have a somewhat deterministic character.[43] The outcome of the 'history of events' is always – in their view – merely the 'froth' on a 'sea' of historical structures devoid of agency.

The Annaliste emphasis on the role of 'mentalités' tends to support the view that cognitive factors must play a part in any convincing theory of change. This has not, however, been true of most applications of structural approaches to International Relations, where as we have seen these have usually seen structure as having a transhistorical regularity, as in core–periphery models.

The recurrence of core–periphery patterning in its simplest political form seems well attested in world history. The work of world-systems analysts has demonstrated how widely it might be possible to recognize such patterns. However, the rigid application of this approach falls foul of both the problems of encompassing cultural diversity, and the problems of encompassing time–space geography. If one allows equal weight to cognitive and cultural factors alongside economics, the causal relevance of economic structures is severely diminished,[44] and the recurrence of core–periphery patterns can easily be explained in terms of mere proximity, or ease of access in terms of time–space geographies.

Consequently, while (at least some) core–periphery relationships seem to exist historically, at least in some aspects of human geography, their explanation in economic terms alone is somewhat problematical.[45] Alternatively, if these relationships are seen in terms of political or cultural relationships, then – while the patterning is more easily explicable – the explanatory strength of a world-systems perspective (rather than the recognition that core–periphery relationships are transhistorically widespread) is undermined. In this view, the economic patterns observed in world-systems analysis are at most 'platforms' in the sense already discussed, rather than the principal determinants of change. Thus, the utility of a world-systems approach is severely limited although this has been the focus for much important work.

The same type of critique can be applied, with only slight modification, to Wilkinson's 'civilizations'. All of the patterns he notes can more readily be interpreted first and foremost as political, cultural, or religious and only secondarily as economic.[46] This is how most archaeologists, for example, would describe his ancient examples.[47] A recurrent problem with both historical structuralist and world-systems analysis, which Wilkinson to some extent avoids, is that political and economic structures are often accorded an existence independent of agency.[48] They are more readily seen as historically contingent and emergent forms.

Consequently, structural approaches are insufficient alone to be a basis for the analysis of long-term change in International Relations. Structure can be both part of change and part of the explanation of change, requiring its own explanations while affording an explanatory framework for other aspects of change. Thus, structural approaches are a source of many useful perspectives on the questions involved, but not a solution to the question of how to study long-term change in International Relations.

Historical particularist approaches

The historical particularist approach has the strength of emphasizing the role of agency and contingency. In this respect it re-emphasizes the strengths of

other approaches, and it can bring to bear some very convincing philosophical arguments in support of its interpretation of the uniqueness of events.

Its theoretical problems derive principally from its opposition to comparison and generalization at any level.[49] This, and its alignment in some
disciplines with discredited theories of causation (such as diffusionism in
anthropology and archaeology),[50] render a historical particularist approach
dubious as an overall explanatory framework for change. If all historical
change is heterogeneous, why are cross-cultural similarities found in anthropological, archaeological and historical records of past societies which had
no contact with each other?

Here the case of the 'Contact-Period' Maori is especially interesting.
When first in contact with Europeans many aspects of Maori culture (and
even material culture) strongly resembled those of Iron Age Europe.[51] This
similarity was not apparent to either culture at the time of contact, but was
first noted in the 1950s by an archaeologist who had previously worked on
the British Iron Age.[52] Rather than being dismissed by later detailed work,
it has been strongly supported by other scholars – drawing on further
supporting data – for a generation after the original publication.[53] Historical
particularism can explain such similarities only by 'chance', but (usually less
striking) examples are widespread across the globe; so is 'chance' sufficient to
account for cross-cultural similarity? In my view, such evidence renders all
entirely 'heterogeneous' explanations of historical change, such as those
based on historical particularism, immediately doubtful. This is not to deny
that historical events are unique in the sense that they occur only once, nor
that agency gives a high degree of heterogeneity to historical trajectories but
these features fail to necessitate a historical particularist approach as such.

Mathematical or formal approaches

Seen as a source of concepts regarding potential forms of change, mathematical approaches present many advantages. The theoretical concepts proposed
by mathematicians, such as systems theory and catastrophe theory, are
closely argued, strictly logical and clearly expressed. They lack internal
contradictions and can be applied to a wide range of situations, being
compatible with many other perspectives.[54]

In this sense, we may usefully employ these concepts in the analysis of
political change. But human societies are unlikely to operate like mathematical equations. The issues of agency and culture, for example, require that
these approaches must be tempered with humanity. They take account of
individual intentionality and the potential capacity of actors to transform the
operational parameters within which they are working.

Such transformation is not always possible, of course, and sometimes may
be very partial even if it can be achieved, but it renders the formal analysis of
human societies using mathematical concepts highly problematic. This can
be resolved by applying these concepts in a conceptual fashion alone, akin to

the use of 'systems-thinking' rather than 'systems-theory'.[55] In this way, such concepts may have their greatest utility to the political scientist, avoiding the mechanistic formalism to which they are otherwise prone.

The failures of behaviouralism and of the over-reliance on quantification alert us to the pitfalls of alternative – formalistic – ways of using mathematics. The interdisciplinary retreat from behaviouralist and quantitative approaches may reassure us that such a critique is well-founded.[56] Of course, the analysis of long-term change in International Relations using mathematical concepts in a non-formal way will inevitably resemble non-'scientific' accounts of change, rather than those of physics, but – in my view – this should not cause us any anxiety. Thus, mathematical *concepts* will be employed here without the adoption of a formal quantitative approach.

Conclusion to review of previous approaches

This review has aimed to draw attention to the strengths and weaknesses of current approaches to long-term change. It can be seen that interdisciplinary trends exist among the approaches to change outlined in the previous two chapters. This enables critiques to be based on these trends, rather than on specific theories in each discipline, while retaining a relevance to many specific approaches.

The recognition that there are aspects of value in almost all, or even perhaps all, of these suggests that any new theory of change might most effectively be built upon these strengths. To achieve this, and to address the post-modernist critique of the whole subject[57] (which has been left unanswered so far), an epistemology will be suggested which enables both the utilization of the theoretical strengths so far identified, and the rational evaluation of hypotheses about change in both the past and the present.

Perspectivism: a post-relativist epistemology

Most scholars in all of the disciplines so far referred to would agree that human perception is, at least partly, subjective. Observation is to some degree coloured by the context in which it is made, whether that context is psychological or ideological.[58] It is the extent and implications of this subjectivity which are in dispute among post-positivist epistemologists and others.[59]

The realization that the observer is subjective and that knowledge is filtered through the lens of perception is in itself no recommendation for the adoption of a relativist epistemology,[60] because it is still possible to perceive the external world and to communicate that perception to others.[61] The failure to encompass the question of interactive communication has (in this regard) been one of the major omissions of post-modernist and other

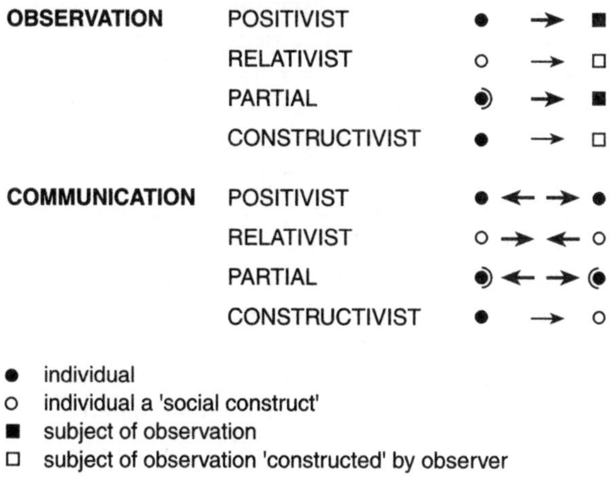

OBSERVATION	POSITIVIST	● → ■
	RELATIVIST	○ → □
	PARTIAL	◗ → ■
	CONSTRUCTIVIST	● → □
COMMUNICATION	POSITIVIST	● ← → ●
	RELATIVIST	○ → ← ○
	PARTIAL	◗ ← → ◖
	CONSTRUCTIVIST	● → ○

● individual
○ individual a 'social construct'
■ subject of observation
□ subject of observation 'constructed' by observer

Fig. 3.2 Differing (simplified) models of subjectivity. Solid arrows indicate direction of communication/observation. Thin arrows indicate 'direction' in which the object of observation/communication is constructed. Bracket indicates subjective filtering of information.

relativist thinkers. Yet these scholars would doubtless be dismayed if one ignored, or misrepresented (as they saw it), their views on the grounds that attempts to communicate them were unintelligible due to the subjectivity of perception. The plurality of possible perceptions of observed apparent external 'facts' (or 'externals') is no reason to doubt that these might have some relationship with that external existence. This is the case even if the existence of externals is itself presumed to be a proposition rather than a fact. Consequently, relativism is at once logically flawed in both proposition and application. Not only is it illogical, but this suggests that *sensu stricto* there can be no relativist epistemology!

In everyday experience, as well as in the whole range of anthropological evidence, the external world (as perceived) is always accorded an existence by human agents: I am yet to meet the 'relativist' who does not eat! That is, reality is – in practice – perceived by all of us as sufficiently 'true' for us to act as if it was certainly true that we must eat to remain healthy. This is the case whether we can demonstrate that truth in philosophy, or whether we prefer a relativistic epistemological view. The perception of reality which all known human societies use in their daily lives is what I term 'everyday reality'. This forms the basis for the epistemology suggested here.

We all live in an 'everyday reality', whether this is the same for each of us, or whether it is perceived partially (or entirely) differently. However, the extent to which that reality impinges on our everyday existence is different depending upon context. For example, compare the relatively comfortable daily life of a scholar on a US campus and a refugee fearing starvation, disease and genocide in a transit camp. To the former, it may seem possible to argue that starvation, pain and death are relativistic concepts – that they exist only conceptually – but to the latter, such an argument is likely to seem at least facile and most likely offensive. Such differences do not merely result in a variety of experience, but in differing perceptions of how 'real' the 'real world' is.

You, the reader, must believe that your perception of communicated information is not completely subjective. That you are reading this book to learn of its contents implies that you believe that it has an existence at least partly external to yourself, and that you can hope to gain information from reading it. Otherwise, the act of reading is merely a meaningless delusion.

In everyday reality, then, there are shared perceptions which you accept can be communicated between individuals. These shared perceptions reinforce our perception of a 'shared reality' and render interpersonal activity a reasonable preference to imagination alone. Communication such as this encourages us to believe that others share, if only partly, our perception of everyday reality. It also enables a consensual knowledge of reality to emerge which, through communication, is acquired by the comparison between individual knowledge and the communicated experience of others. This is then itself communicated among individuals, who can therefore reasonably consider that they share aspects (or all) of the same experience of reality. Consequently, although the reality in which we live is only partially perceived, that perception is partly shared between ourselves and others. Yet the partiality of perception is not identical in all human actors. Different people do not have exactly the same limits to their range of experience and observation; through communication we can expand the limits of our perceptual range.

So the reality of our perception is far from being a narrowly isolated and imaginary world of our own, although some parts of it may be exactly that.[62] Communication encourages a belief in 'consensual realism'. This consensual realism is that everyday reality which emerges from comparing communicated experiences of everyday reality. So that 'consensual realism' itself becomes a consensual reality. In this type of everyday reality, the consensual reality in which practice takes place, none of us are relativists. We all presume that action is capable of achieving an end, at least on some occasions, and is worth undertaking. Even if that action is to eat to avoid hunger, the belief that this action produces a result is itself an acknowledgement of everyday reality, and communication ensures that this can become consensual reality.

If we can perceive a shared reality and communicate this to each other in practice, then we can share to some extent (always, of course, to a limited extent) in the perceptions of others. The plurality of perception becomes, therefore, encompassed within the perception of the world which we individually hold, by the means of communication.

That is, when individuals see the world they do so individually and subjectively. When they can communicate these subjective perceptions to one another, however, and agree upon a shared experience of what constitutes external reality, a consensual reality emerges. There is then the potential for the comparison of differing perceptions with the common perceived external world, the comparison between individual interpretation and consensual reality. We conventionally operate as social actors in terms of shared perceptions of the external world such as these;[63] but if we acknowledge this, then comparison is possible between 'models of the world' and the world as we perceive it.

Consequently, although 'certain knowledge', or 'totally proven hypotheses', are unobtainable in logical enquiry, this does not mean that we have to adopt a relativistic view. If we can share perceptions of external reality and can compare these to form a 'shared reality', then we can also evaluate the relative probabilities of differing hypotheses and, in the same way, add further observations to them simply on the grounds of their ability to encompass that shared realism.

If we can rank interpretations of the world in an order of probability, on the grounds of their ability to encompass observations, then this can form the basis for assigning relative probabilities to different interpretations. To do this, we have simply to compare specific expectations produced by considering the implications of any new interpretation (whether a 'scientific hypothesis' or a belief) with 'shared reality'. In order to arrive at a shared evaluation of these hypotheses, we can communicate the results of our comparisons between ourselves. We can also comment on the means and – if we agree on a logical mode of argumentation – the logic of our evaluations.

We can, therefore, overcome the post-modern critique of reasoned hypothesis-testing by recognizing that 'testing' in a probabilistic manner is possible despite the subjectivity of individual perception and analysis. In this view we might conduct a 'test', by which I mean compare a hypothesis with 'data' (that is, shared perceptions of reality communicated among us), in order to arrive at probabilities from which we may decide on either logical or non-scientific grounds.[64] In the same way as shared perceptions are facilitated by communication because we can communicate our grounds for belief in (or for discounting) a view, we can arrive at shared common perceptions of the credibility of a hypothesis, so long as we can agree upon a shared scale of probability. Such a scale provides a basis for debating the likelihood of it being true or false, but we need to negotiate both criteria of method and the scale itself. All that is required to achieve this is to agree shared criteria, in the same fashion as we can agree 'shared reality', however subjectively. Agreeing upon a 'shared reality' and 'shared criteria' for evaluation in this way enables us to participate in debate about the validity of hypotheses. Yet these criteria (which in International Relations theory we might take as 'logic' and 'reasoned argument') will themselves be amenable to refinement or criticism through communicated shared perceptions or individualistic (partial and subjective) observations. Because communication enables each actor to persuade or dissuade another, once again a consensual basis of evaluation of whether 'facts' fit 'models' can – in theory – be arrived at.

Although we may disagree as to whether we should credit a hypothesis, we can therefore agree as to whether it is a reasonable argument within the constraints of these shared perceptions and as to whether it is supported by the data which we collectively agree exist.[65] We can also potentially agree on the validity of the tests proposed. Consequently, while acknowledging the subjectivity of individual perception and the social context of inquiry it is possible to accept that rational hypothesis-testing by closeness of fit to data can produce a ranking of hypotheses according to probability. This remains the case so long as the majority of observers accept the concepts of logic and an agreed scale of probability.

This produces a method of analysis which is, of course, very similar to the basis of the Anglo-American legal procedure of trial by jury. A proposition is examined in relation to arguments for and against it, and both proposition and arguments are weighed against such evidence as is agreed by those involved to exist. The relevance and reliability of this evidence too is subjected to rigorous source-criticism in a similar fashion, until a body of agreed data is established. Then, according to a set procedure, a decision is given regarding the validity of the proposition being evaluated.

The epistemology used here is based on this approach. It is, therefore, neither positivist nor relativist.[66] For want of a description I shall call it 'perspectivist', because it rests upon the capacity which we have to sharing the perspectives of independent subjective observers through the medium of communication. It follows that the more complete the communication, the more valid a view we have of the perceptions and models held by others.

As this argument may seem somewhat involved, I shall conclude this section by giving a metaphor for perspectivism, so as to clarify this epistemology. Let us imagine two observers standing – implausibly I admit, but this is only a metaphor! – on either side of a large sphere, such as a 'globe'. Neither of them can see over, or around, the sphere and each sees it through a pair of spectacles. The prisms of these both restrict and distort the view of the sphere.

Unless an outside observer, who is not so constrained, informs them of the remainder of the sphere, then the only way in which these two observers can understand the sphere's true character is by learning of the remainder of the sphere from each other. In order to do so, they must communicate as accurately and fully as possible their differing descriptions of what they perceive about it.

This communicated information from the other observer can then be cross-checked by each against what they themselves can see. This may, on occasions, be difficult, because of communication problems, or seemingly irreconcilable differences in perception, but in this fashion a gradual accu-

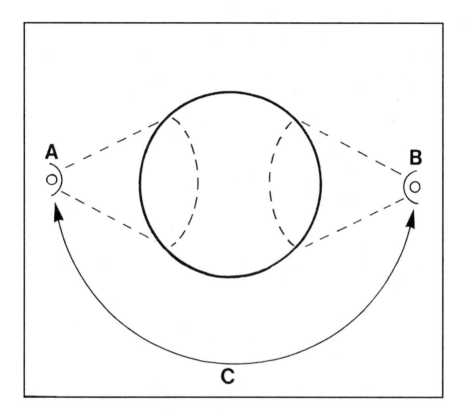

Fig. 3.3   Diagram of the 'perspectivism' metaphor. Observers, shown as **A** and **B**, can supersede the limitations of partial perception, filtered through individual subjectivity (indicated by bracket) through communication **C** (direction indicated by arrow).

mulation of knowledge about the sphere will be achieved over time by each observer. Also, by comparing observations, the observers can assist themselves in their assessments of the way in which the prisms through which they look distort and shape their view of the sphere.

Obviously, the more observers who can contribute information about their observations and the greater the amount of information exchanged about them, the more reliable and complete will be the picture which is built up by each of them in this way. The more exact the descriptions, or precise the language used to express them, the more accurate will be the communication of perspectives, whether or not these contain truth about the sphere. By this method, eventually each observer will learn more about both the sphere and the observer's own (and the others') perspectives. Each observer will be able to evaluate which of these perspectives offers a closer approximation to the true state of the sphere.

So much for metaphor. In practice this epistemological method operates in the following way: hypotheses can be validated or invalidated by the individual undertaking any analysis, by reference to data obtained by themselves or others. That is, the exchange of views and the discussion of both views and data can enhance the abilities of the individual both to validate existing hypotheses and to formulate new hypotheses. Yet all these views remain perspective-dependent, although they may contain perceptions shared with others with whom we are engaged in debate. In communication, these areas of shared observation might become clarified, even if that communication is itself partial and contains elements of distortion.

In areas of agreement a group of individuals may, then, feel that a consensual knowledge – a body of agreed 'fact' as in a court case – has been established which may form a basis for further description or debate. This 'fact' may be a representation of the true external form of the observed data, or it may be a shared but distorted perception of them.

In scholarship, this will mean that we may test our observations against data which both we and others collect, using logical comparison. By establishing the closeness of fit between data and hypothesis, we can generate new observations which include validated (fitting) hypotheses. The credibility of hypotheses tested in this way can be evaluated by the rejection of hypotheses which fail to survive such testing. The credibility of any hypothesis is, therefore, proportional to its ability to survive such tests. The use of agreed forms of argumentation and reasoning, which in scholarly analysis (as already observed) we consider to be logic and rational argument, will further facilitate the structuring and testing of hypotheses so that fuller communication and greater comparability will be achieved.

Consequently, in some – but not necessarily all – cases we can reach a consensual understanding of agreed reality (we do this every day of our lives) and we can recognize for ourselves 'thresholds of belief' and 'thresholds of disbelief' beyond which we consider observations or perspectives credible or to be discarded. These, too, we can communicate to each other and debate between ourselves, so that agreement upon such thresholds is also theoretically achievable. Again, we see exactly this in 'proof beyond reasonable doubt' in legal argument: the point at which the 'threshold of belief' is collectively passed.

That is to say, the aims of conventional academic enquiry may be achieved by conventional academic methods, so long as we recognize that absolute hypothesis-testing is unobtainable by rational means and all logic-based interpretations are interpretations alone. Yet not all such interpretations are equally valid. Cumulative consensual knowledge can be produced by logical argument, and what is describable as (if not strictly) 'empirical research'.[67] This view requires the rejection of relativism, while retaining a belief in the subjectivity of observation, and the adoption of a hypothesis-testing approach, without introducing either logical positivism or Hempel's normative logic of law-based explanation.[68]

Perspectivism, therefore, is an epistemology which requires us to reject both positivism and post-positivistic relativism. It allows us to recognize the potential validity of both scientific investigation and non-scientific forms of knowledge.[69] So this is not a return to 'scientism' any more than to positivism; according to this epistemology, scientific knowledge does not constitute the only source of, or access to, truth.

The success or failure of any field of rational enquiry can, however, be assessed in terms of the accumulation of shared knowledge,[70] as it is perceived by those involved. This may be acquired by a process of addition to existing shared knowledge, or the replacement of one view with another (more collectively credible) one.

Conclusion to epistemological discussion

A perspectivist epistemology enables us to form hypotheses and to test them against observed data. It enables us to evaluate the relative probability of each hypothesis being true or false and, through communication, to evaluate the results of our tests on them. It has the advantage that cumulative acquisition of knowledge by testing can occur rather than, as in Kuhn's view, the wholesale replacement of one hypothesis by another; although such replacement is also seen as a way of advancing knowledge.[71]

Employing a perspectivist paradigm, we can avoid a positivist belief in 'proof by empirical testing' while cumulatively building up a stock of consensual knowledge and shared beliefs. Interestingly for the political scientist, the epistemological approach of perspectivism is philosophically close to the decision-making approach of liberal democracy.[72] In each, the competition of communicated perspectives is subject to debate and consensual evaluation, producing a consensual (if contested) outcome.

As perspectivism provides the same sort of 'truth' by which criminals are imprisoned (and in some US states still executed), it seems a reasonable basis for crediting or discrediting academic hypotheses. This epistemology can now can be used both to form the basis of a new theory for the analysis of long-term change and, as we have seen, for its evaluation against data.

General conclusion to chapter

A perspectivist epistemology also enables us to combine features derived from the approaches already discussed, in theory-building. Thus, using this approach, a new theory of long-term change will be set out.

Notes

1   There has recently been a debate in International Relations over the relevance of epistemological discussion. However, it seems – to me – impossible to conduct an adequate analysis of world politics without clarifying one's

epistemological stance in as explicit a form as possible. For the debate see: Little, R., 1991, 'International Relations and the methodological turn', *Political Studies* 39, 463–78; Smith, S., 1996, 'Positivism and beyond', in S. Smith, K. Booth and M. Zalewski (eds), *International Theory: Positivism and Beyond*, 1–44; Smith, S., 1988, 'Paradigm dominance in International Relations: the development of International Relations as a social science', *Millennium* 16.2, 189–206; Smith, S., 1994, 'Rearranging the deckchairs on the ship called modernity: Rosenberg, epistemology and emancipation', *Millennium* 23.2, 395–405; Hollis, M. and Smith, S., 1996, 'A response: why epistemology matters in international theory', *Review of International Studies* 22, 111–16; Hollis, M. and Smith, S., 1990, *Explaining and Understanding International Relations*; Price, R., 1994, 'Interpretation and disciplinary orthodoxy in International Relations', *Review of International Studies* 20, 201–4; Neufeld, M., 1993, 'Interpretation and the science of International Relations', *Review of International Studies* 19, 39–62; Halliday, F., 1995, 'International Relations and its discontents', *International Affairs* 71.4, 733–46; Hoffman, M., 1987, 'Critical theory and the inter-paradigm debate', *Millennium* 16.2, 231–50; Linklater, A., 1992, 'The question of the next stage in International Relations theory: a critical-theoretical point of view', *Millennium* 21.1, 77–98; Nicholson, M. and Bennett, P., 1994, 'The epistemology of International Relations', in A. J. R. Groom and M. Light (eds), *Contemporary International Relations: A Guide to Theory*, 197–205; Jabri, V. and Chan, S., 1996, 'The ontologist always rings twice: two more stories about structure and agency in reply to Hollis and Smith', *Review of International Relations* 22, 107–10.

2   This is inevitable when discussing human actors because, however 'socially constructed', they remain biological organisms in their engagement with world politics.

3   That is, as all biological organisms have an ecological existence, so must the human body.

4   A point well illustrated by the popular encyclopedia, *The Guinness Book of Records* (ed. R. McWhirter), which lists the upper thresholds of recorded human achievement on a worldwide basis.

5   This point is clear from the history of seafaring also, see: Innis, H., 1950, *Empire and Communications*, Oxford.

6   For the debate regarding the 'socio-biological' basis of action: Wilson, E. O., 1975, *Sociobiology: The New Synthesis*, Cambridge, Mass.; Bock, K., 1980, *Human Nature and History*, New York; Caplan, A. L., (ed.), 1978, *The Sociobiology Debate*, New York; Montague, A. (ed.), 1980, *Sociobiology Examined*; Sahlins, M. D., 1977, *The Use and Abuse of Biology*.

7   Megarry, T., 1995, *Society in Prehistory*, 19–21 (Megarry also cites the 1991 Reith Lectures by S. Jones).

8   A point made by both Megarry and Jones: *ibid.* Cavalli-Sforza, L. L., Menozzi, P. and Piazza, A., 1994, *The History and Geography of Human Genes*, Princeton, NJ.

9   For a socio-biological attempt to confront this major flaw: Durham, W. H., 1978, 'The coevolution of human biology and culture', in V. Reynolds and N. Burton-Jones (eds), *Human Behaviour and Adaptation*, London, 11–32; Durham, W. H., 1991, *Coevolution: Genes, Culture and Human Diversity*, Stanford.

10 Dark, K. R., 1996, 'Ecological change and political crisis', in B. Holden (ed.), *The Ethical Dimensions of Global Change*, 167–80.

11 Wright, L. E, and White, C. D., 1996, 'Human biology in the Classic Maya collapse: evidence from palaeopathology and Palaeodiet', *Journal of World Prehistory* 10.2, 147–198.

12 Baillie, M. G. L., 1995, *A Slice through Time.*

13 Dark, K. R. 1996, 'Ecological change and political crisis', in B. Holden (ed.), *The Ethnical Dimensions of Global Change*, 167–80 (177).

14 As illustrated by the current debate over the causes and 'management' of ecological change.

15 Gamble, C., 1993, *Timewalkers.*

16 For example: Symons, D., 1989, 'A critique of Darwinian anthropology', *Ethology and Sociobiology* 10, 131–44; Alexander, R. D., 1980, *Darwinism and Human Affairs*; Borgerhoff, M. M., 1981, 'Adaptation and evolutionary approaches to anthropology', *Man* 22, 25–41.

17 For example, in Gellner, E., 1964, *Thought and Change*; Giddens, A., 1984, *The Constitution of Society.*

18 That is, the individual is reactive rather than proactive in bringing about change, in regard to non-social factors relating to exogenous environmental change.

19 Eldredge, N., 1986 *Time Frames: The Rethinking of Darwinian Evolution and the Theory of Punctuated Equilibria*, New York; Gould, S. J., 1989, *Wonderful Life*, New York.

20 For the concept of political adaptation: Rosenau, J. N., 1981, *The Study of Political Adaptation.*

21 For example; Gersick, C. J. D., 1991, 'Revolutionary change theories: a multilevel exploration of the punctuated equilibrium paradigm', *Academy of Management Review* 16.1, 10–36; on relevant debates in evolutionary theory see Eldredge, N., 1995, *Reinventing Darwin: the Great Evolutionary Debate.*

22 Eldredge, N. and Gould, S. J., 1972, 'Punctuated Equilibria: an alternative to phyletic gradualism', in T. J. M. Schopf (ed.), *Models in Paleobiology*, San Francisco, 82–115.

23 Scott, A. J. and Storper, M. (eds), 1986, *Production, Work, Territory. The Geographical Anatomy of Industrial Capitalism*, Boston, Mass. Giddens, A., 1995, *A Contemporary Critique of Historical Materialism*, 2nd edn.

24 For instance, on the diverse consequences – and non-consequences – of the Industrial Revolution: Stearns, P. N., 1993, *The Industrial Revolution in World History.*

25 For the more compelling evidence of a role for human individualism: Dosi, G., 1988, 'Sources, procedures and microeconomic effects of innovation', *Journal of Economic Literature* 26, 1120–71.

26 If consequence is taken to demonstrate causality, perhaps politics caused these economic changes?

27 Goldstone, J. A., 1987, 'Cultural orthodoxy, risk and innovation: the divergence of east and west in the early modern world', *Sociological Theory* 5, 119–35; Granovetter, M. S., 1985, 'Economic action and social structure: the problem of embeddedness', *American Journal of Sociology* 91, 481–510; Zukin, S. and Di Maggio, P., 1990, *Structures of Capital: The Social Organization of the Economy*; Burt, R., 1991, *Structural Holes: The Social Structure of Competition,*

Cambridge, Mass.; Lazonick, W., 1991, *Business Organization and the Myth of the Market Economy*; White, H., 1991, 'Comparative economic organization', *Administrative Science Quarterly* 36, 269–96; Coase, R. H., 1992, 'The institutional structure of production', *American Economic Review* 82, 713–19; White, H., 1992, *Identity and control*, Princeton, NJ; Grabner, G., 1993, *The Embedded Firm: On the Socioeconomics Industrial Networks*; Whitley, R., 1994, *The Social Structuring of Forms of Economic Organization: Firms and Markets in Comparative Perspective*; Uzzi, B., 1996, 'The sources and consequences of embeddedness for the economic performance of organizations: the network effect', *American Sociological Review* 61, 674–98.

28   Strange, S., 1986, *Casino Capitalism*; Strange, S., 1988, *States and Markets*; Strange, S., 1990, 'Finance information and power', *Review of International Relations* 16.3, 259–74.

29   For a critical review of Gramsci's own work: Morera, E., 1990, *Gramsci's Historicism*; Ferrira, J. V., 1989, 'Gramsci: Marxism's saviour or false prophet?', *Political Studies* 37, 282–9.

30   Hamilton, G. G. and Biggart, N. W., 1988, 'Market, culture, and authority: a comparative analysis of management and organization in the Far East', *American Journal of Sociology* 94 (Supplement) S52–94; Hirsch, F., 1976, *Social Limits to Growth*, Cambridge, Mass.; Granovetter, M., 1985, 'Economic action and social structure: the problem of embeddedness', *American Journal of Sociology* 91, 481–510; Child, J., 1981, 'Culture, contingency and capitalism in a cross-cultural study of organizations', in L. L. Cummings and B. Shaw (eds), *Research in Organizational Behavior*, Greenwich, 303–56.

31   Jackman, R. W., 1989, 'The politics of economic growth, once again', *Journal of Politics* 51, 646–61; Rosenberg, N. and Frischtak, C., 1984, 'Technological innovation and long waves', *Cambridge Journal of Economics* 8, 7–24; Zysman, J., 1994, 'How institutions create historically rooted trajectories of growth', *Industrial and Corporate Change* 3, 243–83. On economics' own problems with explaining changes, see: Ambrovitz, M., 1993, 'The search for the sources of economic growth: areas of ignorance, old and new', *Journal of Economic History* 53, 217–43.

32   Pounds, N. G., 1994, *An Economic History of Medieval Europe*, 2nd edn, especially 5–8 and 10. Feudalism enmeshed social, economic and political structures.

33   Elster, J., 1983, *Explaining Technical Change*, Cambridge; Jones, E. L., 1988, *Growth Recurring: Economic Change in World History*; Hampden-Turner, C. and Trompenaars, F., 1993, *The Seven Cultures of Capitalism*, New York.

34   Hodges, R. and Whitehouse, D., 1983, *Mohammed, Charlemagne and the Origins of Europe*.

35   Clarkson, L. A., 1985, *Proto-industrialization: The First Phase of Industrialization?* London; Mendels, F. F., 1972, 'Proto-industrialization: the first phase of the industrialization process', *Journal of Economic History* 32, 241–61; Ogilvie, S. and Cerman, M (eds), 1996, *European Proto-industrialization*; Berg, M., 1994, *The Age of Manufactures 1700–1820*, 2nd edn.

36   Cross-cultural psychology is a long-established field within psychology, see for example: Lloyd, B. B., 1972, *Perception and Cognition: A Cross-cultural Perspective*.

37   Schlicht, E., 1990, 'Social psychology: a review article', *The Journal of Institutional and Theoretical Economics* 146.2, 355–62.

38   For example, see the comments of Laver, R. H., 1982, *Perspectives on Social Change*, 3rd edn; Boudon, R., 1986, *Theories of Social Change*.

39   For a compelling illustration: de Gruchy, J. W., 1995, *Christianity and Democracy*.

40   Archer, M. S., 1988, *Culture and Agency*; Cohen, I. J., 1989, *Structuration Theory*.

41   Such was Collingwood's own perspective: Collingwood, R. G., 1946, *The Idea of History*.

42   Keohane, R. O. and Nye, J. (eds), 1977, *Power and Interdependence*, Boston; Keohane, R. O. and Nye, J., 1987, 'Power and interdependence revisited', *International Organization* 41.4, 725–53; Scott, A., 1982, *The Dynamics of Interdependence*; Baldwin, D., 1980, 'Interdependence and power: a conceptual analysis', *International Organization* 34.4, 471–506; McKibbin, W. J. and Sachs, J., 1991, *Global Linkages: Macro-economic Interdependence and Cooperation in the World Economy*, Washington; Rosenau, J. N. and Tromp, H. (eds), 1989, *Interdependence and Conflict in World Politics*, Brookfield, V.; Katzenstein, P. J., 1975, 'International interdependence: some long-term trends and recent changes', *International Organization* 29, 1021–34; Kroll, J. A., 1993, 'The complexity of interdependence', *International Studies Quarterly* 37, 321–47.

43   Although this is avoided by: Giddens, A., 1990, *The Constitution of Society. An Outline of Theory of Structuration*, Chicago.

44   Taylor, M., 1989, 'Structure, culture and action in the explanation of social change', *Politics and Society* 17.2, 115–62; Morrow, J. D., 1988, 'Social choice and system structure in world politics', *World Politics* 41.1, 75–97.

45   Wallerstein, I., 1991, *Geopolitics and Geoculture*; Worsley, P., 1990, 'Models of the modern world system', *Theory, Culture and Society* 7.2–3, 83–96.

46   Wilkinson, D., 1992, 'Cities, civilizations and oikumenes I', *Comparative Civilizations Review* 27, 51–87; Wilkinson, D., 1993, 'Cities, civilizations and oikumenes II', *Comparative Civilizations Review* 28, 41–72.

47   Wenke, R. J., 1990, *Patterns in Prehistory*, 3rd edn, chapters 8–14.

48   Jones, R. J. B., 1996, 'Construction and constraint in the promotion of change in the principles of international conduct', in B. Holden (ed.), *The Ethical Dimensions of Global Change*, 23–39.

49   Joynt, C. B. and Rescher, N., 1961, 'The problem of uniqueness in history', *History and Theory* 1, 150–62. For an interesting discussion of the whole issue: Bebbington, D., 1979, *Patterns in History*.

50   On this: Renfrew, A. C., 1973, *Before Civilization*.

51   Collis, J., 1984, *The European Iron Age*.

52   Fox, A., 1976, *Prehistoric Maori Fortifications on the North Island of New Zealand*, Auckland.

53   Davidson, J., 1984, *The Prehistory of New Zealand*.

54   Nicholson, M., 1989, *Formal Theories in International Relations*; Bennett, P. and Nicholson, M., 1994, 'Formal methods of analysis in IR', in A. J. R. Groom and M. Light (eds), *Contemporary International Relations: A Guide to Theory*, 206–15. For example: Bremmer, S., 1977, *Simulated Worlds*, Princeton; Bremmer, S. (ed.), 1987, *The Globus Model: Simulation of Worldwide Political and Economic Developments*, Frankfurt; Cusack, T. R. and Stoll, R. J., 1990,

Exploring Realpolitik: Probing International Relations Theory with Computer Simulation, Boulder, Colo.; Bennett, P. G., 1995, 'Modelling decisions in International Relations: game, theory and beyond', *Mershon International Studies Review* 39, 19–52; Cederman, L-E., 1995, 'Competing identities: an ecological model of nationality formation', *European Journal of International Relations* 1.3, 331–65; Cederman, L-E., 1994, 'Emergent polarity: Analyzing state-formation and power politics', *International Studies Quarterly* 38, 501–33.

55   For an interesting recent discussion of combining formal and non-formal approaches: Nicholson, M., 1996, *Causes and Consequences in International Relations*.

56   For attempts to build a post-positivist, but non–relativist, epistemology: Bernstein, R., 1983, *Beyond Objectivism and Relativism: Science, Hermeneutics, and Praxis*, Philadelphia; Bhaskar, R., 1989, *Reclaiming Reality*; Gadamer, H. G., 1994, *Truth and Method*, 2nd edn, New York. On the state of contemporary Critical Theory: Bronner, S., 1994, *Critical Theory and its Theorists*. See also: Dancy, J., 1985, *An Introduction to Contemporary Epistemology*; Diggins, J., 1994, *The Promise of Pragmatism: Modernism and The Crisis of Knowledge and Authority*, Chicago; Hollis, M. and Lukes, S. (eds), 1982, *Relativism and Rationality*.

57   Gunnell, J. G., 1995, 'Realizing theory: the philosophy of science revisited', *The Journal of Politics* 57.4, 923–40; Rengger, N. J. 1992, 'No time like the present: postmodernism and political theory', *Political Studies* 40.3, 561–70; Rengger, N. and Hoffman, M., 1992, 'Modernity, Post-modernism and International Relations', in J. Doherty, E. Graham and M. Malek (eds), *Post-modernism and the Social Sciences*, 127–46; Smith, S. 1996, 'Positivism and beyond', in S. Smith, K. Booth, and M. Zalewski (eds), *International Theory: Positivism and Beyond*, 1–44; Hollis, M., 1996, 'The Last Post?' in S. Smith, K. Booth and M. Zalewski (eds), *International Theory: Positivism and Beyond*, 301–8. For more critical views: Brown, C., 1994, 'Turtles all the way down: anti-foundationalism, critical theory and international relations', *Millennium* 23.2, 213–35; Nicholson, M., 1996, 'The continued significance of positivism', in S. Smith, K. Booth and M. Zalewski (eds), *International Theory: Positivism and Beyond*, 128–45.

58   Ashley, R. 1996, 'The achievements of post-structuralism', in S. Smith, K. Booth and M. Zalewski (eds), *International Theory: Positivism and Beyond*, 240–53.

59   Rengger, N. J., 1995, *Political Theory, Modernity and Post-modernity*; Rengger, N. J., 1996, *Duties Beyond Orders*; Rengger, N. J. 1988, 'Going Critical? A response to Hoffman', *Millennium*, 17.1, 81–89; Smith, S., 1996, 'Positivism and beyond', in S. Smith, K. Booth and M. Zalewski (eds), *International Theory: Positivism and Beyond*, 1–44; Biersteker, T., 1989, 'Critical reflections on post-positivism in International Relations', *International Studies Quarterly* 33.3, 263–8; Brown, C., 1994, 'Turtles all the way down: anti-foundationalism, critical theory and international relations', *Millennium* 23.2, 213–35.

60   On the limitations of post-modernism as an epistemological framework: Dews, P., 1986, *Logics of Disintegration*; Giddens, A., 1987, 'Structuralism, post-structuralism and the production of culture', in A. Giddens and J. Turner

(eds), *Social Theory Today*, 195–223; Rosenau, P., 1990, 'Internal logic, external absurdity: postmodernism in political science', *Paradigms* 4.1, 39–57; Rosenau, P. M., 1992, *Post-modernism and the Social Sciences*, Princeton; Brown, C., 1994, 'Critical theory and postmodernism in International Relations', in A. J. R. Groom and M. Light (eds), *Contemporary International Relations: A Guide to Theory*, 56–68; Brown, C., 1994, 'Turtles all the way down: anti-foundationalism, critical theory and international relations', *Millennium* 23.2, 213–35; Gellner, E., 1992, *Postmodernism, Reason and Religion*; Jones, R. J. B., 1991, *Anti-Statism and Critical Theories in International Relations*.

61   Bevir, M., 1994, 'Objectivity in history', *History and Theory* 33, 328–44; Bevir, M., 1996, 'The individual and society', *Political Studies* 64, 102–14 (esp. 111). Bevir stresses the ability to construct partial mutual understanding.

62   Dunne, T., 1995, 'The social construction of international society', *European Journal of International Relations* 1.3, 367–89.

63   For an interesting case of attempts at mutual understanding in a situation of high subjectivity and very 'political' communication: Schwartz, S. B. (ed.), 1995, *Implicit Understanding*.

64   Take the proposition 'the earth is a globe' for example. We cannot 'prove' this for ourselves in a positivist manner, yet we share the perception that it is a 'fact'. I doubt if there are many scholars, whatever their stated epistemological position, who would credit a theory of world politics which asserted that this 'fact' was untrue!

65   The widespread acceptance of logical argument as a basis for philosophical reasoning is a good example of this.

66   That is, it excludes the possibilities of 'total proof' and 'unknowability'. For a similar 'reasoned eclecticism', see: Wight, M., 1991, *International Theory. The Three Traditions*.

67   That is, I use 'empirical' to refer to 'shared reality', not positivistically proven reality.

68   Hempel, C. G., 1959, 'The Function of general laws in history', in P. Gardiner (ed.), *Theories of History*, New York, 344–56.

69   That is, perspectivism allows, for example, for the view that religious truth can be timeless if it is external to human actors.

70   This could, but need not, be in the form of 'facts' or in the form of 'understanding'.

71   Kuhn, T., 1962, *The Structure of Scientific Revolutions*, Chicago. It also avoids the extreme individualism of post-modernism by placing the individual's perception of 'fact', in its social context. In this sense, 'universal truths' can exist if they are universally held to be true or they can be based on external knowledge. Thus, unlike positivism, perspectivism, 'takes religion and emotion seriously', rather than advocating a rigid scepticism of all that is not 'scientific'. However, it also leaves space for wholly 'rationalistic' accounts.

72   That is, both are based on shared views communicated among people, and collective choices about which views to accept or reject.

4

The waves of time? A new theory of change in socio-political systems

Introduction

In this chapter, a new theory of change is outlined. Because it is probably impossible to produce any such theory capable of 'predicting' historical events, this theory will be used here to form the basis of a processual model of long-term change in world politics.[1] By a processual model I mean an idealized representation of the way in which change takes place, rather than assessing the probability of specific events occurring.

Although such a model must account for complex dynamics and encompass change on a very large ('macro-') scale, as we shall see it may be derived from simple logical arguments. In building this model, I shall draw upon many of the fields and approaches mentioned in earlier chapters, alongside both other approaches previously undiscussed in International Relations theory and new theoretical argument specific to the theory of change employed here.

In so doing, I aim not to deride, or 'deconstruct', those studies referred to in earlier chapters, but to use their strengths in combination with these new approaches – within a perspectivist epistemological paradigm – to form the basis of an original theory of change. In my view, many (if not most) of those fields of enquiry have much to offer the International Relations theorist of change. Each of them contains both strengths and weaknesses.

So, it is not my intention simply to apply to the question of change any of the existing 'paradigms' of International Relations theory. Rather, I shall examine this question from 'first principles', building an approach which, if the reader chooses, may then be related to these paradigms. As the approach used here requires some 'label' or 'title' in order to permit its discussion elsewhere, I shall call it 'macrodynamics'. This term is chosen for several reasons. Because the approach adopted here tries to encompass large-scale and long-term change, the prefix 'macro-' seems suitable for it. This also has analogies with the terminology employed by scholars discussing similar scales of analysis, such as macro-economics and macro-history. The second element suggests the essential factor of change, and makes an important link with 'complex dynamics', which we shall see plays a central role in this approach.

The structure of the chapter is as follows. I shall first attempt to resolve a few outstanding issues of definition. Then the conceptual basis for the new theory will be set out. Next, some empirical studies (which have produced apparently confirmatory results) will be examined. Finally, perspectives drawn from those studies will be used in the construction of the specific model to be used here, based on that theory.

Although this theory of change will be applied in this book to build a model for the study of long-term change in international politics, it is important at the outset to make it clear that is has the potential for far wider applicability, both in temporality and in subject of analysis. In this work its application can, therefore, be seen as no more than a preliminary investigation of an approach which might be of use to scholars examining different questions, and which might still be further developed.

Taking complexity seriously

In this analysis I shall refer repeatedly to the concept of 'complex systems'. So this term must at once be defined. Let us start with the 'system'.[2]

A system may, as in systems theory itself, be defined at its simplest as a network of related parts.[3] These may be in constant or occasional relationships with each other and all need not be interrelated at any time, although all may be.

A 'complex' system is 'complex' in the sense that it is 'differentiated'. 'Differentiated' is defined here as meaning 'comprising many parts which have both specialized and related functions'.[4] Take the case of a business: if it has two offices with related functions (such as 'management' and 'accounts') and establishes another five offices with related functions (such as 'marketing' and 'public relations'), then it has become more 'differentiated'. As differentiation is taken here as an index of complexity, then in the terminology used here, it has also become more 'complex'. If it instead contracts to a single office, then it has become less 'differentiated', and so less 'complex'. Plainly, however, differentiation is less easily observed in most 'real world' examples than in this simple example.

This is not to say that the explanation of the origin of these related parts lies in their functional roles. Only that they may be understood as having different roles in the entire network of relationships of which they are part. Nor is it to suggest that every part of a complex system of this sort must be related to every other, either directly or indirectly. Simply, they must bear some degree of relationship to one or more other parts of the same system.[5]

Using this concept of complexity, mathematicians, biologists and economists have seen complex systems as 'nested hierarchies'. By this they mean that these have component parts, like the offices in the example above,

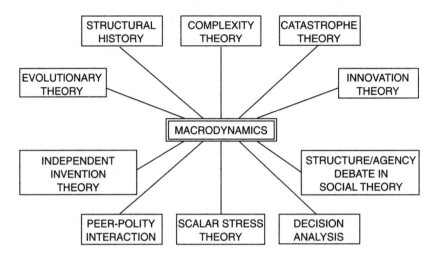

Fig. 4.1   Diagram showing some sources of 'macrodynamic' theory outside of
International Relations theory.

which may be subdivided into sequentially smaller units until one reaches
their basic building blocks. This basic building block is what International
Relations theorists have often seen as the 'unit of analysis'.

In this way one can see an economy, for example, as being comprised of
'sectors' composed of 'industries' composed of 'firms' composed of 'divisions' composed of 'departments' composed of 'individuals'; these are all
parts of the whole system.[6] Yet the concept that complex systems are
intrinsically 'hierarchical', in the sense of being ordered in this way, does not
necessarily mean that they are socially or economically 'ranked', although
this is usually the case in economic reality.[7] It merely suggests that there is a
functional differentiation of decision-making, activity, or the operation of
processes (as for biological processes) which is handled by its sequential
ordering. This means that in biological, mathematical, and economic
examples, complex systems have a hierarchy of parts which operate in what
is often a more or less reflexive fashion.[8]

Work on complex systems such as these in mathematics has shown that
they generally change in the direction of greater rather than lesser complexity if no restraints on this are present. They also exhibit a tendency to
'self-organization': the endogenous ordering into hierarchies giving them a
system-wide form. Complex systems, therefore, exhibit 'morphogenesis'
based on processes that are partly independent of agency, although they
require agents to both initiate them and enact them.

Change in complex systems, whether in the direction of greater or lesser
complexity, therefore produces a 'trajectory' or historical path. Past changes
in the system limit future options and the system appears to 'gather impetus'

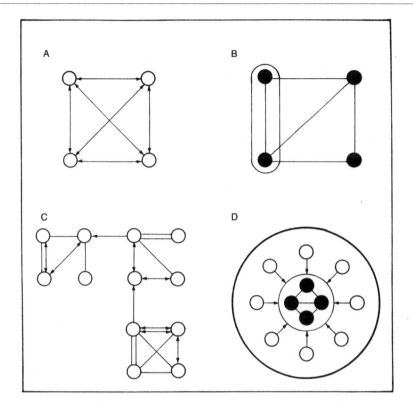

Fig. 4.2 Diagram showing alternative concepts of the 'system'. In systems theory (A) all sub-systems relate to each other. In the Realist system (B), states form systems by inter-state interactions (indicated by lines) and alliances (indicated on left). In the World System (D) it is core:periphery economic relationships which constitute the system. The definition of system in this book is based on the 'complex system' (C). In this, networks of links of various types exist between all parts of the system, but each part is not necessarily linked with all others, or in the same way.

through time by becoming 'path-dependent' in this way. This is another conclusion also supportable on mathematical, biological and evolutionary grounds, and seen in the operation of economic and institutional histories.[9] So, path-dependency will propel a complex system towards greater complexity, while self-organization provides it with aspects of form. These processes cannot initiate systems, nor entirely control their morphology, and can only operate if contextual circumstances permit and if the system does not collapse. But if these processes occur, complexity alone can produce morphogenetic trajectories.

So complex systems are more than simply the 'systems' of 'systems theory', and more than simply descriptive. The theory of complexity can explain some important aspects of how interrelationships produce both form and diachronic dynamics. It can also explain how 'process' can exist in part, independently of both events and structure. However, this is not a 'theory of everything', nor even when considered alone, an adequate theory of the emergence of form (morphogenesis) and dynamics in human societies.

It need hardly be pointed out also, that while complexity in such systems may sometimes be quantifiable, it is more often unquantifiable, even in economic or mathematical systems of this sort. This will especially be the case in human societies, if we see these as complex systems, because patterns of diversity and interrelationship may be constantly shifting, ambiguous and informal.[10] So complexity cannot be used as the basis of a quantifiable mathematical theory of political change in human societies, although it can contribute to understanding how they are organized and change. There are, however, other implications of such an approach.

Allen and others have recently explored the potential for change in complex human, biological and physical systems from an evolutionary perspective.[11] In their view all such systems exhibit what they call 'evolutionary drive', by which they mean, as Allen has recently stressed, 'possibility space'.[12] Possibility space is regarded as the potential options for change open to the system and its parts. This concept refers to the way in which such systems have a greater or lesser degree of possibilities for change, which may or may not be realized.[13]

The concept that such systems are hierarchically structured, in the sense so far mentioned, not only raises the classic International Relations theory question of the 'unit of analysis', but also suggests an answer to this question. This answer lies in the concept of hierarchical structuring of complexity itself, in that this necessitates that the smallest divisible unit must be the basic unit of analysis.

In the case of any study of human societies the basic unit of analysis must therefore be the human individual, simply because it is logically impossible to subdivide that unit any further! By focusing on this 'unit of analysis', as we shall see, it is also possible to avoid the dangers of 'mechanistic' explanation based on the concept of complexity. It ensures that we are aware that politics has 'complex systems' composed of people not electrical components!

This hierarchical understanding of complex systems also suggests that we must adopt a multi-scalar approach, relating people (as the initial 'units of analysis') to other 'units of analysis'. These are often defined in International Relations as including the state and the international system.[14] Each of these units is made up of lower-level units in the form of a set of (social or political) relationships. Such a view necessitates that we think of both states and the 'international system' as human societies rather than as concrete independent entities.[15] It also means that we are able to talk of 'systems' existing at a wide range of levels: from small groups of people to the global networks of relationships visible in contemporary world politics.

To rephrase the same proposition: we must take a complexity-based systemic view of the state and international system, and this means linking both to intra-state levels of analysis. In this sense, the perspective afforded by mathematical, biological and economic studies of systemic complexity conforms to the Pluralist understanding of the state.[16] Yet this analysis is based on drastically different grounds from those usually used in the arguments for Pluralist conceptions of statehood in International Relations theory. Interestingly, however, it coincides too with the anthropological conception of the state as a human societal 'organization'. This suggests another possibility: if we conceive states not only as human societies but also as high-level 'human organizations', is it not possible to apply the same logic to international 'organizations' themselves?[17] If so, we can integrate transnational intra-state and state organizations into this view. So we can see human social (and so political) organization as a continuum of scales within complex systems stretching from the smallest 'social group' (within which the individual is situated) to the largest network of international relationships.

This is not, of course, to claim that all of these organizations represent the same types of units. Nor does it require that we must, on this basis alone, assign equal analytical significance to them when discussing change. Simply, it suggests that we can see differing types of organization in a similar systemic way. This must partly, at least, erode the state–organization and national–international divisions in our thinking about international politics.

Complex systems dynamics also suggests that systemic stability, on any level, is never certain, or a 'given' in analysis, because all complex systems contain 'possibility space' for change. We can see here a convergence of perspectives from both political theory and anthropology with those of mathematics and biology. As one political theorist has recently written of the state:

> It has at best only a tendential (and potential) unity. The multitude of disaggregated decisions, operations and procedures which take place 'within the state' are unified only inasmuch as they are enabled/constrained by the legacy of previous attempts (albeit in different ways) to impose a trajectory on the state through its transformation.[18]

This is very close to a 'complex systemic' perspective on the state as a pathdependent nested hierarchy with possibility space for change!

If complexity theory offers an approach to networks of human relationships, our next task may, therefore, be to clarify how adopting the individual as a basic unit of analysis itself affects the approach taken to change. That is, how can we introduce 'humanity' into 'complexity' in human organizations and interpersonal relationships while retaining the strengths of a 'complexity-based' approach to these? This task may begin with questioning the nature of this 'basic unit of analysis': examining the individual in society.

The individual in society

We have already seen that one of the great triumphs of modern natural science has been the demonstration of human genetic unity. By this I mean showing that humans of varying 'races' and cultures are much more genetically similar than even superficial biological studies had previously suggested. Similarly, cognitive psychology has, albeit less unanimously, reinstated the concept of cognitive individualism.

Together, these studies combine to support the view, which one might in any case adopt on other grounds, that belief in the universality of human-kind and of human cognitive individualism is correct. Put another way: people may be different because they live in different cultures or at different times in history, but they are all still 'people'.

Cross-cultural psychological, anthropological and sociological studies support the view that there are also universal human characteristics, which are not gender-specific, albeit differently expressed in different cultural contexts. For example, recent studies in cross-cultural psychology and sociology have found strong evidence that altruism is one such character-istic.[19]

These studies strongly support the view that the human individual is a 'conscious strategic actor' with 'moral agency'. Physical anthropology shows that there is no biological reason to suppose that this has been different at any time in the history of *homo sapiens sapiens*, the modern human. That is, there is no logical reason to suppose that these 'basic human characteristics' are not transhistorical.

Such a view is not in conflict, of course, with the anthropological discovery of the diversity of human experience and of human cultures. It stresses the essential unity of humanity, not an illusory cultural uniformity in human history. This is a uniformity composed of simple characteristics, such as the ability to choose and the ability to communicate.

A credible theory of change in world politics must, therefore, take into account this transhistorical decision-making potential of human agents. It must also encompass this in a context which does not simply reduce human agency to 'self-interest', and which accounts for the cultural matrix which has resulted in global human cultural diversity.

Humans do not exist in isolation. Human existence is 'social', in that the human agent coexists with other agents, and in relation to other context which affect and to some extent shape agency.[20] This social context of humanity both derives from and requires interaction between individuals based on shared modes of communication, whether verbal or non-verbal. Human societies, and so politics, require organization among individuals. Yet all social and political organization is also formed by the interaction of individuals, whether the form of organization is, for example, 'the tribe', 'the state' or 'the nation'. Organizations both are societies, and are formed within societies, so that social and political organization are inseparable. That is, all 'politics' is strictly 'socio-politics', in the sense that political organization is always a form of social organization.

Yet societies and organizations are also based on the interaction of individuals. Interaction may be through communication, economic exchanges or any other form of peaceful or violent contact. Importantly for the purposes of this book, all societies and organizations are, therefore, both 'complex systems' and (because of interaction) part of other 'complex systems'. Social (and therefore political) change is always change involving the basic unit of the individual, because all these systems are made up of interacting individuals. That is, societies and political units ('polities') do not 'change' as unitary entities, although they may be analysed as unitary entities. Individuals change them, and change is articulated through altered relationships and patterns of interaction.

All change has, then, to be analysed both in terms of individual agency, the choices made by people, and in terms of the contexts in which these decisions are made. This context comprises the role of interaction and communication, the cultural matrix in which they take place and the properties of societies as complex systems. Individual choices cannot be disengaged from a cognitive, cultural, social, economic (and so systemic) context, because that is the context in which all human decision-making operates.[21]

On these grounds too the basic unit of analysis must be the individual in society. Individuals are the basic 'building blocks' of all societies and organizations. This directly links the argument in this section with that of the previous section. It returns to the inter-relationship of social forms, to differentiation, and to the individual as the basic unit of analysis. The discussion in this section reaffirms the role of agency in bringing about change. But this is in the context of systemic dynamics produced in part by the intrinsic properties of complex systems, rather than by human agency alone.

This suggests that humans are not free to make any choice they like, nor that all choices are equally likely at any given time. However, it also suggests that agency plays a central part in the histories, and so trajectories, of states and non-state organizations alike.

Agency must, therefore, be set in its historical and systemic contexts, if events are to be explained.[22] Culture, the details of social organization, economic activities, religious and other beliefs, environment and geography, all provide types of historical contexts within which decision-making may be set. This being said, decisions still derive from agency rather than context.

The indeterminacy of the societal matrix can be demonstrated by the simple observation that similar contexts produce very dissimilar individual histories. That is, people make different decisions under similar circumstances in a 'domestic' (i.e. intra-state) context and the cumulative role of these is to produce cultural diversity.

As we have seen already, this intra-state context can be understood as part of larger (complex) systems going beyond the state. If so – given the self-similarity of complex systems – the observation of heterogeneous decision-making under like circumstances within states implies the centrality of agency and the absence of contextual determinism overall.

While political, social, economic, cultural, religious and other forms of organization and relationship constitute the system, neither these nor agency are determined by each other nor by the system overall. This introduces a paradox. Because of their form, complex socio-political systems are universally similar in terms of the processes which operate within them. They are, however, historically contingent, in that they are made up of differing and changing networks of relationships and organizations.

There is another paradoxical corollary of this argument. If human societies are always organized and interactive, then the form of organization (and the manner of interaction) may be sources of both similarity and difference between them. Both organization and interaction, like the complex system, may impose their own logic on the actors they encompass, without determining decisions or actions.[23] We will return to this point later, but first we must move on to the question of temporalities, before discussing issues of structure, inter-systemic interaction and organisation.

Temporalities of change

Annaliste historiography and studies of complex systems make it clear that it is possible to envisage change operating within human societies at several, to some extent discrete, levels. This does not, however, resolve the question of the temporalities of analysis.

In a complex system, multi-level change must also allow for the reflexive inter-relationship of these levels. However, each level need not change at a similar rate or time, and both approaches imply that change may take place at different rates at different levels, although these may bear some relationship to each other.

So, if 'nested hierarchies' comprise systems which can be understood as a set of complex relationships between an increasing magnitude of levels, then different forms of causation (in addition to different rates of change) may also occur at different hierarchical levels.[24] We have already seen that process (deriving from complexity) and events (deriving from agency) are partly separable, in that processual morphogenetic trajectories can exist independently of agency. However, it would be a mistake to suppose that we can separate events and their causation from processes of systemic change in a complete or discrete manner.

Events take place both within the framework of such processes, and with the capability of transforming processes. Yet process does not compel events to occur, rather than constitute an additional context within which they occur.[25] Process enables events to occur, but also constrains their occurrence. It affords 'windows of opportunity' and periods of processual restraint. These 'windows of opportunity' can open or close to afford actors greater or lesser 'possibility space' and so facilitate or limit the role of agency. In this sense, process can resemble 'structure' in Giddens and Archer's senses.

The distinguishing feature of 'the event' is, of course, its temporality. It is always a short-term phenomenon. However, if events can also alter systemic processes, then the event and the process have no universal causal primacy for each other. Nor is process specific to any given temporality although process can be either short-term or (more usually) long-term in duration.

So, processes can be enacted through events and events can be the basis of process. That is, there is a reflexive relationship between 'the event' and 'the short-term', and through process – the longer term of systemic trajectories. 'Long-term change' (in the sense of change over millennia) in world politics can, therefore, be seen as composed of a series of events. But it can also be seen in terms of processes and trajectories, potentially outlasting the event.

It is, therefore, this processual and systemic approach which perhaps holds the greatest potential for studying long-term change. While events are always short-term happenings, contingent upon circumstances, processes could, theoretically at least, have a long-term existence, even if that existence is not independent of short-term events. This, however, brings us back to the issue of structure, which provides a link between the short-term events and longer-term processual regularities. It is through structure that process is articulated. Structure also enables a clarification of the relationship between agency and events, and also (in part) the sense in which all events are never 'equally likely' to occur.

Coping with structure

The short-term event occurs, as Archer, Giddens and Lloyd have discussed, within a structural context.[26] A clear conceptual framework for under-standing structural effects and the relationship between structure and agency has been provided by their work. Even if their detailed conclusions about this relationship differ, they all agree that structure and agency are capable of transforming each other. They agree that structure forms a context which neither determines human action nor leaves it entirely free of constraint.

Structure consists of many differing, and to some extent disparate, features. These are united by their enabling, co-ordinating and regulatory effects on human behaviour and decision-making.[27] The structure of human agency may, as we have already seen, be afforded by many factors. These include beliefs, cultural contexts, organizational contexts, or environmental or economic factors. However, structure distinctively has the potential, realized or not, both to outlast the event and to articulate process.

'Societies' and 'organizations' are examples of this ability of structure to outlast events, in that societies and organizations are composites of structures and individuals. This combination gives them a distinctive (and temporally situated) character.[28] These structures, societies and organizations come into existence with specific events. The transmission of these structures, such as cultural norms, over generations provides a context for the maintenance of societal characteristics. These are frequently (but not unchangeably) those

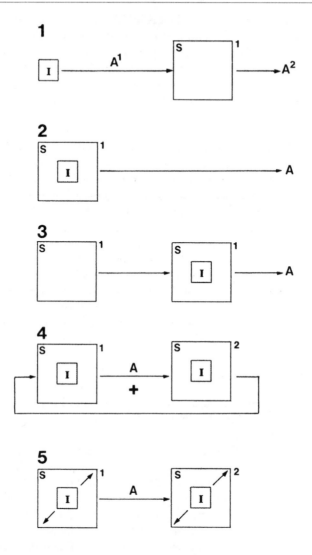

Fig. 4.3   Diagram illustrating some contrasting models of structure and agency. **I** indicates individual; **S** indicates structure; **A** indicates action. The plus sign indicates interaction among individuals.
1. Individual and structure exist separately but structure exists to facilitate the aims of individuals.
2. Individual exists within structural context which determines action (as in economistic determinism).
3. Structure exists before the individual and forms a context which determines action (as in environmental determinism).
4. The 'morphogenetic cycle' of conditioning interaction and modification. (according to Archer)
5. 'Structuration', in which structures are constantly reproduced by action, which they constrain and enable. (according to Giddens)

formed at the outset. Structure can exist as part of agency, tied up with it inextricably through what sociologists have termed 'social reproduction', or it can exist independently of agency, as in the case of geographical structures. A geographical feature, such as a mountain range, may be differently perceived at different points in its existence, and may be assigned differing cultural meanings. But it is a long-term structural feature of the landscape, enabling and constraining action.

Most political, social and economic structures, however, are important in a specific and definable historical period of existence. They are closely associated with specific cultural and political contexts. This is perhaps most clearly illustrated by the case of feudalism.[29] This remained the dominant political structure in Western Europe during the Middle Ages. It shaped events from the parochial to Europe-wide, but ceased to play that role during the start of the Renaissance–Reformation period of European history.[30]

The example of feudalism also enables us to see, perhaps more clearly than in our own period of history, the way in which social and political structures can be intermeshed. In the same way in which social and political organization are inseparable, so social and political structures are inseparable; once again, we see that politics is always socio–politics. The need to form political structure within social structure necessitates that this is the case.

The association of specific structures with specific socio–political systems has, of course, the consequence that the existence of such structures enables the recognition of these systems. This is not to say that no systems share structures; plainly this frequently occurs. Each system has its own unique combination of structures, however, when compared to preceding and following systems. This is, after all, exactly how most Realists and neo-liberals would define the 'Westphalian system', and how historians define 'historical periods'.

In this sense, then, structures bridge the long-term and the short-term and enable systemic recognition. They also reassert the strength of assigning significance to the intermeshing of social and political relationships. Structures, such as institutions, 'regimes' and cultural norms, can persist in the medium-term. They can outlast the event but still need not have a 'long-term' existence. Consequently, structures (often formed by short-term events) construct a medium-term temporality between that of the short-term event and potentially long-term process.[31]

This realization of the 'medium-term' role of structures has implications for our concept of the system, discussed earlier in this chapter. If systems are definable in terms of historically-associated structures, then the emergence and decline of those structures will enable us to trace the origin and decline of systems. This will apply even when these systems are not formally delineated on other grounds, such as by treaties or through conscious mapping.

As political and economic structures are formed within, and constrained by, socio-political systems and have no intrinsic ability to exist outside of those systems, each new socio-political system both brings with it new structures and is definable by the existence of a unique combination of structures.[32] These structures are constituted by the continual reproduction of rules, norms and customs through the enaction of short-term events.

In this sense all socio-political systems can be conceived of as also being networks of regimes, organizational linkages, beliefs, cultural values, and other structures. It follows from this that the relationship between structures, societies, and states means that systems of states cannot be taken as divisible into a discrete dichotomy of 'domestic' and 'inter-state' politics. These categories represent merely levels of structuring and organization within the systemic whole represented by human socio-political organization.[33]

Seen in this way, states and other socio-political systems have a historical (rather than simply analytical) existence. But this is not an existence separate from their components. States and other political units exist in part independently of individual action (in that the action of an individual can seldom cause them to cease existing) but also enmeshed in dynamic socio-political systems. Like larger- and smaller-scale systems, states are also always multi-actor systems, not least because of the large number of potential or active agents within them. This view of the state has an interesting consequence for the study of world politics, however, because, seen in this way, international systems including states are never only 'inter-state systems'. They always contain a multitude of potential agents at the intra-state and inter-state levels.

This also suggests that inter-polity systems not composed of states can be analysed in a similar way to those including states. Both are simply historically-situated, but 'actually existing' forms of socio-political organization. States and other polities are 'systems of systems': they both are made up of, and make up, socio-political systems. Likewise, 'the international system', in the sense of the network of inter-state and transnational interactions above the level of the state and connecting populations of different systems, is simply another level of the systemic hierarchy. Empires too can be considered as similar socio-political systems in the sense of fulfilling all the criteria so far mentioned. The same holds true for inter-imperial systems.

In the theory of complex socio-political systems so far set out in this chapter, all of these types of political relationship can be seen merely as possible levels in the potential range of nested hierarchies of socio-political systems from the smallest social group to the global system. The system is always a system of systems.

The 'system of systems' comprising human socio-political relationships is, however, based ultimately on individuals. Thus, it is the individual to whom we must return in order to build a theory of the processes of socio-political change. In keeping with the basis of complexity theory, this begins with the lowest indivisible unit of analysis and the shortest temporality of change, relating individualistic decision-making – the basis of short-term change – to socio-political systems. If we are to make this link, then as the systems with which we are concerned here are the result of agency, we can use the relationship between decision-making and systemic complexity as a means of relating agency to socio-political systems.

Complexity and decision-making

Decision-making forms a link between the individual, structure and the system, because all socio-political forms derive from agency.[34] This is true whether these decisions are, in some degree, constrained or freely made. Decision-making is, therefore, also central to the understanding of socio-political change on all levels, because all change is inextricably related to agency.

In analysing complex political systems, such as states or international systems, it would be too narrow a stance to claim that 'political' decisions should be privileged in our analysis. As James Rosenau has stressed,[35] we must (at least initially) be willing to discuss and incorporate other types of decision-making in such a study.

The work of decision theorists enables us to understand the means by which decisions are made, and to recognize that procedures of decision-making may also have implications for the emergence and transformation of socio-political complexity. This view is enhanced by recognizing the role of structure in decision-making, as this emphasizes the potential role of context.

If increased socio-political complexity (that is, increased differentiation) emerges through both decision-making and systemic morphogenesis, then it is again clear that the process of the transformation of complex socio-political systems is also explicable partly in terms of decision-making itself. Likewise, as we have seen, processes of systemic change relate to processes of decision-making, and agency shapes the structures and events in the history of socio-political systems. This, once again, emphasizes the centrality of decision-making to the analysis of socio-political change.

Socio-political stability, the replication of existing structures, can only occur due to the 'social reproduction' of these structures by decision-making. The stability, or change, of any socio-political system is, therefore, also closely related to decision-making, and its impacts upon the structural framework within which relationships are maintained in order to constitute the socio-political system. Thus, again, the work of decision theorists is extremely valuable.

Decision-making is essentially a binary process. Any decision may be accepted or not, the latter category comprising both when it is rejected and when it is left unacted upon.[36] In order for socio-political systems to exist diachronically, most decisions have to promote enough systemic or structural stability to maintain the form of the system overall. This is essential for the continued existence ('social reproduction') of the system. Decisions may bring about political change or promote political stability. Stability itself, through the constant reproduction of structure, can play a part in the habitual or regular maintenance of the structures which constitute the framework of activity: the routinization of action.

Routinization of decision-making and structure can both have a role in constraining change. Even when the reproduction of structural frameworks constrains change in this way, these can generate situations which might promote change. For instance, the acceptance or non-acceptance of the 'status quo' in decision-making stimulates either stability or change. Situations prompting decision-making are not responded to 'blindly' or outside of a societal context; but because decision-making is a binary process, even when large numbers of decisions have to be taken each must still rest on a binary choice of acceptance or inaction/rejection.

In this way, intentional decision-making, and its intentional or unintentional consequences, both constitute the socio-political system and the structures which make up its component parts. Decision-making has its own logic, but also the capacity to both reproduce and transform both structures and the system, in terms of events, either by choice or by accident.

Even in a situation of apparent stability, therefore, decision-making constantly occurs. It is required in order to reproduce the existing structures and the networks of relationships between actors and structures.[37] So, stability leads to decision-making as much as does change, and while decisions have to be taken, change always lies latent within each structure and system.

Neither structures nor systems can be conceptualized as static entities, therefore, and they always have the 'possibility space' for change. However, structures and relationships can never be exactly reproduced through time – the same events cannot be entirely reproduced. So change inevitably occurs in any socio-political system. That is, complexity and systemic and structural contingency, combined with human intentionality, generate endogenous socio-political change.

Events from outside the socio-political system also lead to situations in which decisions must be made. In this respect, exogenous factors play their role in decision-making, and so in promoting or limiting change. These exogenously prompted decision-making situations are often conceptualized as 'crises'. They include aspects derived both from agency and from those 'platforms' which give the possibility for specific socio-political systems to emerge.[38] Their impact and relationship to systemic change will depend upon human responses to them, however, and the potential variety of these means that no single outcome is inevitable.[39] The impact of these external factors on the socio-political system is, therefore, primarily to promote decision-making, not to trigger specific responses. There is no reason to suppose that there are identifiable responses always associated even with general types of external 'impacts', such as ecological change.[40]

Even the perception of crisis, or the potential for crisis, can promote decision-making, although this may be no more than the decision to react to, or ignore, the perceived or potential crisis.

At its simplest, this argument could be expressed, then, by the 'common-sense' proposition that people necessarily respond to situations. They usually try to solve their problems, whether these are real or perceived.[41]

Whether in response to endogenous or exogenous factors, decision-making individuals can enact strategies, but they cannot determine the course of events. They can transform socio-political structures, but not determine all types of structural change. So, there is uncertainty and unpredictability in the ability of all human societies to govern their own socio-political systems. The consequences of action may be uncertain and unexpected.

All human interaction also involves decision-making. Such interaction also offers those involved new situations, which promote further decision-making. The greater the number of interactions, the greater the amount of decision-making that must occur.

More efficient communication systems will enhance human interaction. Language, literacy, technologies of transport, and telecommunications, all increase the potential for interaction and therefore for decision-making.[42] Thus individuals must necessarily be faced with a greater range of decision-making situations the more they interact with each other. The more differentiated the structural frameworks and networks of relationships with which they are presented in the course of socio-political reproduction, the more decisions will be needed to enact that reproduction.[43]

So the more complex the system, the more decisions are required to maintain that system. If decision-making also increases with increased interaction, and interaction is greater in more complex systems, then the amount of interaction and degree of complexity are closely related to the amount of decision-making required to reproduce the system diachronically. As the potential for change is latent in each decision that is made, then, the more complex the system the more likely it is to change.

Managing information

To cope with socio-political complexity and interaction, decision-making must depend upon the acquisition and processing of information.[44] Information processing must, therefore, keep pace with the rate of decision-making, as the latter is related to the maintenance of complexity. If it fails to do so, decision-making will be unable to take place rapidly enough to reproduce the system, and collapse in that system will occur. Alternatively, if information cannot be processed rapidly enough for decisions to be made, even though it is available, information overload will occur.[45] If this happens the system is again liable to collapse, due to a failure in the ability of decision-makers to process information rapidly enough.[46]

Information overload can be avoided, however, if the processing of information keeps pace with its acquisition. If information processing and information exchange occur in parallel, then decision-making can respond to the demands of complexity and interaction.[47] These requirements can be met in two ways. More efficient information-acquisition and information-processing capacities can be developed as complexity increases. Or decision-making functions can be ordered – producing the hierarchy found in complex systems – so as to offset increasing demands.[48]

This hierarchical ordering of decision-making must, at least initially, be separated in analysis from 'hierarchical' social ranking of society, as already noted.[49] Information-processing hierarchies may be very different to those of social ranking.[50] As a consequence, di Zerega's comment that because they lack unitary goal-orientation 'democracies are not hierarchies' is patently incorrect, and it is also an incorrect generalization in social terms.[51] Democracies, like other states, represent hierarchical information-processing structures.

The hierarchical ordering of information processing solves the question of equating information acquisition and processing with the requirements of decision-making and structural reproduction.[52] But this ordering does not reduce the amount of overall decision-making. The greater the number of choices involved in the network of relationships and interactions, even if these are part of a multi-layered and highly organized bureaucracy of information analysis and decision-making, the higher the risk of unintended change at some level within it.[53] This is because the risk of such change, deriving from the potential for structures or systems to be inadequately reproduced so as to maintain stability, remains constant. The number of decisions will remain constant even if they are more equitably or efficiently distributed, so the overall amount of decision-making remains proportional to complexity.

Catastrophe theorists and others have noted that increased complexity involving such networks of reliance also produces a characteristic problem.[54] The greater the interdependence of the constituent parts of the system and the more complex its structure, the more difficult it will be to maintain stability, because possibility space for change will be reduced. As discussed in the previous chapter, such systems can be described as 'hypercoherent'.[55]

Hypercoherence occurs when each part of the system becomes so dependent upon each other that change in any part produces instability in the system as a whole. In this view, too, increased complexity also bears a close relationship to increased propensity for change.

The overall amount of decision-making in any given time-span (the 'rate of decision-making') will, as we have seen, increase with complexity, and more complex socio-political systems will require a higher rate of decision-making to reproduce and maintain them. Complexity and the rate of decision-making, therefore, stand in a proportional relationship and are proportional to both the propensity for change and the probability of collapse.

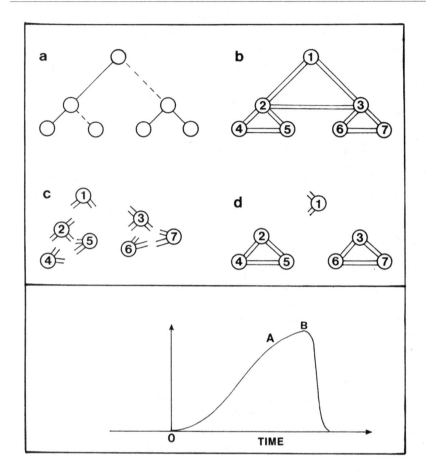

Fig. 4.4   Diagram showing the concept of hypercoherence in complex systems and catastrophic change. The exact systemic relationships shown are for illustrative purposes only. **a** shows a complex system, **b** a similar system which is 'hypercoherent': each part is dependent on the others. **c** illustrates that change in any part of system **b** can produce sudden collapse in the whole system. **d** shows an alternative to **c**, where sudden change in **b** causes the hypercoherent system to 'decompose' into lower-level entities. The inset diagram illustrates catastrophic change: a trajectory slowly grows less able to sustain change, at point **A**, the possibilities for change ('possibility space') begin to decrease rapidly, at **B** sudden collapse occurs.

To summarize this argument so far: complex socio-political systems will exhibit an internal dynamic which leads them to increase in complexity. The rate of decision-making must, necessarily, keep pace with this increased complexity, but the more complex the system is, the more liable it is to collapse.

Increased complexity also necessitates more efficient information processing in order to respond to decision-making requirements produced by
its own degree of complexity and the structures which it employs. So
growth in complexity coincides with an increase in the efficiency of
information-processing paralleling socio-political networks.[56] That is, both
decision-making and information processing must keep pace with the level
of complexity if immediate collapse is to be avoided.

Innovation and the rate of change

This understanding of the relationship between agency, structure and
systemic processes can be both clarified and expanded upon by further
considering the question of the rate of change. As we have already seen,
changes in socio-political complexity derive from agency, that is, from the
innovation of new structures, organizations and other forms of socio-
political differentiation.

As greater socio-political complexity requires more decision-making, it
gives more opportunity for socio-political innovation to occur. Innovation
theorists suggest that the likelihood of initial adoption or rejection of
innovations remains broadly constant over time.[57] If so, then since the rate of
information processing is proportional to the degree of complexity, as
complexity increases so will the rate at which innovations are adopted. This
coincides with the view that greater decision-making at first gives more
'possibility space' for change in more complex socio-political system.
However, of course, this possibility space begins to close increasingly rapidly
as the system becomes more complex. Thus, these factors must be set beside
the increasing 'coherence' of a more complex socio-political system.[58] So
that, if complexity is paralleled by the efficiency of information-processing,
complexity will grow with increasing speed until possibility space for change
begins to close as the system becomes hypercoherent.

So, complex socio-political systems become more complex, and potentially more 'coherent', faster. This rate of change will slow proportionately
if the degree of complexity decreases, but while complexity increases so will
potential instability. As the system becomes more complex, the range of
possible decisions promoting further growth will decrease, so that an
increasingly complex system will become increasingly 'path-dependent' and
lose its adaptive flexibility.

Hypercoherent 'option-narrowing' of this sort, if not stopped, will
eventually precipitate collapse, and when collapse occurs it will, as catastrophe theorists have shown, be a sudden and revolutionary process rather than
a slow 'winding down' of growth.[59] That is, socio-political complexity will
rise to the point of catastrophe, because of the endogenous logic of the
growth of complexity itself, in a path-dependent trajectory, and then
suddenly collapse.[60]

When they decline due to hypercoherence, such systems will necessarily do so at a rate proportional to their declining complexity. As the rate of change remains proportional to the level of complexity, decline in complexity will occur increasingly slowly, although the shift to a decline mode will be sudden. In the same way, growth in complexity operates increasingly rapidly from an equally sudden and discrete starting point. This starting point may itself, according to the theory of 'initial states', be crucial for the exact form of the emergent system and highly dependent on historically-specific circumstances.

As innovation is based on decision-making and prompted by interaction, this may also permit an understanding of how one socio-political system succeeds another in diachronic terms. If innovation is a constant process (increasing with complexity), and given a correlation between the rate of decision-making and the rate of change, the point at which the innovation of new systems, structures and organizations is most likely will coincide with the maximum point of growth of the system. This will be close to the point immediately prior to the point of catastrophe, when the system will enter decline mode and the rate of change will begin slowing down.

Thus, the collapse of the initial system into catastrophe and the high rate of innovation existing at (and close to) this point suggest that the successor system is liable to form at this point. Those participating in this new socio-political system have the advantage of greater possibility space for change, and the path-dependent dynamic of increasing complexity. Those participating in the previous system, which is hypercoherent or in a state of decline, have fewer possibilities for decision-making, and the enhanced path-dependent trajectory of this system has now 'switched' to a decline mode. So when an endogenous process of socio-political succession occurs in this way, the point of emergence of the new system is likely to coincide with the point of initial decline of the previous system. For a while the two systems will coexist, as the earlier system declines at an increasingly rapid rate and the new system emerges rapidly.

This enables us to generate a successional model of endogenous socio-political change, where the successor system might follow a similar trajectory to that of the system which it replaces. In time it too will collapse and be replaced by another socio-political system.

It must be remembered that what is 'catastrophic collapse' of this sort may not seem 'catastrophic' (or even collapse), in the conventional use of these terms, to those involved or to other contemporary observers. Nor is such change *determined* to occur at any specific point by systemic processes. The entire sequence is, in every case, both historically situated and contingent. The events and structures involved may be dissimilar, and if similar changes occur these may operate on very different time-scales; so processually similar sequences of this sort may be historically heterogeneous above the processual level. It would also be possible for those involved to avert catastrophic collapse altogether by reversing or mitigating the processes leading to it. This would have to be achieved prior to the narrowing of options to those which, while leading to catastrophe, are necessary for the reproduction of systemic complexity. However, it means that collapse is not 'determined' nor inevitable.

Nor is the point of initiation of systemic transformation, or of the successor system itself, determined by this processual logic. Socio-political systems are reproduced by decision-making, as are the interactions and structures which constitute them. So decision-making always has the potential both to transform existing structures and systems and to produce new structures or systems.

Thus, we need not expect to discover this 'ideal' pattern of succession in every case; it could only occur if no other factors intervened to prevent this sequence of changes. For such a sequence to occur would require that this process override all other socio-political factors, such as the effects of war or ecological change. On theoretical grounds, it might be expected that such a situation would rarely occur. However once begun, subsequent systems in the same trajectory might be expected to be more likely (due to path-dependency) to continue this sequence.

So the processual regularities identified in this chapter present us with another paradox regarding change in socio-political systems. Change, according to this view, is both contingent and contextual, but transhistorical and cross-cultural.

It is possible to express the idealized version of this sequence graphically. When we do so we can see that this generates a series of modal curves, which I shall hereafter refer to as 'waves'. Each of these waves interlocks with a second originating at (or close to) that point in time where the preceding one was most complex. This is, of course, a simplified graphic representation of the dynamical trajectory that this model proposes, taking no account of the non-deterministic transformative potential which we have noted exists within it.

The term 'waves' – which carries implications of both instability and indeterminacy – is a far more accurate description of such patterns than the more usual term 'cycles'. The latter tends to suggest a 'circular' process of change continuously generating like patterns in a deterministic fashion, unlike that found here. However, in this and the following chapters the adjective 'cyclical' is used as a shorthand term for 'wave-like', without implying any such associations.

As already shown, path-dependency, routine and the need to maintain the structures and organizations within systems, all promote this sequence. So such a pattern of socio-political succession *could* occur in reality, but need not do so. If it occurs at all, of course, then we may expect such factors to prompt its continued replication through time, producing a cyclical pattern of similar diachronic waves. These need not continue throughout the entire duration of a system's existence, because the factors which produce them might vary over time, or cease to operate, even while the same processes continue.

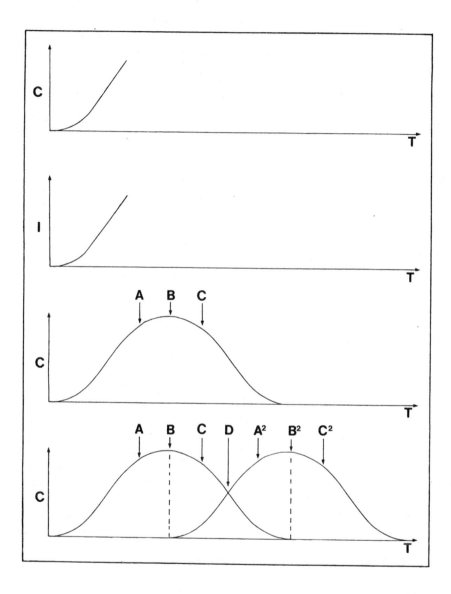

Fig. 4.5   Graphs of the relationship between the rate of change and rising complexity, and between the rate of information-exchange and the rate of change. **T** represents time, **C** represents complexity and **I** rate of information processing if complexity is rising. In 3, **A** indicates the point at which growth in complexity will begin to slow, as hypercoherence takes affect. **B** represents the point at which catastrophic change to 'decline' mode will occur. **C** shows the point where the rate of decline will begin to accelerate. A new system is likely to emerge at or close to point **B**, and begins to supersede the previous trajectory at point **D**. It will then prescribe an identical trajectory: indicated by points $\mathbf{A^2}$, $\mathbf{B^2}$ and $\mathbf{C^2}$.

A series of simple arguments, based on non-deterministic principles and on an understanding of complex systems, agency and structure, can be used in this way to generate a multi-scalar model of the relative chronology and process of the emergence and decline of socio-political systems. This suggests that both cyclical and (perhaps more usually) non-cyclical change can result from these processes. Process alone, it seems, might both facilitate and constrain both agency and structure.

The 'amplitude' of these waves is not fixed as in the diagram here. Rather it may vary in each separate wave. Thus, it might be expected that such a cyclical pattern would be more likely to occur the more complex the system involved, simply because greater complexity would reduce possibility space and increase path-dependency. Consequently, cyclicality may be more common in socio-political systems that are highly complex than in less complex systems. As such, it may be that the closer to the limits of information-processing possible under specific circumstances the system becomes, the greater the probability of cyclicality.

The hypothesis does not have an in-built absolute chronology, so that the 'wavelength' for different systems may vary. On the grounds of complexity theory, we might assume that this might bear some relation to the circumstances of systemic formation: the 'initial state' of the system.

The implicit relative chronology means that, in the sequence produced, the frequency of the cyclical waves so generated will be constant. This leaves the content and character of the changes involved – that is to say, the short-term – as a matter of historically specific explication. The model is of process rather than event; but of processes which form a logical framework within which events occur, and which stand in a reflexive relationship to the events which they encompass. Structures, events, and processes are produced by historically-specific decision-making because they are the products of the interplay of intentionality and contextual circumstances.

Before applying this approach to analysing world politics, it may be useful to examine some 'empirical' data which show that the relationships between information exchange and socio-political complexity suggested here are well attested in anthropological and other evidence for human societies.

Empirical evidence for macrodynamics

This model can be both supported and further developed by examining the anthropological work of Johnson, Kosse and others on the relationship between scale and socio-political complexity, briefly referred to in Chapter 2. This provides strong empirical support for the validity of major aspects of the theory, and suggests some ways in which it might be further elaborated.

The first aspect of their work which is of special interest is that it strongly suggests a firm relationship in anthropological data between the scale of socio-political organization, the mode of information processing and the form of socio-political organization.[61] These are also, on empirical grounds, strong reasons for correlating increasing organizational 'stress' with increasing scale, leading to increased organizational fragility and the risk of sudden, dramatic, collapse after relatively long periods of more gradual growth in scale.

Scale, differentiation, information processing and vulnerability

While most hunter-gatherer social groups are small and egalitarian, larger societies universally tend to be ranked in some way.[62] There seem to be extremely well-documented thresholds of group-size, broadly definable in demographic terms, at which political organization alters form.[63]

The evidence for this is too extensive to discuss in detail here, but examples will show how strong a case is possible on anthropological grounds. Ember found that in 24 societies there was a close correlation between increasing group-size and political differentiation.[64] Carneiro examined 46 communities, discovering that size and the type of political organization were closely correlated.[65] On the basis of 106 ethnographically documented societies, Upham has also shown that increasing group-size correlated with increased political organization.[66] Likewise, Narroll's earlier work had suggested that communities of more than 500 people usually have centralized political organization.[67]

This cross-cultural and transhistorical characteristic of the correlation between scale, socio-political differentiation and the form of political organization does not correlate with specific ecological or economic contexts. Rather, it seems to be based on exactly the same factors which we have already been discussing: information processing and interpersonal interaction.[68]

A series of independent empirical studies undertaken in several disciplines have also shown that there is a consistent 'span of control' (a group which can be managed by an individual) which serves to regulate information-processing capabilities across a wide range of anthropological and historical examples.[69] This group (consistently about five people) is recognizable as a building block for information-processing hierarchies in a wide range of human societies.

Many detailed studies have been undertaken by anthropologists and organizational analysts to examine this proposition. These support the conclusion that societies and organizations can be seen to contain such information-processing hierarchies. Examples include the studies by Pugh on businesses in the UK;[70] by Klatzky on US businesses;[71] by Jones on native African groups;[72] by Skinner on imperial China;[73] by Johnson on a wide range of ethnographic examples worldwide;[74] and by Mayhew and Levinger.[75]

The work of the latter two scholars adds the observation that the larger (and as these studies show, therefore, in our terms more complex) the system the more it becomes 'point vulnerable'; that is, it is more liable to change. Mayhew and Levinger's work has been supported by another detailed study undertaken by Williamson.[76] This also found that the number of organizational levels in a ranked information-processing system correlated with the loss of control by the managers of that system. Williamson identifies this as the result of distorted information flows through the system, which can only be alleviated by new technologies of information processing.

Similar work undertaken elsewhere in organizational analysis has confirmed a consistent relationship between the number of levels of bureaucracy in an organization and the stages of decision-making hierarchies.[77] These do not exist in a wholly uniform manner, however, as the work of Pugh and others has shown. Thus, while the concept of scalar levels can be widely corroborated by empirical studies, the form of these is contingent on their exact circumstances of formation.[78]

These studies show a relationship between information-processing capabilities, socio-political scale and differentiation and the likelihood of change. They, therefore, offer strong empirical evidence for central aspects of this model, from detailed examination of a wide range of data by many different scholars.

Further work in this area has produced results which seem to confirm other aspects of the model presented here. This work is supported by other anthropological studies of the issue of scale and political organization, relating these − once again − to information-processing capacities. In an important recent anthropological study, for example, Kosse has shown that changes in information-processing capabilities exist at definable demographic thresholds of 5 people, 10–25 people, 125–175 people, and then a limit of face-to-face communication at about 500 people; while another similar threshold is at 2500 people, with ranked information processing required for groups of over 3000.[79] This correlates well the anthropological work of Lekson, suggesting the same threshold for the specialization of social functions, and with other evidence that most hunter-gatherer bands range from 25 to 500 people in size, so conforming to the generalization of a 500-person threshold for face-to-face communication.

Perhaps the most remarkable confirmation of the validity of linking socio-political complexity, scale and information processing has, however, recently been published in Fletcher's study of the long-term development of urbanism.[80] Fletcher sets out data relating to the growth of urbanism world-wide over the past 15,000 years to the present. This shows a series of shifts in scale and complexity correlating with changes in communication exactly as such studies suggest, but using a huge quantity of new data from anthropology, history and archaeology.

In each case, the constraints of scale and increasing complexity seem to be overcome by changes in communication and socio-political organization.

This is, of course, so far very much what would be expected. However, these studies note further correlations which are of interest here.

The politics of increasing scale

The principal contribution from these studies which elaborates, rather than simply supports, the theory is in relation to the political consequences of increasing scale. Johnson's key theoretical point in examining this data was that increasing scale promoted increasing 'stress' on the groups of people involved.[81] By this he meant that they become less politically stable as their scale increases. This instability, he argues, derives from internal loss of consensus and increased public dissatisfaction with 'group performance'. This is reminiscent of the economist Mancur Olson's observation that the growth of interest groups (analogous to 'internal divisions' in Johnson's scheme) in periods of relative political stability, leads to internal conflicts which prompted endogenous crises and political decline.[82] Both agree that scalar growth promotes internal instability.

Kosse and Fletcher both support the 'scalar stress' perspective developed by Johnson on the basis of their own data, and this conclusion is further supported by Mayhew and Levinger's study. Kosse also notes that in intergroup competition larger organizations tend to have a 'competitive advantage'.[83] This, she argues, means that larger organizations will tend to expand their political control in conflict situations, and their smaller counterparts will tend to combine to form larger groups to gain this advantage. If so, she suggests, we should see the emergence of larger but fewer political groups, when examined over a long time-scale.

Such a conclusion seems historically problematical given the rise to global empire of a range of small European states, notably Britain, Holland and Portugal. An alternative interpretation of the same data, preferred here, is – as Lazonic and West have argued – that a degree of systemic (for example, 'state') integration, rather than size alone, increases competitive advantage while, as we have seen, over-integration increases instability.[84] So more integrated systems, including more integrated states, would have a competitive advantage over less integrated polities, including smaller polities, up to the point at which they became hypercoherent.

There seem to be some historical, anthropological and archaeological evidence to credit the view that the average size of political units has been increasing over a very long period of human history. In an interesting – if problematical – attempt to quantify the changing numbers of human political groups over time, Carneiro found a long-term trend which seems to show exactly this pattern.[85] Carneiro attempted to estimate the number of independent political groups existing in 100 BC, AD 500 and AD 1976, from which there seems to have been exactly the gradual pattern of size-increase but decrease in number of polities which Kosse's hypothesis suggests. This pattern has also been recognized, in somewhat different data, by Sander-

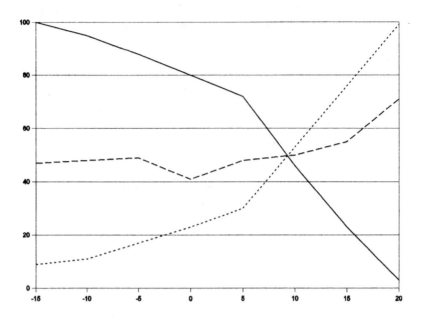

Fig. 4.6   Graph showing growth in size and decrease in number of political units over time as reconstructed by Carneiro and Kosse, against Eckhardt's plot (based on the work of Dupuy and Dupuy) of the increase in recorded warfare over time (in centuries BC and AD indicated on horizontal axis).

son,[86] whose work supports the view that urban size and the size of the largest political units have grown proportionally over the last 5000 years. If competitive advantage in inter-polity interaction is achievable through increased integration or scalar increase, then this pattern is easily explicable.

However, the proliferation of small states in the twentieth century would seem to undermine this view. This may enable a modification to be made to this interpretation. The propensity for collapse found in complex socio-political systems (noted earlier in this chapter) may explain this apparent anomaly because there are two possible choices – if there are no changes in information-processing capabilities – facing groups which begin to exceed the scalar possibilities of their current organization form. The first is collapse, the fission into smaller groups; the second, to shift to larger political units with a different form of socio-political organization. If each choice was being taken by different polities or at different times then the observable pattern in political history would result. Thus, a fusion of scalar perspectives based on unit size and those based on socio-political complexity may offer a convincing interpretation of this evidence.

Intriguingly, Carneiro and Kosse's graph of political scale can be compared with the (albeit, like Carneiro's study, methodologically problematical) graphs produced by Eckhardt, showing the increasing destructiveness and frequency of war over much the same period.[87] Perhaps these two trends bear some relationship to each other, if both may be credited, in that states can prosecute war more effectively than non-state groups. This is supported by Johnson's suggestion that increased dispute frequency may be related to increased scalar stress. That is, larger socio-political systems may be more violence-prone. If so, as world politics becomes dominated by increasingly large-scale units, both the likelihood of violence and the ability of those polities to prosecute war increase.

A further reason for increased conflict with increased organizational scale among socio-political groups may be found in the work of van der Leeuw. His work suggests that collective information processing will stimulate scalar socio-political growth so long as the system involved is able to acquire new information.[88] This will act, in his view, as a stimulus to territorial expansion, economic intensification, and specialization. So large complex socio-political groups may have both more internal stresses and greater competitive advantages as opposed to neighbouring less complex groups.[89] They may have an internal dynamic of expansion and economic change, and an increasing willingness to resort to violence.

Thus an internal dynamic of exploration and acquisition will lead to the expansion of the larger groups, at the expense of smaller groups in their peripheries. This may prompt conflict with other small neighbouring groups but, if so, the likely outcome will favour the larger group. Combined with the approach so far suggested here, this might imply that more complex socio-political systems are also more 'expansive', in addition to being faster-changing, than less complex social forms.

Increasingly large political units also have the advantage, according to Johnson, of offering both 'informational' and economic 'economies of scale'. This relates to a point made by Kosse, building on work by Rambo, that larger units may be more economically cost-effective for their inhabitants than smaller groups in terms of time–energy expenditure, but that upper thresholds for this also exist. Similar conclusions were reached by Kennedy (in his 'imperial overstretch' model) and by Tainter in his study of the collapse of complex societies.[90]

This 'economy of scale' might be expected to give an impetus to more rapid technological development in larger groups. This coincides well with the apparent correlation between state-societies and both industrial and proto-industrial scales of production. However, clearly the potential for fission might act as a barrier to the continual increase of socio-political scale, a factor reinforced by cultural and other differences between groups.

The shift to a larger scale of socio-political organization is, as we have seen, not the only response to increased complexity. In examining data from egalitarian and other non-state groups, Cohen also notes that these will break into smaller groups as an alternative strategy to accommodate increases in scale[91] thus showing that the shift to new political forms is not determined, but a strategic group-response to internal pressures. In this sense, these groups exhibit evidence of adaptation but this is neither deterministic nor a reaction to exogenous stimuli.

Instead, as Johnson points out, in complex systems endogenous increases in scale can increase either 'the probability of systems collapse or the development of hierarchical organization'.[92] As he also noted, the shifts in political scale correlated with increased societal scale are neither deterministic nor uniformly timed. As he puts it, 'alternative structural arrangements are possible to resolve the same underlying problems',[93] noting that 'stress builds slowly, but its resolution in either collapse or development is likely to be much more rapid'.[94]

The results of these studies might, therefore, be added to those produced by the theoretical discussion in this chapter. This is facilitated by the close relationship between socio-political complexity and polity size. However, it is important that one must not confuse system complexity and the size of political units. These are not the same thing, but rather they are related variables. Both can be explained with reference to changing modes of information exchange and information processing. One cannot simply 'read off' complexity as unit size or vice versa; only through shifts in communication and information processing are increases in unit size possible.

In studies of the transition from kin-based to chiefdom societies the key measure of scale has been population size. This affords an apparently 'absolute' measure of size, and demographic scale can be seen to correlate with the changes both from kin-based to chiefdom forms of organization and from the chiefdom to the state. Once above the level of the state, more sophisticated modes of information exchange and processing render population size far less useful as a measure of scale. Likewise, the effects of population increase no longer seem to include changes in the essential form of socio-political organization. This may be because these new media of communication and data processing enable the state to encompass a far wider demographic range than other forms of polity, or because the faster rate of technological innovation and territorial expansion 'dampen' the effects of increasing population size.

If systemic complexity and the size of political units are separable, however, then increase or decrease in each cannot necessarily be correlated. Thus, the cyclical patterning which we have seen to be possible in complexity need not be found in either demography or the size of political units. These are related, but not identical, factors linked by foundations in the possibilities afforded by differing forms of communication and information processing.

The lack of similar approaches in International Relations

Combining the results of data-based and theoretical studies in this way, therefore, permits the construction of a model which will explain some important aspects of world politics from a long-term perspective. It is, then, surprising that so far such approaches have been almost totally unused in International Relations, although it is worth noting that there are many similarities in general terms with Rosenau's 'turbulence' model (summarized in Chapter 1). 'Turbulence' might well be seen as an effect produced when scale exceeds information-processing capabilities.

Otherwise, there are few studies which have employed similar approaches. John P. Lewis has pointed out that scale has largely been ignored in International Relations theory.[95] In a much more restricted study than that here, Lewis (writing as an economist rather than a political scientist) drew attention to the 'consequences of giantism' for India. His aim is to show on empirical grounds that because it is 'large', India is 'cumbersome', and that it is possible to understand this in terms of the 'span of control'. Lewis does not seem to have been especially familiar with the considerable literature on this concept, describing a large body of material as 'thin' and quoting only a few of those studies published at the time of his paper. His conclusions are nonetheless fascinating. This case-study led him to propose that, faced with 'giantism', the government has only two options, other than political fission, which he finally sees as another possibility in the conclusion to his article. It must either decentralize, or delegate decision-making to non-governmental actors.

Lewis's study, despite its limitations, empirically replicates similar results to several of those produced by the independent studies reviewed here. Once again it supports the theory's validity by relating it to empirical data unused in its formation. Yet Lewis's study was not aimed at connecting this observation to general theoretical arguments regarding world politics, nor at issues of understanding change as a whole.

Huang recently used an empirical, historical, method to examine the role of information processing (on rather different grounds) in the collapse of the Soviet Union and in current changes in China.[96] However, this examination was again not the basis for a wider theoretical discussion of the implications. In his study, change and information processing are closely connected, with collapse explained in terms of inadequate information-processing capabilities.

So those empirically based studies in International Relations which have examined similar issues to those discussed here have produced conclusions which also support some of those so far proposed in this chapter. This also shows how such approaches have generally been overlooked in this discipline as ways of examining change.

Interaction between socio-political systems

The dynamics of socio-political systems themselves can be readily accommodated within the theory so far proposed, but leave partly unanswered the question of how exogenous factors relate to these endogenous processes.

International Relations scholars are well acquainted with a wide range of such factors: war, trade, diplomacy and migration. We have seen how these can lead to 'crises' promoting internal decision-making, but what of their other effects?

Two types of inter-systemic interaction may be seen as of special interest to questions of change in world politics. The first is transnational interaction, by which I mean contact between individuals who (at some socio-political level) are within separate polities. This is of interest to the analyst of change because there is no doubt that transnational interaction between human social groups has the ability to facilitate changes among them. We see this in terms of religious change, for example, where believers of one religion convert those of another by means of interaction between the populations of two or more political units. These interactions may then restructure social or economic organization within polities, in addition to resulting in religious changes among their populations. This, of course, applies to many aspects of secular interaction also, such as the adoption of new technologies or even clothing fashions. Such interactions include missions, trade, population movements, and personal contacts.

In this way, transnational interaction results in change. This further highlights the problems with assigning causal primacy to 'exogenous' factors. If these transnational interactions promote change from within a polity, in what sense is this change 'exogenous' to it? But there is a further point of theoretical interest here, in that interaction itself does not directly result in change; change comes from its effects on those within the polity concerned. People choose either to accept or to reject innovations intro-duced from 'outside' their socio-political group, they choose to believe or disbelieve in religions, and they choose to undertake or reject commercial transactions. That is, change may originate in transnational contacts, but if change occurs it is as a result of endogenous processes, not an automatic 'stimulus–response' mechanism.

International Relations theorists have, of course, been especially inter-ested in a second type of 'exogenous' change: interaction between polities or other forms of socio-political systems, such as 'civilizations'. Despite a long-standing interest in questions of inter-polity interaction, International Relations has a surprisingly restricted range of approaches which address the questions of interaction between polities and their consequences.[97]

Interdependence and regime theories can be applied, or core–periphery approaches used, or these issues can be addressed in terms of competition or co-operation, within the Realist or neo-Liberal paradigms. In other dis-ciplines, especially since the demise of diffusionism in archaeology, anthropology and history, there are an equally restricted range of approaches to inter-polity interaction. Among these, 'Peer Polity Interaction' ('PPI') may hold special significance in this context. It is an individualistically based approach and directly relates both transnational and inter-polity interactions both to each other and to change. This approach is very compatible with

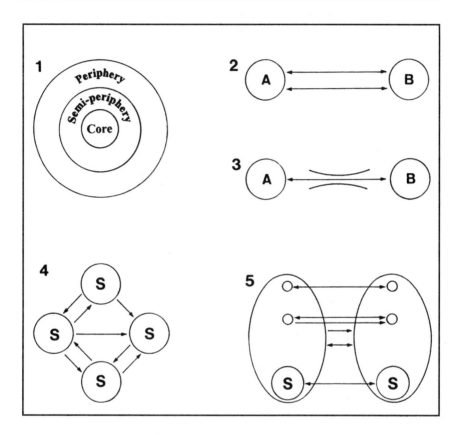

Fig. 4.7 Diagram showing differing models of regional interaction.
1. The World System, where relations of exploitation and dominance structure the system.
2. Interdependence between two states or geographical areas (**A** and **B**), where multiple channels of two-way interaction promote mutual reliance.
3. International Regime, where voluntary participation promotes structures shaping interaction between actors.
4. The Realist model of interaction between competing unitary state actors (**S**).
5. Peer-Polity Interaction: interaction is multi-channelled and multi-level. It can be between states (**S**), individuals (small circles) or other actors and can take a wide range of forms. However, interaction at all levels and in all forms promotes convergence.

that employed here, because it focuses on the 'flow of information of various kinds between polities',[98] and is applicable at many systemic levels.

PPI sees the effect of interaction between individuals and socio-political organizations (including states) as promoting similarities between them.[99] The greater the amount of interaction between socio-political organizations (whether in the form of transnational contacts, inter-polity trade, diplomacy, political or economic competition, or war) the more this will promote similarities between the groups involved. So inter-unit systems (for example) will develop distinctive cultural features through time, and the participant actors may increasingly share both political characteristics and structures of interaction. Clearly, this approach may easily be incorporated into the model here.

Before this can be achieved, however, two qualifications must be made to this approach. First, it cannot be taken to have a law-like universality. Such interactions may promote greater similarities, and will usually have this effect, but this cannot be anticipated in every case because of the role of agency in establishing patterns of political change. This fits well with the religious example used above: religious contacts will frequently promote the growth of inter-polity religious similarities, as might be seen in the cases of the expansion of Christianity and Islam, but this is not always the case.

Secondly, the effects of each type of interaction will not be similar beyond this general level of analysis. For instance, warfare may prompt more rapid technological change to counter enemy technologies, but this may not result from cultural contacts.

Modified in this way, a version of PPI enables us to combine the strengths of approaches developed within International Relations, such as regime theory, and to incorporate these with the specific aspects of this model.[100] It also has the advantage that it does not pre-decide that inter-polity contacts must be predominantly co-operative or competitive in character – simply that mutual similarities are likely to result from them.

But such contacts exclude one important form of interaction between socio-political systems: those instances in world history where a polity or system is not incorporated within a successor, but destroyed by invasion and conquest. The model already set out enables us to incorporate these cases with ease. If the socio-political system (on any level) is destroyed by human, or for that matter other (such as ecological) reasons, then we can simply observe the termination of one socio-political trajectory and the start of another. If a component of the system is destroyed, this might, but need not, affect the system overall, unless it is already hypercoherent. If so, this might trigger systemic collapse.

So such instances pose no problem for the model set out here. Of course, it is also noteworthy that historians, anthropologists and archaeologists have been able to show that systemic destruction of this sort is usually a feature of a system already beginning to collapse as the result of endogenous processes. Even invading 'barbarians' usually seem to have 'taken over' existing polities, not destroyed them.

Following such rare phases of conquest and replacement as occur, two outcomes are possible. Either the conquest will impose an existing trajectory of its own or a new endogenously based trajectory will start.

This approach to interaction between polities emphasizes the essential feature of all such interaction. It is not between abstract entities (such as states) but between people,. who may or may not be representatives of polities. Consequently, conquest and systemic destruction are here assigned a relatively minor role. Systems do break down – we have seen that this is inherent in their complexity – but not usually as a result of conquest.

Conclusion

The model presented here can be seen to offer a non-deterministic approach based on an understanding of complex systems and the interplay of structure and agency. It incorporates an individualistic basis with a totalizing perspective which places the emphasis in bringing about socio-political change on endogenous socio-political processes but which also connects these with economic and ecological factors.

In the next chapters this macrodynamic theory of change will be applied to data relating to world politics. This will set out a new interpretation for long-term global socio-political change which both examines the central themes of the emergence and history of the state and the 'international system', and places a new emphasis on other forms of socio-political organization which have existed in the past.

Notes

1 Westcott, J. H., (ed.), 1986, *Predictability in Science and Society*.
2 For complex systems see, for example: Serra, R. and Zaharini, G., 1990, *Complex Systems and Cognitive Processes*, Berlin; Waldrop, M. M., 1992, *Complexity: The Emerging Science at the Edge of Chaos*; Gell-Mann, M., 1994, *The Quark and the Jaguar: Adventures in the Simple and the Complex*, New York; Coveney, P. and Highfield, R., 1995, *Frontiers of Complexity: The Search for Order in a Chaotic World*; Khalil, E. L. and Boulding, K. E. (eds), 1996, *Evolution, Order and Complexity*; Lewin, R., 1992, *Complexity: Life at the Edge of Chaos*, New York; la Porte, T. R. (ed.), 1975, *Organized Social Complexity: Challenge to Politics and Policy*, Princeton, Perrow, C., 1986, *Complex Organizations: A Critical Essay*, 3rd edn; Nicholis G. and Prigogine, I., 1989, *Exploring Complexity*, New York; Holland, J. H., 1995, *Hidden Order. How Adaptation Builds Complexity*, New York.
3 Little, R., 1985, 'The systems approach', in S. Smith (ed.), *International Relations: British and American Approaches*, Oxford, 70–91. However, note that 'complex systems' are not simply a re-working of the 'systems' of 'systems theory', having origins in different aspects of mathematics, and assigning different properties to systems, which are defined in different terms from those used conventionally in systems theory.
4 For earlier approaches to complexity in human socio-political organization: Lawrence, P. and Lorsch, J., 1967, 'Differentiation and integration in complex organizations', *Administrative Science Quarterly* 12, 1–47; Simon, H. A., 1973, 'The organization of complex systems', in H. H. Pattee (ed.), *Hierarchy Theory: The Challenge of Complex Systems*, New York, 3–27. On differentiation, also see: Luhmann, N., 1982, *The Differentiation of Society*, New York.

5   This is unlike the always 'holistic' relationships of systems theory's 'sub-systems'. For an example of a 'systems theory' approach to these relationships, by way of contrast, see: Haas, M., 1970, 'International subsystems: stability and polarity', *American Political Science Review* 64.1, 93–103.

6   The analogy is made by: Clark, N., Perez-Trejo, F. and Allen, P., 1995, *Evolutionary Dynamics and Sustainable Development*.

7   Allen, T. F. H. and Starr, T. B., 1982, *Hierarchy, Perspectives for Ecological Complexity*, Chicago; Blau, P. M., 1968, 'The hierarchy of authority in organisations', *American Journal of Sociology* 37, 453–67; Blau, P. M., 1970, 'A formal theory of differentiation in organizations', *American Sociological Review* 35, 201–18; Holling, C. S., 1987, 'Simplifying the complex: the paradigms of ecological function and structure', *European Journal of Operational Research* 30, 139–46. See also: Radner, R., 1992, 'Hierarchy, the economics of managing', *Journal of Economic Literature* 30.3, 1382–1415.

8   For the way in which such processes can produce unexpected consequences (albeit seen from a system-theory perspective): Forrester, J., 1971, 'Counter-intuititive behavior of social systems', *Technology Review* 73, 53–68.

9   Arthur, W. B., Ermoliev, Y. M. and Kaniovski, Y. M., 1987, 'Path dependent processes and the emergence of macro-structure', *European Journal of Operation Research* 30.2, 294–303; Hauser, J., Jessop, B. and Nielsen, K. (eds), 1995, *Strategic Choice and Path-Dependency in Post-Socialism*; David, P. A., 1988, *Path Dependence: Putting the Past into the Future of Economics*, Stanford, Calif.

10 On the role of interaction in shifting social and political relationships: Claessen, H. J. M. and Van De Velde, P., 1985, 'Sociopolitical evolution as complex interaction', in J. J. M. Claessen, P. van de Velde and M. E. Smith (eds), *Development and Decline: The Evolution of Sociopolitical Organization*, South Hadley, Mass.

11 Allen, P. M. and Sanglier, M., 1981, 'Urban evolution, self-organisation and decision-making', *Environment and Planning* A21, 167–183; Allen, P. M. and Perez-Trejo, F., 1992, 'Strategic planning of complex economic systems', *Review of Political Economy* 4.3, 275–290; Allen, P. M., and McGlade, J. M., 1987, 'Evolutionary drive: the effect of microscopic diversity, error making and noise', *Foundations of Physics* 17.7, 723–728.

12 Clark, N., Perez-Trejo, F. and Allen, P., 1995, *Evolutionary Dynamics and Sustainable Development*.

13 That is, options for change are latent in any situation, but both may not be chosen by actors, and may exist only within a limited range of possibilities.

14 For a subtler view: Brown, S., 1996, *International Relations in a Changing Global System*, 2nd edn, p. 166.

15 Ware, R. B., 1996, 'Set theory, self-consciousness and the state', *Contemporary Political Studies* 3, 1638–49.

16 Krasner, S., 1984, 'Approaches to the state: alternative conceptions and historical dynamics', *Comparative Politics* 16.2, 223–46.

17 Seen in this way, both states and other socio-political organizations may be related to a wider body of scholarly literature regarding organizations, culture and change. For example: Porras, J. and Silvers, R., 1991, 'Organizational development and transformation', *Annual Review of Psychology* 42, 51–78; Porras, J. and Robertson, P., 1992, 'Organizational development: theory, practice and research', in M. Dunnette and L. Hough (eds), *Handbook of*

Industrial and Organizational Psychology, 2nd edn, Vol. 3, Palo Alto, Calif., pp. 719–822; Mohrman, A. *et al.*, (eds), 1989, *Large-Scale Organizational Change*, San Francisco; Fombrun, C., 1986, 'Structural dynamics within and between organizations', *Administrative Science Quarterly* 31, 403–21; Menard, C., 1994, 'Organizations as coordinating devices', *Metroeconomica* 45.3, 224–47. For a related discussion from within 'IR': Rosenau, J. N., 1996, 'Powerful tendencies, startling discrepancies and elusive dynamics: the challenge of studying world politics in a turbulent era', *Australian Journal of International Affairs* 50.1 23–30.

18 Hay, C., 1994, 'Crisis and the discursive unification of the state', *Contemporary Political Studies 1994*, 236–55.

19 Piliavin, J. A. and Charng, H-W., 1990, 'Altruism: a review of recent research', *Annual Review of Sociology* 16, 27–65.

20 Lake, D. *et al.*, 1996, 'Choice and Action', *Journal of Evolutionary Economics* 6, 43–76; Gaenslen, F., 1986, 'Culture and decision making in China, Japan, Russia and the United States', *World Politics* 39.1, 78–103; Smircich, L., 1983, 'Concepts of culture in organization analysis', *Administrative Science Quarterly* 28, 339–358; Schneider, B. (ed.), 1990, *Organizational Climate and Culture*, San Francisco; Schein, E. H., 1990, 'Organizational Culture', *American Psychologist* 45, 109–19; Dennison, D. R., 1990, *Corporate Culture and Organizational Effectiveness*, New York; Hofstede, G., 1991, *Cultures and Organisations: Software of the Mind*. Note Robert Keohane's comment that 'we must understand the context of action before we can understand the action itself': Keohane, R., 1984 *After Hegemony*, Princeton, p. 258. See also: Lapid, Y. and Kratochwil, F. (eds), 1996, *The Return of Culture and Identity in IR Theory*, Boulder, Colo.

21 Bevir, M., 1996, 'The individual and society', *Political Studies* 64, 102–14; Pomper, P., 1996, 'Historians and individual agency', *History and Theory* 35.3, 281–308.

22 Kratochwil, F. W., 1989, *Rules, Norms and Decisions*. For 'event history': Abbot, A., 1983, 'Sequences of social events: concepts and methods for the analysis of order in social processes', *Historical Methods* 16, 129–47; Brass, D. J., 1984, 'Being in the right place: a structural analysis of individual influence in an organisation', *Administrative Science Quarterly* 29, 518–39.

23 For the effects of organization on individual decision-makers, and on group decision-making: Miller, G., 1992, *Managerial Dilemmas: The Political Economy of Hierarchy*; Carzo, R. and Yanouzas, J. N., 1969, 'Effects of flat and tall organisation structure', *Administrative Science Quarterly* 14, 178–91; Cumings, L. L., Huber, G. P. and Arendt, E., 1974, 'Effects of size and spatial arrangements on group decision-making', *Academy of Management Journal* 17, 460–75; Menard, C., 1994, 'Organizations as coordinating devices', *Metroeconomica* 45.3, 224–47; Dosi, G. and Malerba, F., 1996, 'Organizational learning and institutional embeddedness', in G. Dosi and F. Malerba (eds), *Organization and Strategy in the Evolution of Enterprise*, 1–26; McPherson, M. J., Popielarz, P. A. and Drobnic, S., 1992, 'Social networks and organizational dynamics', *American Sociological Review* 57, 153–70. See also: Fligstein, N. and Freeland, R., 1995, 'Theoretical and comparative perspectives on corporate organisations', *Annual Review of Sociology* 21, 21–43; Aoki, M., 1986, 'Horizontal vs. vertical information structure of the firm', *American Economic Review* 76, 971–83.

24   George, D. A. R., 1990, 'Chaos and complexity in economics', *Journal of Economic Surveys* 4.4, 397–414; Kuran, T., 1989, 'Sparks and prairie fires: a theory of unanticipated political revolution', *Public Choice* 61, 41–74.

25   See, for example, Campanella, M. (ed.), 1988, *Between Rationality and Cognition: Policy Making under Conditions of Uncertainty, Complexity and Turbulence*, Torino; Alexander, J. C. *et al.* (eds), 1987, *The Micro–Macro Link*, Berkeley, Calif.

26   There has also been a recent debate over the relationship between agency and structure in world politics. For example, see: Carlsnaes, W., 1992, 'The agency–structure problem in foreign policy analysis', *International Studies Quarterly* 36, 245–70; Hollis, M. and Smith, S., 1994, 'Two stories about structure and agency', *Review of International Studies* 20.3, 241–51; Hollis, M. and Smith, S., 1992, 'Structure and agency: further comment', *Review of International Studies* 18.2, 187–8; Hollis, M. and Smith, S., 1991, 'Beware of gurus: structure and action in International Relations', *Review of International Studies* 17.4, 393–410; Wendt, A., 1987, 'The agent–structure problem in International Relations theory', *International Organization* 41.3, 335–70.

27   Thompson, G. *et al.*, 1991, *Markets, Hierarchies and Networks. The Coordination of Social Life*; Weick, K. E., 1985, 'Sources of order in underorganized systems: themes in recent organizational theory', in Y. S. Lincoln (ed.), *Organizational theory and inquiry*, Beverley Hills, Calif., 103–36. Note also: Krasner, S. D., 1982, 'Structural causes and regime consequences: regimes as intervening variables', *International Organization* 36, 185–205.

28   Waller, T., 1988, 'The concept of habit in economic analysis', *Economic Issues* 22, 113–26; Onuf, N. G., 1989, *World of Our Making: Rules and Rule in Social Theory and International Relations*, Columbia SC; Zucker, L. G., 1991, 'The role of institutionalization in cultural persistence', in W. W. Powell and P. J. Di Maggio (eds), *The New Institutionalism in Organizational Analysis*, Chicago, 83–107. Note, however, that the dynamics of structures can have a degree of autonomy through self-organization: Rosen, R., 1979, 'Morphogenesis in biological and social systems', in A. C. Renfrew and K. Cooke (eds), *Transformations*, New York, pp. 91–111. On self-organization see, for example: Zuiderhout, R. W. L., 1990, 'Chaos and the dynamics of self-organization', *Human Systems Management* 9, 225–38; Yates, F. E., 1987, *Self-organizing Systems*, New York.

29   For a recent discussion from an International Relations theory viewpoint: Fisher, M., 1992, 'Feudal Europe 800–1300: communal discourse and conflictual practices', *International Organization* 46.2, 427–66; For a recent historical account, Reynolds, S., 1994, *Fiefs and Vassals*.

30   Deibert, R. J., 1996, 'Typographica: the medium and the medieval-to-modern transformation', *Review of International Studies* 22.1, 29–56.

31   For a clear illustration of how these forms of regularity structure events: Ruggie, J. G., 1982, 'International regimes, transactions and change: embedded liberalism in the post war economic order', *International Organization* 36.2, 379–415; Kratochwil, F. W., 1989, *Rules, Norms and Decisions*.

32   Collins, R., 1981, 'On the microfoundations of macrosociology', *American Journal of Sociology* 86, 984–1014; Schelling, C., 1978, *Micromotives and Macrobehavior*, New York.

33 Alger, C. F., 1984–5, 'Bridging the micro and the macro in International Relations research', *Alternatives* 10, 319–44.

34 For a recent discussion: Lieshaut, R., 1996, *Between Anarchy and Hierarchy*. See also: Anderson, P. A., 1987, 'What do decision makers do when they make a foreign policy decision? Implications for the comparative study of foreign policy', in C. F. Herman, C. W. Kegley and J. N. Rosenau (eds), *New Directions in the Study of Foreign Policy*, 285–308.

35 Rosenau, J. N., 1990, *Turbulence in World Politics*.

36 Decision-making theory is outlined in Zey, M. (ed.), 1992, *Decision Making*, Newbury Park, CA.

37 Starbuck, W. H., 1983, 'Organizations as action generators', *American Sociological Review* 48, 91–102; Miner, A. S., 1990, 'Structural evolution through idiosyncratic jobs the potential for unplanned learning', *Organization Science* 1, 195–210.

38 For example, see: Phillips, W. and Rimkunas, R., 1978, 'The concept of crisis in international politics', *Journal of Peace Research* 15, 259–72; Porter, R. and Teich, M. (eds), 1986, *Revolution in History*.

39 Pierson, P., 1993, 'When effect becomes cause: policy feedback and political change', *World Politics* 45, 595–628; Prechel, H., 1994, 'Economic crisis and the centralization of control', *American Sociological Review* 59, 723–45; Sutton, R. I. and Kahn, R. L., 1987, 'Prediction, understanding and control as antidotes to organizational stress', in J. W. Lorsch (ed.), *Handbook of Organizational Behavior*, Englewood Cliffs, NJ, 272–85.

40 Goodman, L. D. and Burke, W., 1991, 'Creating successful organizational change', *Organizational Dynamics*, 5–17.

41 Tallman, I. and Gray, L. N., 1990, 'Choices, decisions and problem solving', *Theory and Research in Organizational Theory*, 161–94.

42 Huber, G. P., 1984, 'The nature and design of post-industrial organizations', *Management Science* 30, 928–51. On the consequences of higher-speed communications: Kern, S., 1983, *The Culture of Time and Space 1880–1918*. See also: Fligstein, N., 1990, *The Transformation of Corporate Control*, Cambridge, Mass.

43 Lopez, L. A., 1988, 'Informal exchange networks informal systems: a theoretical model', *American Anthropologist* 90.1, 42–55; Athanassiades, J. C., 1973, 'The distortion of upward communication in hierarchical organizations', *Academy of Management Journal* 16, 207–26; Arrow, K. J., 1985, 'Informational structure of the firm', *American Economic Review* 75, 303–7.

44 Von Krogh, G. and Roos, J. (eds), 1996, *Managing Knowledge*; Walsham, G., 1993, *Interpreting Information Systems in Organisations*, New York; Stinchcombe, A. L., 1990, *Information and Organizations*, Berkeley; Casson, M. C., 1997, *Information and Organization*.

45 Demski, J. S. and Sappington, D. E. M., 1987, 'Hierarchical regulatory control', *Rand Journal of Economics* 18, 369–83; Arrow, K., 1964, 'Control in large organizations', *Management Science* 10.3, 397–408; Williamson, O. E., 1967, 'Hierarchical control and optimum firm size', *The Journal of Political Economy* 75, 123–38; Crozier, M. and Thoenig, J. C., 1976, 'The regulation of complex organized systems', *Administrative Science Quarterly* 21, 54–70; Geanakoplos, J. and Milgrom, P., 1991, 'A theory of hierarchies based on limited managerial attention', *Journal of Japanese and International Economics* 5, 205–25;

McAfee, R. P. and McMillan, J., 1995, 'Organizational diseconomies of scale', *Journal of Economics and Management Strategy* 4.3, 399–426.

46   This effect has been widely recognized. See, for example: Crozier, M. and Thoenig, J. C., 1976, 'The regulation of complex organized systems', *Administrative Science Quarterly* 21, 547–70.

47   Herper, M., 1985, 'The state and public bureaucracies: a comparative and historical perspective', *Comparative Studies in Society and History* 27, 86–110; van der Leeuw, S. E. and McGlade, J., 1993, 'Information coherence et dynamiques urbaines', in B. Lepetit and D. Pumain (eds), *Temporalités Urbaines*, Paris, 195–242; Sah, R. and Stiglitz, J. E., 1986, 'The architecture of economic systems: hierarchies and polyarchies', *American Economic Review* 76.4, 716–27; Tirole, J., 1986, 'Hierarchies and bureaucracies', *Journal of Law, Economics and Organization* 2.3, 181–214.

48   Simon, H. A., 1973, 'The organization of complex systems', in H. H. Pattee (ed.), *Hierarchy Theory*, New York, 3–27; Simon, H. A., 1962, 'The architecture of complexity', *Proceedings of the American Philosophical Society* 106, 467–82; Laurent, A., 1978, 'Managerial subordinacy: a neglected aspect of organizational hierarchy', *Academy of Management Review* 3, 220–30.

49   See also: Vrba, E. S. and Eldredge, N., 1984, 'Individuals, hierarchies and processes: toward a more complete evolutionary theory', *Palaeobiology* 10, 146–71.

50   Klegg, S., 1981, 'Organization and control', *Administrative Science Quarterly* 26, 545–62; Klegg, S. and Dunkerley, D., 1980, *Organization, Class and Control*; Galbraith, J. R., 1974, 'Organisation design: an information-processing view', *Interfaces* 4, 28–36; Galbraith, J. R., 1977, *Organization Design*, Reading, Mass.

51   Di Zerega, G., 1995 'Democracies and peace: the self-organizing foundation for the democratic peace', *The Review of Politics* 57.2, 279–309.

52   Pattee, H. H. (ed.), 1973, *Hierarchy Theory: The Challenge of Complex Systems*, New York; Chandler, A. D., 1992, 'Organizational capabilities and the economic history of the industrial enterprise', *Journal of Economic Perspectives* 6, 79–100; Blau, P. M., 1968, 'The hierarchy of authority in organizations', *American Journal of Sociology* 37, 453–67; Demski, J. and Sappington, D., 1987, 'Hierarchical regulatory control', *RAND Journal of Economics* 18, 369–83; Casson, M. and Wadeson, N., 1996, 'Information strategies and the theory of the firm', *International Journal of the Economics of Business* 3.3, 307–30.

53   Athanassiades, J. C., 1973 'The distortion of upward communication in hierarchical organizations', *Academy of Management Journal* 16, 207–26.

54   Zeeman, E. C., 1982, 'Decision making and evolution', in C. Renfrew, M. J. Rowlands and B. A. Segraves (eds), *Theory and Explanation in Archaeology*, New York and London, 315–46.

55   Flannery, K. V., 1972, 'The cultural evolution of civilizations', *Annual Review of Ecology and Systematics* 3, 399–425.

56   On the potential for these to reinforce group identities and shared concepts of community, through the communication of beliefs: Jones, P., 1991, *Groups Beliefs and Identities*.

57   For an convenient introduction: Spratt, D. A., 1989, 'Innovation theory made plain', in *The Process of Innovation*, edited by S. E. van der Leeuw and

R. Torrence, 245–57. For an overview of innovation theory: Grohaugh, K. and Kaufmann, G. (eds), 1988, *Innovation: A Cross-Disciplinary Perspective*.

58   Olson, M., 1971, 'Rapid growth as a destabilizing force', in J. C. Davis (ed.), *When Men Revolt and Why*, New York, 215–27.

59   Zeeman, E. C., 1980, 'Catastrophe models in administration', *Association for Institutional Research. Annual Forum Proceedings* 3, 9–24; van der Leeuw, S. E., 1987, 'Revolutions revisited', in L. Manzanilla (ed.), *Studies in Neolithic and Urban Revolutions*, 217–43; Gersick, C. J. G., 1991, 'Revolutionary change theories: a multilevel exploration of the punctuated equilibrium paradigm', *Academy of Management Review* 16.1, 10–36. See also: Ruse, M., 1989, 'Is the theory of punctuated equilibria a new paradigm?' *Journal of Social and Biological Structures* 12, 195–212; Eldredge, N., 1986 *Time Frames: The Rethinking of Darwinian Evolution and the Theory of Punctuated Equilibria*, New York; Eldredge, N., 1989, 'Punctuated equilibria, rates of change and large-scale entities in evolutionary systems', *Journal of Social and Biological Sciences*, 173–84; Gould, S. J., 1982 'the meaning of punctuated equilibria and its role in validating a hierarchical approach to macroevolution', in R. Milkman (ed.), *Perspectives on Evolution*, Sunderland Mass., 83–104.

60   That is: the system is path-dependent due to both its structural and dynamical properties. For a discussion of the relationship between path-dependency and structure: Ermolieu, A. B. and Kaniovski, Y., 1987, 'Path dependent processes and the emergence of macro structure', *European Journal of Operational Research* 30, 294–304.

61   In addition to the examples given in the text here, note: Campbell, F. and Akers, R. L., 1970, 'Organizational size, complexity and the administrative component in occupational associations', *The Sociological Quarterly* 11, 435–51; Hart, P., 1982, 'The size and growth of firms', *Economica* 29, 29–39; Hymer, S. and Pashigian, P., 1962, 'Firm size and rate of growth', *Journal of Political Economy* 70, 536–69; Kumar, M., 1985, 'Growth, acquisition activity and firm size: evidence from the United Kingdom', *Journal of Industrial Economics* 33, 327–38; Reinmann, B. C., 1973, 'On the dimensions of bureaucratic structure: an empirical reappraisal', *Administrative Science Quarterly* 18, 462–76.

62   Carneiro, R. L., 1967, 'On the relationship between size of population and complexity of social organization', *Southwestern Journal of Anthropology* 23, 234–43. See also: Rosenberg, M., 1994, 'Pattern, process and hierarchy in the evolution of culture', *Journal of Anthropological Archaeology* 13, 307–40.

63   Johnson, G. A., 1978, 'Information sources and the development of decision-making organisations', in C. L. Redman *et al.* (eds), *Social Archaeology: Beyond Subsistence and Dating*, New York, 87–112; Johnson, G. A., 1982, 'Organizational structure and scalar stress', in C. Renfrew, M. Rowlands and B. A. Segraves (eds), *Theory and Explanation in Archaeology* New York, 389–421.

64   Ember, M., 1963, 'The relationship between economic and political development in nonindustrial societies', *Ethnology* 2, 228–48.

65   Carneiro, R. L., 1967, 'On the relationship between size of population and complexity of social organization', *Southwestern Journal of Anthropology* 23, 234–43.

66   Upham, S., 1990, 'Analog or digital? Toward a generic framework for explaining the development of emergent political systems', in S. Upham (ed.), *The Evolution of Political Systems*, 87–115.

67   Narroll, R., 1956, 'A preliminary index of social development', *American Anthropologist* 58, 687–715.

68   For comparison: Laserson, M. H., 1988, 'Organizational growth of small firms: an outcome of markets and hierarchies', *American Sociological Review* 53, 330–42.

69   Child, J., 1984, *Organization*, 2nd edn, 58–84.

70   Pugh, D. S. *et al.*, 1968, 'Dimensions of organization structure', *Administrative Science Quarterly* 13, 65–105.

71   Klatzky, S. R., 1970, 'Relationship of organizational size to complexity and coordination', *Administrative Science Quarterly* 15, 428–48.

72   Jones, G. J., 1966, 'Chiefly succession in Basutoland', in J. Goody (ed.), *Succession to High Office*, 57–81.

73   Skinner, G. W., 1977, 'Cities and the hierarchy of local systems', in G. W. Skinner (ed.), *The City in Late Imperial China*, Stanford, 276–351.

74   Johnsonn, G. A., 1978, 'Information sources and the development of decision-making organisations', in C. L. Redman, *et al.* (eds), *Social Archaeology: Beyond Subsistence and Dating*, New York, 87–112.

75   Mayhew, B., 1973, 'System size and ruling elites', *American Sociological Review* 78, 468–75; Mayhew, B., 1972, 'System size and structural differentiation of military organisations; testing a harmonic series model of the division of labor', *American Journal of Sociology* 77, 750–765; Mayhew, B. and Levinger, R. L., 1976, 'Size and density of interaction in human aggregates', *American Journal of Sociology* 82, 86–110; Mayhew, B. H. and Levinger, R. L., 1976, 'On the emergence of oligarchy in human interaction', *American Journal of Sociology* 81, 1017–49.

76   Williamson, O. E., 1967, 'Hierarchical control and optimum firm-size', *Journal of Political Economy* 75, 123–38; Williamson, O. E. (ed.), 1995, *Organization Theory*, 2nd edn.

77   For other studies supporting this conclusion from an organizational analysis perspective: Urwick, L. F., 1956, 'The manager's span of control', *Harvard Business Review* 34, 39–47; Reimann, B. C., 1973, 'On the dimensions of bureaucratic Structure: an empirical reappraisal', *Administrative Science Quarterly* 18, 462–76; Scott, R. W., 1975, 'Organizational structure', *Annual Review of Sociology* 1, 1–20; McAfee, R. P. and McMillan, J., 1995, 'Organizational diseconomies of scale', *Journal of Economic and Management Strategy* 4.3, 399–426; Geanakoplos, J. and Milgrom, P., 1991, 'A theory of hierarchies based on limited managerial attention', *Journal of Japanese and International Economics* 5, 205–25. For the general disciplinary context of all these studies: Bedeian, A., 1987, 'Organization theory: current controversies, issues and direction', in C. L. Cooper and I. T. Robertson (eds), *Review of Industrial and Organizational Psychology*, Chichester, 110–40; Levinthal, D., 1990, 'Organizational adaptation and environmental selection: inter-related processes of change', *Organization Science* 2, 140–5.

78   Pugh, D. D. *et al.*, 1968, 'Dimensions of organization structure', *Administrative Science Quarterly* 13, 65–105.

79   For Kosse's views: Kosse, K., 1990, 'Group size and social complexity. Thresholds in the long-term memory', *Journal of Anthropological Archaeology* 9, 275–303; Kosse, K., 1994, 'The evolution of large, complex groups: a hypothesis', *Journal of Anthropological Archaeology* 13, 35–50.

80   Fletcher, R., 1995, *The Limits of Settlement Growth.*
81   Johnson, G. A., 1982, 'Organizational structure and scalar stress', in C. Renfrew, M. Rowlands and B. A. Segraves (eds), *Theory and Explanation in Archaeology*, 389–421, New York.
82   Olson, M., 1982, *The Rise and Decline of Nations*, New Haven, CT.
83   This is a central argument in: Kosse, K., 1994, 'The evolution of large, complex groups: a hypothesis', *Journal of Anthropological Archaeology* 13, 35–50.
84   Lazonic, W. and West, J., 1995, 'Organizational integration and competitive advantage: explaining strategy and performance in American industry', *Industrial and Corporate Change*, 4.1, 229; Meier, R. L., 1972, 'Communications stress', *Annual Review of Ecology and Systematics* 3, 289–314.
85   Carneiro, R. L., 1978, 'Political expansion as an expression of the principle of competitive exclusion', in R. Cohen and R. Elman (eds), *The Anthropology of Political Evolution*, 205–44, Philadelphia.
86   Sanderson, S. K. 1995, *Social Transformations*, Cambridge, MA.
87   Eckhardt, W., 1992, *Civilizations, Empires and Wars.*
88   Van der Leeuw, S. E., 1981, 'Information flows, flow structures and the explanation of change in human institutions', in S. E. van der Leeuw (ed.), *Archaeological Approaches to the Study of Complexity*, Amsterdam 230–312. For a detailed case-study employing van der Leeuw's perspective: van der Leeuw, S. E., 1993, 'Decision-making in the Roman Empire during the Republic', in P. Brun, S. E. van der Leeuw and C. R. Whittaker (eds), *Frontiers d'empire*, 65–93.
89   See also: Wirsing, R., 1973, 'Political power and information: a cross-cultural study', *American Anthropologist* 75, 147–78.
90   Tainter, J. A., 1988, *The Collapse of Complex Societies.*
91   Cohen, M. N., 1977, *The Food Crisis in Prehistory*, New Haven, Conn.; Cohen, M. N., 1981, 'Pacific Coast foragers: affluent or overcrowded?', *Senri Ethnological Studies* 9, 275–95.
92   Johnson, G. A., 1982, 'Organizational structure and scalar stress', in C. Renfrew, M. Rowlands and B. A. Segraves (eds), *Theory and Explanation in Archaeology*, 389–421, New York.
93   *Ibid.*
94   *Ibid.*
95   Lewis, J. P., 1991, 'Some consequences of giantism. The case of India', *World Politics* 43, 367–89.
96   Huang, Y., 1994, 'Information, bureaucracy and economic reform in China and the Soviet Union', *World Politics* 47, 102–34. See also the analogous conclusions of: Solnick, S. L., 1996, 'The breakdown of hierarchies in the Soviet Union and China. A neo-institutional perspective', *World Politics* 48, 209–38.
97   Krasner, S. D. (ed.), 1983 *International Regimes*, Ithaca; Simmons, A., 1987, 'Theories of international regimes', *International Organization* 41, 491–517; Young, O., 1986, 'International regimes: toward a new theory of institutions', *World Politics* 39, 115–7. For the relationship between this body of work on 'regimes' and earlier concepts of international order and interaction in International Relations theory: Evans, T. and Wilson, P., 1992, 'Regime theory and the English school of International Relations: a comparison', *Millennium*

21.3, 329–51; Hansenclever, A., Mayer, P. and Rittberger, V., 1996, 'Interests, power, knowledge: the study of international regimes', *Mershon International Studies Review* 40.2, 177–228.

98 Renfrew, C., 1986, 'Introduction: peer polity interaction and socio-political change', in C. Renfrew and J. F. Cherry (eds), *Peer Polity Interaction and Socio-Political Change*, 1–18 (8).

99 Renfrew, C., 1986, 'Introduction: peer polity interaction and socio-political change', in C. Renfrew and J. F. Cherry (eds), *Peer Polity Interaction and Socio-Political Change*, 1–18. For analogous work supporting this conclusion: Bikhchandani, S., Hirshleifer, D. and Welch, I, 1992, 'A theory of fads, fashion, custom and cultural change in informational cascades', *Journal of Political Economy* 100.5, 992–1026. For two examples of interactionally established societal norms: Solow, B. L., 1991, *Slavery and the Rise of the Atlantic System*; Sullivan, R. J., 1990, 'The revolution of ideas: widespread patenting and invention during the English Industrial Revolution', *Journal of Economic History* 50, 349–62; Weenig, M. W. H. and Midden, C. J. H., 1991, 'Communication network influences on information diffusion and persuasion', *Journal of Personality and Social Psychology* 61, 734–42; Burt, R. S., 1992, *Social Contagion*, Cambridge, Mass.

100 Notably, this disengages regime formation and the adoption of cultural and other similarities from notions of political or economic leadership and hegemony. On leadership and regimes: Young, O. R., 1991, 'Political leadership and regime formation: on the development of institutions in international society', *International Organization* 43.5, 281–308. It also permits regime analysis to be applied to the formation of relationships within, as well between, socio-political systems, whether states or 'international systems'. For the use of regime analysis in a similar way: Huizenga, F. D., 1995, 'Regime analysis: a rule-based method for studying institutions', *Administration and Society* 27.3, 361–78.

5

The origins of international relations: non-state societies

Introduction

In this chapter I shall apply the theory proposed in the previous chapter to non-state societies from both the past and present. These range from the earliest human societies to those on the brink of state-formation. The less complex of these societies (which are not necessarily the earliest) will provide an important test for the relationship between organizational scale and the rate of change. If the model is correct, political change should occur only very slowly in them and they should display an absence of cyclicality. Cyclical processes of change should become noticeable only (if at all) with increasing socio-political complexity above the level at which 'sequential hierarchy' (in Johnson's terms) emerges. In order to achieve this, however, one needs to examine the range of non-state societies and their complexity, in the terms so far described.

It must be stressed at the outset that, while the classification of non-state polities adopted here is my own, this is based on long-recognized anthropological terminology.[1] In employing this terminology it is worth noting that no implication of evolutionary sequence or value-judgement is implicit in this use of the classifications adopted. They refer only to types of political organization rather than stages in human history, although there is (as will become clear) a sequential dimension to the first occurrence of these types. However, many of these types coexist today, and more were contemporary in the past. Thus, they do not represent a linear 'progression' from simple to more complex, with each type replacing a less complex one.

Kin-based societies

All non-state polities in the past can be divided, at the most general level, into two groups.[2] The first is that of the kin-based society. In such societies social and political organization is based on the grounds of kin alone, with kin-groups often defined much more broadly than in the modern West. In the simplest of such societies, called 'bands' by anthropologists,[3] there is very little trace of formal political organization and of differentiation in tasks and skills.[4] Such groups include, for example, the earliest human societies and those of non–state modern peoples (such as the Australian Aborigines in the nineteenth century); the Inuit ('Eskimo') prior to Westernization; the earliest European societies in the Palaeolithic and Mesolithic periods; and the !Kung bushmen at the time of their first contact with Europeans.[5]

Kin-based societies can be organized tribally, with the kinship and shared culture converging to afford social identities, or without such political divisions simply as 'peoples'.[6] These societies can often have a degree of political leadership within what is characteristically an essentially egalitarian society. For example, in Papua New Guinea, prior to the twentieth century, there was the so-called 'big-man' form of leadership.[7] In 'big-man' societies there is no regular position of leadership, but individuals could take pre-eminent roles in society on personal grounds. This form of political organization has proved remarkably enduring, and still exists today in the tribal societies of the Highlands of Papua New Guinea. Tribes can, how-ever, have no political leadership at all and represent, by definition, only self-defining cultural groups.

Economic forms associated with kin-based societies also vary. Kin-based societies can be hunter-gatherers, either sedentary or mobile, or pastoralists or farmers.[8] Crafts specialization and mass-production are always absent, and their settlements are not highly nucleated into towns or cities.

Such societies still exist in some parts of the world today, but it must be recalled that for the majority of human history kin-based political organiza-tion was universal.[9] This was the form of organization which accompanied human migrations throughout the world in prehistory, producing a world-wide range of human societies.[10] The development of tribalism seems, although this cannot be demonstrated unambiguously, to be a secondary aspect of such societies. This may have emerged in conjunction with the definition of specific territories and geopolitical identities in given loca-tions.[11] It could be said that strong political differences between groups emerged at the tribal level whereas politics in band societies was essentially concerned with personalities and family connections. In this sense, the change from bands to tribes can be seen as accompanied by social differ-entiation, whereas economic and ecological changes do not accompany this transition in a consistent manner.

Tribes and bands are not necessarily comprised of merely a handful of people, but there are demographic thresholds which can be recognized, as has already been mentioned. As these have played a part in building the model in the previous chapter, little weight will be placed on them here, for fear of circular reasoning. However, one piece of evidence not employed in building the model may be permissible, the apparent size-range of big-man groups at 300–500 individuals.[12] This is interesting, in that these figures represent the absolute top of the scale for both face-to-face contact and for hunter-gatherer groups. What is especially significant for this chapter is that kin-based societies – both bands and tribes – show no trace of dramatic changes in either their way of life or their political organization over very long periods of time. This is a remarkably stable political form.

That is not to say that political upheavals and inter-tribal warfare are absent from such societies. Nor are relations between tribes in peacetime always friendly but the effects of leadership change (such as it is), war and conflict are not to eliminate one tribe or establish the subservience of one band to others. Consequently, while inter-group warfare is attested from the Neolithic period onwards, there is no strong argument that this promoted the emergence of larger groups or the disappearance of defeated groups in kin-based societies.

Consequently, low levels of differentiation in social and economic activities, and the very gradual and slight evidence for change in the political and social organization of these groups are, as the theory suggests, found together. These features correlate with a low level of political centralization. Fried[13] has pointed out that no known human society has no evidence of leadership at any time, but in kin-based societies this is entirely contingent and based on individuals. This is equally true of both bands and tribes. !Kung bushmen have leaders, but these are spokespeople for specific groups or residential communities, not tribal kings. Even in 'big-man' societies rank is based on the individual and individual accomplishments, not on an established position continually existing, or if one prefers, continuously reproduced, in society, except as a latent structural potential.[14]

This coincidence of characteristics can be widely demonstrated: native North America also affords some especially illuminating examples of kin-based types of social organization. The Iroquois were a sedentary native American people,[15] sharing common cultural customs and linguistic features, but tribally organized. They were not, however, governed by a recognizable and regularly constituted élite, but instead had leaders whose position was based on personal factors and contingent upon situation. This enabled political actions to be taken, wars fought, and the well-known 'League' of Iroquois groups established, but it was not the basis of state-formation or other dramatic political change.[16] Even the coming of guns and European contact did not transform these patterns within Iroquois society itself although, of course, the consequences of European colonization were ultimately to terminate them. As Milner has recently made clear, this inter-group hostility and shifting pattern of tribal alliances was a widespread feature of native American groups. However, as in indigenous Pacific societies, it was not one producing the 'rise and fall' of political units, but rather a flux of alternating relationships.[17]

Another native American example of the kin-based political type is afforded by the Cherokee, whose leaders were 'self-made' individuals.[18] This tribe coexisted with those having both kin-based and non-kin-based political organization, showing that each does not preclude alternative forms of socio-political organization.

Moving further south, and into the present, there is, for example, the

Mekranoti-Kayapo in Brazil.[19] Being a kin-based society, access to external
contacts is the key factor in allowing the emergence of individuals as leaders.
Because these contacts are liable to change, and access to them is not
restricted to leaders, this position is personalized, not formalized. Likewise
leadership is also highly contingent, again due to factional and individual
competition, in the Akwe-Shavante, another Brazilian group.[20]

This brief survey, then, illustrates that this point can be made by a very
great quantity of anthropological and archaeological data regarding kin-
based societies. They characteristically have low levels of differentiation;
they have one, or at most two, levels of decision-making above that of the
individual and they exhibit change in the form of their political organization
only of a gradual and long-term character. This change when it is most
clearly seen – in the emergence of tribalism – comprises a scalar change
accompanied by a change in social and economic differentiation (complexity) which produces new types of political circumstances.

On this level of socio-political organization therefore, the model proposed earlier seems to fit much empirical data from cases world-wide. These
appear to illustrate a slow rate of change in groups with low levels of socio-
political complexity, in which major transformations of political
organizations seem to be absent over millennia. Although one may be able
to recognize a transition from less to more complex kin-based societies in
the emergence of tribalism, this cannot be correlated with any common
factor other than an increase in scale and other dimensions of complexity.
The major transition which separates these kin-based societies from other
non-state societies is also associated with scalar changes and increased
differentiation.[21] For this we need to examine more differentiated kin-based
groups, whether tribal agriculturalist/pastoralist societies, or those where a
concentration of resources enables sedentism to arise among hunter-
gatherer groups.

The transition to governed society

The most complex hunter-gatherer groups can be both sedentary and
populous in comparison to the generality of similar bands. For an example of
such a group, one may take the Taremuit, coastal 'eskimos'. They have
leaders who retain their role as a more formal part of the social order, unlike
those of the groups so far discussed.[22] Perhaps the most informative example
is that of the western coast of North America, however, where the abundant
maritime resources of the area permitted sedentism among pre-Contact
hunter-gatherers, who have been seen as archetypal of similar societies.[23]

Arnold[24] and others have pointed out that these abundant resources could
only be exploited by communities with a clear division of labour (i.e.
differentiation) and the division of tasks into operative stages. This implies
social, or at least economic, organization beyond that found in most other

hunter-gatherer groups. These communities also had 'some of the highest population density figures for hunter-gatherers anywhere in the world'.[25] While some have seen them as having regularly constituted government, it has recently been pointed out that evidence for their political organization more closely resembles the 'big-man' societies of Melanesia than formalized leadership.

Other scholars have noted that in abundant environments elsewhere, there seem to have been similar sedentary 'complex hunter-gatherers'. For example, the Calusa in Florida, coastal communities of hunter-gatherers in prehistoric Peru,[26] in Japan and (in the Mesolithic period) on the Danish coast in Europe, may all have been communities of this sort.[27] Archaeological evidence seems to support the view that large sedentary hunter-gatherer populations could have been far more widespread in prehistory than current interpretations allow. These seems to represent the scalar limits of hunter-gatherers in both population density and economic form, without the emergence of permanent government.

Ecological and economic factors undeniably afforded the opportunity to develop socio-political complexity on the north-west coast of America and elsewhere, but they did not necessitate this. Interestingly, Ames has argued that rather than looking to such factors, the development of socio-political complexity among these communities should be explained using an information-processing model based on that of Johnson.[28] These communities can be seen both to closely accord with expectations produced by the model and to demonstrate the potential of being aware of the role of ecological and economic platforms, enabling the operation of socio-political processes.

These examples illustrate, then, the relationship between high populations, differentiation of economic and social activities, and ecological possibilism. The fact that such changes did not occur everywhere and at all times, when such economic and ecological circumstances were present, suggests that the emergence of complex hunter-gatherer societies is not attributable to either economics or ecological factors alone: agency has to be incorporated in its explanation. It also suggests a strong relationship between political scale and political change. In kin-based societies it is a general rule that the bigger the group the more complex it seems to be.[29]

The earliest regularly governed societies

This brings us to another type of non-state society: the chiefdom. The chiefdom has seldom been discussed by political scientists.[30] It is, however, a major focus of research in anthropology and in archaeology, especially in the USA, the UK and Scandinavia.[31] As such it is both a well-studied and an amply evidenced form of non-state socio-political organization.

It was probably Kalervo Oberg who first employed the concept of the chiefdom in anthropology,[32] but it is widely known through Service's studies of political evolution.[33] The concept of the chiefdom has been variously defined in detail, and the following definition tries to encompass those aspects which would be generally agreed upon by anthropologists and archaeologists alike. It is based mostly on ethnographic accounts, and especially on Pacific, North American and African evidence.

Chiefdoms are socially differentiated and ranked societies, with regularized government involving a (often hereditary) leader. Frequently they retain kin-based elements in the social structure but have an agricultural or pastoralist basis. As such they may be either sedentary (as in almost all cases) or mobile, as in the form of the Hunnic groups which invaded Late Roman Europe and the Chinese empire alike.[34] The chiefdom encompasses, therefore, all other known non-state societies.

Chiefdoms have been usually found to have common economic characteristics relating to the differentiation of economic activities beyond the level connected with the most complex hunter-gatherers.[35] There are no certain examples of chiefdoms with hunter-gatherer economies, nor of proto-industrial or industrialized chiefdoms. So, chiefdoms exist within an economic range, as is the case for kin-based societies, but this range (as in that example) is extremely wide.[36] What is clear is that all chiefdoms are more socially and economically differentiated than other kin-based societies, and that they have regularized leadership. It is not generally true that chiefs derive their position from economic wealth; rather this formal leadership represents the regularization of the contingent leadership of hunter-gatherer groups: that is, chiefdoms arise at the transition from sequential to simultaneous hierarchy.

Chiefs frequently employ symbols of rank and build public works to represent themselves, their dynasties, or their communities. They generally promote crafts-specialization in connection with both display and chiefly life-styles, but these derive from chiefly patronage not vice versa.[37]

Chiefs are often highly competitive, warring against neighbouring groups and engaging in competitive patterns of exchange. The use of such interregional contacts may play an important part in maintaining chiefdoms, and some may even come into existence through migration and conquest of neighbouring areas. However, chiefdoms generally exhibit cultural similarities derived from protracted contacts, rather than being politically transformed by them.

Chiefdoms seem to encompass a wide range of world societies, mostly not now surviving, from the Neolithic period to the modern period.[38] Chiefdoms are, therefore, extremely widely spread across the globe, occurring at some time on all continents (except for Australasia) which support substantial human populations.

The breadth of this societal type has to be appreciated. Chiefdoms include the less politically complex of the medieval kingdoms of Europe; the Ancient Polynesian societies; some pre-colonial African kingdoms; and many native North American groups.[39] They seem to have been widespread in Europe until the establishment of the Roman Empire, and beyond the Rhine until the eighth century AD or later.[40]

The category of chiefdoms, therefore, contains a wide diversity of specific political forms, sharing features in common. This diversity makes the chiefdom especially useful for the purposes of evaluating the theory advanced in the previous chapter. Whereas chiefdoms clearly cannot be equated with economic or ecological similarities – and the details of the histories involved suggest that they are highly contingent – can we, in fact, identify the processes anticipated by the model in the trajectories of chiefdoms?

To examine this question I shall divide chiefdoms, like kin-based societies, into more or less complex categories based on their social and economic differentiation. This will form the basis for discussing chiefdoms in relation to the model proposed in the previous chapter, and for examining the diachronic aspects of this political form.

Although these are of course broad categories, chiefdoms can be divided into less complex, which I shall call simply 'chiefdoms', and more complex, which I shall call 'over-chiefdoms'. These types will be useful in comparing the characteristics of the trajectories of each sort of chiefdom, although the limitations of such a basis categorization must, of course, be appreciated.

To illustrate this, I shall discuss two examples of each category. In each case one will be selected from Europe and one from a non-European society, for reasons which will become apparent. In the first group, the chiefdoms of early Christian Ireland (in the seventh and eighth centuries AD) and Polynesia (in the eighteenth and nineteenth centuries AD) will be analysed. In the second, those of later prehistoric continental Europe (in the first millennia BC and AD) and Africa (in the nineteenth century) will be discussed.

Chiefdoms

The early Christian societies of Ireland originated in the fifth century AD, when they derived their religion and much of their material culture from contact with Roman Britain, as the story of St. Patrick famously illustrates.[41] These societies had probably been organized along tribal lines since at least the Bronze Age, and had traditions of having comprised large tribal zones prior to the formation of their early Christian political units.[42] The latter were small – approximately 150 (called *tuatha*) existed simultaneously – and culturally distinguished from each other by histories and legends about their origins and relationships. These differences formed the basis for kinship-based, but highly ranked, societies with crafts specialization and established hereditary leadership. The scale of each political unit meant that inter-group conflict was often of a limited scope, and total populations may have been in the lower thousands.

Leadership, while regularized, was not dissimilar in several respects to that of a 'big-man' society, insofar as access to chiefly status rested upon personalized factors and individual success, and was supported by extremely slight resources. Irish chiefs (*ri*) were, however, bound by the regularized requirements of office, unlike 'big-men', and these included inter-group warfare and acts of generosity to their subjects.

The chiefdom in Ireland, then, is closely analogous to the pattern already suggested as characteristic of the chiefdom in general. Chiefs had limited ability to rule and yet a recognized right to leadership. Their function was to be judges, symbols of the chiefdom, and to lead war-parties against neighbouring rulers. There was no notion of statehood, although chiefs could establish dominance over each other and build short-lived polities larger in size than most *tuatha*.

The Polynesian case offers the classic instance of a chiefly society.[43] This offers a clear contrast, in ecological and economic terms, to Ireland. Although agricultural societies existed in Pacific island contexts, these grew different crops, involved contrasting economic organization and, of course, existed in environmentally very dissimilar locations from those of Ireland.

Probably the most widely discussed of the Pacific societies is the Hawaiian chiefdom, but others existed on Tonga, Tahiti and other island groups. As in Ireland, chiefs in Polynesia were partly selected by descent, and a similar role was attached to genealogical knowledge for this purpose. Hawaiian society was ranked and had well-defined concepts of leadership, involving hereditary chiefs. The Hawaiian chiefs ruled a population providing much evidence of specialization both in social and economic contexts. This population – probably about 200,000 – was the largest in Polynesia, but was divided between four chiefdoms. In Hawaii, as in Ireland, greater and lesser chiefs existed as a hierarchy of political control.

In other areas of Polynesia smaller chiefdoms were equally well established. In Tonga, chiefs were effective rulers with hereditary dynasties lasting generations. In the one well-documented case, a Tongan dynasty ruled from *c* AD 950 to *c*. 1500: that is, for a period equivalent to the entire European Middle Ages. In Tahiti, there was a rigid class structure and established leadership. Tahiti seems to have been the focus of six chiefdoms in the eighteenth century, with a combined population comprising about 30,000 people when Europeans arrived, under harsh and formalized rulership. Like Hawaii, Tahiti had an economy encompassing specialized production and was highly socially differentiated.

The Polynesian and Irish examples both illustrate the defining characteristics of the chiefdom. They also illustrate how such political units are characteristic of specific scales of organization, with populations for chiefdoms of above 500 people but below 10,000.

In all these cases chiefdoms proved very enduring. Although there were political changes, both in the ruling dynasties and in the units themselves, these did not occur often. Most chiefdoms survived for centuries, and the inter-chiefdom systems of political contact which they built up were even more enduring. In each case they were terminated only by foreign invasion.

This conforms with theoretical expectations: chiefdoms change more frequently than complex hunter-gatherer groups, but still very slowly, and they exhibit both higher populations and greater political instability than kin-based societies. If the model is correct, over-chiefdoms, those which are more complex, should be faster-changing, larger and more volatile than other chiefdoms or kin-based polities.

Over-chiefdoms

The Zulu represent a group which went from a chiefdom to an over-chiefdom form of socio-political organization within the scope of historical sources.[44] They began as a conventional chiefdom, with small political units similar in scale to those of early Christian Ireland. These were hereditary and kin-based but had clear-cut group leadership.

Around 1800 this warring system of chiefdoms was integrated politically by the success of one chief who subdued his neighbours and brought them under his rule, again much in the manner which we have seen in Irish 'over-kingship'. This was accompanied by administrative and organizational changes, increasing social ranking and specialization.

This was built upon in the next generation by the famous Zulu ruler Shaka, who established all Zulu chiefdoms under one 'superchiefdom' comprising about 100,000 people. This was also accompanied by administrative changes, consolidating and elaborating those of his predecessor. The unpopularity of Shaka's rule led to his assassination in 1828, which was followed by civil war. A new Zulu state – with much more elaborate administration and bureaucracy – established after this, lost independence to the British in 1880.

The Zulu example illustrates a chiefdom becoming a state, and shows one way in which chiefdoms can increase in complexity. It shows that political reorganization was accompanied by changes in the centralization of control, in social organization and in the rise of new means of information processing in the form of new governmental levels. These are closely connected to changes in scale and to an increasing rate of socio-political change.

The example of northern Europe in the late prehistoric period also shows this.[45] At about 1000 BC this area was probably made up of many small chiefdoms, and even at the end of the Western Roman Empire, c. 400 AD, the characteristic political organization of Europe outside the Roman world was the chiefdom.

These chiefdoms can be most accurately reconstructed in the period of the Roman conquest, when it is clear that Britain, Gaul (modern France) and 'Germania' (the part of Europe north of the Rhine) were organized in this fashion. In Britain and Gaul, tribal groups had their own chiefs in established leadership based on hereditary succession. The construction of large-scale 'public works' and the ability of chiefs to act as judges and warleaders seems well evidenced. There were many other social groups, and an economy containing a wide range of specialists, with the majority of the population engaged in agriculture or pastoralism.

In Germania it seems that some groups were already chiefdoms in the first century BC, but at the start of the millennium others seem to have been organized as complex kin-based groups, albeit with agricultural economies.[46] Late Roman (third–fifth century AD) records of these make it clear that by that time they had (at least for the most part) acquired chiefdom characteristics similar to those of the Britons and Gauls during the early Roman period.

The societies beyond the Roman Empire in the first century BC and the first century AD were therefore composed of many chiefdoms, but among these were over-chiefdoms. The description of the Gauls provided by Caesar attests that state-like characteristics (but not states) were being developed by them during the period prior to the Roman conquest. Archaeological evidence both supports this view and may extend it to parts of Eastern Britain. In these areas the emergence of large political centres associated with long-distance trade and intensive craftworking may attest increased economic specialization and organization. The Gallic evidence also encompasses hints of political change within Gallic kingdoms, including the growth of bureaucracy and perhaps the adoption of aspects of literacy for administrative purposes.

Caesar himself gives us (possibly unreliable) figures for the populations involved in the barbarian groups which he fought, and further population estimates are given by other ancient writers. Patterson has recently summarized the range of these as 14,000–263,000.[47] If these ancient writers present anything like reliable accounts of these populations (and they might well have had reason to exaggerate) then the larger of these would be broadly comparable to Shaka's Zulu 'superchiefdom'. It is, however, interesting that during the barbarian migrations of the fourth and fifth centuries, comparable scales of population are noted by Roman authors;[48] so perhaps Caesar's figures approximate to the numbers involved.

Similar evidence is available for Britain at the end of the pre-Roman period. Large centres of political control and crafts specialization emerged in the immediately pre-Roman period and there is again evidence of a dense population and substantial agricultural surplus.[49] Direct written sources are of less help in reconstructing social organization in Britain, but this was plainly a highly differentiated society. Writing is again evidenced for the first time, but its purpose in British Iron Age society is unclear. By the end of the Iron Age, however, the long-stable pattern of British tribal (or more accurately 'chiefly') politics was being disrupted by the rise of a large over-chiefdom. This came to encompass much of southeast England, and was threatening enough to neighbouring rulers to prompt them to seek Roman assistance.

So in these two examples we can, again, see evidence of a rise in the scale of political organization correlating with changes in political centralization, with social and economic differentiation (that is, complexity), and with the rise of new approaches to administration and information-processing. In both cases these new polities seem to have been much less stable than those they replaced, as both Caesar and the rapidly shifting pattern of dynastic politics in Britain attest.

Still more interesting in this context, perhaps, is the result of recent work on socio-political change in late Iron Age Europe. In two independent studies, archaeologists have found evidence of the cyclical growth and collapse of socio-political systems.[50] These studies support the view that the more complex polities of later prehistoric Europe were less stable than those of earlier prehistory, where no such patterns have been convincingly shown.

Sadly, no equivalent study is available for the Zulu kingdom, but that the volatility of this increased as it became more complex during the nineteenth century has already been noted. These two examples, therefore, provide instances of more complex chiefdoms changing more rapidly over time than less complex chiefdoms.

The examples discussed suggest that chiefdoms are also faster changing and less stable than complex hunter-gatherer groups. They show that chiefdoms are larger and more strongly socially and economically differentiated than such groups and that the extent of their internal differentiation increases if they become over-chiefdoms. The population figures for over-chiefdoms apparently indicate a range of 100,000–300,000. This is, of course, far larger than the range for chiefdoms, at 500–10,000 people. A question, perhaps, might arise as to the relationship between groups of intermediate size (10,000–100,000) and these categories. This is, however, illusory given the partial character of population data for non-literate (or only occasionally literate) populations, from which few demographic records characteristically survive. So, the range for chiefdoms overall seems to be from 500 to 500,000 people, and the transition to over-chiefdoms probably occurs in the part of that range between 10,000 and 100,000 people.

This, of course, also raises a key difference affecting the estimation of scale between chiefdoms and both over-chiefdoms and states. In non-literate societies all communication has to be based either on personal contact or the use of symbols conveying relatively simple messages compared to language. This means that in such societies communication over long distances and between large groups is necessarily slow and personalized. In literate societies, communication of detailed information over long distances is possible and information can be readily distributed to large groups. Consequently, while population estimates may effectively represent scale in chiefdoms and tribes, the use of writing makes such a correlation unreliable as a guide to scale in literate societies. Another time–space geography takes hold, constrained by means of communication rather than absolute population size. This does not mean, as we have seen, that scalar factors are unimportant, merely that the equation of scale and population size is invalid in larger socio-political systems. This represents, in itself, a fundamental socio-political transformation taking place within the chiefdom range, as full literacy emerges with the origins of the state.

Change occurs more slowly in chiefdoms than in over-chiefdoms. The latter exhibit higher levels of volatility, and (apparently) also cyclical patterns of growth and decline. The contrast between rapid changes in the rise and fall of the Zulu kingdoms and the slow pattern of large-scale change, rather than simply dynastic politics, in Ireland during the seventh and eighth centuries makes this clear. While these differences in the rate of change cannot be demonstrated in quantitative terms, there seem, therefore, strong arguments for supposing that the model suggested in the previous chapter does fit these examples.

In his analysis of the emergence of chiefdoms, Spencer has argued that two of the concepts developed by Johnson are especially useful in understanding the origins of chiefly rule.[51] Spencer suggests that the emergence of chiefdoms represents the transition from sequential to simultaneous hierarchy. However, he stresses that this transition is not determined to an increased scale, but results from the interplay of scale, information processing and agency.

From chiefdoms to over-chiefdoms

The process of change which we have seen in the examples discussed here is evidenced much more widely among chiefdoms. There are also examples in which the transition from chiefdom to over-chiefdom, and then to state, can be charted in some detail. Perhaps one of the clearest examples of this is the case of the Anglo-Saxon kingdoms. Thus, a brief discussion of this example may serve to illustrate a wider range of possible cases where we may trace such a sequence of development.[52]

When first reliably attested in textual sources in the seventh century, the Anglo-Saxon kingdoms were clearly, in the sense used here, chiefdoms.[53] Prior to the late sixth century archaeological evidence suggests that these were chiefdoms, with very small-scale – although chiefly – organization and low levels of socio-political differentiation. From the later sixth century onward, however, these small chiefdoms coalesced to form larger units. These were more sharply ranked societies with crafts specialization and greater social diversity. Their leaders held recognized office and built both palaces and other public monuments, including 'Offa's Dyke', a long defensive earthwork which runs along the present English–Welsh border.

They fought with both one another and non-Anglo-Saxon groups and engaged in trade with overseas merchants.

The Anglo-Saxon kingdoms of the seventh century existed in a regional socio-political system alongside state-societies. Interaction with these introduced the Christian religion, and along with it the use of literacy for record-keeping and the production of royal laws, proclamations and histories as they attempted to emulate continental states.

Like the over-chiefdoms of later prehistory, these kingdoms increased the areas under their control through conquest, so building larger polities. These polities then began to develop state attributes (including bureaucracy and urbanism) very rapidly during the eighth century. Thus, the polities attacked by the Vikings from the end of that century onward were already states.

The Anglo-Saxon example, then, adheres to the pattern of change already seen operating in chiefdom societies but helps us trace the incorporation of an over-chiefdom into a regional socio-political system dominated by states. It emphasizes that chiefdoms do not exist in isolation; they occur either as regional 'chiefly' systems, or in regional systems alongside other types of polity. Such 'regional systems' of chiefdoms emerge with chiefdoms, but are also found among over-chiefdoms.

It must not be supposed that chronological 'lateness' (or 'Europeanness' for that matter) is more likely to have produced over-chiefdoms rather than chiefdoms. Another example from the British Isles of a later 'regional chiefly system' illustrates this very effectively.

Many Scottish people still today associate themselves with 'clans', but in the early modern and medieval periods these 'clans' were effectively functioning chiefdoms.[54] They were territorially based, small in geographical extent, and little affected by feudal concepts despite their medieval situation. In the clan, kinship was 'at the core', and the clan leader was a hereditary chief with legal and military duties. Competitive, and often warring, clans were not urbanized or bureaucratic. Chiefs did not wield a monopoly of legitimate force, in a society in which feuding was common among families.

The Scottish clan was based on an agricultural economy with evidence of crafts specialization, but without any mass-production. The existence of regularized leadership attests the chiefdom character of clans, but the absence of state characteristics is equally certain. The Scottish clans may, therefore, be classified as chiefdoms, but even in the eighteenth century they were not over-chiefdoms. The Scottish clan system alerts us to the way in which chiefdoms can function alongside states and in any chronological period. They also survived as polities for generations, despite their unstable leadership. This was a society in which leaders might easily be killed or deposed, but where the clan system itself plainly operated successfully for centuries. Its circumstances of foundation are unclear, so its exact duration cannot be ascertained.

However, it is clear that throughout its existence the clan-system existed within a broader regional system, comprised partly of states – a 'regional state system'. Consequently, this example also illustrates both the way in which chiefly systems can exist within regional state systems, and how distinctive cultural and socio-political groupings can form sub-regions within these.

There is also a definable progressive trajectory common to all political systems which include chiefdoms. The chiefdom is impossible without the pre-existence of a complex kin-based society and the complex kin-based society in every case seems to derive from an earlier simpler kin-based group. But all these types of socio-political organization coexisted and specific polities of each type continued to exist after others – whether more, or less, complex – had already collapsed. The period in which each type of society formed may, however, be more sequential, as the earliest chiefdoms preceded the earliest over-chiefdoms and the earliest over-chiefdoms probably preceded the earliest states.

From chiefdom to the state

The origins of the state (which may help us to understand both the nature and trajectories of state societies) obviously forms a key point of interest for scholars of International Relations examining long-term, large-scale, change.[55] As is implicit in the foregoing account of the earliest chiefdoms, states usually emerged from changes in chiefdom societies, unless they were imposed by an already-formed state in a process of territorial expansion.

An understanding of 'regional chiefly systems' is a prerequisite to a long-term perspective on the state and (as we shall see) the inter-state system. For it was in these 'regional chiefly systems' that 'regional state systems' originated.

Defining the state

The state has been variously defined. Political theorists, historians, archaeologists and anthropologists have all used different definitions of statehood.[56] Here, the state will be defined in an anthropological way. First, because this affords the most useful definition when examining transhistorical data. Secondly, because it can be readily combined with the anthropological terminology used in the earlier parts of this chapter.[57]

According to anthropological definitions the state has the monopoly of legitimate force, a centralized bureaucratic mode of government, and an urban-centred settlement-pattern. These criteria can be used to recognize states whether in the past or the present, allowing for the subdivision of these into types of state (centrally-planned, nation-state, and the like). In this respect a kingdom might be either a chiefdom or a state, and the subdivision of the category 'state' is analogous to the subdivision of kin-based societies and chiefdoms into distinct types.

The variety of forms which these defining features can take has to be stressed. Bureaucracy may be organized around a secular or religious 'civil service', or a dispensation of administration to members of a family or clan, or to aristocrats or 'sub-kings'. Urbanism may consist of large, populous trading places but towns could also be different in form: 'administrative villages' of bureaucrats and rulers, perhaps with attendant craftworkers, servants and so on.

The anthropological definition of the state poses its own problems, however, and these have been discussed at length by other scholars elsewhere. These difficulties relate especially to two factors: the transhistoricity of the 'state' as a category of political organization, and its relationship to literacy. Obviously both of these factors are extremely important here.

Gledhill has drawn attention to the problems posed both by transhistorical definitions of the state and by 'privileging' the modern state so as to separate it as a distinct category from earlier states, as would Hall.[58] Even a superficial reading of anthropological literature will cast doubt upon any such artificial division. It also highlights the wide variation in the political forms sharing the features so far mentioned as characteristic of the state.

An especially problematical area, arising from anthropological and archaeological studies, is whether states can exist without literacy.[59] This is not necessitated by the model proposed here, although of course one might expect states to use literacy in information processing if the model is correct. It is, however, possible to imagine a state organized without the need for literacy, if alternative solutions to information processing were adopted. However, the correlation between literacy and statehood is a useful means of validating the model. If the model is correct in seeing states as a means of organizing information processing in large-scale societies efficiently enough to permit their continued existence, then literacy would be expected in most (albeit not necessarily all) states.

The explanation of state-formation as a global process of change according to the model employed in this chapter is simple. In this view, the state is a scalar adaptation of the chiefdom. This explains the greater central control, more bureaucracy and larger settlements. It also explains the economic features suggested, as these too can be seen as the products of greater scale and larger populations.

This obviously relates closely to the arguments over whether we should associate states and literacy. If bureaucratization is a prerequisite of statehood, and the intensification of information processing – as the intensification of production – would be supposed to accompany this, then the association between literacy and states might be expected to be close. So, we might expect to find further evidence of literacy and record-keeping, alongside intensified division of activities, at the earliest sites associated with the independent development of states. If, however, bureaucracy was able to function without literacy there is no reason why it would not be possible to organize a state society without writing. That is, although literacy might be employed in the government of most states, we cannot use literacy as an identifier of the state. Alternative solutions to scalar stresses of information-

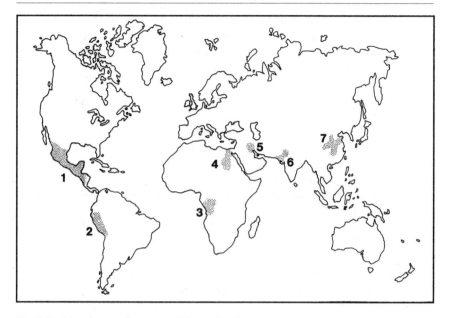

Fig. 5.1   Map showing locations of the earliest known independent instances of state-formation. The Indus Valley (6) is shown although it is not certainly independent of Mesopotamia (5). In sub-Saharan Africa, Kongo (3) is shown as the first certain state but there could have been earlier independently-formed sub-Saharan African states. Other areas shown are Mesoamerica (1), Peru (2), Egypt (4) and China (7).

processing could have been found without recourse to literacy. This focuses attention on the earliest, independently developed, states.

These may occur in seven distinct regions: Mesopotamia, Mesoamerica, Peru, Egypt, the Indus Valley, China and sub-Saharan Africa. These centres were not (with the possible exception of the Indus Valley and Egypt) in contact with one another during the relevant periods.

Mesopotamia[60]

The earliest Mesopotamian states were small city-states rather than large-scale polities. These were interlinked by a series of relationships in both political and cultural terms. From these relationships, trading networks seem to have developed. The earliest city-state was Warka or Uruk. Warka/Uruk seems to have made a rapid transition to statehood, with associated social and economic diversification, settlement nucleation (including the urbanization of neighbouring sites) and literacy. These prompted the swift formation of, not 'a state' at Warka/Uruk, but an inter-state system composed of similar city-states, with political relationships between them from the outset: the 'Sumerian civilization'. In Mesopotamia, then, 'the state' did not emerge separately in many places, but the 'inter-state system' emerged as an entity after an initial phase of urban city-state formation.

The effectively simultaneous origin of the inter-state system is of special significance for the political scientist: 'international relations' emerge along with the state. A similar pattern can be seen in other zones of independent state-formation.

Mesoamerica[61]

Yoffee has pointed out that a similar pattern is visible in Mesoamerica to that of Mesopotamia, in the emergence of many small city-states. In Meso-america the earliest such state appears to have formed in the valley of Oaxaca in about 200 BC. This was accompanied, as Blanton has pointed out, by rapid population rise, economic intensification, specialization and urbanization – the settlement at Monte Alabán seems to have housed *circa* 17,000 people at *c.* 200 BC. It also seems to be associated with the emergence of 'hieroglyphic' writing.

Another, near contemporary, development in the growth of the Meso-american state was the formation of a city-state in the valley of Mexico at Teotihuacan, beginning in about 150 BC. This city-state was centred on a planned city of about 13 square kilometres. This had a population including craftspeople and administrators, and trading areas apparently occupied by foreign merchants, including one clearly linking the city with Oaxaca.

Although within the same 'regional chiefly system', these developments were, to a great extent, independent of each other and also of the emergence of the Maya in the first two centuries BC. Although in the past claimed to be non-urbanized, the Maya had large 'urban' centres containing thousands of inhabitants. These developed simultaneously with rapid population increase, intensified crafts specialization, and literacy. Such centres were the basis for the centralized administration of a large, and to a great degree culturally homogenous, area as a series of polities. The political history of these groups is becoming known in some detail as their writings are deciphered. These enable us to recognize many aspects of Mayan politics, including inter-state rivalry and war. So that the Maya, like the other Mesoamericans and the Mesopotamians, developed an inter-state system very soon after the state itself.

The rapid growth of states and inter-state systems in Mesoamerica, then, conforms in most part with the pattern found in Mesopotamia. The association between scalar increase, increasing social and economic differ-entiation, the origins of literacy, and the emergence of states is striking. It is also remarkable that swiftly subsequent to the earliest evidence of the state, inter-state systems emerge in both cases.

Peru[62]

The origins of Andean state-formation (in what is now Peru) date from the first millennium AD. Once again a series of polities seem to have emerged broadly contemporaneously. These, of which the best known are the Mochica and Nasca, show evidence of urbanism, and of large-scale centralized organization and social and economic complexity which may well exceed that of the over-chiefdom. Although their organizational structure is unclear in detail, it may be that they can be classified as states.

This ambiguity over whether these polities were states is resolved in the case of their successors, the two larger political units of Huari and Tiahuanaco, which both emerged *circa* AD 600. These were almost certainly centralized, ranked, and probably bureaucratic societies with large urban centres and a high level of social and economic specialization. As such they may be classified as states without hesitation. Whichever of these examples we choose to see as the earliest Andean states, plainly they conform to the model proposed here. They also again illustrate the emergence of the state and inter-state system broadly contemporaneously.

The Indus Valley[63]

It is unclear whether the city-states which developed in the Indus Valley *c.* 2700 BC were independent of developments in Mesopotamia, and the societies which formed the context of this change were certainly in contact with those of Mesopotamia. However, they may be included here as an illustration of the same pattern of initial city-state formation.

Again, these were formed by the rapid growth of cities, of which the largest (Mohenjo-daro) perhaps had about 40,000 inhabitants. This shows some evidence of planning and crafts specialization; and inscriptions and administrative buildings indicate a literate bureaucracy, alongside very extensive social differentiation.

Again, we have an example of the rapid growth of urbanism, the state, increased 'complexity' in social organization and the economy alongside the rise of bureaucracy and literacy. However, in this case it seems likely that the relationship between pre-state Harappan (that is, Indus Valley) groups and Mesopotamia preclude this as an example of independent state-formation.

Egypt[64]

The first Egyptian state came into existence *c.* 3100–2700 BC, perhaps – but again not indubitably – independently of those founded in Mesopotamia. By the end of this period of formation the state was organized as a literate, bureaucratically administered, urban-based society with established political leadership and extensive social and economic differentiation. This 'Old Kingdom' state, then, closely conforms to the expectations of the model. However, it is again unclear whether it emerged independently of the states of Mesopotamia or as a consequence of interactions between complex non-state societies in Egypt and the Mesopotamian states.

China[65]

The earliest Chinese state probably dates from *c*. 1500 BC and was accompanied by the widespread use of literacy, the emergence of bureaucracy, the growth of urbanism, the rapid growth of population, and intensified social and economic complexity.

In this period China was still disunited, and the neighbouring kingdoms resulting from the transition to statehood competed for dominance. So, dynasties coexisted producing a distinctive inter-state system in East Asia formed within a common cultural zone.

Thus, like the other early states so far discussed, the growth of the Chinese state coincides with increased decision-making and information-processing capabilities. The Chinese system demonstrates, again, that these developments were both independent of each other and yet similar in processual terms. Again, several states emerged in the same area broadly simultaneously.

Sub-Saharan Africa[66]

It is, however, mistaken to assume that states never emerged in isolation or that the origin of the state was even approximately contemporary in all parts of the world. This point is clarified by examining sub-Saharan Africa state-formation.

Independent state-formation almost certainly occurred in sub-Saharan Africa, although it is often neglected when discussing the initial process of state-formation. However, not all of those polities conventionally referred to as 'states' by African historians can truly be accorded such a title by the criteria used here. Nor is it clear which instance of possible state-formation in this area is to be assigned chronological primacy.

Consequently, the African case has to be discussed rather than simply stated. The possible chronological and geographical range of options for the designation 'the earliest independently-founded state in sub-Saharan Africa' is extremely broad.

In the southern part of the area, some hold that state-formation first occurred in the Zimbabwe region during the Middle Ages. Not all scholars would agree that this political unit was in fact a state rather than a chiefdom, despite its magnificent urban centre at Great Zimbabwe. It is unclear whether the process of state-formation is represented in this area by the town at Mapungubwe, or whether this was the centre of an over-chiefdom. This defended settlement provides evidence of crafts specialization and social diversification accompanying clear suggestions of established leadership, but there is no suggestion of bureaucracy.

The shift from Mapungubwe to the site of Zimbabwe is much more likely to represent the transition to statehood, but even this remains problematical.[67] The main site shows indications of both social diversification and economic specialization, alongside increased population and long-distance trade, in the thirteenth and fourteenth centuries. The city was large, perhaps 18,000 people inhabited it, but there is no evidence for bureaucracy. Thus, the question remains as to whether Zimbabwe was a city-state, or an over-chiefdom analogous to those of later prehistoric and medieval Europe.

Zimbabwe was, however, not the only African polity to develop independently. In the fifteenth century the kingdoms of Kongo, Loango and Tio existed as a political system in central Africa. The kingdom of Kongo – comprising 250 square miles – was populous, with over 500,000 inhabitants. Political leadership was both 'simultaneous' and (although non-literate) bureaucratically organized, with a high degree of centralization apparent. While Kongo may be designated a state, the others of these political units were clearly chiefdoms, lacking the features defining the state. In this respect, despite the impressive ruins of Zimbabwe, Kongo was more certainly a state according to the criteria used here.

Elsewhere in central Africa state-formation did not occur at such an early date. The commonest pre-colonial form of political organisation was the chiefdom, as among the Luba. Even the south of sub-Saharan Africa, apart from Zimbabwe, is without other societies showing potential evidence of independent state-formation.

The north-west of Africa provided the setting for a much earlier groups of kingdoms, arguably state-societies, including Ghana and Gao. The exact dates and circumstances of the origins of these are sadly uncertain, although they are first recorded in the seventh century. Some of the West African kingdoms are probably classifiable as states, but the concept of statehood may have been introduced into this area by contact between West African chiefdoms and the Middle Eastern states. So, while these sub-Saharan African polities, notably Igbo-Ukwa, could have developed independently of Middle Eastern contacts, only then coming to trade with the Middle Eastern states, this is uncertain.[68] However, as their early history is currently under study, hopefully it will become clearer whether they – rather than Kongo – are the earliest independently-formed sub-Saharan African states.

This brief review of African evidence for initial state-formation demonstrates how difficult it is to recognize the first independently-formed sub-Saharan states. The state clearly emerged independently in sub-Saharan Africa, but when and where depends upon the degree of importance attached to hints of bureaucratization and the other attributes used to define the state as a political form.

In my view, therefore, the earliest *certainly* attested sub-Saharan state is Kongo, although the West African polities may well have been much earlier states independent of Mediterranean contacts. As such, while the state may originate in sub-Saharan Africa in isolation, it is still closely associated with sudden changes in the scale of political organization and the growth of new administrative procedures. Significantly, however, these were non-literate societies, showing convincingly that literacy is not a prerequisite for statehood.

Conclusion

This review shows that there are very strong grounds to interconnect changes in political form from chiefdoms to states with changes in scale and in information processing.[69] It suggests that both are associated with increased social and economic differentiation. The model proposed in the previous chapter can, then, explain the existence of the political forms so far examined and account for transitions between them. It is, of course, notable that the heterogeneity of individual trajectories of political history expected on the grounds of this model, and the importance attached to endogenous emergence of political forms, are both borne out by this study.

Interestingly, in every case we see state-formation occurring within a regional system of chiefdoms. New states become part of a new regional system composed either of chiefdoms and states or of states alone.

The existence of pre-existing cultural zones among the chiefdoms involved in state-formation is another common characteristic. This suggests that, from the outset, states must be considered in the context of transnational regional cultures rather than as isolated political entities devoid of cultural context.

Such observations, based on historical and archaeological data, obviously have direct relevance to many key questions of International Relations theory. They affect not only how we see the state, but how we conceptualize the relationship between the state, transnational cultures, and the inter-state system. This also enables us to consider the diachronic trajectories of these regional inter-state systems in the next chapter. By focusing on a sequential approach we will be able to ascertain, for example, if the cyclicality apparently associated with increasing complexity in Europe is evidenced in later systems in this area.

This chapter has served both to introduce the context of later 'international' regional state systems and the processes of change affecting them. It has also contributed to the validation of the model proposed here. It hardly need be said at this point that either economic or ecological approaches alone would be incapable of explaining so many aspects of these apparently contrasting political changes. The 'state', then, did not originate – at least in most cases – as an isolated polity, but as part of (and within) a 'regional system'. This is the first time that this has been recognized, let alone explained.

Notes

1   For an important recent anthropological discussion of this: Upham, S. (ed.), 1990, *The Evolution of Political Systems. Sociopolitics in Small-scale Sedentary Societies*, Cambridge.

2   On the danger of over-classifying these: Feinman, G. and Neitzel, J., 1985, 'Too many types: an overview of prestate societies in the Americas', *Advances in Archaeological Theory and Method* 7, 39–102.

3   Wenke, R. J., 1990, *Patterns in Prehistory*, 3rd edn, 282–3.

4   Begeler, E., 1978, 'Sex, status and authority in egalitarian society', *American Anthropologist* 80, 571–88; Price, T. D. and Feinman, G. M., 1995 (eds), *The Foundations of Social Inequality*, New York; Wright, H., 1984, 'Prestate political formations', in T. Earle (ed.), *On the Evolution of Complex Societies*, Malibu, 41–77. See also: Clark, J. E. and Parry, W. J., 1990, 'Craft specialization and cultural complexity', *Research in Economic Anthropology* 12, 289–346.

5   Lee, R. B., 1979, *The !Kung San*; Lee, R. B., 1984, *The Dobe !Kung*, New York; Barnard, A., 1983, 'Contemporary hunter-gatherers: current theoretical issues in ecology and social organization', *Annual Review of Anthropology* 12, 193–214; Leacock, E. and Lee, R. (eds), 1982, *Politics and History in Band Societies*; Kent, S. (ed.), 1996, *Cultural Diversity among Twentieth Century Foragers*.

6   Helm, J. (ed), 1968, *Essay on the Problem of the Tribe*, Washington, Seattle; although note that some alleged 'tribes' are the construct of modern anthropologists! On this, see: Vansina, J., 1990, *Paths in the Rainforest*, Madison, Wis., esp. 246–7.

7   Sillitoe, P., 1978, 'Bigmen and War in New Guinea', *Man* 13, 252–71; van Beskell, M. A. *et al.* (eds), 1986, *Approaches to 'Big Man' Systems*.

8   Davis, L. B. and Reeves, B. O. K. (eds) 1989, *Hunters of the Recent Past*; Lee, R. B. and De Vore, I. (eds), 1968, *Man the Hunter*, Chicago; Ingold, T., Riches, D. and Woodburn, J. (eds), 1991, *Hunters and Gatherers*.

9   Note its late survival in Europe also: Odner, K., 1992, *The Varanger Saami*, Oslo.

10 Gamble, C. 1993, *Timewalkers*.

11 This included inter-group warfare: Haas, J. (ed.), 1990, *The Anthropology of War*; Chagnon, N., 1988, 'Life histories, blood revenge and warfare in a tribal population', *Science* 239, 985–92; see also his 1965, *Yanomano, the Fierce People*, New York.

12 Johnson, A. W. and Earle, T., 1987, *The Evolution of Human Societies*, Stanford.

13 Fried, M. H., 1967, *The Evolution of Political Society*, New York.

14 Sahlins, M., 1963, 'Poor man, rich man, big man, chief: political types in Melanesia and Polynesia', *Comparative Studies in Society and History* 5, 285–303; Bakel, M. A., Hagesteijn, R. R. and van der Velde, P. (eds), 1986, *Private Politics: A Multidisciplinary Approach to 'Big Man' Systems*, Leiden.

15 Snow, D. R., 1996, *The Iroquois*.

16 Crawford, N. C., 1994, 'A security regime among democracies, cooperation among Iroquois nations', *International Organization* 48.3, 345–85; Bonhage-Freund, M. T. and Kurland, J. A., 1994, 'Tit-for-tat among the Iroquois: a game theoretic perspective on inter-tribal political organization', *Journal of Anthropological Archaeology* 13, 278–305; Jennings, F. (ed.), 1985, *The History and Culture of Iroquois Diplomacy*, Syracuse, NY; Richter, D. K. and Merrell, J. N., (eds), 1987, *The Iroquois and their Neighbours 1600–1800*, Syracuse, NY.

17 Redmond, E. M., 1994, *Tribal and Chiefly War in South America*, Michigan; Trigger, B. G. (ed.), 1978, *Handbook of North American Indians*, Washington, DC.

18 Royce, C. C., 1887, 'The Cherokee nation of Indians', in J. W. Powell (ed.), *Fifth Annual Report of the Bureau of Ethnology 1883–1884*, Washington.

19 Werner, D., 1981, 'Are some people more equal than others? Status inequality among the Mekranoti Indians of Central Brazil', *Journal of Anthropological Research* 37, 360–73.

20 Maybury-Lewis, D., 1974, *Akwe-Shavante Society*.

21 Ames, K., 1985, 'Hierarchies, stress and logistical strategies among hunter-gatherers in north western North America', in T. D. Price and J. A. Brown (eds), *Prehistoric Hunter-gatherers: The Emergence of Cultural Complexity*, Orlando, 155–80; Arnold, J. E., 1991, 'Transformation of a regional economy: sociopolitical evolution and the production of valuables in southern California', *Antiquity* 65, 953–62; Arnold, J. E. 1992, 'Complex hunter-gatherer-fishers of prehistoric California: chiefs, specialists and maritime adaptations of the Channel Islands', *American Antiquity* 57, 60–84; Mascher, H. D. G., 1991, 'The emergence of cultural complexity on the northern North-west Coast', *Antiquity* 65, 924–34; Yesner, D., 1980, 'Maritime hunter-gatherers: ecology and prehistory', *Current Anthropology* 21, 727–50; Hayden, B. and Gargett, R., 1990, 'Big man, big heart? A Mesoamerican view of the emergence of complex society', *Ancient Mesoamerica* 1, 3–20; Flanagan, J. G., 1989, 'Hierarchy in simple "egalitarian" societies', *Annual Review of Anthropology* 18, 245–66; Braun, D., 1990, 'Selection and evolution in non-hierarchical organization', in S. Upham (ed.), *The Evolution of Political Systems*, 62–86.

22 Ames, K. M., 1981, 'The evolution of social ranking on the northwest coast of North America', *American Antiquity* 46, 789–805; Matson, R. G. and Coupland, G., 1995, *Prehistory of the Northwest Coast*, New York.

23 Koyama, S. and Thomas, D. H. (eds), 1981, *Affluent Foragers*, Osaka; Keeley, L. H., 1988, 'Hunter-gatherer complexity and "population pressure": a cross-cultural analysis', *Journal of Anthropological Archaeology* 7, 373–411; Arnold, J. E., 1985, 'Economic specialization in prehistory: methods of documenting the age of lithic craft specialization', in S. C. Vetik (ed.), *Lithic Resource Procurement*, Carbondale, Ill., 37–58.

24 Arnold, J. E., 1985, 'Economic specialization in prehistory: methods of documenting the age of lithic craft specialization', in S. C. Vetik (ed.), *Lithic Resource Procurement*, Carbondale, Ill, 37–58.

25 *Ibid.*

26 Widmer, R. J., 1988, *The Evolution of the Calusa: Nonagricultural Chiefdom on the Southwest Coast of Florida*; Marquardt, W. H., 1988, 'Politics and production among the Calusa of south Florida', in T. Ingold, D. Riches and J. Woodburn (eds), *Hunters and Gatherers I: History, Evolution and Social Change*, 161–88; Quilter, J. 1991, 'Late Preceramic Peru', *Journal of World Prehistory* 5, 387–438.

27 Arnold, J. E., 1993, 'Labor and the Rise of Complex Hunter-Gatherers', *Journal of Anthropological Archaeology* 12, 75–119.

28 Ames, K. M., 1991, 'The archaeology of the *longue durée*: temporal and spatial scale in the evolution of social complexity on the southern Northwest Coast', *Antiquity* 65, 935–45; Ames, K., 1985, 'Hierarchies, stress and logistical strategies among hunter-gatherers in north western North America', in T. D. Price and J. A. Brown (eds), *Prehistoric Hunter-gatherers: The Emergence of Cultural Complexity*, Orlando, 155–80.

29 The whole issue is discussed by: Price, T. D. and Brown, J. A., (eds), 1985,

Prehistoric Hunter-Gatherers: The Emergence of Cultural Complexity, New York; Cohen, M. N., 1985, 'Prehistoric hunter-gatherers: the meaning of social complexity', in T. D. Price and J. A. Brown (eds), *Prehistoric Hunter-Gatherers: The Emergence of Cultural Complexity*, Orlando, 99–119.

30   So far as I am aware the only political scientists to have discussed chiefdoms are Yale Ferguson and Christopher Chase-Dunn.

31   Earle, T. K., 1987, 'Chiefdoms in archaeological and ethnological perspective', *Annual Review of Anthropology* 16, 279–308; Jones, G. D. and Kautz, R. R., 1981, *The Transition to Statehood in the New World*. See also: Gregg, S. A. (ed.), 1991, *Between Bands and States*, Carbondale, Ill.; Pauketat, T., 1994, *The Ascent of Chiefs: Cahokia and Mississippian Politics in North America*, Tuscalosa; Drennan, R. D. and Uribe, C. A. (eds), 1987, *Chiefdoms in the Americas*, Latham, Mass.; Drennan, R. D., 1987, 'Pre-Hispanic chiefdom trajectories in Mesoamerica, Central America, and northern South America', in R. D. Drennan and C. Uribe (eds), *Chiefdoms in the Americas*, Lanham, MD, 263–87.

32   Oberg, K., 1955, 'Types of social structure among the lowland tribes of south and central America', *American Anthropologist* 57, 472.

33   Service, E. R., 1975, *The Origins of the State and Civilization*, New York.

34   Thompson, E. A., 1948, *A History of Attila and the Huns*.

35   Drennan, R. D. and Uribe, C. A., (eds), 1987, *Chiefdoms in the Americas*, Latham, Mass.; Earle, T. (ed.), 1991, *Chiefdoms: Power, Economy and Ideology*, Cambridge.

36   Clark, J. E. and Parry, W. J., 1990, 'Craft specialization and cultural complexity', *Research in Economic Anthropology* 12, 289–346.

37   Renfrew, C. and Shennan, S. (eds), 1982, *Ranking, Resource and Exchange*, Cambridge.

38   For some further examples: Roosevelt, A. C., 1987, 'Chiefdoms in the Amazon and Oronoco', in R. D. Drennan and C. A. Uribe (eds), 1987, *Chiefdoms in the Americas*, Latham, Mass., 133–85; Redmond, E. M. and Spencer, C. S., 1994, 'Pre-Columbian chiefdoms', *National Geographic Research and Exploration* 10, 422–39; Spencer, C. S. and Redmond, E. M., 1992, 'Prehistoric chiefdoms of the western Venezuelan Llanos', *World Archaeology* 24, 134–57; Drennan, R. D., 1987, 'Pre-Hispanic chiefdom trajectories in Mesoamerica, Central America and northern South America', in R. D. Drennan and C. Uribe (eds), 1987, *Chiefdom in the Americas*, Latham, Mass., 263–87.

39   Carneiro, R. L., 1981, 'The chiefdom: precursor of the state', in G. D. Jones and R. R. Kautz, *The Transition to Statehood in the New World*, 37–79; Hodges, R., 1982, *Dark Age Economics*, chapter 10.

40   Hedeager, L., 1992, *Iron Age Societies*.

41   Dumville, D. N. *et al.*, 1993, *Saint Patrick* AD 493–1993; Croinin, D. O., 1995, *Early Medieval Ireland 400–1200*.

42   For the 'Early Christian period' literary convention that Ireland was divided into large provinces in prehistory: Rees, A. and Rees, B., 1961, *Celtic Heritage*, 120–1. For society in Ireland prior to the fifth century AD: O'Kelly, M. J., 1989, *Early Ireland*.

43   Kirch, P. V., 1989, *The Evolution of Polynesian Chiefdoms*; Sahlins, M. D., 1958,

Social Stratification in Polynesia, Seattle; Bellwood, P., 2nd. edn., *The Polynesians*.

44 Maylam, P., 1986, *A History of the African People of South Africa*, New York; Curtin, P. *et al.*, 1995, *African History*, 2nd edn, 269–73; Davenport, T. R. H., 1991, *South Africa: A Modern History*, 4th edn; Worden, N., 1994, *The Making of Modern South Africa*; Iliffe, J., 1995, *Africans*, 174–5.

45 Recently analysed in: Arnold, B. and Gibson, D. B. (eds), 1995, *Celtic Chiefdom, Celtic State*, Cambridge. See also: Gibson, D. and Geselowitz, M. N., 1988 (eds), *Tribe and Polity in Late Prehistoric Europe*, New York.

46 Todd, M., 1992, *The Early Germans*; Roymans, N., 1990, *Tribal Societies in Northern Gaul*, Amsterdam; Kristiansen, K. and Jensen, J., 1994, *Europe in the First Millennium* BC, Sheffield.

47 Patterson, N. T., 1995, 'Clans are not primordial: pre-Viking Irish society and the modelling of pre-Roman societies in northern Europe', in B. Arnold and D. B. Gibson (eds), *Celtic Chiefdom, Celtic State*, Cambridge, 129–36 (136).

48 Goffart, W., 1980, *Barbarians and Romans* AD *418–584*, Princeton, NJ, 33 and 231–4.

49 Haselgrove, C., 1995, 'Late Iron Age society in Britain and north-east Europe: structural transformation or superficial change?' in B. Arnold and D. B. Gibson (eds), *Celtic Chiefdom, Celtic State*, 81–7.

50 Kristiansen, K., 1991 'Chiefdoms, states and systems of social evolution', in T. Earle (ed.), *Chiefdoms: Power, Economy, and Ideology*, Cambridge, 16–43; Parker-Pearson, M., 1984, 'Economic and ideological change: cyclical growth in the pre-state societies of Jutland', in D. Miller and C. Tilley (eds), *Ideology, Power and Prehistory*, 69–92. Note also the suggestion of 'cyclical chiefdoms' in the first millennium AD in Europe, proposed by Hodges, R., 1982, *Dark Age Economics*, 187–8.

51 See also: Spencer, C. S., 1987, 'Rethinking the chiefdom', in R. D. Drennan and C. Uribe (eds), 1987, *Chiefdoms in the Americas*, Latham, Mass., 1–9.

52 Campbell, J. (ed.), 1982, *The Anglo-Saxons*; Hodges, R., 1989, *The Anglo-Saxon Achievement*; Yorke, B., 1990, *Kings and Kingdoms of Early Anglo-Saxon England*; Sawyer, P., 1978, *From Roman Britain to Norman England*.

53 Hodges, R., 1982, *Dark Age Economics*, 187.

54 Dodgshon, R. A., 1995, 'Modelling chiefdoms in the Scottish Highlands and islands prior to the '45', in B. Arnold and D. B. Gibson (eds), *Celtic Chiefdom, Celtic State*, 99–109; Dodgshon, R. A., 1981, *Land and Society in Early Scotland*; Houston, R. A. B. and Whyte, I. D. (eds), 1989, *Scottish Society 1500–1800*.

55 For important anthropological discussions: Haas, J., 1982, *The Evolution of the Prehistoric State*, New York; Carneiro, R. L., 1970, 'A theory of the origin of the state', *Science* 169, 733–8; Claessen, H. J. M. and Skalnik, P. (eds), 1978, *The Early State*, The Hague. For a recent archaeological discussion of this problem in general: Trigger, B., 1993, *Ancient Civilizations: Ancient Egypt in Context*, Cairo.

56 For instance: Torstendahl, R., 1992, *State Theory and State History*; Abrams, P., 1988, 'Notes on the difficulty of studying the state', *Journal of Historical Sociology* 1.1, 58–89; McCarnoy, M., 1984, *The State and Political Theory*, Princeton; Jessop, B., 1990, *State Theory*; Held, D., 1989, *Political Theory and*

the Modern State; Doorbros, M. and Kaviras, S. (eds), 1996, *Dynamics of State-Formation*.

57 Perhaps the classic anthropological definitions of the state are those by Service and Claessen: Claessen, H. J. M. and Skalnik, P., (eds), 197, *The Early State*, The Hague; Service, E., 1971, *Primitive Social Organisation: An Evolutionary Perspective*, 2nd edn, New York; Service, E. R., 1975, *Origins of the State and Civilization*, New York.

58 Hall, J. A., 1985, *Powers and Liberties*.

59 Gledhill, J., 1995, 'Introduction: the comparative analysis of social and political transitions', in J. Gledhill, B. Bender and M. T. Larsen, *State and Society*, 1–29.

60 Postgate, N., 1994, *Early Mesopotamia*; Blanton, R. E. *et al.* 1993, *Ancient Mesopotamia*, 2nd edn; Maisels, C. K., 1990, *The Emergence of Civilization*; Stein, G. and Rothman, *The Organizational Dynamics of Complexity*, Madison, Wis.; Oates, J., 1996, 'A prehistoric communication revolution' *Cambridge Archaeological Journal* 6.1, 165–76.

61 Sharer, R. J., 1994, *The Ancient Maya*; Coe, M. D., 1993, *Breaking the Maya Code*; Culbert, T. P., (ed.), 1991, *Classic Maya Political History: Hieroglyphic and Archaeological Evidence*; Kowalewski, S. A., 1990, 'The evolution of complexity in the valley of Oaxaca', *Annual Review of Anthropology* 19, 39–58; Adams, R. E. W., 1996, *Prehistoric Mesoamerica*, 2nd edn, Oklahoma; Fowler, W. R. (ed.), 1991, *The Formation of Complex Society in Southwest Mesoamerica*, Boca Raton, Fla.

62 Haas, J., Pozorski, S. and Pozorski, T. (eds), 1987, *The Origins and Development of the Andean State*; Keatinge, R. W., 1988, *Peruvian Prehistory*.

63 Allchin, R. and Allchin, B., 1982, *The Rise of Civilization in India and Pakistan*; Possehl, G. L. (ed), 1993, *Harrapan Civilization*.

64 Kemp, B., 1991, *Ancient Egypt*; Adams, W. Y., 1984, 'The first colonial empire: Egypt in Nubia 3200–1200 BC', *Comparative Studies in Society and History* 26.1, 36–71; Bard, K. A., 1994, *From Farmers to Pharaohs*; Trigger, B. G., Kemp, B. J., O'Connor, D. and Lloyd, A. B., 1983, *Ancient Egypt: A Social History*; Spencer, A. J., 1993, *Early Egypt: The Rise of Civilisation in the Nile Valley*; Knapp, A. B., 1988, *The History and Culture of Ancient Western Asia and Egypt*, Chicago.

65 Rawson, J. (ed.), 1997, *Mysteries of Ancient China*, provides an authoritative account of Chinese state-formation. See also: Fairbank, J. K., 1992, *China: A New History*, Cambridge, Mass., chapters 1 and 2; Keightley, D. N., 1983, *The Origins of Chinese Civilization*, Berkeley, Calif.; Chang, K. C., 1977, *The Archaeology of Ancient China*, 3rd edn, New Haven, Conn.; Barnes, G. L., 1993, *China, Korea and Japan*.

66 Eisenstadt, S. N., Abitbol, M. and Chazan, N. (eds), 1988, *The Early State in African Perspective*, Leiden; Phillipson, D. W., 1993, *African Archaeology*, 2nd edn; Connah, G., 1987, *African Civilization*; Mokhtar, G. (ed.), 1981, *General History of Africa. Vol. II: Ancient Civilizations*, Paris; Shinnie, M., 1965, *Ancient African Kingdoms*.

67 Garlake, P. S., 1973, *Great Zimbabwe*; Garlake, P. S., 1976, 'Great Zimbabwe: a reappraisal', *Proceedings of the African Congress of Prehistory and Quaternary Studies*, Addis Ababa, 221–6. See also Juma, A. M., 1996, 'The Swahili and the

Mediterranean worlds: pottery of the late Roman period in Zanzibar', *Antiquity* 70, 148–54.

68   Ajayi, J. F. A. and Crowder, M. (eds), 1972, *A History of West Africa*, New York.

69   A recent, acclaimed, study has demonstrated that literacy originated in the context of state record-keeping: Postgate, N., Wang, T. and Wilkinson, T., 1995, 'The evidence for early writing: utilitarian or ceremonial?' *Antiquity* 69, 459–80.

6

Cyclical states: the long-term dynamics of socio-political systems in the age of the state

Introduction

The formation of states and inter-state systems introduced a fundamental change into global political organization. But this did not equally affect all peoples at all times since the foundation of the earliest state. Hunter-gatherer bands and tribes coexisted with chiefdoms before the state-formation, and they both continued to coexist with states for millennia.

In the period in which states have been the largest polities, referred to here as 'the age of the state', regional systems have consequently been (in part) inter-state systems. These 'regional state systems' are easily observed in world history, and – at simplest – can be seen to be organized in two ways: as a system of independent states, or as an imperial systems. The empire is unusual as a form of political organization, in that it is both a 'state' and composed of a relationship between states or other polities, which have become politically controlled by one of their number. This seldom, if ever, forms the entirety of such a system but may comprise its principal state actor.

The empire, in the 'age of the state', may be seen as having an analogous relationship to the independent state found in other inter-state systems, as has the over-chiefdom to the chiefdom. In each case, the larger polity is composed of a system of smaller polities, in which one (usually the largest) of these controls the others so as to comprise a far larger political unit. In this sense, empires are 'over-states'!

By using historical and archaeological materials it is possible to reconstruct outline histories of all known states and empires. Thus, the history of regional systems in 'the age of the state' can be traced from its origins to the present.

Analysing regional state systems

In the same way as analysis of the political unit may proceed from its constituent parts, it is logical to analyse the internal organization of these two types of regional state system by beginning with their components. These include states themselves and other intra-state and transnational actors. But regional state systems also comprise other constituents, such as cultures, religions and languages. Consequently regional state systems are never simply groups of states in a specific region. They also comprise a range of other constituting units and structures, and a network of relationships between these.

Some of these are constrained by the geopolitics of statehood, so that they occur only within the borders of specific states. Intra-state components of this sort include economic organizations, institutions, customs and languages. Others have a transnational character, such as social movements and religions. These exist alongside – and interwoven with – inter-state relationships.

Such transnational factors can play no less a role in constituting relationships between individuals and non-state organizations than in shaping inter-state interactions. Non-state organizations, such as firms, can also enact networks of linkages which transcend the borders of political units, yet which help to constitute the set of relationships forming the regional system.

So, each regional state system, although it is (in part) an inter-state system or empire is also made up of a much more complex set of relationships. It is always a multi-actor and multi-scalar system operating within a context of religious, cultural, economic and other factors, which may help both to constitute and to constrain it. Regional state systems are, therefore, neither state-centric, nor simply economic 'world-systems'.

Nor are they static entities; they are by definition constantly shifting networks of relationships. By this, I do not mean that regional state systems have no discernible geopolitical or historical unity, only that they are constantly changing.

Such systems may exhibit forms of 'self-organization' by internal dynamical processes or based on structural characteristics. The former are those organizational properties of such regional systems which arise as a result of endogenous systemic processes. As we have also seen, these processes, founded in human interaction, operate in a multi-scalar fashion, so that they exist on an intra-state and inter-state level, as well as transnationally. They pervade the dynamics of all regional systems, whether based on states or not, at all times.

So, regional state systems can be analysed both in part and as unified wholes. But they are only such unified entities as an outcome of their complex and ever-changing multi-actor and multi-structural relationships. These relationships run through every level and linkage from the individual to the regional system in general.

This, therefore, presents a paradox going beyond the dichotomy of holism and atomism.[1] It is one which is not readily encompassed by simply focusing on 'the state' as a unit of analysis. Nor can it be resolved by focusing

on economic networks as the sole basis of defining inter-state and transnational relationships.

Historically, regional state systems were geographically constrained due
to time, geographical and technological limitations. For this reason regional
state systems, prior to the rise of global empires, comprised distinctive
geographical zones of socio-political activity. Within these regional state
systems, as we have already seen, there might be sub-regions definable on
cultural, religious, societal or economic, grounds, or in relation to specifics
of their political history or organization. These were not distinct 'regional
systems' where networks of regular contact were limited by technology or
time:geography, but rather sub-divisions within such regional systems.

If the regional state system is potentially unstable and capable of exhibiting
cyclical growth and decline, then approaches which assume systemic
stability among states in international politics are fundamentally flawed.
Likewise, attempts to build future regional systems based on an assumption
of inter-state stability may be called into question. So, even at this point, it
is clear that if the model proposed in chapter 4 is correct, the implications for
the dynamics of contemporary world politics and the theory of International
Relations are wide-ranging.

Cyclicality and regional state systems

This chapter presents an investigation of the trajectories of such regional
state systems. This gives an opportunity both to evaluate the model proposed and to apply it to a database relating to the history of world politics
after the establishment of states and inter-state systems. In chapter 5 we saw
that the model very adequately explains the trajectories and socio-political
units already discussed. It can also account for the origins of the state and
inter-state system. It can therefore explain how the 'age of states' came about
in the first place, rather than simply take it as a 'given'. Here the model will
be used to investigate the development of regional state systems, with special
reference to the possibility of cyclicality raised in chapter 4.

A few issues regarding the character of the proposed cyclicality need,
perhaps, to be clarified. First, it was suggested that complex socio-political
systems could, but need not, exhibit cyclical patterns of growth and decline.
However, this process of cyclical growth and collapse is non-deterministic:
it is merely one possible resolution of the scalar dynamic observed, which
could also produce non-cyclical growth and decline. Like shifts to larger-
scale political units, cyclicality is merely a possible consequence of the
increased scale of the system, not an inevitable and universal property of all
socio-political systems. Unlike such scalar shifts, cyclicality is an unintended
rather than consciously-chosen option, resulting from the processual properties of the systems involved. Here we may see morphogenetic processes
overriding the role of agency, and path-dependency producing trajectory.

If it is present at all, cyclicality in the growth and decline of states or regional systems is clearly of special note to scholars of International Relations. This raises the question of how we may recognize cyclicality, and how we may validate other aspects of this model in relation to regional state systems.

Recognizing cyclical regularities

To recognize a cyclical pattern in regional state systems, one must identify repetitive phases of near-equal length in the growth and decline of complexity in these systems. These would be expected to be specific to individual trajectories, not universally shared between them. They would not be expected to be closely connected with absolute population numbers or absolute geopolitical extent.[2]

The apparent problem, that socio-political complexity cannot be reduced to quantifiable variables, such as geopolitical extent of population numbers, is illusory for the methodology adopted here. The lack of 'measures' presents no problems for a historically based methodology. If methodologies of testing are based on historiographical rather than mathematical principles, and a perspectivist paradigm of validation, then 'quantifiability' is not the crucial criterion for verifiability. Nor can problems of the selectivity of writing such an account present serious theoretical problems: all historical and political science accounts unavoidably 'select' information. If one did not select information in this way one would be required to encompass all possible data, which in this case would mean the whole of world history! Likewise, to argue against 'selectivity' in historical writing and political science implies that only a total knowledge of a situation (which is not humanly possible) is required in order to render an interpretation credible. In practice, no scholar does this.

The consequence of this, of course, is that the fact that the resulting pattern is 'an interpretation' does not mean that it has not been observed in a rigorous fashion. International Relations scholars employ historical interpretations to support the majority of their theories and hypotheses. In fact, most International Relations theory itself is usually debated in terms of closeness of fit to historical interpretations, although these may be so widely credited as to be assumed as fact by political scientists.

Likewise, historians and anthropologists have long recognized widely credited patterns identified in this way without recourse to numerical methods. Such patterns may lack formal mathematical 'proof', but as we have already seen, formally 'proving' any hypothesis in this way may be much more problematical than simply showing that it is probably true! Here I shall opt for the 'probable truth' of history against the 'absolute' positivistic proof of mathematics.

Causally relating historical changes in the rise and decline of regional state systems to the model is possible due to several properties which all such systems possess. For instance, one can examine the constituent polities within a regional system. As the regional state system is partly composed of states, then success or failure in inter-state competition suggests that a pre-eminent state will often be visible in any inter-state system, as Modelski and others have noted.

By this, I do not mean to imply that such competition is universal. The expansionist dynamic of socio-political complexity suggests that this is likely, however, to be a widespread response to conflicting expansionist ambitions. In this respect, Realist theory may find some support, in that inter-state competition may be a widespread characteristic of regional state systems. Where a fundamental difference lies is that here inter-state com-petition is seen as a variable generalization, not a universal law. The rise and decline of historically-specific forms of these regional state systems can, therefore, be traced, in part, by charting the rise and decline of such leading states when they are identifiable.

However, by far the most useful way to chart changes in the complexity of regional state systems is simply by recognizing that those characteristics which make them distinctive as periods in history – their socio-political institutions or structures – can be seen to emerge over time, reach a period of greatest complexity and then decline, in an entirely 'historical' way. Thus, one can (without recourse to attempts at quantification) recognize the growth and decline of socio-political complexity.

These characteristics combine, therefore, to show that phases in regional state systems may be broadly definable as what historians (and others) would refer to as 'periods' of regional history, as was noted in chapter 4. Con-sequently, comparison with the periodization of regional systemic histories will render a straightforward test of this model, as well as give an opportunity for its application to an extensively-studied database.

Defining the regional system in geographical terms

This brings us to the question of how to identify the spatial limits of regional state systems. In chapter 4, we saw that these can be defined in relation to shared structures and patterns of contact. Here, the latter will be used as a simple way of differentiating between systems.

We have already seen that the earliest states emerged independently in sub-Saharan Africa, the Americas, the Middle East, China, and perhaps also elsewhere in Asia and Africa. In every certain case there seems strong grounds for the argument that initial state-formation produced an inter-state system almost from the first. This enabled a regional state system to develop, although it was regional chiefly systems which gave rise to the state, not the state which initiated these regional systems.

As we have seen, technology and time–geography limited regular contact between these systems for most of their histories. It is, therefore, logical to use this geographical separation to divide these systems as analytically distinct. The validity of this approach is, of course, reinforced by the physical separation of the Middle East, Americas, East Asia and sub-Saharan Africa from each other in terms of regular sustained political contacts during much of human history.

However, regional state systems can be defined more closely if we combine such limitations on regular contact with the requirement that a regional state system should have distinctive structures. By combining these two features – the limitation of regular contact and the existence of distinctive structures – one arrives at five regional state systems which existed prior to the 'expansion of Europe' in the fifteenth century AD. Each of these derives from one certainly independent case of initial state-formation. That deriving from the earliest state-formation, in Mesopotamia, I shall refer to as the 'Old World' system; that deriving from state-formation in China, I shall call the Chinese system; state-formation in sub-Saharan Africa gave rise to a sub-Saharan regional state system. In the Americas two distinct regional state systems – the Mesoamerican and South American – can be recognized. The two other areas in which possibly independent state-formation occurred (the Indus Valley and Egypt) are included here in the Old World system, with which they were rapidly in contact. Of these regional state systems, all but the Old World and Chinese systems are easily differentiated by the absence of contact, and structural differences contrast these latter systems.

In discussing the development of regional state systems it seems logical to examine the subsequent trajectories of these distinct systems. However, one further system – the significance of which to the long-term development of world politics is obvious – has also a claim to special attention: that of western Europe. This is not an independent regional system in the sense that this term is used here. It did not originate independently to these other developments: it was a secondary consequence of the Middle Eastern trajectory and remained closely linked to it. Rather, it is a 'sub-regional system' in the sense which has already been discussed.

One might define another 'sub-regional system' linked to that of the Middle East and western Europe: the eastern European and Eurasian system. In both this area and western Europe the origins of the regional state system ultimately derive from that of the Middle East. Although these sub-regions have also had to some extent distinctive histories, together they form an 'Old World' regional state system with a single origin.

There is a strong case for *analytically* exploiting this sub-regionality to test the model presented here. If regional state systems share common processes and trajectories, then one should see not only like processes, but the same trajectory, in each of these cases.

So, western Europe will form our first and – for reasons which will become clear – most detailed case-study. Then, this sub-region will be compared with another sub-region of the same regional system: the Middle East. This will permit the type of comparison referred to above. Then, to contrast with the 'Old World' regional trajectory, three other regions

(China, sub-Saharan Africa and Mesoamerica) will be discussed in turn. This is not to imply that no other regional state systems, or even analytically divisible 'sub-regional' systems, are visible in world history. Simply, these will serve as examples of the whole.

Although sub-regions have, by their very nature, somewhat shifting (and often only vaguely defined) limits, both western Europe and the Middle East are widely referred to as distinct 'regions' by political scientists, historians and geographers. Thus, this division need not present any serious definitional problems here. However, it is worth noting that for historical reasons, which will also become clear, I include the continent of Europe east of the Adriatic and south of the Danube in the 'Middle East'.

Obviously, in any such review of millennia of political history, the histories provided here are merely outlines of the principal changes. However, in terms of both processes and events, they will enable us to relate the trajectories discussed to the model. Consequently, there is, of course, a wealth of more detailed data which one might use to elaborate the brief descriptions given here, but space does not permit such a discussion.

Western Europe

The western European sub-regional state system was late established. The earliest states in the north-western Mediterranean, and the earliest, therefore, in the western part of this region, are those of pre-Roman Italy.[3] The first of these was the Etruscan state of the eighth century BC, which was historically the most important polity in northern Italy until its suppression by Rome in 510 BC.[4] In the south of Italy and on the southern coast of western Europe elsewhere, city-states were established by Greek colonists, but these did not prompt local urbanization or state-formation.[5]

Rome itself rose from a city-state to being dominant in Italy between the eighth and sixth centuries BC.[6] By the third century BC it was the leading polity in Italy. Following its leadership of the other Italian states in the first Punic War (264–241 BC) this position was strongly established, and the next century provided Rome with its first western provinces, in Sicily, Spain, and the Balearic islands.[7] After the defeat of Carthage in the second Punic War (146 BC) a large area of north west Africa was also added to the Roman state.[8]

This pattern of conquest and political expansion led Rome to acquire new eastern provinces during the second century BC. In 120 BC, or earlier, the southern coastal area of Gaul (what is today France) was added to the Roman Republican empire.[9] The conquest of Gaul was achieved in the last half of the first century BC.[10]

The establishment of the state in most of western Europe, outside Italy, was, therefore, the result of the expansion of the Roman state to form the Roman Empire. So, it is at this point that the start of the western European 'sub-regional' trajectory may be identified. The last two centuries BC, therefore, saw the establishment of the Roman state as dominant in most of western Europe south of the Rhine, and in much of the eastern Mediterranean and north Africa. It is only at this point, therefore, that we may begin to identify a distinctively western European trajectory which can be examined in more detail, albeit of course still in briefest outline, given the purpose of this account.

The origins of the western European sub-regional system

The first millennium opened with two defining events, the Birth of Christ and the accession of the first Roman emperor (Augustus). While the first was soon to affect the whole of the Old World, the arrival of the Roman state into western European politics occurred immediately after the Augustan period. Augustus died in AD 14, and by AD 100 a pan-European political framework was established for the first time.[11] In this framework, political change throughout Europe and beyond – from Ireland to Mesopotamia and from Scandinavia to the Sahara – was linked by the dominance of the Roman state and of its economic and diplomatic contacts.[12] This survived until the year AD 410, when Rome, and effective rule of western Europe, passed to barbarian kings, who established a different political order.[13] Their system, comprising both states and chiefdoms, was almost equally extensive. For example, Frankish contacts demonstrably extended from Ireland to Scandinavia and to Constantinople (modern Istanbul) in the east.[14]

Thus, at both its start and end the Roman Empire can be seen as the origin of a distinctive 'Old World' regional state system, unifying western Europe and the Middle East. That this was succeeded by another raises the question of possible cyclicality.

The Roman empire lasted almost exactly 400 (396) years. If we use this to provide a chronology for a possible wave in this regional system as might be anticipated in the proposed model, then there 'should' be a sequence of overlapping 'waves' of growth and decline originating at *c.* 400 and *c.* 200 respectively.

These provide us with a series of points at which to evaluate the relationship between the expectations of the model and well-attested historical trajectory: the start, middle and end of each wave. I shall call these points 'test points' without the presumption that the 'test' in each case is an absolute one.

One remaining question is how to correlate with the historical sequence the rise and decline of structures and actors associated with specific systems. This arises because the test points chosen will be expressed as dates, whereas what are being sought are processes. Consequently, the expression of test points as dates must be taken as indicative of where to seek events expressing these processes, rather than precise points to correlate exactly with specific events. The essential forms which change might take are: 'rise' (an increase in complexity), 'decline' (a decrease in complexity) or, when complexity has reached its highest level in a trajectory, 'apex'.

As processes, not events, are being sought in this analysis, exact correlation with these test points is less significant than similarity between the processual expectations produced by the model and the historical sequence. Nevertheless, potentially indicative events will be included as a guide to processes, but the exact selection of specific events is less important to the argument than that they illustrate process. It must be remembered that processually-identical trajectories might include dissimilar events, so like events cannot be expected in different trajectories. In order to examine the validity of this model in relation to the western European trajectory, as this originated in the Roman period, it is with the Roman Empire that we must begin.

The Roman Empire[15]

The test points for the period 0 to AD 400 are at AD 100, where we would expect a rapid rise of the Roman system, AD 200, at which time we would expect it to be at its apex, and for a successor system to begin slowly to emerge. At AD 300, we would expect the decline of the early Roman system to be acute, but the rise of the successor system to become more rapid. By AD 400, which is not admissible as a test point for the early Roman system as it was used to form the chronology, we would expect the successor system to be at its apex. In the historical sequence, we find that these points do correlate with periods of observed historical processes. The rapid growth of the Empire *circa* AD 100 is attested by two observations: first, that the Empire reached what were to be its outer borders by 117, and began to consolidate its hold on Britain and Gaul at around this time. Mommsen observed that the years following AD 100 (the Antonine period) represented the height of Roman imperial grandeur. This period came to both a climax and an end in 193, when the Empire embarked upon the increasingly severe crisis of the third century. This point of apex followed by systemic collapse closely coincides with the expectations produced by the model. At AD 300, we see the rapid rise of a successor system. This is usually attributed to the changes in Imperial structure, policy, security and economics under Diocletian and Constantine the Great, between 284 and 337. Perhaps the first such transformative change in the structure of the Empire was, however, the universal freedom and citizenship granted to free-born natives of the Empire by Caracalla in AD 212.

In the fourth century, Late Roman socio-political structures continued to emerge. This period arguably reached its height at the end of the fourth century in the reign of Theodosius I, the last ruler of an undivided Roman Empire. The Theodosian phase of imperial success was short-lived, as collapse in the West followed in the early fifth century: in AD 410 Rome itself fell.

So, although we are unable to use AD 400 as a test point for the end of the Roman Empire, it is interesting that it was also the apex of the new system emerging around AD 200 and becoming dominant about AD 300. Consequently, although history (like our model) does not permit the exact precision of dates when one is discussing broad processes of change, it is possible to point to a close correlation between these phases of fundamental transformation and the expectations produced by this model.

Late Antiquity[16]

The successor system has been characterized by historians as the Late Antique period. The Late Antique period was characterized by the existence of a sub-Roman system and social, economic and cultural structures. 'Sub-Roman' in this context means derived from, and continuous to, those of the Late Roman world. The dominant sub-Roman or Late Antique state, both in Europe and the Middle East, was the Byzantine Empire. This was, as contemporaries recognized, merely the surviving, eastern, part of the Roman Empire. In Europe, this state formed merely part of a wider multi-state network, having a hegemonic role among its component states and chiefdoms. Because of this, in this period the Western system was very closely tied to the trajectory of the Byzantine state.

We have already seen that the historical sequence correlates well with the expected changes at AD 200, 300 and 400. The 'Late Antique' system emerged after about AD 200, with a rapid rise around AD 300, and its apex was *circa* AD 400. We would also expect the system to be in rapid decline after about AD 500, and to collapse circa AD 600. This is, again, what we find.

The early Byzantine state began to decline after the reigns of Anastasius and Justin I, perhaps especially during the reign of Justinian I, AD 527 to 565. Severe decline did indeed occur around AD 600: between 613 and the 640s first Persian, and then Arab, attacks ended Byzantine rule throughout most of the Middle East. All of these changes impacted upon the system. However, it was the collapse of Byzantine intervention in the West during the last decades of the sixth century which brought about an end to the period of Byzantine hegemony. At the same time, the newly independent Western kingdoms asserted themselves and their culture in what has been called the 'seventh-century transformation' which brought the period to an end. Scholars from Pirenne onwards have seen this as a fundamental period of change, separating the world of Antiquity from that of the Middle Ages.

Plainly these processes closely coincide with the expectations of the model. So too does their relationship, in both chronological and political terms, with the partly contemporary emergence and decline of the barbarian successor states of western Europe.

The barbarian kingdoms[17]

This encompasses the 'Migration Period' system of 'barbarian' (that is, non-Roman) kingdoms. It is a period sometimes described as the 'Dark Ages' of Europe. The barbarians, migrating into what had been the Western Roman Empire, were chiefdom societies with a Germanic Iron Age culture. However, their élites swiftly took control of the apparatus of Roman bureaucratic government throughout most of Europe. The polities which these élites ruled then rapidly developed the attributes of states, although retaining kingship as an institution.

The kingdoms which formed in western Europe were, therefore, state-societies built from within the administrative ruins of the Roman Empire. They were united by sharing common social, cultural and economic structures deriving from a synthesis of both their 'barbarian' and Roman backgrounds.

In the fifth century, western Europe contained many kingdoms, among which the Goths and Franks were the dominant groups. The Goths were divided into two competing kingdoms: those of the Ostrogoths in Italy and the Visigoths in Spain. The Merovingian dynasty which ruled the Franks gained control of what is today France. After the end of Ostrogothic rule in Italy, the Frankish kingdom became the dominant 'barbarian' state in the Late Antique western Europe. Following the collapse of the Byzantine invasion of the West *circa* AD 570, the Franks were unchallenged as the political and military leaders of western Europe.

On the basis of the model alone, one would expect that the new system would emerge around AD 400. It would be expected to show rapid growth, in contrast to the steep decline of the Late Antique system, *circa* AD 500. Then rapid development would be expected, rising to an apex at about AD 600.

This is exactly what we see in the historical record. The Ostrogothic kingdom of Italy was founded as soon as Alaric seized Rome. The kingdoms of the Franks and Visigoths became established during the course of the fifth century, so that both were in existence by AD 500. The sixth century was characterized by the consolidation of these kingdoms, while the collapse of Byzantine intervention in the West (following the Lombardic invasion of 568) led to the consolidation of Frankish hegemony.

Interestingly, this relationship can be clearly documented by a Frankish official source. For around 40 years in the late sixth and early seventh century, the Frankish kings struck coins in the names of Byzantine emperors. However, from the reign of Chlothar II (584–628) Frankish coins bore only the names of Frankish rulers. They no longer needed to legitimate their currency by reference to the Byzantine empire.

The early Middle Ages[18]

As we have seen, there is wide historical agreement that a new medieval system began to emerge during the seventh century. The regional system which emerged between the seventh and twelfth centuries, therefore, included states developed from the barbarian kingdoms of the period AD 400–800. Major structural changes had, however, transformed both their internal socio-political and economic organization and their external relations.

These new states began, from the seventh century onwards, to develop market economies and inter-state regularized exchange. Integration into a complex network of dynastic and diplomatic contacts throughout Europe consolidated the new regional system. During the period, the geographical size of the constituent states generally grew, and the resources at the disposal of new, larger and more centralized administrations increased. Of these states, by far the most politically important in Europe was still the Frankish kingdom, which came to establish an empire of its own in western Europe.

The expected points of change are at AD 600, for the emergence of the system, 700, for its rapid rise, 800, its apex, and 900, for its rapid decline. We have already seen that the system did, in fact, emerge around AD 600. To judge from the chronology of the rapid development of those characteristics (market economy, etc.) distinguishing this from the preceding system, c. AD 700 did mark the start of an intensification of its growth.

The Frankish kingdom was dramatically changed in the two generations following Charles Martel's victory over the Arabs in 732 and the subsequent replacement of the Merovingian by the Carolingian dynasty. These changes reached a climax in the reign of Charlemagne, in 768–814. Charlemagne established a Frankish empire, dominating western Europe in both political and military terms. It is usually said that this phase of Frankish history reached its height when Charlemagne was crowned as a new western 'Roman' emperor at Rome on Christmas Day, AD 800.

There is obviously a remarkably close chronological correlation between the rise of the Frankish empire and the expectations of change based on the model alone. However, for our purposes, it is not the correlation between the expected apex at c. 800 and the coronation of Charlemagne which is of especial interest. More significant still is that the growth of this system to its apex is, according to most historians, exactly as we might expect on the grounds of the model.

Charlemagne's empire collapsed very rapidly, although Frankish kings long maintained an important role in European politics. By the 880s it was irrevocably split, the eastern area – which we now call Germany – coming permanently under the rule of dynasties in competition with that of the Franks. So the expectation of rapid decline at about AD 900 is also met by this historical sequence.

The Viking Age[19]

The brief period of Carolingian empire was followed by immediate challenge due to the emergence of the Vikings on the European stage. The

Vikings were raiders and settlers from among the 'Iron Age' peoples of Scandinavia. They had for centuries existed within the western European network of regional interactions. For example, it is now clear that Scandinavian interactions with the Anglo-Saxons and Franks began in the sixth century or earlier.

Consequently, while representing an external foe for many European polities, the Vikings can be seen to transform the system from within. This occurred in two main ways: by gaining political and military dominance over parts of the territory of existing states, and by prompting their internal reorganization in the face of the 'Viking threat'. So structural transformation accompanied these political changes, both within and outside those areas controlled by the Vikings. Thus, historians usually characterize the period of Viking activity as a 'Viking Age' around the North Sea and beyond, even where there were no Viking kingdoms.

The expected points of change in this period are the emergence of the system at *circa* AD 800, its rapid rise to after 900, an apex at about 1000, and rapid decline after 1100. The fit between these expectations and the historical sequence is, once again, very close.

The first recorded Viking raid is that on the monastery of Lindisfarne in 793. The ninth century saw a constant pattern of Viking activity, with the settlement of Normandy beginning in 911, and that of Iceland between the 870s and 930s. These changes were paralleled by responses from existing western European kingdoms. So, for example, it was in the late ninth century also that King Alfred the Great was reorganizing southern England to resist Viking aggression. That is, both inside and outside of territories under Viking rule, a new 'Viking Age' system was clearly being formed at these times. This included new actors, structures, and polities.

In the reign of Cnut (1016–35) a formal Scandinavian (Viking) empire was established, bringing the North Sea area under a single ruler. But this empire was shortlived, and despite successes by the Normans (a Viking kingdom in origin) throughout the eleventh century, by 1100 the Viking Age was beginning to come to an end. In 1085 a final attempt at Viking conquest of Britain failed, and the last major Norman gain was the conquest of Sicily in 1091. In Scandinavia the Viking Age lasted perhaps another century, and the conventional end for this period, there, is usually set at *c.* 1200.

The medieval feudal system[20]

In most of Europe the last traces of the Viking Age system were fading in the twelfth century. By 1200 they had been replaced by the feudal order, even in Scandinavia. The following period of European history is characterized by the development of the states originating in the seventh-century transformation to form large feudal kingdoms ruled by relatively stable monarchies. These acknowledged a theoretical allegiance to the concept of the unity of Christendom. The feudal mode of social and economic organization distinguishes this period, often simply known as the 'Middle Ages'. To many today it forms the archetype for perceptions of medieval life, although some scholars (especially historians) use the term 'Middle Ages' for earlier periods also.

On the basis of the model, we would expect this system to begin *circa* 1000, rising rapidly after 1100 to an apex about 1200 and rapid collapse after 1300. The start of the Middle Ages is, as already mentioned, a matter over which historians have not reached a consensus. However, the beginning of this period (whether we designate it the Middle Ages, or the Late Medieval Period) is usually put in the eleventh century. As we have seen, the end of the Viking period can be identified as beginning with the end of Cnut's rule in 1035. Others, such as Brooke, have seen the end of the tenth century – that is to say, from 962 onwards (and especially the rule of Otto, 962–73) – as marking the emergence of a new phase in medieval history. The early eleventh century certainly marked a change in the geographical scope of the sub-regional system, with the collapse of Moslem control in Spain from 1002 onwards. So it would be relatively uncontroversial to begin this period *circa* AD 1000.

The rapid rise of the new system at about 1100 is evidenced by the extension of feudalism into eastern Europe at this time. The proclamation of the First Crusade in 1095 and the subsequent capture of Jerusalem by the Crusaders in 1099 also gave the feudal system a new extent. Feudal 'Europe' thereafter stretched from Anglo-Norman Ireland (the Norman invasion was in 1086) to Russia and the borders of the Arab world.

This system can be seen to have reached its height in the reigns of Louis IX of France and Frederick II of Germany. The extent of the system also reached its furthest limits during this period, following the sack of Constantinople in 1204. This set up the medieval feudal lords of the 'Latin Empire' as rulers of the Aegean and of most of what had been the Byzantine empire in 1200. There is, therefore, again a close agreement between the well established sequence of European history and the expectations produced by this model. An expected rapid decline *c.* 1300 is also attested by the collapse of European feudalism in the eastern Mediterranean, ending with the loss of the last Crusader kingdom in 1291.

In Europe itself, the feudal order was already declining before the Black Death of the 1340s, which further exacerbated the decline. It was shaken by the displacement of the Pope by the French kings in 1309, and Papal authority was disputed by European rulers throughout the century, in the Great Schism. This, lasting until 1417, may be seen as clearly constituting systemic decline from the period of relatively stable relations within Europe since 1000. By 1356, Emperor Charles IV had effectively disestablished the German empire beyond his own realms. In 1337 England and France embarked upon the Hundred Years War. AD 1300, then, seems to meet all the expectations of systemic decline produced by the model, with the feudal system in general collapse.

The Renaissance system[21]

The end of the Middle Ages in Europe is usually associated with the Renaissance of the fifteenth century. By the end of the fifteenth century the political, social and economic organization of Europe had been radically changed from that of twelfth-century feudalism.

The expected points of change are at AD 1500, 1600 and 1700, with the system beginning at 1400 and ending about 1800. Historically the start of the period is, again, debatable, as one might expect given the internal transition of existing medieval states into their Renaissance successors. Key changes were, however, happening close to 1400, such as the end of the Great Schism (1414–18), and a new extensity is visible in, for example, the beginnings of post-medieval European intervention in Africa (1415). European exploration and the Renaissance itself characterized the fifteenth century, attesting a continued growth in extensity and a dramatic increase in social and economic differentiation.

Martin Luther initiated the European Reformation in 1517. This transformed both the religious life of Europe and, consequently, the relationship between the European states and the Papacy. The rise of the Habsburgs after 1519 initiated another major change in European politics. Habsburg domains expanded throughout the sixteenth century, to reach their greatest extent in its last decades. When the famous Armada was sent against England in 1588, for example, it was from Habsburg Spain. The height of Habsburg dominance and expansionism therefore closely correlates with the expected apex of the system at about 1600. The rapid collapse of their challenge to the north-west European states occurred during the Thirty Years War of 1614–48.

The year 1648 is itself conventionally taken to mark the start of the modern 'international system', following the Congress of Westphalia. A major systemic change at this date, originating the successor system from within its predecessor, again closely coincides with the expectations of the model if we take the transformative change as the start, rather than the end, of the Thirty Years War.

The last point at which change would be expected in this sequence is at 1700. At this point we would expect to see the rapid decline of the system beginning in the fifteenth century. The Nine Years War of 1689–97, the 'Glorious Revolution' of 1688, and the War of Spanish Succession culminating in the treaties of Utrecht and Radstadt (1713–14), all suggest rapid systemic change in this period. These changes replaced the Habsburgs with Britain and France as key state-actors in the system. The events of the fifteenth to eighteenth centuries can, therefore, be seen to coincide with our expectations.

The modern system[22]

The Westphalian system is usually supposed to characterize the modern period. While the character of this change is debatable, in this period even Roman Catholic states were free of temporal allegiance to the Papacy, and mutual sovereignty was generally recognized. The attendant structural changes included the establishment of regular diplomacy and treaty relationships regulating the system.

Expected changes are at 1700, 1800 and 1900, with the end of the system close to AD 2000. It would be expected that a new system emerging close to 1800 would be at its height close to AD 2000, but begin to collapse very rapidly thereafter. In view of the recent nature of these changes (the transformations expected at about 2000 might still, of course, be in the future) I shall consider all of these changes in a single section.

We have seen that there is agreement that the modern system originated as a result of the Thirty Years War. Most scholars consider the Westphalian system still to exist in the last decade of the twentieth century. Many scholars (especially, recently, Zacher[23]) have seen the Westphalian system in steep decline in the twentieth century.

The first test point is at 1700, as already mentioned in connection with Habsburg decline. At this time too, we see the rapid rise of the European 'Great Powers' of the early and mid-nineteenth century: Britain and France. The years surrounding 1800 were, indeed, an apex of the interstate system dominated by Franco-British rivalry. This was, of course, especially the case during the period from the French Revolution in 1789 to the Battle of Waterloo in 1815. The so-called Concert of Europe, which followed, lasted until our next test point at *circa* 1900. The 'Concert' is generally seen as ending in the Great War of 1914–18, but during the nineteenth century relations between European states had steadily deteriorated. The emergence of a unified Germany, and the re-orientation of Franco-German relations after the Treaty of Frankfurt of 1871 (following the Franco-Prussian war), intensified imperial rivalry from the 1870s onwards.

These rivalries and contests were resolved in favour of Britain after 1918. Thereafter, both Germany and France went into steep decline. However, a newly globalized 'European' system dominated by the United States – with Britain as its ally – began to emerge after 1900. The rise of United States dominance in the 'European' system became more pronounced after 1945, which may be seen as terminating Franco-German struggles for control.

In the Cold War, American hegemony reached its zenith, with the security and economy of Europe strongly interlinked with that of the United States, and extensive Americanization occurring inside European states. The West European states, therefore, became part of a system centred upon an extra-European state for the first time, a transformation in this relationship occurring with the end of the Cold War.

It might be supposed that a new system would emerge to replace this

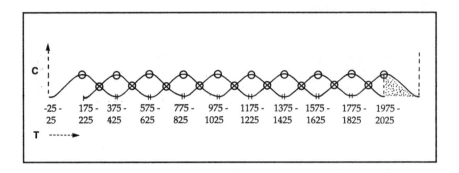

Fig. 6.1   Graph showing possible waves of complexity for the Old World system. Dates
on horizontal scale are those discussed in the text. Open circles indicate possible stress
points. Note: levels of complexity are shown to illustrate the 'waves' anticipated by the
model, rather than as an absolute scale or for comparison between successive periods of
the trajectory. **C** = complexity. **T** = time.

c. AD 2000. Such a post–Cold War western European system may be
forming, with the rise of the European Union. However, as we shall see in
the next chapter, the new global scale of the 'European' system may mean
that it is now too narrow a focus to concentrate merely on its strictly
European component.

Interestingly, on the grounds of the model, we would expect to see the
system in decline *c.* 2000, as emerging close to 1800, although rising only
slowly until 1900. The United States came into existence in 1776, defeating
the last attempt at European intervention in 1840. In 1823, the US President
had already declared the 'Monroe Doctrine', that the United States would
oppose any European intervention in the Americas. It was only in *c.* 1900
that America began to play a decisive role in European affairs, a role
emphasized in 1919 by Wilson's role at Versailles. According to this model,
the apex of US political, cultural and economic dominance should be *circa*
2000. Many scholars have identified the end either of the Cold War or of
that in the Gulf as the height of US political and military supremacy.
Consequently, the emergence and history of the modern western European
system again closely correlates with the expectations produced by this
model.

Conclusion to the examination of the western European trajectory

The historical sequence from Western Europe over the whole of the last
2000 years therefore shows a close correlation with the expectations produced by this model. The only specifically 'European' addition was in its
chronological calibration, with reference to the earliest state system to

encompass western Europe. Unless this model is an accurate depiction of the processes of long-term socio-political change on this level, there is no reason why such correlation should 'work'. For example, there is no reason why it should be possible to model the rise and decline of the modern system with reference to the duration of the Roman empire.

It must be stressed that, other than the operation of the sort of processes discussed in this book, there is no reason why these successive sequences should have a similar chronology. Their economic and ecological contexts were strikingly different, as were the detailed structures of the states and 'international systems' involved. There are no otherwise identified 'long-cycles' of either politics or economics which might credibly lie behind such patterns of change.

It might, of course, be argued that even although each of these test points correlates with the historical sequence, they still represent only a small number of possible correlations. However, it must be recalled that there was only a one in four chance of correlation at each point.

An interesting aspect of this western European trajectory has already been referred to. This is the way in which (following the expansion of the European empires) it 'globalized' in the period after c. 1400. This had the effect of eliminating other systemic trajectories. With the exception, perhaps, of that of China, these were absorbed into the 'Old World' system, so as to render this a 'global system' rather than simply a regional system. How this occurred will be discussed at greater length in the next chapter, but here it is noteworthy that the final two waves of this trajectory have had a global character. The globalization of the 'Old World' system has, therefore, apparently introduced a cyclicality into the global system of today. If so, it is a remarkable testimony to the enduring significance of long-term processes of change in shaping world politics that this derives from specific events in Europe two millennia ago.

The observation that the western European sub-regional system has expanded to encompass other regional systems, however, presupposes that there were other regional state systems prior to this point. It also raises the possibility that these had their own historical sequences forming distinctive trajectories until they were absorbed into that of Europe. These systems, therefore, provide further examples against which this model can be compared. However, before we examine those regional systems long distinct from that of Europe, it is worth examining the history of the Middle East.

The Middle East is simply another part (another 'sub-region') of the 'Old World' regional system, and the only other area which shares the common Roman background to western Europe. It was also in this area that the concept of the state originated in the 'Old World' regional system. Thus, if the cyclical pattern so far identified is the result of system-wide processes, the Middle East would be expected to show the same pattern of historical change as that found in western Europe. This might begin at one of two points. The cyclical pattern of change could originate with initial state-formation either in the ancient Middle East or in the Roman imperial period itself, as seems to be the case in Europe.

We can, therefore, further evaluate the validity of this pattern in general, and clarify its origins, by examining the Middle Eastern sequence with it in mind. This has, of course, also an intrinsic interest, given the centrality of the Middle East to the study of world politics, especially in a long-term perspective.

The Middle East

The Middle Eastern sequence is closely related to the western European sequence from the Bronze Age onwards, although as one would expect the relationship between the two varies considerably over the millennia. The state, as we saw in the previous chapter, originated independently in the Middle East, and it is from these developments that all European states ultimately derive their political form.

The earliest Middle Eastern systems[24]

We have already seen that the state originated in the fourth millennium BC in Mesopotamia, and perhaps also independently in Egypt. The origin of the state in the Middle East was very rapidly accompanied by the origin of an inter-state system, and the two processes were inextricably linked by the consolidation of non–city-state polities from coalitions of city-states. The first evidence of inter-state relations comes, therefore, from the fourth millennium BC also, with the diplomatic relations between these polities.

By the late fourth millennium these city-states were organized as a recognizable regional system: the Sumerian 'civilization'. The Sumerian 'civilization' is aptly named, as it was a system based on city-states which shared common cultural, social and economic features. This system was also characterized by other much less 'civilized' aspects than this title might imply, including inter-state warfare from the fourth millennium BC onward! Conflict afforded the opportunity for one of these states to rise to prominence: the city of Akkad.

The Akkadian state became a major regional actor in *c.* 2350 BC, after almost a thousand years of competitive interaction between these city-states. This was a state with grand expansionist ambitions, which soon established an imperial system by subjugating its neighbours.

The Akkadian empire was culturally and socially distinct from earlier societies, but similar to the earlier Mesopotamian states in political organization. In *c.* 2200 BC the Akkadian empire fragmented into rival polities, having been both internally divided and under attack by non-state peoples.

The Akkadian collapse led to a period of hiatus, in which no larger polities formed to take its place. This period ended in 2100 BC when the city of Ur established control over most of the former Akkadian area.

Ur was more successful in establishing a flourishing economic system. Like the Akkadians, the rulers of Ur brought about social and cultural changes, but it too collapsed after about a century, in *c.* 2004 BC. The area then once again fragmented into smaller polities, which were encompassed within the Babylonian empire in *c.* 1800 BC. The Babylonian empire may be dated from 1792–*c.* 1600 BC. This, too, brought new social and cultural structures, but once again fragmented into smaller polities.

By the middle of the first millennium BC the Middle East had a clearly defined inter-state system composed of small states encompassing both the polities of Mesopotamia and those which had been developing in Anatolia and Egypt, to which we shall shortly return.

This system passed into a 'dark age' (a period of scant written evidence) *c.* 1100–900 BC, ending with the establishment of the Assyrian empire (*c.* 883–609 BC). This empire, lasting for almost 300 years, re-formed the Middle Eastern system around itself.

The ensuing period of political fragmentation was ended with the rise of the Persian empire in *c.* 550 BC. Persia became the single most important state in Anatolia and Mesopotamia for nearly 250 years until its destruction by the Macedonian king, Alexander ('the Great') in 331 BC. The collapse of Alexander's empire permitted the rise of a new Persian dynasty with a distinctive set of cultural values, the Seleucids. This was, in turn, destroyed by the Parthian empire in 141 BC.

The Parthians themselves were replaced by a new Persian state, the Sassanian empire, in the AD 220s. This proved even more enduring, collapsing only when the Arab invasion swept it away in AD 637.

Consequently, the sequence in Mesopotamia does not show evidence of a 400-year wave until the Sassanian period. Prior to the rise of the Persian state it is, however, interesting to observe that there is some evidence of a regular pattern of growth and decline on a different – 100–200-year – wave. After the collapse of the first Persian empire, however, this pattern ceased.

The collapse of the Persian empire, due to Alexander's invasion, serves to introduce contemporary developments further west, but still within what I have referred to here as the Middle East. These took place in three key areas: the Aegean, Anatolia and Egypt. However, such are the problems surrounding Ancient Egyptian chronology at present that it may be worth concentrating on the former areas.

In the Aegean the state had emerged in two distinct locations: on Crete and in mainland Greece. The Cretan state originated in *c.* 2000 BC, and is today referred to as the Minoan civilization. This was destroyed, after nearly 650 years of existence, in 1450 BC, perhaps due to a natural catastrophe. On mainland Greece the first state was that today designated the Mycenean civilization, which was less long-lasting, from the sixteenth to the fourteenth centuries BC. The Myceneans were, in many respects, successors to the

Minoans, but they were followed by a 'dark age' equivalent to that affecting Mesopotamia and Anatolia. This lasted until the eighth century, when the Greek city-states emerged.

These earlier developments were discontinuous with, but laid the basis for, the emergence of the Greek city-state system in the eighth and seventh centuries. This was consolidated and geographically expanded through the seventh and sixth centuries to form the basis for the Classical Greek city-state system of the fifth and fourth centuries BC.

Although famed for its cultural achievements, the Greek city-state system was not long-lasting. It survived for less than two centuries, amid much political conflict and warfare. The rise of Macedon, a northern Greek kingdom less politically complex than the city-states to its south, brought an end to the city-state system in 338 BC. The Macedonian empire extended Greek 'civilization' across Anatolia, into north Africa, and beyond, but was short-lived, ending with Alexander the Great's death in 324 BC.

The fragmentation of this empire, however, produced a new socio-political system. This was the network of Greek-speaking states usually referred to as 'the Hellenistic world'. These dominated Anatolia and the Aegean from the death of Alexander to the Roman conquest, which brought this system to an end in the first century BC.

The Aegean states, therefore, proved longer-lasting than those of Meso-potamia. Again, there are hints of diachronic regularities, in that the Classical and Hellenistic systems both lasted approximately 300 years, after a clear break with the Mycenaean past, but two examples are probably insufficient to claim evidence for cyclicality. Importantly, the pre-Roman Aegean sequence also lacks any evidence of a 400-year wave.

These developments in the Aegean took place at the same time as changes in Anatolia. The Anatolia sequence was, of course, more closely linked to that of Mesopotamia. The 'dark age' of the mid-first millennium BC was followed by the rise of the Hittite empire. This began in c. 1350 BC, but the empire – although extensive – was brief. It had collapsed by 1200 BC, when the region returned to political fragmentation between rival smaller states until its conquest by Persia in the sixth century BC. Following Alexander's conquests it became part of the Macedonian empire, and then part of the Hellenistic system until the Roman takeover of the area.

It has, of course, to be noted that the development of these three areas must be brought together as a single trajectory from the Bronze Age onwards, as their politics were from that point so interlinked as to intermesh their political histories. This observation does not invalidate a discussion, for convenience, of the region in terms of different areas as has been under-taken. However, it stresses the importance of drawing these together in evaluating the possibility of a cyclical pattern in the overall trajectory.

On this basis, it is clear that the Middle East also lacks evidence of a 400-year wave prior to the first millennium AD. If there was a wave in Middle Eastern politics, it does not predate the Roman period. Such evidence could, of course, cast doubt upon the possibility of such a wave itself, or it may suggest that it is present only after the Roman conquest, when we have seen evidence of it operating in western Europe. This option can, of course, easily be examined, by continuing our investigation of the Middle Eastern trajectory.

The Roman period[25]

If a 400-year wave beginning in the Roman period exists in the 'Old World' regional system, the Middle East 'should' show an identical wave to that found in the western European trajectory from the Roman conquest onwards. In the Roman period itself this region has, of course, the same test points as for Europe. It is important to note, however, that the foundation of the Eastern Roman Empire, with its capital at Constantinople, separated the Roman-period histories of western Europe and the Middle East. It was this political decision on behalf of the Roman imperial government which was to form the basis for the Middle Eastern sequence in the period from the fifth to the ninth centuries, so this seems an appropriate place to continue our examination of the Middle Eastern sequence.

The early Byzantine Empire[26]

The effects of Byzantine rule in this region were different from those in the West. The Eastern Roman Empire (the 'Byzantine Empire'), as it is called by modern scholars, was at its height in the fifth century, which saw the unchallenged rule of the Byzantines in the Aegean and Anatolia. From Greece to Egypt, the Byzantine Empire was both integrating new populations, increasing in social differentiation and specialism, and growing in prestige and resources at AD 500. It continued to do so through the sixth century under Justinian I. His reconquest of North Africa and Italy in the sixth century established a Byzantine hegemony in the Middle East which was at its height prior to the reign of Phocas (AD 602–10), and saw the Empire at its greatest extent. This closely coincides with the expectations of rapid rise in the fifth century (to AD 500) with an apex at c. 600.

The early Arab system[27]

The test points for the third wave are at AD 700, 800, 900 and 1000, with the system beginning close to AD 600. Byzantine domination had been replaced by the growth of a system centred on Arabia after 600. In the seventh century, from 610 onwards, the Byzantine empire collapsed in the face of Arab invasion, although the causes of the collapse, which began prior to Arab incursions, seem to have been internal.

The rapid rise of the successor system is attested by the progress of the Arab conquests during the seventh century. Jerusalem was captured in 638. Egypt fell in the same decade and the Arabs raided into Asia Minor. A decade later Cyprus and Rhodes fell, and by the 690s Armenia and the African provinces of the empire were lost.

Rapid rise in the extensity of the Arab system at AD 700 is attested by both these conquests and those of the first decades of the eighth century. In the first decade of the eighth century, the Arabs invaded and conquered the majority of Spain, and they were raiding as far as Poitiers in the 730s.

We would expect the peak of this system to be around AD 800. The late eighth century did, in fact, mark the height of Arab control, the period of Harun-al-Rashid, Caliph of Baghdad.

The Abbasid period[28]

According to our expectations from the model, the successor system has to have emerged near to the peak of the previous system at AD 800. This represented a period of dynastic change within the Arab world from the Umayyad to the Abbasid dynasties. The Abbasids, under Al-Mansur, founded their capital at Baghdad in the 760s. However, from 817 into the later ninth century, civil war and revolution characterized their reign. The period around 800 also saw the foundation of the North African dynasties, the Idrisids and Aghlabids. Our next test point is at AD 900, when we should expect rapid decline of the system. By 900 the Abbasids were in crisis.

The revival of the Byzantine Empire[29]

The expected test points are rapid rise at AD 900, an apex at 1000, and decline by 1200. This period is almost exactly that usually seen to characterize the Middle Byzantine Empire. During the ninth century the emergence of Carolingian hegemony in the west and the revival of the Byzantines in the east culminated in the return of a dominant Byzantine state in Asia Minor. The Byzantine resurgence gathered pace after the decisive victory won in northern Asia Minor in AD 863, and the recruitment of the Bulgarians to the Byzantine cause in 864. Although the Bulgarians turned against the Byzantines from the 890s onwards, during the 930s and 940s the Byzantines made steady gains of territory. In the 950s and 960s the Byzantine empire, under Nicephorus Phocas, continued to make gains, including the reconquest of Crete and Cyprus. The greatest period of Byzantine resurgence was yet to come, during the reign of Basil II (963–1025). Basil's reign coincides well with our expected apex point at AD 1000.

We would expect this to be followed by collapse during the eleventh century, becoming more rapid after 1100. The first Arab attack after Basil's death was in the early 1030s. This was easily repelled, but the expansion of the Seljuk empire brought about the reduction of Byzantine control in Anatolia for a while to no more than a Black Sea coastal strip.

The 'Crusader' system[30]

We would expect a new system to emerge at the height of the previous period, AD 1000. Test points for this sequence are at 1100, 1200 and 1300.

The Turkish Seljuk empire ruled from 1037 to 1109, replacing both the Byzantines and the Arab states in Anatolia and as far east as the Oxus. The Seljuks emerged in the early eleventh century and gained a substantial victory over the Byzantines at Manzikert in 1071. Their rise coincides closely (if not exactly) with the expected test points at AD 1000 and 1100.

However, another component of the successor system was also emerging in the eleventh century, in western Europe. The first European crusade, capturing Jerusalem in 1099, followed rapidly on the period of Byzantine resurgence under Basil II and the emergence of the Seljuks. It must be recalled that the European invasion of the Middle East represented *intra-systemic* change within the regional system as a whole. Crusading transformed the Middle Eastern system in both socio-political and cultural terms, with Arab control of the eastern Mediterranean severely decreased. Crusader strength grew in contrast to that of the Byzantines and Seljuks.

After the capture of Constantinople in 1204, Europeans ruled what had been the Byzantine Aegean as the 'Latin Empire'. Although Moslems (led by Saladin) took Jerusalem in 1187, a few years later, in 1206–27, Genghis Khan struck at the heart of Arabia. Persia was overrun in 1231 and by 1258 Baghdad fell.

These changes coincided, however, with the collapse of the Latin empire, Byzantine reconquest began in 1224, and by 1261 Constantinople had been recaptured. Mongol expansion into the Middle East was halted by the battle of Ayn Jalut in 1260. The Mamluks, who were responsible for the defeat of the Mongols in 1260, gradually took control of the Crusader kingdoms. The first major towns fell in 1265, and the conquest was completed by 1291. The resurgence of Moslem polities in the Middle East at the end of the thirteenth century, following an initial decline of crusader domination in the decades after 1200, closely fits our test points for AD 1200 and 1300.

The Turkish system[31]

It was not the Mamluks who were to rise to dominance, however, but another Moslem group: the Ottomans. Test points for this wave are at 1400, 1500, and 1600.

The Ottomans, founded by Othman (1288–1326), destroyed the Byzantine empire with the conquests of Mohammed 'the Conqueror' (1451–81). Rising rapidly after 1300, to effectively form the Middle Eastern socio-political system on their own (Turkic) lines by 1400, the growth of the Ottoman empire correlates well with the expectations of the model.

Two key events in the Ottoman takeover coincide with the test point at 1400. In 1389 they defeated the Serbs at Kosovo, and in 1393 the Bulgarian empire, giving them control of the Balkans. Kosovo and its aftermath have long been seen by historians as pivotal points in Ottoman history. The destruction of the Byzantine empire proved to be a transformative aspect of Middle Eastern history. After 1453 the Ottomans found themselves rulers of the entire Middle East, without serious threat from neighbouring states. The emergence of the Ottoman system between 1393 and 1453 therefore coincides well with the expected test at 1400.

The Ottoman empire[32]

From the fifteenth to nineteenth centuries, the Ottoman empire constituted the basis of the Middle Eastern system. Test points are at 1400, 1500, 1600, and 1700, with the system expected to end close to 1800.

We have seen that Ottoman supremacy was achieved between the 1390s and 1450s, with the periods of Mohammed the Conqueror and his successor Selim (1512–20) constituting a phase of rapid growth around 1500. Important, too, is that following its humiliating defeat by Tamerlane in 1402, the Ottoman empire was reorganized under Mohammed I (1413–21). The reign of Suleiman 'the Magnificent' (1520–66) is usually seen as the height of the empire. The test points at 1400 and 1500 coincide, therefore, with the broad sweep of Ottoman history, although the apex of the Ottoman empire occurs, perhaps, too early in the sixteenth century to be considered a fit to the test point at AD 1600. As we shall see, its relationship to the successor system is, however, exactly as we would expect on the basis of the model.

The return of the West[33]

From the late sixteenth century the Ottoman empire began to decline. The next period is characterized by the return of Western domination of the Middle East. There are test points at AD 1700, 1800, and 1900, with the system originating close to the apex of the previous wave at AD 1600.

The first of these test points fits Middle Eastern history very closely. It has been claimed that Suleiman was followed by thirteen incompetent successors, but the successor system was not to be found in the Moslem world. Close to the height of Ottoman control, Western intervention in the Middle East returned with a major defeat for the Ottomans at Lepanto in 1571.

We would expect rapid decline of the Ottoman system at AD 1700. In 1699 Ottoman control of Hungary ended, with further territorial losses in 1718. These began a gradual process of diminution in the European part of the Ottoman realms.

Ottoman collapse would be expected at about AD 1800. At first, one might suppose that this test was not met by the historical sequence. The Ottoman empire survived until the early twentieth century. The period around 1800, however, marked a drastic change in the relationship between the Ottomans and the West.

By 1800, the core areas of the Ottoman empire appeared to be under threat of Western invasion. Nor was the Moslem world able to guarantee its safety. In 1799, it was the British who guaranteed the integrity of the Ottoman empire, in opposition to the continued expansion of other European nations into the Middle East.

Nor were Western gains to cease at 1800. After the Congress of Vienna (1815), the British themselves took the Ionian islands as part of the settlement at the treaty of Adrianople (1829). Russia gained Georgia and eastern Armenia, along with smaller areas, at the same time. Following the Greek war of independence (1821–32) a 'European' state was again established in the Aegean.

Between the late eighteenth century and 1829, the relationship between the West and the Ottomans had been transformed by major losses of territory from the Ottomans to the 'sphere of influence' (or direct control) of European states. The expectations produced by the model of an end to the fifteenth-century Ottoman system (although not the Ottoman sultanate), and the emergence of a Western-dominated system reaching its height at around 1800 are, therefore, met. The nineteenth century was, of course, to see the continued collapse of the 'sick man of Europe' (the Ottomans) in the face of Western imperialism.

The final test point prior to the end of this wave is at AD 1900. Here, we would expect rapid collapse of the new (European) system and the rapid rise of a successor. Following its involvement in World War I, the Ottoman empire collapsed completely to be replaced by a modernized Turkish state. After World War I Western involvement again intensified. The British had occupied Egypt in 1882, the French controlled what had once been Arab-ruled North Africa, and Libya passed into the hands of the Italians in 1911. Following World War I, Syria, Iraq and Transjordan were in European hands, and Greece was granted additional territories.

The modern Middle Eastern system[34]

European control of Middle Eastern territory had largely ceased by 1950. As we have seen, however, new states of a 'European' form began to be established with the foundation of Greece in 1832. The successor system comprised states which were no longer under direct Turkish or European control. Nor were they, in the twentieth century, part of the 'sphere of influence' of European states in the same sense as before.

The origins of modern Turkey (founded by Atatürk in 1922) started the establishment of these independent Middle Eastern states. A characteristic of these states was their adoption, to a greater or lesser extent, of Western political organization. This process had led, by the 1990s, to the majority of Middle Eastern states (excepting Iran and, to a lesser extent, the Arabian peninsula) being organized on Western lines. Although the imperial period ended, European and American involvement in the sub-region remained. On the grounds of the model alone, we would expect the current form of western domination of Middle Eastern politics to end, for this wave at least, close to AD 2000. It is, however, too soon to say whether this will, or will not, occur and so impossible to form a test at this point.

Conclusion to the examination of the Middle Eastern trajectory

While the pre-Roman evidence from this region showed no trace of a 400-year wave such as was found in the Western European trajectory, the evidence provided by the Roman and later periods in the Middle East seems to confirm the existence of this wave in that sub-region also. This shows a general correlation between the expectations produced by applying the model to the western European sequence and the historical sequence in the Middle East. This examination strongly suggests that, as in the western European sequence, a 400-year wave is visible in the Middle Eastern trajectory after the start of the Roman imperial period. The only point at which the Middle Eastern sequence might be considered to differ greatly from this expectation was at AD 1600.

The Chinese regional state system – that originating as a consequence of initial state formation in China itself – provides a clear example of a trajectory separate from that of the 'Old World' system evidenced above. This, therefore, gives a case against which this, apparently general, 400-year wave in the development of regional state systems may be evaluated. For the most part, China did not pass under direct European rule at any time in its history. As such, it might be expected to show a different periodicity to that of the 'Old World' trajectory, whether the model is valid or not.[35]

The region encompassed by the 'Chinese regional state system' was comprised not simply of China but several neighbouring states. Thus Japan and Korea, as well as those parts of south-east Asia in which the earliest statehood originated from a Chinese rather than South Asian (that is, 'Old World') source, must be seen as within this system. However, the systemic trajectory may be illustrated by examining the sequence from China itself, which in territorial and political terms formed the main part of this system

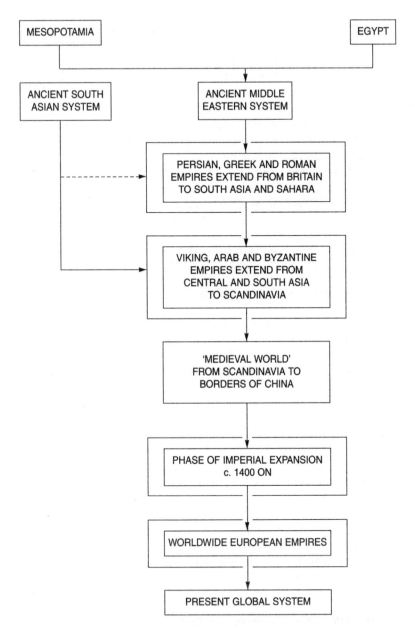

Fig. 6.2   Diagram illustrating, in simplified form, the emergence of the Old World regional system. Double outlining indicates periods in which large parts of the system were encompassed in empires. Arrows indicate chronological succession, not causal relationships or origins. Note that the South Asian system did not derive from the state-formation in the Indus Valley, but from state-formation in the first millennium BC in the Ganges Valley, it may have been integrated into the Old World system in the Roman period (broken horizontal line) or later during first millennium AD (solid horizontal line).

throughout its existence prior to European colonial expansion. Thus, the Chinese sequence will be used here to stand for the overall trajectory of the regional state system in general.

If the model is correct, that sequence might also be cyclical. If the observed 400-year periodicity is the product of a shared 'Old World' trajectory – as argued – then China would be expected to lack such a pattern, even if cyclical change based on identical processes were evidenced. If, however, the wave were based on global ecological or economic factors, then an identical pattern would be expected. In order to examine this, mere chronologies of regional systemic socio-political change will suffice, as these can serve to show the existence or lack of a 400-year wave.

Consequently, China provides us with an excellent opportunity to explore further whether this wave is a specifically 'Old World' or a more general pattern, and to explore the utility and validity of this model. China, of course, has an even better-documented political history than that of Europe and the Middle East, facilitating such an approach.

The Chinese regional state system

Although China is usually discussed as if a single state, it was in origin a multi-state regional system with common cultural foundations. This was consolidated at some periods in its history into an empire, whether formally declared or not.[36] China, therefore, might be taken – in passing – to illustrate the validity of equating imperial and other regional systems. It shows how easily a regional state system can shift between these two forms of political organization.

Thus China demonstrates the falsity of separating the state rigidly from the regional system. In China, these have, at different times, been both separate and the same political entities.[37] So, this example both serves the general purpose outlined so far, and helps to validate the breaking down of political, social and cultural divisions, and divisions between intra-state, inter-state and imperial political systems, into a multi-scalar systemic approach. Interestingly, China also illustrates the validity of using historical periodization to recognize changes in socio-political complexity, as each new dynasty or historical period was associated with distinctive structures and socio-political forms.

The formation of the Chinese system

The origins of this regional state system lie in the Neolithic period, when centralized (but not certainly bureaucratic) polities emerged in eastern and central China.[38] These changes were accompanied by intensified division of labour and other indices of complexity such as economic specialization, but it is as yet unclear whether any of them should be classified as a state.

The Neolithic period lasted until around 1500 BC. It is in the next period that both statehood and chronology become more clearly defined.

Shang China[39]

The Shang period lasted from *c.* 1500 to 1050 BC (450 years) and was marked by greatly increased bureaucracy and political scale, alongside intensified urbanization. Economic specialization increased (with, for example, specialized silk-production emerging) and a monetary economy was established. Literacy is also first evidenced at this period.

There is, therefore, no difficulty with classifying the Shang as a state society, and it will be taken here as the first certain Chinese state-society. As such we may note it conforms to our expectation regarding new forms of information processing emerging alongside new forms of social complexity. It is uncertain whether all of the Shang cultural zone was a single state or whether, as is more likely, this comprised a culturally homogenous inter-state system.

The Zhou states[40]

The next phase of Chinese political history of note here is the Zhou which developed in *c.* 1050 BC as a successor to the Shang. The Zhou overthrew the Shang, and established a new and larger inter-state system, with a similarly homogenous culture but a more layered bureaucratic government and a more strongly ranked society.

After ruling China for approximately 280 years, the Zhou states splintered into many rival political groups in *c.* 771 BC, but the Zhou exercised nominal authority over these for another 368 years until 221. Among these new states were the Qin, who were later to rise to prominence. Consequently, it is possible to take the Zhou period as lasting either about 280 or 780 years.

The Spring and Autumn and Warring States periods and the rise of Qin[41]

Spring and Autumn and Warring States periods represent little more than a development of the late (or Eastern) Zhou period, and could be reclassified as representing a single period of Chinese history characterized by fierce inter-state rivalry. This was ended by the rise of the Qin state.

This state established a single Chinese empire in 221 BC, but it was very short-lived, collapsing in 206 BC. Despite its brief duration, the Qin established the structures of the bureaucratic, centrally controlled and literate state throughout its domains. However, the collapse of Qin through rebellion was rapidly followed by the rise of a new dynasty, the Han.

Han China[42]

The Han period developed out of the reconsolidation of the Qin state in 206 BC and was in existence until AD 220. The history of this period is divisible into two main phases: the Western and Eastern. The Western Han state was modelled on the Qin empire and overtly expansionist in character.

This phase came to an end in AD 9, when the focus of the Han shifted to the Eastern Han dynasty, but the Han period can be interpreted as being a single period of 426 years.

Disunity and attempts at re-unification

The end of the Han period was followed by a long phase of political fragmentation and attempted re-unification, with first the 'Three Kingdoms' (AD 220–280) and then subsequent polities ruling part but not all of China. There was a brief period of attempted unification under the Jin dynasty, during the period AD 280–316, but this rapidly led to more civil war and political disunity. In the north of China, invasion by non-Chinese peoples prompted a dramatic collapse in population and socio-political complexity, as this is understood in this book. This resulted in the emergence of around 20 rival polities in the Yellow River Basin (once the core of the Chinese empire) alone.

This period came to an end when northern China was re-unified under the Wei, but this too split first into Eastern and Western parts, and then into the Northern Qi and Northern Zhou. Consequently, fragmentation continued to characterize Chinese politics until the rise of the Sui dynasty among the Northern Zhou. This restored political unification in 589, after a period of 369 years.

The Sui and T'ang[43]

The Sui, AD 589–618, and T'ang, 618–907, dynasties may be considered together, as they represent a continuum within a single state. The dynastic designation represents only its internal development, rather than the establishment of a successor state. Together these lasted 318 years, although the latter part of this period was once again characterized by political fragmentation and civil war. This ended with the period of the Five Dynasties, from 907 to 960. It is unclear whether this ought to be counted with the T'ang period or as a separate transitional phase but the political disunity which it represents was terminated by the development of the Song.

Song China[44]

The Song period, AD 960–1279, can also be divided into two phases: a 'northern' phase 960–1126, and a 'southern' phase 1129–1279. These lasted

166 and 150 years respectively, but can be seen as a single 'Song' period of 316 years. The Song period was brought to an end by the Mongol conquest of China in 1279, which established the relatively short-lived Yuan dynasty.

Yuan China[45]

The Yuan period marks a clear break in the endogenous Chinese trajectory in that it represents a period of foreign rule of the whole Chinese system. It was, however, short-lived compared to earlier periods of Chinese polities, lasting only 90 years. Peasant revolution established a new Chinese state organized on different lines to its predecessors in many important respects.

The Ming period[46]

The new Chinese state is known, after its rulers, as Ming China. This empire re-united the majority of what was the Chinese empire in pre-Mongol times and ruled China for 276 years before itself ending in revolution. The Ming period, from 1368–1644, therefore represents the re-foundation of the Chinese state rather than a clear continuity from the imperial past. However, the revolution which overthrew it did not seek to replace the state as such, but rather to alter its domestic socio-political organization.

Qin China[47]

This uprising did not itself establish a new state but led to the opportunity for the Qin to seize control of China and found their own dynasty. This commenced in 1644 and came to an end with the establishment of the Chinese republic in 1911, after 267 years.

Modern China[48]

It is by no means clear that we should see the Chinese communist revolution as marking the end of the period of the period begun in 1911, because it too results – as did that revolution – from the Westernization of Chinese politics and the modernization of Chinese society and culture. Consequently, I shall group these two recent phases of Chinese history together as 'Modern China'.

Conclusion to examination of the Chinese trajectory

The Chinese trajectory is especially interesting in contrast to the previous examples because it shows a very different periodicity. Whereas the

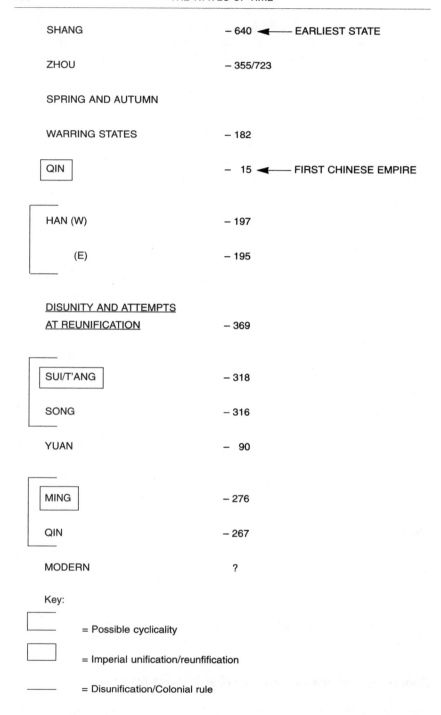

Fig. 6.3 Possible waves in China.

examples so far discussed evidence a 400-year cyclical pattern, this is not present in China. Instead, we see that discontinuities in Chinese history have led to a series of relatively short, but still remarkably regular, phases of development.

The first of these begins with the Sui/T'ang-Song periods which may each have lasted for about 318 years. Then there is a break at the Yuan period, with another two periods of similar duration (this time 276 and 267 years) following this during the Ming and Qing periods. Thus, except for a brief period of disruption by Mongol rule (which might be expected to end the trajectory), the political history of China could either be seen to comprise a series of 300 year waves or two distinct phases comprising pairs of periods. These were dissimilar in chronology to the 'Old World' wave, but the last ends at the very point at which China entered the 'Old World' system, by adopting European concepts of governance and statehood.[49] Thereafter, Chinese rulers, whether capitalist or Maoist, adopted European concepts of the state and European modes of government alongside European cultural forms, such as Marxism itself!

If so, China may have entered into the cyclical 'Old World' systemic trajectory at this point. This may, therefore, suggest that China will also show indications of rapid systemic decline c. 2000, according to that trajectory, and some specialists have argued that these indications are visible in the 1990s. It is possible, however, that the lack of direct European rule has left China as the only part of the contemporary world still operating outside of this system. This latter conclusion seems, however, less plausible than the former, given the inclusion of modern China in other aspects of the contemporary socio-political and economic system, and given the evidence of Westernization in Chinese culture during the twentieth century.

The distinctive Chinese cyclical patterning exhibited until 1911 has not, however, always been a feature of Chinese politics. In the trajectories of the earliest Chinese states, the Shang and Zhou seem to be of a much longer duration. In these periods there is inadequate evidence of cyclicality; however, this was terminated by the Spring and Autumn/Warring States periods.

Chinese evidence , then, may go to demonstrate that cyclicality is not an inherent property of regional state systems. On the basis of the examples so far examined it would seem, while not universal, to be a common feature of such systems. This is, of course, what we would expect on the basis of the model proposed in this book.

The key change in the case of China, shifting the trajectory from a non-cyclical to a cyclical mode, seems to have been unification under a single political authority. Perhaps this helps us to explain the cyclicality of the 'Old World' regional state system. Perhaps it was the unified political control afforded by the Roman imperial system which set in place the necessary circumstances for a cyclical 'Old World' regional trajectory.

It is also interesting to see the much greater role that political revolution played in China's development than in the 'Old World' system. This must alert us to the possibility that different trajectories might have other distinctive transhistorical political characteristics. Perhaps transhistorical political culture can precipitate, although not determine, the mode of transition between successive periods. A useful further evaluation of the generality of these patterns can be achieved by examining data from Africa.

Africa[50]

The independent origin of statehood south of the Sahara has been discussed earlier. It is also clear that, with the exception of a few coastal polities, the states of this region were not in regular contact with Europeans for the majority of the pre-colonial period. Consequently, it is interesting to ask what patterning – if any – can be discerned in the African trajectory represented by these political units.

The political trajectories of sub-Saharan African states are so historically different as to preclude the approach to discussing regional political development so far adopted in this chapter. This is because the African states of this region do not show evidence of successive patterns of state-formation and collapse. That is, although states frequently formed, especially in west Africa, when these states collapsed they were not replaced by successor states but by non-state societies. So, cyclical patterning – like inter-state imperialism – is absent from this trajectory.

This does not mean that sub-Saharan states were especially short-lived, or less fully developed than those of Europe or the Middle East. For example, Benin – famed for its artwork – lasted for 400 years. Dahomey lasted two centuries or so. Kongo, the earliest sub-Saharan African state which can be undeniably assigned that title, collapsed after about 300 years in AD 1710. Likewise the Asante state had no successor when it collapsed after approximately 200 years in the 1880s.

So, while successive sequences of state-formation and state-collapse are not visible in the African trajectory, there were many long-lived African states. This means that inter-state systems did, of course, exist when these states were juxtaposed. More frequently, however, these states existed in local systems comprised of other – non-state – units such as chiefdoms and tribes.

This, of course, raises the question of the implications of the African evidence for the model. Such sequences do not refute the proposed model, as the states involved show a coincidence between bureaucratization, the growth of social and economic complexity and increased scale. They also rise and decline in the wave-like fashion expected on theoretical grounds. But the opportunities for political innovation facilitated by the most complex stages of state-growth were seemingly not acted upon to construct cyclicality in this regional system.

The examination of the African trajectory suggests that the growth of social complexity, itself, cannot determine recurrent waves of growth and collapse. Instead, the African case seems to fit another aspect of the model: that the cyclical growth and collapse of socio-political complexity *can*, but *need not*, occur. It also conforms with the view that the likelihood of cyclical patterning in such trajectories is dependent upon the specifics of the trajectories involved. More specifically, it seems possible that those areas which are, at least partly, unified by imperialism – such as the Middle East, China and western Europe – are those which have regional state systems with cyclical trajectories. Perhaps isolated state-formation leads to patterns such as that exhibited in sub-Saharan Africa. In order to examine this possibility, another case-study is especially illuminating: that of the 'pre-Contact' Mesoamerican system. There states did not form in isolation, so a successive pattern of states would be expected according to this view; but imperialism was absent until the latest pre-Contact period of the trajectory. So the pattern 'should' be non-cyclical if it is imperialism which, in some fashion, causes this sequential trajectory.

The Mesoamerican regional state system

The emergence of state-society in the Valley of Mexico began a long pre-colonial Mesoamerican trajectory.[51] The dominance of Teotihuacan, lasted from *circa* 150 BC until AD 650, a period of roughly 800 years.[52] The next stage of this Mesoamerican political trajectory is characterized by the existence of the Mayan states.

The Maya[53]

The Mayan states were a network of polities of various sizes, united by a common culture and religion. These seem to have been derived from the earlier regional system, and were clearly from the outset literate bureaucratic polities with centralized political organization and evidence of large urban centres. The Maya states survived in the lowlands from *circa* 250 BC, rising to an apex around AD 600, and then declining until about 900. In the northern part of the Mayan area Mayan 'civilisation' survived after this date. The Maya collapse led to the emergence of competing smaller polities, one of which – the Toltecs – rose to pre-eminence.

The Toltecs[54]

The establishment of the Toltec dominance over these lesser states was accomplished in the tenth century AD. The Toltec domain was extended both to areas which had been severely affected by the Mayan collapse, and to areas where this was, to some extent, still an ongoing process. They too were conquered (*c.* 1156) by another polity – the Chicimec – and their polity fragmented once more into rival states. The Toltec collapse was followed once more by political fragmentation, and this too was eventually replaced, by the emergence of the Aztec state.

The Aztecs[55]

The Aztecs had been present in Mesoamerica since the twelfth century, but established their pre-eminence during the fifteenth century. The foundation of their empire can be dated from the establishment of their capital in the early thirteenth century. The destruction of the Aztec state by the Spanish may be dated to the capture of the Aztec capital in 1519. Thereafter, Mesoamerica became part of the Spanish empire and linked to the 'Old World' regional state system already discussed. The Aztec empire, then, was the last of the pre-colonial Mesoamerican states.

Conclusion to Mesoamerican case-study

It is interesting to note that Mesoamerica, unlike the 'Old World' and China, does not exhibit what seems to be a cyclical pattern of growth and decline.[56] In this respect, Mesoamerica supports the evidence from Africa that cyclicality is not an intrinsic property of the regional state system. However, in Mesoamerica the state and the inter-state system emerged together, as in the Middle East, whereas in Africa, states formed largely in isolation. Consequently, as we can see, a successive sequence of states is evidenced in Mesoamerica. But neither the Mesoamerican nor the sub-Saharan African regional system was unified under a single polity, even if the Toltec and Aztec kingdoms were both expansive and hegemonic. So, this case further supports the view that long-term cyclical trajectories in regional state systems seem to originate in periods of large-scale political unification.

Conclusion

The studies presented above suggest that 400-year cyclical patterning can be discerned in the 'Old World' system. Another, but different, wave can be identified in the Chinese system. However, all other systems were not cyclical, as the evidence from Africa and Mesoamerica shows.

These regional systems were all eventually incorporated into a single global system, based on the 'Old World' regional system, and more specifically that of the western European sub-region. By that time, this regional system had a well-established 400-year wave.

This wave, it must be stressed, has never been previously identified. The recognition of such a potentially significant pattern stresses the value of a long-term approach, and shows its relevance to contemporary world politics. If this wave existed, it probably exists today.

So, the formation of new states resulting from twentieth-century decolonization took place within a global system which may already have developed an internal dynamic of cyclical change. This may, then, provide an interesting context for analysing change occurring in the present.

To return to a long-term perspective. Regional state systems can, therefore, endogenously generate cyclical patterns of formation and collapse. While all such systems have the potential for cyclicality, in practice the formation of empire seems closely linked to the emergence of these waves. The reason for this is unclear. However, a possible explanation is to be found by comparing empires and over-chiefdoms. In each case cyclicality is seen, while this is absent from other regional systems. A common feature of these types of political organization is that they exist at the upper thresholds of organizational scale, employing specific forms of communication and information processing. It seems likely therefore, that cyclicality in both cases is a consequence of scalar stress, as scale exceeds information-processing capacity.

Once established, these waves can endure for very long periods of time. They far outlast the polities which brought them into existence. Such waves are not 'determined' by the structure of the system, or by the processes of change which produce them. They are simply the consequence of scalar limitations on socio-political growth. Once established, however, the path-dependent character of these systemic trajectories makes it more likely that waves (once started) will continue, than cease. Thus, cyclical trajectories are produced.

As we have seen, there is no common global periodicity for such waves until the globalization of the 'Old World' system due, once again, to imperial expansion. These processes, therefore, were (and are) contingent upon the maintenance of specific historically-situated political forms: the state, the inter-state system, and the empire. Specific political changes centuries in the past may also fundamentally affect the way that the global systemic trajectory still operates today.

It must be stressed that these processes make some forms of change more likely than others, but not inevitable. The forms of polity adopted and the forms of change which occurred are, simply solutions of problems posed by the limitations of information-processing under historically-specific circumstances. But these were not determined by process, nor were they inevitable. Alternatives were, and are, always available, and whether they were or are chosen is ultimately a matter of agency rather than structure or underlying process. Once choices have been made, however, these have potentially long-lasting and wide-ranging consequences. In the next chapter we shall see that changes in information processing and in the scale of socio-politics, resulting from global imperialism and the globalization of the 'Old World' system, may again be transforming the political organization of human societies. These patterns could even be changing once again, in a way analogous to that attendant upon the initial stages of state-formation itself.

Notes

1   As such it supersedes a Pluralist–Structuralist division based on these grounds.
2   As demonstrated by: Nelson, B. A., 1995, 'Complexity, hierarchy and scale: a controlled comparison between Chaco Canyon, New Mexico and La Que-mada, Zacatecas', *American Antiquity* 60.4, 596–618.
3   Holloway, R. R., 1994, *The Archaeology of Early Rome and Latium*.
4   Spivey, N. and Stoddart, S., 1994, *Etruscan Italy*.
5   Tsetskhladze, G. R. and de Angelis, F. (eds), 1988, *The Archaeology of Greek Colonisation*.
6   Cornell, T. J., 1995, *The Beginnings of Rome*; David, J-M., 1996, *The Roman Conquest of Italy*.
7   Scullard, H. J., 1991, *A History of the Roman World 753 to 146 BC*.
8   Smith, P. J., 1993, *Scipio Africanus and Rome's Invasion of Africa*, Gieben.
9   Crawford, M., 1978, *The Roman Republic*; Badian, E., 1968, *Roman Imperialism in the Late Republic*; Harris, W. V., 1979, *War and Imperialism in Republican Rome*.
10 King, A., 1992, *Roman Gaul and Germany*.
11 On the growth of the Roman Empire between Augustus and the end of the first century AD see: Jones, A. H. M., 1970, *Augustus*; Syme, R., 1939, *The Roman Revolution*; Erington, R. M., 1971, *The Dawn of Empire*; Scullard, A., 1982, *From the Gracchi to Nero*; Cornell, T. and Matthews, J., 1982, *Atlas of the Roman World*, 74–81, 84 and 106–7.
12 For example, see: Parker, A. J., 1987, 'Trade within the Empire and beyond the frontiers', in J. Wacher (ed.), 1987 *The Roman World*, 2 vols, vol. II, 635–57; Elton, H., 1996, *Frontiers of the Roman Empire*.
13 Collins, R., 1991, *Early Medieval Europe 300–1000*, 45–57 and 75–99.
14 James, E., 1992, *The Origins of France*, 110–11 and 135–7; Wood, I., 1994, *The Merovingian Kingdoms 450–751*, 159–80.
15 Wacher, J. (ed.), 1987, *The Roman World*; Cornell, T. and Matthews, J. 1982, *Atlas of the Roman World*.Garzetti, A., 1974, *From Tiberius to the Antonines* covers the period to AD 192. For the later Roman period see: Jones, A. J. M., 1964, *The Later Roman Empire 284–602*, 2 vols. The intervening period is discussed, in part, by MacMullen, R., 1976, *Roman Government's Response to Crisis AD 235–337*; Lintott, A., 1993, *Imperium Romanum*.
16 Herrin, J., 1987, *The Formation of Christendom*; Hodges, R. and Whitehouse, D., 1983, *Mohammed, Charlemagne and the Origins of Europe*.
17 Wood, 1994, *The Merovingian Kingdoms 450–751*; James, 1992, *The Origins of*

France; Collins, R., 1983, *Early Medieval Spain*; Collins, R., 1991, *Early Medieval Europe*; Wickham, C., 1981, *Early Medieval Italy*.

18   *Ibid.*

19   Roesdahl, E., 1991, *The Vikings*; Graham-Campbell, J., 1989, *The Viking World*, 2nd edn; Foote, P. G. and Wilson, D. M., 1970, *The Viking Achievement*, 2nd edn, New York; Jones, G., 1984, *A History of the Vikings*, 2nd edn. On the Normans prior to 1066, see: Bates, D., 1982, *Normandy Before 1066.*

20   Platt, C, 1979, *The Atlas of Medieval Man*; Brooke, C., 1987, *Europe in the Central Middle Ages 962–1154*, 2nd edn; Bloch, M., 1961, *Feudal Society*, transl. L. A. Manyon; Folz, R., 1969, *The Concept of Empire in Western Europe from the Fifth to the Fourteenth Century*, transl. S. A. Ogilvie; Hallam, E. M., 1980, *Capetian France 987–1328*; Mundy, J. H., 1973, *Europe in the High Middle Ages 1150–1309*; Hay, D., 1989, *Europe in the Fourteenth and Fifteenth Centuries*, 2nd edn; Waley, D., 1985, *Later Medieval Europe.*

21   Hay, D., 1989, *Europe in the Fourteenth and Fifteenth Centuries*; Potter, G. R., (ed.), 1961, *The Renaissance 1493–1520*; Elton, G. R., (ed.), 1958, *The Reformation 1520–1529*; Elton, G. R., 1963, *Reformation Europe 1517–1559*; Pounds, N. J. G., 1979, *An Historical Geography of Europe 1500–1840*; Mamatey, V. S., 1978, *Rise of he Habsburg Empire 1526–1815*, 2nd edn, New York; Wilson, C., 1976, *The Transformation of Europe 1558–1648*; Wedgewood, C. V., 1964, *The Thirty Years War*, 2nd edn; Kann, R. A., 1974, *A History of the Habsburg Empire 1526–1918*, Berkeley; Davis, C. S. L., 1995, *Peace, Print and Protestantism 1450–1558*, rev. edn; Cameron, E., 1991, *The European Reformation.*

22   McKay, D. and Scott, H. M., 1983, *The Rise of the Great Powers 1648–1815*; Anderson, M. S., 1976, *Europe in the Eighteenth Century 1713–83*; Ford, F. L., 1967, *Europe 1780–1830*; Hearder, H., 1966, *Europe in the Nineteenth Century 1830–1880*; Roberts, J., 1967, *Europe 1880–1945*; Kissinger, H., 1964, *A World Restored*, New York; Calvocoressi, P., 1991, *World Politics Since 1945*, 6th edn; Mason, J. W., 1985, *The Dissolution of the Austro-Hungarian Empire 1867–1918*; Chamberlain, M. E., 1985, *Decolonization*; Holland, R. F., 1985, *European Decolonisation 1918–1981: An Introductory Survey*; Urwin, D. W., 1968, *Western Europe Since 1945*; Bridges, F. R., and Bullen, R., 1980, *The Great Powers and the European States System 1815–1914*; Hyam, R., 1975, *Britain's Imperial Century 1815–1914*; Gulic, E. V., 1967, *Europe's Classical Balance of Power*, 2nd edn, New York; Joll, J., 1990, *Europe since 1870*, 4th edn; Schroeder, P. W., 1996, *The Transformation of European Politics 1763–1848.*

23   Zacher, M. W., 1992, 'The decaying pillars of the Westphalian temple: implications for international order and governance', in J. N. Rosenau and E-O. Czempiel (eds), *Governance Without Government: Order and Change in World Politics*, 58–101.

24   Powell, A. (ed.), 1995, *The Greek World*; Curtis, J. (ed.), 1993, *Early Mesopotamia and Iran*; Crawford, H., 1991, *Sumer and the Sumerians*; Dickinson, O., 1994, *The Aegean Bronze Age*; Aubet, M. E., 1993, *The Phoenicians and the West: Politics, Colonies and Trade*; Saggs, H. W. F., 1995, *Babylonians*; Osborne, R., 1996, *Greece in the Making: 1200–479* BC; Martin, T. R., 1996, *Ancient Greece*, Yale.

25   Millar, F., 1994, *The Roman Near East 31* BC–AD *337*, Cambridge, Mass.

26   Herrin, J., 1987, *The Formation of Christendom*, 16–219; Mango, C., 1980,

Byzantium. The Empire of the New Rome; Browning, R., 1980, *The Byzantine Empire*, esp. 7–23; Browning, R., 1971, *Justinian and Theodora*; Cameron, A., 1993, *The Mediterranean World in Late Antiquity* AD *395–600*; Grabar, A., 1966, *Byzantium from the Death of Theodosius to the Rise of Islam*.

27 Browning, R., 1980, *The Byzantine Empire*, 23–74; Stratos, A. N., 1968–75 *Byzantium in the Seventh Century*, 3 vols, Amsterdam: B. Lewis, 1958, *The Arabs in History*, 4th edn.

28 Hodges, R. and Whitehouse, D., *Mohammed, Charlemagne and the Origins of Europe* 122–57; Shaban, M. A., 1971, *The Abbasid Revolution*.

29 Jenkins, R., 1966, *Byzantium: The Imperial Centuries* AD *600–1071*; Browning, R., *The Byzantine Empire*, 77–95.

30 Angold, M., 1984, *The Byzantine Empire 1025–1204: A Political History*; Friendly, A., 1971, *The Dreadful Day: The Battle of Manzikert 1071*; Mayer, H. E., 1972, *The Crusades*, transl. J. Gillingham; Prawer, J., 1972, *The Latin Kingdom of Jerusalem*; Smail, R. C., 1956, *The Crusaders in Syria and the Holy Land*; Richards, D. S., 1973, *Islamic History 950–1150*; Lock, P., 1995, *The Franks in the Aegean 1204–1500*.

31 Wittek, P., 1938, *The Rise of the Ottoman Empire*; Inalcik, H., 1973, *The Ottoman Empire: The Classical Age 1300–1600*, New York.

32 Cook, M. A., (ed.), 1976, *A History of the Ottoman Empire to 1730*; Shaw, S. J. (with E. K. Shaw), 1976–7, *History of the Ottoman Empire and Modern Turkey* 2 vols; Runciman, S., 1965, *The Fall of Constantinople 1453*.

33 Lewis, B., 1968, *The Emergence of Modern Turkey*, 2nd edn; Anderson, M. S., 1966, *The Eastern Question 1774–1923*; Crawley, M., 1955, *Greek Independence 1832–33*; Overdale, R., 1992, *The Middle East since 1914*; Palmer, A. P., 1992, *The Decline and Fall of the Ottoman Empire*.

34 Calvocoressi, P., 1991, *World Politics since 1945*, 287–388; Hourani, A., Khoury, P. S. and Wilson, M. C. (eds), 1993, *The Modern Middle East*; Kedourie, E., 1992, *Politics in the Middle East*; Lawless, R. I., 1980, *The Middle East in the Twentieth Century*; Bill, J. A. and Springborg, R., 1994, *Politics in the Middle East*, 4th edn; Owen, R., 1992, *State, Power and Politics in the Making of the Modern Middle East*.

35 Taylor, P. J., 1989, *Political Geography*, 93, fig. 3.1.

36 Hucker, C. O., 1995, *China's Imperial Past*; Songqiao, Z., 1994, *Geography of China*, New York; Gernet, J., 1996, *A History of Chinese Civilization*, transl. J. R. Foster and C. Hortmann, 2nd edn.

37 Note, however, that a related and interconnected regional system formed in South and Southeast Asia, as recently discussed by: Allchin, R. *et al.*, 1995, *The Archaeology of Early Historic South Asia: The Emergence of Cities and States*. See also, Richards, J., 1996, *The Mughal Empire*.

38 Rawson, J. (ed.), 1997, *Mysteries of Ancient China*. See also: Barnes, G. L., 1993, *China, Korea and Japan*.

39 Nelson, S. M. (ed.), 1995, *Archaeology of Northeast China*; Chang, K. C., 1980, *Shang Civilization*, New Haven, CT.

40 Shu, C-Y. and Linduf, K., 1988, *Western Chou Civilization*, New Haven, CT.

41 Lewis, M. E., 1990, *Sanctioned Violence in Early China*.

42 Twitchett, D. and Lowe, E. (eds), 1986, *The Cambridge History of China Vol. I: Qin and Han*; Zhongshu, W., 1982, *Han Civilization*.

43   Twitchett, D. (ed.), 1979, *The Cambridge History of China Vol. II; Sui and T'ang China, 589–906.*

44   Fairbank, J. K., 1992, *China: A New History*, Cambridge, Mass., chapters 4 and 5.

45   Morgan, D., 1986, *The Mongols*; Langlois, J. D., 1981, *China Under Mongol Rule*, Princeton; Endicott-West, E., 1989, *Mongolian Rule in China.*

46   Mote, F. F. and Twitchett, D. (eds) 1988, *The Cambridge History of China Vol. VIII: Ming China 1368–1644*; Dreyer, E., 1982, *Early Ming China: A Political History, 1355–1435*, Stanford.

47   Wakeman, F., 1985, *The Great Enterprise*, Berkeley, Calif.; Fairbank, J. K., 1992, *China: A New History*, Cambridge, MA, chapters 7–12.

48   Mackerras, C., Taneja, P. and Young, G., 1994, *China Since 1978*, Melbourne; Moise, E. E., 1994, *Modern China.*

49   Fairbank, J. K., 1992, *China: A New History*, Harvard, chapters 13–21.

50   Curtin, P. *et al.*, 1995, *African History*, 2nd edn; Mokhtar, G. (ed.), 1981 *General History of Africa. Vol. II: Ancient Civilizations*, Paris; Hrbek, I. (ed.), 1992, *General History of Africa. Vol. III Africa from the Seventh to the Eleventh Century.*

51   Bruhns, K. O., 1994, *Ancient South America*; Fieder, S. J., 1992, *Prehistory of the Americas*; Weaver, M. P., 1993, *The Aztecs, Maya, and their Predecessors*, New York.

52   Millon, R., 1988, 'The last years of Teotihuacan dominance', in n. Yoffee and G. Cowgill (eds), *The Collapse of Ancient States and Civilizations*, Tucson, 102–64; Coe, M., 1992; *Breaking the Maya Code*; Sharer, R. J., 1994, *The Ancient Maya*; Fash, W. L., 1994, 'Changing perspectives on Maya civilization', *Annual Review of Anthropology* 23, 181–208.

53   Culbert, P. T. (ed.), 1973, *The Classic Maya Collapse*, Albuquerque; Schele, L. and Friedel, D., 1990, *A Forest of Kings: The Untold Story of the Ancient Maya*, New York; Coe, M. D., 1993, *The Maya.*

54   Fox, J. W., 1987, *Maya Postclassic State Formation*, Cambridge.

55   Hodge, M. G. and Smith, M. E. (eds), 1993, *Economies and Polities of the Aztec Realm*, Albany, NY; Smith, M. E., 1987, 'The expansion of the Aztec Empire: a case study in the correlation of diachronic archaeological and ethnohistorical data', *American Antiquity* 52, 37–54. Note also: Smith, M. E., 1987, 'Archaeology and the Aztec economy: the social scientific use of archaeological data', *Social Science History* 11, 237–59; Conrad, G. and Demarest, A. A., 1988, *Religion and Empire*, Cambridge; Carrasco, P., 1991, 'The territorial structure of the Aztec empire', in H. R. Harvey (ed.), *Land and Politics in the Valley of Mexico: A Two Thousand Year Perspective*, Albuquerque, 93–112; Clendinnen, I., 1993, *The Aztecs;* Smith, M. E., 1996, *The Aztecs.*

56   Coe, M. D., 1993, *The Maya*, 142.

7

Volatile networks: socio-political dynamics in the age of the global system

Introduction: the three ages of global politics

The previous chapter concentrated on regional state systems. It is obvious that their trajectories have played a very important role in global political history for millennia. However, this is not to say that the state was the only significant actor at any point in this long history. Nor was the state itself an unchanging entity. Different types of states existed at different times, while sharing the defining characteristics of this socio-political form.

To envisage a chronologically definable 'age of the state' does not, therefore, require that one must imagine state organization to be unchanging. It is merely requires belief in two propositions. First, that states and empires (as a form of state) are transhistorically identifiable by the presence of those few basic characteristics already discussed. Second, that they have been the largest directly administered political units since the earliest states emerged.

In an earlier chapter, we saw that another form of socio-political organization (the chiefdom) held the same place in an earlier period – an 'age of the chiefdom'. This socio-political form also changed from polity to polity, and through time. For example, Shaka's Zulu kingdom and the Hawaiian chiefdoms encountered by Cook were dissimilar in many detailed aspects of their organization. But both were chiefdoms.

As we have seen, a wide variation is found among political organizations capable of being classified as 'chiefdoms'. One would, on this basis, expect that the state might also exhibit wide variations in form. Thus, the role of the state and the role of the chiefdom are in this respect comparable, as was the role of the kin-based mode of organization in pre-chiefly societies.

Consequently, there have been at least three ages of global socio-politics: the 'age of kin-based politics', the 'age of the chiefdom' and the 'age of the state'. In the latter two periods earlier socio-political forms did not immediately die out; they persisted for millennia. Thus, while this view of large-scale long-term political development implies that eventual transition to a new socio-political form succeeding the state may be considered likely, this is not likely to mean the end of the state.

The paradoxical character of international politics

Again, long-term socio-politics presents us with a series of paradoxes and puzzles. There is a definable progression in socio–political scale and speed of growth, but smaller-scale political units persist for centuries after larger units emerge. While the overall rate of change increases, we saw in the last chapter that path-dependency renders the trajectories of regional (and then global) state systems potentially cyclical. These systems always included, but were never solely composed of, states. Chiefdoms, states and empires are trans-historically comparable as political forms, but not 'like units' in all respects. This raises a further paradox of the relationship between comparability and incomparability in socio–political forms.

We have also seen that macrodynamic analysis might be applied at many different scales or 'levels'. So a single state might be analysed in this fashion, as representing another scalar level in the system of systems. Alternatively, the approaches used here to examine regional systems might equally be applied to the analysis of specific non-state actors. However, they too have to be seen as forming part of a larger systems and, like states, made up of yet smaller systems. As we have seen, such non-state actors, and the sets of relationships they help to shape, also play a central role in defining and maintaining the unity of regional systems.

Even in an age of states, therefore, the state, non-state and structural contexts of international politics are strictly inseparable. Here is another paradox, therefore, because (in an 'age of states') although regional systems will appear to be composed of states, states did not originate these regional systems. Instead, states formed within the networks of cultural, religious, social, and economic relationships making up earlier, chiefly, regional systems.[1] Such non-state factors prompted the formation of states as administrative units, and shaped the form both of states and of intra-state and other non-state organizations. States, therefore, were from the first enmeshed in an ever-changing network of social, cultural, religious and economic beliefs, values, institutions and relationships. So, the state and the social system, the social and the religious and cultural system, and each of these and the economic system, are interlinked. Yet not all these links are equally strong at all times, nor is every linkage capable of affecting all others in every way. So, these are not the holistic systems of general systems theory, with their constant feedback flows. Rather, they are ever-shifting complex webs of relationships where agency, structure, process and trajectory combine to form contingent 'states', in both senses. In such systems politics, social organization, economics, culture and religion (for example) are closely connected, but despite these linkages, each operates along a (to some extent) differing trajectory.

When we introduce change into this picture, further paradoxes become clear. There is a 'determined indeterminism' in individualistic action, coexisting with the reflexivity of structures also having diachronic unities of existence. This operates alongside an individualistic basis for macro-level systemic change, producing cross-cultural and transhistorical processual regularities. Thus, socio-political comparability and incomparability, determinism and indeterminism, micro- and macro-levels, and the possibilities of historical particularism and cross-cultural generalizations, may all be in a paradoxical rather than oppositional relationship.

We see a similar set of paradoxes when discussing the probability and trajectories of change. While highly unstable, and ever-changing, polities (be they chiefdoms or states) and structures provide both continuity and stability. But systemic change is both ever-present and definable as a periodic, even spasmodic, phenomenon. Change is not always explicable in similar terms on the level of events, but shared processes are widespread and play a central role in bringing about such changes. It is possible to treat the whole as a multi-scalar unity, or to divide it into 'levels of analysis', with equal merit and 'reality'.

These points stress that the fundamental task for the analyst of change in international politics is to grasp this pattern of paradoxes. It is not a task for which any of the existing theories of International Relations completely prepares one. It is, therefore, unsurprising that so much of the theory which has been found useful here derives from sources other than this discipline.

They also challenge existing assumptions about the possibility and role of universals in explaining change. Here processual universals are argued to exist, but change proceeds in terms of historically specific (albeit in part structurally constrained) events. So all events are not equally likely at any time but true predictability by social science means is impossible. In this view, hierarchical information processing bestows on all complex socio-political systems a propensity for change in specific processual ways. But this does not mean that any specific type of change is certain to come about, or that it will occur at a specific time. Change remains fundamentally located in the individual actor, often operating through the means of organizational structures to achieve the aims and objectives sought.

So, changes are explicable on a processual level as well as by other means, but processual analysis of this sort is not deterministic in the sense that specific changes are inevitable. It could not tell us beforehand, for example, whether Caesar would cross the Rubicon, or whether John Kennedy would be shot in Dallas. Such events usually lie beyond the limits of predictability, even if identical processes of change operated in both the past and the present. However, the future is not wholly unpredictable by these means. If a trajectory or a process has existed over millennia, this holds out the possibility that it will continue into the future. Path-dependency will enhance this likelihood. Thus, there is yet another paradox – the unpredictability of future events, and the probability of future processes and trajectories being the same as at least some of those in existence today.

This is seen very clearly when we discuss the role of scalar increases resulting in stresses prompting change. Increased scale does not necessitate either change at any given moment nor change in any given way. However, if the limits of information processing are exceeded by scalar increase, change will have to occur as a result. In this sense change is 'determined' by increased scale but such determinism is extremely 'weak', in part because its possible outcomes are so wide-ranging.

In this respect we see that scale presents the actor with problems requiring strategic action to overcome them. This also illustrates another aspect of the macrodynamic approach. Process need not be recognized by actors to affect their decisions. So, scalar stresses need not be consciously identified as such to have a major role in prompting change. That is, people do not think one day 'socio-political organization is too big' or 'we have exceeded our information-processing threshold'; the effects are more indirect and filtered through other perceptions. In this case, these may be factors such as 'the rise of separatism', 'increased factionalism', 'social disorder', or the 'loss of control'. Such issues can be resolved in many ways, and these will be chosen by the specific actors involved, rather than being determined by other factors. The basis of this response is simple human problem-solving, but the sources of the contexts prompting this are long-term processes of change.

Macrodynamic processes as the 'tectonics' of world politics

This means that human socio-political diversity, as well as socio-political change, can be explained by reference to these factors. Processual factors such as those discussed in this book are, I suggest, Gaddis's 'tectonics' of international politics. By this Gaddis means factors which produce the 'inexplicable' changes which he observes in the twentieth century.[2] As he points out, such factors can be seen in operation, but are seldom understood by the actors upon whom they operate. He says of them: 'explanations have to be sought in processes which lie outside our normal range of perception. These processes may operate on a different timescale from the one to which we are accustomed'. This seems to me a clear analogy for the processes discussed in this book.

Interestingly, 'plate tectonics' have been used by Fletcher as an analogy for the way in which information-processing structures affect urban form and development. As he points out, the significance of the effects of plate tectonics were recognized prior to the recognition of the character of such processes.[3]

Another possible metaphor for the effects of long-term processes such as these on world politics is that of an iceberg. We can easily see the obvious surface bulk of ice (the contemporary history of our own period in history) but cannot so readily recognize the significance of the far greater extent of ice beneath the sea – the more distant past. In order to discover the significance of this it is necessary to look beneath the waves of time.

The role of these underlying processes is seen – for instance – very clearly in the case of the formation of the earliest states. Such states (according to the model set out here) originated as a means of organizing human communities on a scale above that of the chiefdom. The shift from chiefdom to state organization was analogous to the shift from kin-based societies (such as those of hunter-gatherers) to that of the chiefdom. In each case the scalar shifts were not determined by the trajectories involved. Probably their causes were not perceived in terms of underlying processes by any of those involved. There were always other solutions to the problems of scale involved, and other societies which took these solutions. So, the !Kung remained a kin-based society as the state formed in Kongo, and the Hawaiians were a chiefdom when Captain Cook arrived.

On the basis of this model there is no reason to assume that the choices taken by any of these groups of people were necessarily more 'progressive' or inevitable, but neither should we assume the opposite. All that is required here is that one recognizes that these were choices which human groups made in response to common scalar processes, whether these choices were made collectively, governmentally or under coercion.

Nor were these apparently 'progressive' shifts unilinear or unidirectional changes. The state could 'revert' to a chiefdom, as it did in sub-Saharan Africa and early Anglo-Saxon England, and the chiefdom could revert to a kin-based society. Yet, they were not entirely reversible. Over time there came to be fewer kin-based societies as more chiefdoms developed. No state is known to have returned to being a kin-based society in its entirety. There has, therefore, been a 'progressive' element to the trajectories involved, if by 'progress' one means that socio-political complexity has generally increased over the span of human history. Those few kin-based societies surviving today live inside states, and no entirely independent chiefdom still survives. Yet this is a very recent aspect of world politics, one of the later twentieth century. When Marx wrote, independent chiefdoms were widespread in Africa, South America, and the South Pacific, and many kin-based groups remained unknown to the European world. The last major areas of independent stateless politics were those parts of South America and Melanesia only 'explored' by Europeans or their descendants in the half-century 1930–80.

The present phase of world politics, in which the 'Old World' regional state system state came to form the basis of a global state system, is, therefore, a product of European imperialism. As we have seen, there are grounds for believing that it has transferred the long-running wave of European systemic change into this global system. Consequently, both this pattern of cyclicality, and the realization that this global system will be the focus of any future scalar shifts, render a long-term perspective on contemporary world politics of central importance to their study.

In conclusion, therefore, it is worth – in brief – examining how the global system of today emerged, and whether this too has resulted in scalar shift in socio-political organization. As we have seen, the origins of this global system lie in the expansion of the 'Old World' regional state system to bring into its control extra-European empires.[4] The growth of imperialism and imperial economies in turn brought European economic organization to the extra-European world. This meant that by 1900 there was no continent on which European states were not the principal political actors, even where they were not directly in control.

The recent character of these changes is easy to take for granted and easy to see as inevitable. But there is no reason to suppose that this was always the only possible solution to scalar problems facing Europeans. It is important to recall that other regional systems need not have been colonized had other choices been made, and a multi-systemic world could, perhaps, potentially have existed today.

The consequences of empire

The 'globalization' of the 'Old World' system has already been discussed briefly here and much debated in International Relations. It is the focus of a great amount of scholarly attention worldwide.[5] While it seems true that – to some extent – claims of globalization (in society and culture for instance) have been greatly overstated,[6] there is no doubt that the political system of every continent is now based on the European system,[7] due either to colonization or to so-called 'modernization', which has effectively meant 'Westernization'.[8] In terms of the form of political organization, then, the world has globalized – or, more correctly, 'Europeanized' – but this is not equally applicable to all aspects of human activity, so that localized structures and other contexts for action necessitate a wide diversity in the shape which this has taken in any specific society.[9]

A consequence of the globalization of the 'Old World' system has been to bring new areas into the realm of statehood. It has also established the Westphalian inter-state system as the framework for an 'international system' of worldwide proportions. Like all preceding regional systems, this 'global system' has, of course, other dimensions beyond its political organization as a series of interconnected states.

It has also acquired Europeanized economic and cultural institutions, even where these coexist with or are transformed through local cultures and economies. The spread of economic interlinkages and transnational relations of the world economy are well known to International Relations scholars.

Within this system, the spread of European cultural traits is also highly visible and (especially among sociologists and anthropologists) is another much-discussed feature of the contemporary world.[10] The spread of European culture forms, however, an interesting starting-point from which to relate these changes to the model so far discussed, simply because it has a largely been a characteristic of the period after the collapse of European empires.

European culture, like European political systems and for that matter Europeans themselves, has been able to spread around the globe primarily

due to new technologies of communication. These have permitted interaction on a larger scale than ever before, whether seen in terms of numbers
of participants or geographical scope. It was not simply 'technology' which
enabled European empires to form, but these specific technologies of
communication.[11] The means of communication, not those of conquest or
production, permitted Europeans to rule empires on which the 'sun never
set', because they could travel to and from them, and could transfer
resources and messages between them.

   This immediately locks the development of global European imperialism
into the model so far proposed, but the connections which may be forged
run far deeper than communication alone. The ability to communicate
globally facilitates a global scale of political organization. It also led to a scalar
increase in the socio-political organization of the European state (which was
met through the means of imperialism), so that where communication
provided opportunities for expansion these were often seized. The initial
response to these new opportunities was, therefore, a scalar increase in the
size of those polities within which such technological changes occurred. As
the technologies involved were specific to Europe, this occurred in European polities.

   According to the model, then, there is nothing historically surprising
about the 'imperial age', given the expansionist character of regional socio-
political systems and their dependence on communication as a limit to scalar
stresses. Interestingly, Fletcher has recently noted that, at the same point as
Europe experienced its Industrial Revolution, another scalar increase took
place in European urbanism.[12] Thus, scalar demographic and organizational
increases and economics began to prompt further growth in each other as
demand increased. The European empires and the European industrial
economies could, then, develop in parallel as a consequence of the same
scalar factors. Yet they were not determined to do so – economics alone did
not shape political change – and nor was such a development inevitable.
Simply, changes in technologies of communication (resulting from agency-
based innovation) led to new socio-political and economic opportunities.
These were taken in ways which led to shifts in the form of both socio-
political and economic organization. These gave the opportunities for new
resource-platforms to be created by mass-production on a far greater scale
than previously achieved. This enabled population increase and industrialization, which then supported each other, leading to further scalar
increases.

   So the global empires did not form as an outcome of irresistible pressures
of economics, technology or demography. They were the consequences of
agency, and facilitated by new communication methods again resulting from
individual agency. As a consequence of such changes we can again see
changes in nucleation and in patterns of interaction, the use of trains and
eventually cars, permitting the growth of even larger cities and networks of
distribution.[13] These could rely for employment on the increased scale of the

industrial economy and the services for which they in turn generated a need. The use of new communicative technologies and methods, such as printed newspapers and eventually telecommunications, enabled information exchange in the industrial city and industrial empire alike.[14]

Thus, in Europe the changes in technology and economic organization resulting from the Industrial Revolution consolidated the results of changes in technology and organization resulting from earlier (post-medieval) phases of economic growth. It is easy to assign these causal primacy in explaining European colonization and expansion, but the Industrial Revolution occurred after this was already under way.[15] These earlier changes, too, can be seen to result not from some preceding and fundamental economic shift but as a consequence of the cultural and religious changes resulting from the Renaissance and Reformation in Europe.[16] This in turn occurred at a cyclical point in the systems trajectory. So did the systemic wave cause these changes?

The answer must be no, in that the cyclical patterning afforded only the opportunity for changes to take place, not a deterministic requirement for them to occur or to adopt the forms chosen. These forms can be closely related to individualistic behaviour – religious reform in the case of the Reformation and cultural changes in the Renaissance – producing changes in the beliefs, perceptions, and cultural values of those who participated in such international systemic transformations.[17] The rediscovery of Classical science was, for example, one such consequence.

Without specific acts and actors all of these changes would have taken a different form. For example, without Martin Luther the Reformation would have been different, even if we accept that it would have still occurred. Whether the causes of these changes were intentional or unintentional, historically specific events can equally be understood in processual terms, as agency, and through the lens of structure.

There is another observation which this approach permits and which clarifies the character of these changes. This is the effects of these changes on the state itself as a form of socio-political organization. The Reformation and Renaissance are not merely connected with socio-economic changes in European states but with the rise of the nation-state and the origins of the Westphalian state-system. Many scholars have, for instance, pointed to the close relationship between the origins of liberal democracy and both the Reformation and Renaissance.[18] It can, therefore, be claimed that the state of the Westphalian system was domestically restructured by these changes. It also seems that the regional state system itself in Europe henceforth derived its conceptual basis from them, albeit indirectly.

It was also possible for these 'new' states to build extra-European empires more readily than ever before, as we have seen. This produced a restructuring of their external relations which occurred during the same period in which European states took on the new domestic structures of liberal democracy and industrial economics. Consequently, as the European system expanded, although not all of these structures involved were found in all of its states, these structures became more widespread. They rapidly spread within the system. Thus the two waves of the Westphalian inter-state system identified here share the common threads of the growth of liberal democratic government and that of the globalization of European concepts of politics in general. That is, the origins of the contemporary global system can be related to the processes of change discussed in detail here.

The rise of empire and the industrial age which followed it, are, therefore, easily accommodated within the model. However, these have to be seen as historically specific outcomes resulting from responses to processual regularities. They are not, in this view, assigned the ultimate causality in relation to each other which is often assumed.

Decolonization and the emergence of successor states[19]

We have already seen that collapse of the imperial system is explicable by using the model. This can be understood as a consequence of long-term processual trajectories inherent (it seems) in the 'Old World' regional system. Likewise, the rise of new successor states in the wake of collapse is equally explicable in this way.

The formation of many smaller independent states is explicable as an alternative solution to the global scale of the 'European' global state system following the collapse of empire. After empire two possible solutions to the scalar problems of imperial collapse might have been seized upon: the formation of new empires (perhaps by non-Europeans) or the fission of large imperial polities into smaller states.

Two areas in which empire was replaced by 'empire' were, of course, Russia and China. There, pre-existing empires were effectively geopolitically replicated rather than fragmented.[20] The internal reorganization of these can be seen as the discovery of alternative solutions to the scalar problems of political organization, the exact forms chosen being the outcome of historically specific factors and local structures.[21]

So, when the USSR collapsed – according to this model – the successor was likely to be either another Russian empire (this could still occur at the time of writing) or a series of smaller states, probably defined along preexisting identities. The latter is what has so far occurred.[22] This, of course, alerts us to the possibility of similar changes in China, or even the USA. However, we must recall that distinct trajectories may produce different results as differing solutions are found to shared processual problems.[23]

Another especially visible aspect of the later twentieth-century global system is also explicable in these terms: the rise of international institutions.[24] The scale of the global system enables a simple but comprehensive explanation to be proposed for the rise of both international institutions and other transnational actors in the twentieth century.[25] This is the need to cope with scales of information processing and global governance resulting from the emergence of a worldwide inter-state system.[26] This readily fits the chronology of the rise of such institutions and firms during the period of imperial decline. As such, they are part of the emergent global systemic trajectory which we have seen is identifiable in the period *c*. 1900–2000. This is, of course, the period in which the nineteenth-century empires ceased to exist.

The model can, therefore, enable a coherent explanation and interpretation of large-scale changes in world political history, in general terms, from the earliest societies to the fall of the soviet system. It can do so without a complete rewriting of world political history and without recourse to determinism. It is, of course, fascinating to speculate on the implications of this model for the future development of the global system in detail. However, I shall leave that, for the most part, for another work but perhaps here is an apt place to make some preliminary comments on the implications for the future of the nation-state and the prospects for global governance.

How long can this go on?

Will the current revolution in communications again have a transformative effect? The role of international communications has already facilitated major changes in the way in which information is used in international politics:[27] the rise of global news media and mass interest in distant political situations and global issues among the 'general public' in many parts of the world.[28] These, in turn, permit the rise of international 'public opinion' and are perhaps encouraging the growth of a global 'civil society'.[29]

While such features are not universally distributed among the world's population, nor were any of the other changes which have already been discussed. Their effectiveness has certainly been enhanced by the spread of liberal democracy and free-market economics.[30] These have produced a capacity for international attitudes to both governmental and non-governmental action to have serious political consequences.[31]

The development of electronic communications has meant that global communication of this sort, established in the nineteenth century, is being revolutionized once again, this is facilitating interaction and engagement on an unprecedented scale.[32] Yet geographical growth is no longer (for the most part) a possible buffer to scalar increases in political units. They cannot expand territorially to accommodate increased population or other aspects of scalar growth, with the ease with which this could be achieved by the largest nineteenth-century empires.

This change in the ease of communications, then, will probably bring about new dangers and new opportunities for transforming the global socio-political system.[33] The 400-year wave of rise and decline found in the regional state system might persist, bringing global rather than regional collapse. Alternatively, the form of socio-political organization might be transformed so as to avoid this catastrophe. Such a transformation might involve a shift in the form of political organization, or in the manner in which societies are spatially or socially organized.[34] One option for such a shift – 'the decline of the nation-state' – has been widely heralded for a generation, but the state does not appear to be obviously 'declining' globally: there are still very many states and potential states attempting to form.[35]

However, to focus on the persistence of a socio-political form at a time of scalar shift is perhaps to forget the lessons of long-term analysis as we have seen them here. Similar changes occur as similar responses to scalar stress are adopted, but not all at the same time. Not all societies will respond to similar stresses in the same ways, or even feel those stresses at the same points in time. Alternatively, other processes than the decline of the state as a form of socio-political organization might be represented, such as a change in the role and organization of states and their relationships to non-state actors.[36]

Consequently, one might see here another paradox: the 'decline' of the nation-state may be evidenced, but this does not necessitate either a 'world without states' or that nation-states will be replaced by non-state forms of organization. A new type of state might be emerging, or perhaps there are alternative solutions which might be adopted to accommodate the shift in scale. For example, these options could include the development of a new tier of global governance, at the regional level for instance, or the formation of global structures of administration relieving states of some of the pressures produced by increased scale.[37] They might involve new transnational institutions (which might absorb the consequences of such changes), or they might be in changes in the distribution of administrative functions to intra-state bodies or devolved intra-state regional units.

Alternatively, the system might be fragmenting into many smaller states once more, so that the size of individual units might be decreasing to accommodate new levels of information. It is not necessary to argue that these changes are mutually exclusive. Differing socio-political groups need not share the same types of change for us to see that all the possibilities may exist at present. Members of differing societies might or might not opt for different solutions to these scalar problems, depending on a wide range of factors including inter-state and transnational interactions. Alternatively, the elimination of communication time might fundamentally transform the processes involved. This might then alter the whole processual character of world politics. If there are changes in the very processes of change then the waves of state politics seen in the previous chapter may be ending rather than continuing into the next millennium.

It does not seem immediately apparent which of these interpretations is the most credible. However, I doubt if the latter is under way at present, given the apparently ongoing similarities between observable changes in world politics and the cyclical processes of the 'Old World' regional state system discussed here. Political fragmentation seems well attested, but so too can one point to many regional integrationist projects and attempts at global governance. Thus, perhaps all solutions are being simultaneously tried, and perhaps some or all will succeed.

Conclusion

This book has aimed to investigate the processes of long-term global change from a fresh point of view. I have hoped to link individual agency with macrodynamic processes to understand the way in which people can form their own histories but are constrained by the past. Yet there are similarities between the problems and issues which individuals face at all periods in human history, as well as contrasts. Such similarities derive from processual factors and enduring environmental and other structures.

This book is intended, as was mentioned earlier, only as a preliminary study of what is inevitably a vast subject. Yet, the potential for the study of international politics in examining long-term processes of change seems to me almost equally huge. I hope others will apply the macrodynamic framework of analysis suggested here to their problems and questions, both to seek new answers and to develop this approach further.

In this analysis we have seen how complexity, information processing and decision-making construct fundamental processes of change which have transhistorical roles in the formation of socio-political trajectories. Such an approach can overcome many long-established but false contrasts: between determinism and freewill, between structure and agency, between the short- and long-term temporalities of analysis and between the levels at which that analysis is undertaken. This leads to the realization that understanding change in world politics, as in other aspects of life, involves an engagement with a series of paradoxes as well as fundamental questions.

I hope also to have shown the potential of such a long-term analysis of world politics. Long-term studies in International Relations are only begin-ning. In the future, the past will become even more important to the study of the present.

Notes

1   This introduces a further paradox: states both are 'social constructs', produced by such contexts, and have a structural (institutional) existence as part of that context. For the state as social construct: Biersteker, T. J. and Weber, C. (eds), 1996, *State Sovereignty as Social Construct*.

2   Gaddis, J. L., 1992, *The United States and the End of the Cold War*, Oxford, New York and Toronto, p. 155.

3   Fletcher, R., 1995, *The Limits of Settlement Growth*, p. 91.

4   Classically discussed in: Wolf, E. R., 1982, *Europe and the People Without History*, Berkeley. See also: Boxer, C. R., 1965, *The Dutch Seaborne Empire*

1600–1800, New York; Boxer, C. R., 1973, *The Portuguese Seaborne Empire 1415–1825*; Fieldhouse, D. K., 1967, *The Colonial Empires: A Comparative Study from the Eighteenth Century*, New York; Fieldhouse, D. K., 1982, *The Colonial Empires*, 2nd edn; Phillips, J. R. S., 1988, *The Medieval Expansion of Europe*; Scammell, G. V., 1989, *The First Imperial Age (1400–1715)*; Scammell, G. V., 1981, *The World Encompassed*; Thomson, J. E., 1994, *Merceneries, Pirates, and Sovereigns: State-building and Extra-territorial Violence in Early Modern Europe*, Princeton, NJ; Rosecrance, R., 1991, *The Rise of the Trading State: Commerce and Conquest in the Modern World*, New York.

5   Robertson, R., 1987, 'Globalization theory and civilizational analysis', *Comparative Civilizations Review* 17, 20–30; Robertson, R., 1992, *Globalization: Social Theory and Global Culture*; Spyby, T., 1995, *Globalization and World Society*.

6   Jones, R. J. B., 1995, *Globalization and Interdependence in the International Political Economy;* Germain, R. (ed.), 1997, *Globalization and its Critics*.

7   By which I mean that the European Westphalian state-system and the concept of the nation-state have spread to encompass the globe. Calvocoressi, P., 1993, *World Politics since 1945*; Weiss, L. and Hobson, J. M., 1995, *States and Economic Development. A Comparative Historical Analysis*.

8   Smith, A. D., 1990, 'Towards a global culture?' *Theory, Culture and Society* 7, 171–93; van Lave, T., 1987, *The World Revolution of Westernization: The Twentieth Century, a Global Perspective*.

9   Stalling, B. (ed.), 1995, *Global Change, Regional Response. The New International Context of Development*.

10 Lipschutz, R. D., 1992, 'Reconstructing world politics: the emergence of global civil society', *Millennium* 21, 389–420; Ghils, P., 1992, 'International civil society: international non-governmental organizations in the international system', *International Social Science Journal* 133, 417–29.

11 Cipolla, C. M., 1965, *Guns, Sails and Empire*, New York: Smith, A. K., 1991, *Creating a World Economy: Merchant Capital, Colonialism and World Trade 1400–1825*, Boulder, Colo.; Headrick, D. R., 1981, *The Tools of Empire*.

12 Fletcher, R., 1995, *The Limits of Settlement Growth*, pp. 89 and 209–11.

13 Fletcher, R., 1995, *The Limits of Settlement Growth*, p. 9.

14 *Ibid.*

15 The exact starting-date of European colonialism is unclear, but well before *c.* 1750: Phillips, J. R. S., 1988, *The Medieval Expansion of Europe*; Scammell, G. V., 1989, *The First Imperial Age (1400–1715)*.

16 Tracy, J. D., 1991, *The Political Economy of Merchant Empires*; Tracy, J. D. (ed.), 1990, *The Rise of Merchant Empire: Long-distance Trade in the Early Modern World 1350–1750*; Cipolla, C. M., 1976, *Before the Industrial Revolution: European Society and Economy 1000–1700*.

17 Zacher, M. W., 1992, 'The decaying pillars of the Westphalian temple: implications for international order and governance', in J. N. Rosenau and E-O. Czempiel (eds), *Governance without Government: Order and Change in World Politics*, 58–101.

18 *Ibid.*

19 Chamberlain, M. E., 1985, *Decolonization*; Strong, D., 1991, 'Global patterns of decolonization 1500–1987', *International Studies Quarterly* 35, 429–45;

Dunbabin, J. P. D., 1994, *The Post-Imperial Age*; Holland, R. F., 1985, *European Decolonization 1918–1981: An Introductory Survey*.

20 On the fragmentation of the Soviet Empire and its constituent sub-units: Simon, G., 1996, 'The end of the Soviet Union, causes and relational contexts', *Aussenpolitik* 47.1, 9–21.

21 Contrast Asian and North American experience, for example. Palat, R. A. (ed.), 1993, *Pacific Asia and the Future of the World System*, Westport; Thompson, R. C., 1994, *The Pacific Basin Since 1945*.

22 On the collapse: Motyl, A. J., 1992, 'From imperial decay to imperial collapse: the fall of the Soviet Empire in comparative perspective', in R. L. Rudolph and D. F. Good (eds), *The Hapsburg Empire and the Soviet Union*, New York, 15–43. Featherstone, M. (ed.), 1990, *Global Culture, Nationalism, Globalization and Modernity*; Smith, A. D., 1995, *Nations and Nationalism in a Global Era*.

23 Dark, K., 1996, 'United States decline in global perspective: comparing processes of change in the USA, USSR and China', *Contemporary Political Studies* 1, 1–12.

24 Taylor, P., 1993, *International Organisation in the Modern World*. See also: Mansbach, R. W., Ferguson, Y. H. and Lampert, D. E., 1976, *The Web of World Politics: Nonstate Actors in the Global System*, Englewood Cliffs, NJ.

25 Risse-Kappen, T., 1995, *Bringing Transnational Relations Back In*.

26 Zacher, M. W. and Sutton, B. A., 1995, *Governing Global Networks*, Cambridge; Dark, K., 1996, 'United States decline in global perspective: comparing processes of change in the USA, USSR and China', *Contemporary Political Studies* 1, 1–12.

27 Held, D., 1995, *Democracy and the Global Order*; Axford, B., 1995 *The Global System*; Brunn, S. and Leinbach, T., 1991, *Collapsing Space and Time*; Garrett, G. and Lange, P., 1995, 'Internationalization, institutions, and political change', *International Organization* 49.4, 627–55.

28 Shaw, M., 1994, *Global Society and International Relations*.

29 Shaw, M., 1994, *Global Society and International Relations*; Gillis, P., 1992, 'International civil society: interchange, non-governmental organizations in the international system', *International Social Science Journal* 133, 417–79; Shaw, M., 1992, 'Global society and global responsibility: the theoretical, historical and political limits of international society', *Millennium* 21.3, 421–34.

30 Carnoy, M. *et al.*, 1993, *The World Economy in the Information Age*; Mowlana, H., 1985, *International Flow of Information: A Global Report and Analysis*, Paris; Smith, N. and Dennis, W., 1987, 'The restructuring of geographical scale: coalescence and fragmentation of the northern core region', *Economic Geography* 63, 160–82; Ward, B., 1989, 'Telecommunications and the globalization of financial services', *Professional Geographer* 41.3, 257–71; Dicken, P., 1992, *Global Shift: The Internationalization of Economic Activity*, New York; OECD, 1992, *Globalization of Industrial Activities*.

31 Macadam, D., McCarthy, J. D. and Zald, M. (eds), 1996, *Comparative Perspectives on Social Movements*; Hill, C., 1996, 'World opinion and the empire of circumstance', *International Affairs* 72.1, 109–31; Melucci, A., 1989, *Nomads and the Present: Social Movements and Individual Needs in Contemporary Society*; McGrew, A., 1992, 'A global society', in S. Hall, D. Held and T. McGrew (eds), *Modernity and its Futures*, 62–113.

32 Castells, M., 1989, *The Informational City*. For new dangers: Williams, P. and

Black, S., 1994, 'Transnational threats: drug trafficking and weapons proliferation', *Contemporary Security Policy* 15, 127–51.

33   For its effects, and possible effects: Krasner, S. D., 1991, 'Global communications and national power: life on the Pareto frontier', *World Politics* 43, 336–66; Tonn, B. E. and Feldman, D., 'Non-spatial government', *Futures* 27.1, 11–36; Cioffi-Revilla, C., Merritt, R. L. and Zinnes, D. A. (eds), 1987, *Communication and Interaction in Global Politics*, Newburn Park, Calif.; Mowlana, H., 1986, *Global Information and World Communication: New Frontiers in International Relations*; Spiro, P. J., 1995, 'New global communities: non-governmental organizations in international decision-making institutions', in B. Roberts (ed.), *Order and Disorder After the Cold War*, 251–62; Aronson, J. D., 1996, 'The consequences of free trade in information flows', *International Affairs* 72.2, 311–28; Lazlo, E., 1991, *The Age of Bifurcation: Understanding the Changing World*, Philadelphia; Melucci, A., 1996, *Challenging Codes. Collective Action in the Information Age*; Brunn, S. and Leinbach, T. (eds), 1991, *Collapsing Space and Time*; Mowlana, H., 1997, *Global Information and World Communication*.

34   For example see: Wriston, W. B., 1992, *The Twilight of Sovereignty: How the Information Revolution is Transforming our World*, New York; Ohmae, K., 1990, *The Borderless World*; Tonn, B. E. and Feldman, D., 1996, 'Non-spatial government' *Futures* 27.1, 11–36.

35   For contrasting views: Barkin, J. S. and Cronin, B., 1994, 'The state and the nation: changing norms and the rules of sovereignty in International Relations', *International Organization* 48.1, 107–30; McGrew, T. G. and Lewis, P. G., 1992, *Global Politics*; Holt, I., 1994, 'The permanent crisis of a divided mankind: contemporary crisis of the nation state in historical perspective', *Political Studies* 42, 166–235; Camilleri, J. and Falk, J., 1991, *The end of sovereignty?*; Sklair, L., 1991, *Sociology and the Global System*; Strange, S., 1996, *The Retreat of the State*; Mann, M., 1993, 'Nation states in Europe and other continents: diversifying, developing, not dying', *Proceedings of the American Academy of Arts and Sciences* 122.3, 115–40; Held, D., 1989, 'The decline of the nation-state', in S. Hall and M. Jacques (eds), *New Times*, 191–224; Strange, S., 1996, *The Retreat of the State*; McCarthy, P. and Jones, E. (eds), 1996, *Disintegration or Transformation?*; Dunn, J. M. (ed.), 1995, *Contemporary Crisis of the Nation State*.

36   For a 'world-systems' view: Goldgeier, J. M. and McFaul, M., 1992, 'A tale of two worlds: core and periphery in the post-Cold War era', *International Organization* 46.2, 467–91.

37   Hirst, P. and Thompson, G., 1992, 'The problem of "globalization", international economic relations, national economic management and the formation of trading blocs', *Economy and Society* 21, 357–96; Cox, R., 1994, 'Global restructuring: making sense of the changing international political economy', in R. Stubbs and G. Underhill (eds), *Political Economy and the Changing Global Order*, 45–59.

Bibliography

Unless otherwise noted, all books are published in the United Kingdom.

Abbot, A., 1983, 'Sequences of social events: concepts and methods for the analysis of order in social processes', *Historical Methods* 16, 129–47.

Abrams, P., 1983, *Historical Sociology*, Ithaca.

Abrams, P., 1988, 'Notes on the difficulty of studying the state', *Journal of Historical Sociology* 1.1, 58–89.

Adams, R. E. W., 1996, *Prehistoric Mesoamerica*, 2nd edn, Stillwater, OK.

Adams, W. Y., 1984, 'The first colonial empire: Egypt in Nubia 3200–1200 BC', *Comparative Studies in Society and History* 26.1, 36–71.

Adler, B. and Crawford, B. (eds), 1991, *Progress in Post-War International Relations*.

Agnew, J., 1994, 'The territorial trap: the geographical assumptions of international relations theory', *Review of International Political Economy* 1.1, 53–80.

Agnew, J. A. and Corbridge, S., 1989, 'The new geopolitics: the dynamics of geopolitical disorder', in R. J. Johnston and P. J. Taylor (eds), *A World in Crisis? Geographical Perspectives*, 266–88.

Ajayi, J. F. A. and Crowder, M. (eds), 1972, *A History of West Africa*, New York.

Alexander, J. C. *et al.* (eds), 1987, *The Micro-Macro Link*, Berkeley, CA.

Alexander, R. D., 1980, *Darwinism and Human Affairs*

Alger, C. F., 1984–85, 'Bridging the micro and the macro in international relations research', *Alternatives* 10, 319–44

Allan, P. and Goldmann, K. (eds), 1992, *The End of The Cold War: Evaluating Theories of International Relations*, Dordrecht

Allchin, R. and Allchin, B., 1982, *The Rise of Civilization in India and Pakistan*

Allchin, R. *et al.*, 1995, *The Archaeology of Early Historic South Asia: The Emergence of Cities and States*

Allen, P. M., 1982, 'The genesis of structure in social systems', in A. C. Renfrew, M. J. Rowlands and B. A. Segraves (eds), *Theory and Explanation in Archaeology*, New York, 347–74

Allen, P. M. and McGlade, J. M., 1987, 'Evolutionary drive: the effect of microscopic diversity, error making and noise', *Foundations of Physics* 17.7, 723–8

Allen, P. M. and Perez-Trejo, F., 1992, 'Strategic planning of complex economic systems', *Review of Political Economy* 4.3, 275–90

Allen, P. M. and Sanglier, M., 1981, 'Urban evolution, self-organisation and decision-making', *Environment and Planning* A21, 167–83

Allen, T. F. H. and Starr, T. B., 1982, *Hierarchy, Perspectives for Ecological Complexity*, Chicago

Althusser, L., 1977, *For Marx*

Ambrovitz, M., 1993, 'The search for the sources of economic growth: areas of ignorance, old and new', *Journal of Economic History* 53, 217–43

Ames, K. M., 1981, 'The evolution of social ranking on the northwest coast of North America', *American Antiquity* 46, 789–805

Ames, K. M., 1985, 'Hierarchies, stress and logistical strategies among hunter-gatherers in north western north America', in T. D. Price and J. A. Brown (eds), *Prehistoric Hunter-gatherers: The Emergence of Cultural Complexity*, Orlando, 155–80

Ames, K. M., 1991, 'The archaeology of the *longue durée*: temporal and spatial scale in the evolution of social complexity on the southern Northwest Coast', *Antiquity* 65, 935–45

Amin, A. (ed.), 1994, *PostFordism: A Reader*

Anderson, M. S., 1966, *The Eastern Question 1774–1923*

Anderson, M. S., 1976, *Europe in the Eighteenth Century 1713–83*

Anderson, P., 1974, *Passages from Antiquity to Feudalism*

Anderson, P., 1974, *Lineages of the Absolutist State*

Anderson, P. A., 1987, 'What do decision makers do when they make a foreign policy decision? Implications for the comparative study of foreign policy', in C. F. Herman, C. W. Kegley and J. N. Rosenau (eds), *New Directions in the Study of Foreign Policy*, 285–308

Anderson, P. W., Arrow, K. J. and Pines, D. (eds), 1988, *The Economy as an Evolving Complex System*, Reading, MA

Angold, M., 1984, *The Byzantine Empire 1025–1204: A Political History*

Aoki, M., 1986, 'Horizontal vs. vertical information structure of the firm', *American Economic Review* 76, 971–83

Archer, M. S., 1988, *Culture and Agency*

Archer, M. S. 1995, *Realist Social Theory: the Morphogenetic Approach*

Arnold, J. E., 1985, 'Economic spcialization in prehistory: methods of documenting the age of lithic craft specialization', in S. C. Vetik (ed.), *Lithic Resource Procurement*, Carbondale, IL, 37–58

Arnold, J. E., 1991, 'Transformation of a regional economy: sociopolitical evolution and the production of valuables in southern California', *Antiquity* 65, 953–62

Arnold, J. E. 1992, 'Complex hunter-gatherer-fishers of prehistoric California: chiefs, specialists and maritime adaptations of the Channel

Islands', *American Antiquity* 57, 60–84

Arnold, J. E., 1993, 'Labor and the rise of complex hunter-gatherers', *Journal of Anthropological Archaeology* 12, 75–119

Arnold, B. and Gibson, D. B. (eds), 1995, *Celtic Chiefdom, Celtic State*, Cambridge

Aron, R., 1968, *Progress and Disillusion*, New York

Aron, R., 1968, *Main Currents in Sociological Thought 2*, New York

Aronson, J. D., 1996, 'The consequences of free trade in information flows', *International Affairs* 72.2, 311–28

Arrighi, G., Hopkins, T. K. and Wallerstein, I. 1989, *Antisystemic Movements*, London and New York

Arrighi, G., 1994, *The Long Twentieth Century*, London and New York

Arrow, K., 1964, 'Control in large organizations', *Management Science* 10.3, 397–408

Arrow, K. J., 1985, 'Informational structure of the firm', *American Economic Review* 75, 303–7

Arthur, W. B., Ermoliev, Y. M. and Kaniovski, Y. M., 1987, 'Path dependent processes and the emergence of macro-structure', *European Journal of Operational Research* 30.2, 294–303

Ashley, R. 1996, 'The achievements of post-structuralism', in S. Smith, K. Booth and M. Zalewski (eds), *International Theory: Positivism and Beyond*, 240–53

Athanassiades, J. C., 1973, 'The distortion of upward communication in hierarchical organizations', *Academy of Management Journal* 16, 207–26

Aubet, M. E., 1993, *The Phoenicians and the West: Politics, Colonies and Trade*

Axford, B., 1995, *The Global System*

Badian, E., 1968, *Roman Imperialism in the Late Republic*

Baillie, M. G. L., 1995, *A Slice through Time*

Bakel, M. A., Hagesteijn, R. R. and Van der Velde, P. (eds), 1986, *Private Politics: A Multidisciplinary Approach to 'Big Man' Systems*, Leiden

Baldwin, D. (ed.), 1993, *Neorealism and Neoliberalism: The Contemporary Debate*

Baldwin, D., 1980, 'Interdependence and power: a conceptual analysis', *International Organization* 34.4, 471–506

Bard, K. A., 1994, *From Farmers to Pharaohs*

Barkin, J. S. and Cronin, B., 1994, 'The state and the nation: changing norms and the rules of sovereignty in international relations', *International Organization* 48.1, 107–30

Barnard, A., 1983, 'Contemporary hunter-gatherers: current theoretical issues in ecology and social organization', *Annual Review of Anthropology* 12, 193–214

Barnard, A. and Spencer, J. (eds), 1996, *Encyclopedia of Social and Cultural Anthropology*

Barnes, G. L., 1993, *China, Korea and Japan*

Barr, K., 1979, 'Long waves: a selective annotated bibliography', *Review* 2.4, 675–718

Bates, D., 1982, *Normandy Before 1066*

Bawden, G., 1996, *The Moche*

Bebbington, D., 1979, *Patterns in History*

Beck, N., 1991, 'The illusion of cycles in international relations', *International Studies Quarterly* 35.4, 455–76

Bedeian, A., 1987, 'Organization theory: current controversies, issues and direction', in C. L. Cooper and I. T. Robertson (eds), *Review of Industrial and Organizational Psychology*, Chichester, 110–40

Begeler, E., 1978, 'Sex, status and authority in egalitarian society', *American Anthropologist* 80, 571–88

Bell, J. A., 1994, *Reconstructing Prehistory*, Philadelphia

Bellwood, P., 1987, *The Polynesians*, 2nd edn

Bennett, P. and Nicholson, M., 1994, 'Formal methods of analysis in IR', in A. J. R. Groom and M. Light (eds), *Contemporary International Relations: A Guide to Theory*, 206–15

Bennett, P. G., 1995, 'Modelling decisions in international relations: game, theory and beyond', *Mershon International Studies Review* 39, 19–52

Berg, M., 1994, *The Age of Manufactures 1700–1820*, 2nd edn

Berge, P., Pomeau, Y. and Vidal, C., 1984, *Order within Chaos: Towards a Deterministic Approach to Turbulence*, New York

Bergesen, A. (ed.), 1983, *Crises in the World System*, Beberley Hills, CA

Bergesen, A. (ed.), 1980, *Studies of the World System*, New York

Bergesen, A. and Schoenberg, R., 1980, 'Long waves of colonial expansion and contraction, 1415–1969', in Bergesen, A. (ed.), *Studies of the Modern World System*, New York, 231–77

Bergesen, A., 1980, 'From utilitarianism to globology: the shift from the individual to the world as a whole as the primordial unit of analysis', in A. Bergeson (ed.), *Studies of the Modern World System*, New York, 231–77

Bernstein, R., 1983, *Beyond Objectivism and Relativism: Science, Hermeneutics, and Praxis*, Philadelphia

Berry, B. J. L., 1991, *Long-wave Rhythms in Economic Development and Political Behavior*, Baltimore, MD

Bevir, M., 1994, 'Objectivity in history', *History and Theory* 33, 328–44

Bevir, M., 1996, 'The individual and society', *Political Studies* 64, 102–14

Bhaskar, R., 1989, *Reclaiming Reality*

Biersteker, T. 1989, 'Critical reflections on post-positivism in international relations', *International Studies Quarterly* 33.3, 263–8

Biersteker, T. J. and Weber, C. (eds), 1996, *State Sovereignty as a Social Construct*

Bikhchandani, S., Hirshleifer, D. and Welch, I., 1992, 'A theory of fads, fashion, custom and cultural change in informational cascades', *Journal of Political Economy* 100.5, 992–1026

Bill, J. A. and Springborg, R., 1994, *Politics in the Middle East*, 4th edn.

Bird, J., 1989, *The Changing Worlds of Geography*

Blachman, M. J. and Puchala, D. J., 1991, 'When empires meet. The long peace in long-term perspective', in C. W. Kegley (ed.), *The Long Post-War Peace*, New York, 177–201

Blanton, R. E. *et al.*, 1993, *Ancient Mesopotamia*, 2nd edn.

Blau, P. M., 1968, 'The hierarchy of authority in organizations', *American Journal of Sociology* 37, 453–67

Blau, P. M., 1970, 'A formal theory of differentiation in organisations', *American Sociological Review* 35, 201–18

Bloch, M., 1961, *Feudal Society*, Transl. L. A. Manyon

Bock, K., 1980, *Human Nature and History*, New York

Bonhage-Freund, M. T. and Kurland, J. A., 1994, 'Tit-for-tat among the Iroquois: a game theoretic perspective on inter-tribal political organization', *Journal of Anthropological Archaeology* 13, 278–305

Booth, D. (ed.), 1994, *Rethinking Social Development*

Borgerhoff, M. M., 1981, 'Adaptation and evolutionary approaches to anthropology', *Man* 22, 25–41

Boswell, T. and Sweat, M., 1991, 'Hegemony, long waves, and major wars: a time series analysis of systemic dynamics', *International Studies Quarterly* 35, 123–49

Boudon, R., 1986, *Theories of Social Change*

Bourdieu, P. 1972, *Outlines of a Theory of Practice*

Boxer, C. R., 1965, *The Dutch Seaborne Empire 1600–1800*, New York

Boxer, C. R., 1973, *The Portuguese Seaborne Empire 1415–1825*

Boyd, R. and Richerson, P. J., 1985, *Culture and the Evolutionary Process*, Chicago

Boyd, R. and Richerson, P. J., 1992, 'How microevolutionary processes give rise to history', in M. H. and D. V. Nitecki (edds), *History and Evolution*, New York, 179–209

Brands H. W., 1992, 'Fractal history, or Clio and the chaotics', *Diplomatic History*, 495–510

Brass, D. J., 1984, 'Being in the right place: a structural analysis of individual influence in an organisation', *Administrative Science Quarterly* 29, 518–39

Braudel, F., 1981–4, *Civilization and Capitalism 15th-18th Century*, 3 vols

Braudel, F., 1975, *The Mediterranean and the Mediterranean World in the Age of Philip II*, 2 vols

Braun, D., 1990, 'Selection and evolution in non-hierarchical organization', in S. Upham (ed.), *The Evolution of Political Systems*, 62–86

Braybrooke, D., 1987, *Meeting Needs*, Princeton, NJ

Bremmer, S. (ed.), 1987, *The Globus Model: Simulation of Worldwide Political and Economic Developments*, Frankfurt

Bremmer, S., 1977, *Simulated Worlds*, Princeton, NJ

Brewin, C., 1992, 'Research in a global context: a discussion of Toynbee's legacy', *Review of International Studies* 18.2, 115–30

Bridges, F. R. and Bullen, R. 1980, *The Great Powers and the European States*

System 1815–1914

Bromley, S., 1994, *Rethinking Middle East Politics*

Bronner, S., 1994, *Critical Theory and its Theorists*

Brooke, C., 1987, *Europe in the Central Middle Ages 962–1154*, 2nd end.

Brown, C. 1994, 'Turtles all the way down: anti-foundationalism, critical theory and international relations', *Millennium* 23.2, 213–35

Brown, C., 1996, 'International relations theory and international distributive justice', *Politics* 16.1, 1–8

Brown, C., 1994, 'Critical theory and postmodernism in international relations', in A. J. R. Groom and M. Light (eds), *Contemporary International Relations: A Guide to Theory*, 56–68

Brown, C., 1997, *Understanding International Relations*

Brown, L. R. *et al.*, 1994, *Vital Signs*

Brown, M. E. *et al.* (eds), 1995, *The Perils of Anarchy*, Cambridge, MA

Brown, S., 1984, 'The world polity and the nation-state system', *International Journal* 39, 509–28

Brown, S., 1996, *International Relations in a Changing Global System*, 2nd edn.

Browning, R., 1971, *Justinian and Theodora*

Browning, R., 1980, *The Byzantine Empire*

Bruhns, K. O., 1994, *Ancient South America*

Brunn, S. and Leinbach, T. (eds), 1991, *Collapsing Space and Time*

Bryant, C. G. A. and Jary, D. (eds), 1990, *Giddens' Theory of Structuration: A Critical Appreciation*, London and New York

Buckley, W., 1987, *Sociology and Modern Systems Theory*

Bull, H., 1977, *The Anarchical Society: A Study of Order in World Politics*, New York

Bulmer, M., 1994, *Theoretical Evolutionary Ecology*, Sunderland, MA

Burchill, S. and Linklater, A., *et al.*, 1996, *Theories of International Relations*

Burke, P., 1992, *History and Social Theory*

Burns, A. F. and Mitchell, W. C., 1946, *Measuring Business Cycles*, New York

Burt, R., 1991, *Structural Holes: The Social Structure of Competition*, Cambridge, MA

Burt, R. S., 1992, *Social Contagion*, Cambridge, MA

Burton, J. W., 1965, *International Relations: A General Theory*

Burton, J. W., 1972, *World Society*

Burton, J. W., 1983, 'The individual as the unit of explanation in international relations', *International Studies Newsletter* 10, 14–17

Burton, J. W. 1983, *Dear Survivors*

Burton, J. W. (ed), 1990, *Conflict: Human Needs Theory*

Buzan, B., 1993, 'From international system to international society: structural and regime theory meet the English School', *International Organization* 47.3, 327–52

Buzan, B., 1995, 'The level of analysis problem in international relations reconsidered', in K. Booth and S. Smith (eds), *International Relations Theory Today*, 198–216

Buzan, B., 1996, 'The timeless wisdom of Realism', in S. Smith, K. Booth and M. Zalewski (eds), *International Theory: Positivism and Beyond*, 47–65

Buzan, B., Jones, C. A. and Little, R., 1993, *The Logic of Anarchy*, New York

Buzan, B. and Jones, R. J. B. (eds), 1981, *Change and the Study of International Relations*

Buzan, B. and Little, R., 1994, 'The idea of international system: theory meets history', *International Political Science Review* 15.3, 23–56

Callinicos, A., 1988, *Making History: Agency, Structure, and Change in Social Theory*, Ithaca, NY

Calvocoressi, P., 1996, *World Politics Since 1945* (7th edn)

Cameron, A., 1993, *The Mediterranean World in Late Antiquity AD 395–600*

Cameron, E., 1991, *The European Reformation*

Camilleri, J. and Falk, J., 1991, *The End of Sovereignty?*

Campanella, M. (ed.), 1988, *Between Rationality and Cognition: Policy Making under Conditions of Uncertainty, Complexity and Turbulence*, Torino

Campbell, F. and Akers, R. L., 1970, 'Organizational size, complexity and the administrative component in occupational associations', *Sociological Quarterly* 11, 435-51

Campbell, J. (ed.), 1982, *The Anglo-Saxons*

Caplan, A. L. (ed.), 1978, *The Sociobiology Debate*, New York

Carlsnaes, W., 1992, 'The agency-structure problem in foreign policy analysis', *International Studies Quarterly* 36, 245–70

Carneiro, R. L., 1967, 'On the relationship between size of population and complexity of social organization', *Southwestern Journal of Anthropology* 23, 234-43

Carneiro, R. L., 1970, 'A theory of the origin of the state', *Science* 169, 733–8

Carneiro, R. L., 1978, 'Political Expansion as an Expression of the Principle of Competitive Exclusion', in R. Cohen and R. Elman (eds), *The Anthropology of Political Evolution*, Philadelphia, 205–44

Carneiro, R. L., 1981, 'The chiefdom: precursor of the state', in G. D. Jones and R. R. Kautz (eds), *The Transition to Statehood in the New World*, 37–79

Carneiro, R. L., 1987, 'Cross currents in the theory of state-formation', *American Ethnologist* 14, 756–70

Carnoy, M. *et al.*, 1993, *The World Economy in the Information Age*

Carrasco, P., 1991, 'The territorial structure of the Aztec empire', in H. R. Harvey (ed.), *Land and Politics in the Valley of Mexico: A Two Thousand Year Perspective*, Albuquerque, 93–112

Carzo, R. and Yanouzas, J. N., 1969, 'Effects of flat and tall organisation structure', *Administrative Science Quarterly* 14, 178–91

Casson, M., 1990, 'Entrepreneurial culture as a competitive advantage', *Research in Global Business Management*, 1, 139–51

Casson, M., 1993, 'Cultural determinants of economic performance', *Journal of Comparative Economics* 17, 418–42

Casson, M., 1997, *Information and Organization*

Casson, M. and Wadeson, N., 1996, 'Information strategies and the theory of the firm', *International Journal of the Economics of Business* 3.3, 307–30

Castells, M., 1989, *The Informational City*

Cavalli-Sforza, L. L., Menozzi, P. and Piazza, A., 1994, *The History and Geography of Human Genes*, Princeton, NJ

Cederman, L-E., 1994, 'Emergent polarity: Analyzing state-formation and power politics', *International Studies Quarterly* 38, 501–33

Cederman, L-E., 1995, 'Competing identities: an ecological model of nationality formation', *European Journal of International Relations* 1.3, 331–65

Cerny, P. G., 1990, *The Changing Architecture of Politics: Structure, Agency and the Future of the State*, Newbury Park, CA

Cerny, P. G. (ed.), 1993, *Finance and World Politics: Markets, Regimes and States in the Post-Hegemoninc Era*

Chagnon, N., 1965, *Yanomano: The Fierce People*, New York

Chagnon, N., 1988, 'Life histories, blood revenge and warfare in a tribal population', *Science* 239, 985–92

Chamberlain, M. E., 1985, *Decolonization*

Champion, T. C., 1989, *Centre and Periphery*

Chandler, A. D., 1992, 'Organizational capabilities and the economic history of the industrial enterprise', *Journal of Economic Perspectives* 6, 79–100

Chang, K. C., 1980, *Shang Civilization*, New Haven, CT

Chang, K. C., 1977, *The Archaeology of Ancient China*, 3rd edn, New Haven, CT

Chase-Dunn, C., 1981, 'Interstate system and capitalist world-economy: one logic or two?', *International Studies Quarterly* 25.1, 19–42

Chase-Dunn, C., 1990, *Global Formation: Structures of the World Economy*, Cambridge, MA

Chase-Dunn, C., 1992, 'The comparative study of world-systems', *Review* 15.3, 313–33.

Chase-Dunn, C., 1993, 'Comparing world-systems: concepts and working hypotheses', *Social Forces* 71.4, 851–86

Chase-Dunn, C., 1994, 'The historical evolution of world-systems', *Sociological Enquiry* 64.3, 257–80

Chase-Dunn, C. and Hall, T. D. (eds), 1991, *Core/Periphery Relations in PreCapitalist Worlds*, Boulder, CO

Chase-Dunn, C. and Hall, T. D., 1997, *Rise and Demise*, Boulder, CO

Chase-Dunn, C. and Rubinson, R., 1977, 'Toward a structural perspective on the world system', *Politics and Society* 7.4, 453–76

Checkland, P., 1981, *Systems Thinking, Systems Practice*

Child, J., 1984, *Organization*, 2nd edn, 58–84

Child, J., 1981, 'Culture, contingency and capitalism in a cross-cultural study of organizations', in L. L. Cummings and B. Shaw (eds), *Research in Organizational Behavior*, Greenwich, CT, 303–56

Chirot, D., 1994, *How Societies Change*, Thousand Oaks, CA

Cioffi-Revilla, C., Merritt, R. L. and Zinnes, D. A. (eds), 1987, *Communication and Interaction in Global Politics*, Newbury Park, CA

Cioffi-Revilla, C. and Lai, D., 1995, 'War and politics in Ancient China, 2700 BC to 722 BC', *Journal of Conflict Resolution*, 39, 467–94

Cioffi-Revilla, C. 1991, 'The long-range analysis of war', *Journal of Interdisciplinary History*, 21, 603–29

Cipolla, C. M., 1965, *Guns, Sails and Empire*, New York

Cipolla, C. M., 1976, *Before the Industrial Revolution: European Society and Economy 1000–1700*

Claessen, H. J. M. and Skalnik, P. (eds), 1978, *The Early State*, The Hague

Claessen, H. J. M. and van de Velde, P., 1985, 'Sociopolitical evolution as complex interaction', in H. J. M. Claessen, P. van de Velde and M. E. Smith (eds), *Development and Decline: The Evolution of Sociopolitical Organization*, South Hadley, MA

Clark, N., Perez-Trejo, F. and Allen, P., 1995, *Evolutionary Dynamics and Sustainable Development*

Clark, J. E. and Parry, W. J., 1990, 'Craft specialization and cultural complexity', *Research in Economic Anthropology* 12, 289–346

Clarkson, L. A., 1985, *Proto-industrialization: The First Phase of Industrialization?*

Clendinnen, I., 1993, *The Aztecs*

Cloke, P., Philo, C. and Sadler, D., 1991, *Approaching Human Geography*

Coase, R. H., 1992, 'The institutional structure of production', *American Economic Review* 82, 713–19

Coe, M. D., 1993, *The Maya*

Coe, M. D., 1993, *Breaking the Maya Code*

Cohen, S. B., 1994, 'Geopolitics in the new world era: a new perspective on an old discipline', in G. J. Demco and W. B. Wood (eds), *Reordering the World*, Boulder, CO, 15–48

Cohen, I. J., 1989, *Structuration Theory: Anthony Giddens and the Constitution of Social Life*, London and New York

Cohen, R. and Service, E. (eds), 1978, *Signs of the State: The Anthropology of Political Evolution*, Philadelphia

Cohen, M. N., 1988, *The Food Crisis in Prehistory*, New Haven, CT

Cohen, M. N., 1981, 'Pacific coast foragers: affluent or overcrowded?', *Senri Ethnological Studies* 9, 275–95

Cohen, M. N., 1985, 'Prehistoric hunter-gatherers: the meaning of social complexity', in T. D. Price and J. A. Brown (eds), *Prehistoric Hunter-*

Gatherers: The Emergence of Cultural Complexity, Orlando, 99–119

Collingwood, R. G., 1946, *The Idea of History*

Collingwood, R. G. and Richmond, I. A., 1969, *The Archaeology of Roman Britain*

Collins, Randall, 1981, 'On the microfoundations of macrosociology', *American Journal of Sociology* 86, 984–1014

Collins, Randall, 1986, *Weberian Sociological Theory*

Collins Randall and Waller, D., 1992, 'What theories predicted the state breakdowns and the revolutions of the Soviet bloc?' *Research in Social Movements, Conflicts and Change* 14, 31–47

Collins, Roger, 1983, *Early Medieval Spain*

Collins, Roger, 1991, *Early Medieval Europe 300–1000*

Collis, J., 1984, *The European Iron Age*

Colomy, P. (ed.), 1992, *The Dynamics of Social Systems*

Comte, A., 1858, *The Positive Philosophy*, New York

Connah, G., 1987, *African Civilization*

Conrad, G. and Demarest, A. A., 1988, *Religion and Empire*, Cambridge

Cook, M. A. (ed.), 1976, *A History of the Ottoman Empire to 1730*

Cornell, T. and Matthews, J., 1982, *Atlas of the Roman World*

Cornell, T. J., 1995, *The Beginnings of Rome*

Coveney, P. and Highfield, R., 1995, *Frontiers of Complexity: The Search for Order in a Chaotic World*

Cox, M., 1994, 'Rethinking the end of the Cold War', *Review of International Studies* 20, 187–200

Cox, R., 1994, 'Global restructuring: making sense of the changing international political economy', in R. Stubbs and G. Underhill (eds), *Political Economy and the Changing Global Order*, 45–59

Cox, R. W. 1986, 'Social forces states and world orders: beyond International Relations theory', in R. D. Keohane (ed.), *Neorealism and its Critics*, New York, 204–54

Cox, R. W., 1983, 'Gramsci, hegemony and international relations: an essay in method', *Millennium* 12.2, 165–75

Cox, R. W., 1987, *Production, Power and World Order*, New York

Cox, R. W., 1997, *The New Realism*

Cox, R. W. and Sinclair, T. J., 1996, *Approaches to World Order*

Crawford, H., 1991, *Sumer and the Sumerians*

Crawford, M., 1978, *The Roman Republic*

Crawford, N. C., 1994, 'A security regime among democracies, cooperation among Iroquois nations', *International Organization* 48.3, 345–85

Crawley, M., 1955, *Greek Independence 1832–33*

Croinin, D. O., 1995, *Early Medieval Ireland 400–1200*

Crozier, M. and Thoenig, J. C., 1976, 'The regulation of complex organized systems', *Administrative Science Quarterly* 21, 547–70

Culbert, T. P. (ed.), 1991, *Classic Maya Political History: Hieroglyphic and Archaeological Evidence*

Culbert, P. T. (ed.), 1973, *The Classic Maya Collapse*, Albuquerque

Cumings, L. L., Huber, G. P. and Arendt, E., 1974, 'Effects of size and spatial arrangements on group decision-making', *Academy of Management Journal* 17, 460–75

Curtin, P. *et al.*, 1995, *African History*, 2nd edn

Curtis, J. (ed.), 1993, *Early Mesopotamia and Iran*

Cusack, T. R. and Stoll, R. J., 1990, *Exploring Realpolitik: Probing International Relations Theory with Computer Simulation*, Boulder, CO

Czempiel, E.-O. and Rosenau, J. N. (eds), 1989, *Global Changes and Theoretical Challenges*, Lexington, Mass.

Dahrendorf, R., 1959, *Class and Class Conflict in Industrial Society*, Stanford

Dahrendorf, R., 1979, *Life Chances*

Dancy, J., 1985, *An Introduction to Contemporary Epistemology*

Dark, K. R., 1995, *Theoretical Archaeology*

Dark, K. R., 1996, 'Defining global change', in B. Holden, (ed.), *The Ethical Dimensions of Global Change*, 8–19

Dark, K. R., 1996, 'Ecological Change and Political Crisis', in B. Holden (ed.), *The Ethical Dimensions of Global Change*, 167–80

Dark, K. R., 1996, 'United States decline in global perspective: comparing processes of change in the USA, USSR and China', *Contemporary Political Studies* 1, 1–12

Dark, K. R., forthcoming, 'Problems and possibilities in the long-term analysis of International Relations' (BISA Long-Term Change Conference Paper 1995)

Dark, K. R. with Harris, A. L., 1996, *The New World and the New World Order*

Davenport, T. R. H., 1991, *South Africa: A Modern History*, 4th edn

David, J-M., 1996, *The Roman Conquest of Italy*

David, P. A., 1988, *Path Dependence: Putting the Past into the Future of Economics*, Stanford, CA

Davidson, J., 1984, *The Prehistory of New Zealand*

Davis, C. S. L., 1995, *Peace, Print and Protestantism 1450–1558*, rev. edn.

Davis, L. B. and Reeves, B. O. K. (eds) 1989, *Hunters of the Recent Past*

de Gruchy, J. W., 1995, *Christianity and Democracy*

Dear, J., 1988, 'The postmodern challenge: reconstructing human geography', *Transactions of the Institute of British Geographers* 13, 262–74

Deibert, R. J., 1996, 'Typographica: the medium and the medieval-to-modern transformation', *Review of International Studies* 22.1, 29–56

Demski, J. S. and Sappington, D. E. M., 1987, 'Hierarchical regulatory control', *RAND Journal of Economics* 18, 369–83

Dennison, D. R., 1990, *Corporate Culture and Organizational Effectiveness*, New York

Deudney, D. and Ikenberry, G. J., 1991, 'Soviet reform and the end of the Cold War: explaining large-scale historical change', *Review of International Studies* 17.3, 225–50

Devetak, R. 1996, 'Critical theory', in S. Burchill and A. Linklater *et al.*

(eds) *Theories of International Relations*, 145–178

Devetak, R., 1996, 'Postmodernism', S. Burchill and A. Linklater *et al.* (eds) *Theories of International Relations*, 179–209

Dews, P., 1986, *Logics of Disintegration*

Di Zerega, G., 1995, 'Democracies and peace: the self-organizing foundation for democratic peace', *Review of Politics* 57.2, 279–309

Dicken, P., 1992, *Global Shift: The Internationalization of Economic Activity*, New York

Dickinson, O., 1994, *The Aegean Bronze Age*

Diggins, J., 1994, *The Promise of Pragmatism: Modernism and The Crisis of Knowledge and Authority*, Chicago

Docherty, T. (ed.), 1993, *Postmodernism: A Reader*

Dodgshon, R. A., 1981, *Land and Society in Early Scotland*

Dodgshon, R. A., 1995, 'Modelling chiefdoms in the Scottish Highlands and islands prior to the '45', in B. Arnold and D. B. Gibson (eds), *Celtic Chiefdom, Celtic State*, 99–109

Doorbros, M. and Kaviras, S. (eds), 1996, *Dynamics of State-Formation*

Doran, C. F., 1991, *Systems in Crisis*

Doran, C. and Parsons, W., 1980, 'War and the cycle of relative power', *American Political Science Review* 74, 947–65

Dosi, G., 1988, 'Sources, procedures and microeconomic effects of innovation', *Journal of Economic Literature* 26, 1120–71

Dosi, G. and Malerba, F., 1996, 'Organizational learning and institutional embeddedness', in G. Dosi and F. Malerba (eds), *Organization and Strategy in the Evolution of Enterprise*, 1–26

Dougherty, J. E. and Pfaltzgraff, R. C., 1990, *Contending Theories of International Relations*, 4th edn, New York

Doyal, L. and Gough, I., 1991, *A Theory of Human Needs*

Doyle, M., 1986, 'Liberalism and world politics', *American Political Science Review* 80, 1151–62

Doyle, M., 1995, 'Liberalism and world politics revisited', in C. Kegley (ed.), *Controversies in International Relations Theory*, 83–106

Drennan, R. D. and Uribe, C. A. (eds), 1987, *Chiefdoms in the Americas*, Latham, MA

Drennan, R. D., 1987, 'Pre-Hispanic chiefdom trajectories in Mesoamerica, Central America, and northern South America', in R. D. Drennan and C. A. Uribe (eds), *Chiefdoms in the Americas*, Lanham, MD, 263–87

Dreyer, E., 1982, *Early Ming China: A Political History, 1355–1435*, Stanford

Dumville, D. N. *et al.*, 1993, *Saint Patrick, AD 493–1993*

Dunbabin, J. P. D., 1994, *The Post-Imperial Age*

Duncan, J. and Ley, D., 1982, 'Structural Marxism and human geography: a critical perspective', *Annals of the Association of American Geographers* 72, 30–59

Dunn, J. M. (ed.), 1995, *Contemporary Crisis of the Nation State*

Dunne, T., 1995, 'The social construction of international society', *European Journal of International Relations* 1.3, 367–89

Durham, W. H., 1978, 'The coevolution of human biology and culture', in V. Reynolds and N. Burton-Jones (eds), *Human Behaviour and Adaptation*, London, 11–32

Durham, W. H., 1991, *Coevolution: Genes, Culture and Human Diversity*, Stanford

Durkheim, E., 1933, *The Division of Labor in Society*, trans. by G. Simpson, New York

Earle, T. K., 1987, 'Chiefdoms in archaeological and ethnological perspective', *Annual Review of Anthropology* 16, 279–308

Earle, T. (ed.), 1991, *Chiefdoms: Power, Economy and Ideology*, Cambridge

Eckhardt, W., 1992, *Civilizations, Empires and Wars*

Eisenstadt, S. N. (ed.), 1968, *The Protestant Ethic and Modernization*, New York

Eisenstadt, S. N., Abitbol, M. and Chazan, N. (eds), 1988, *The Early State in African Perspective*, Leiden

Eldredge, N., 1985, *Unfinished Synthesis: Biological Hierarchies and Modern Evolutionary Thought*

Eldredge, N., 1986, *Time Frames: The Rethinking of Darwinian Evolution and the Theory of Punctuated Equilibria*, New York

Eldredge, N., 1989, 'Punctuated equilibria, rates of change and large-scale entities in evolutionary systems', *Journal of social and Biological Sciences*, 173–84

Eldredge, N., 1995, *Reinventing Darwin: The Great Evolutionary Debate*

Eldredge, N. and Gould, S. J., 1972, 'Punctuated equilibria: an alternative to phyletic gradualism', in T. J. M. Schopf (ed.), *Models in Paleobiology*, San Francisco, 82–115

Elton, G. R. (ed.), 1958, *The Reformation 1520–1529*

Elton, G. R., 1963, *Reformation Europe 1517–1559*

Elton, H., 1996, *Frontiers of the Roman Empire*

Elster, J., 1983, *Explaining Technical Change*, Cambridge

Ember, M., 1963, 'The relationship between economic and political development in nonindustrial societies', *Ethnology* 2, 228–48

Endicott-West, E., 1989, *Mongolian Rule in China*

Erington, R. M., 1971, *The Dawn of Empire*

Ermolieu, A. B. and Kaniovski, Y., 1987, 'Path dependent processes and the emergence of macro struture', *European Journal of Operational Research* 30, 294–304

Evans, T. and Wilson, P., 1992, 'Regime theory and the English School of international relations: a comparison', *Millennium* 21.3, 329–51

Fairbank, J. K., 1992, *China: A New History*, Cambridge, MA

Falk, R., 1978, 'The world order models project and its critics', *International Organization*, 31, 531–45

Falk, R., 1987, *The Promise of World Order*

Falk, R., 1995, *On Humane Governance. Towards a new global politics: the WOMP report of the Global Civilization Project*

Fash, W. L., 1994, 'Changing perspectives on Maya civilization', *Annual Review of Anthropology* 23, 181–208

Featherstone, M. (ed.), 1990, *Global Culture, Nationalism, Globalization and Modernity*

Feinman, G. and Neitzel, J., 1985, 'Too many types: an overview of prestate societies in the Americas', *Advances in Archaeological Theory and Method* 7, 39–102

Ferguson, Y. H. and Mansbach, R. W., 1996, 'Political space and West-phalian States in a world of "polities": beyond inside/outside', *Global Governance* 2.2, 261–87

Ferguson, Y. H. and Mansbach, R. W., 1996, *Polities: Authority, Identities and Change*, Columbia, CA

Ferrira, J. V., 1989, 'Gramsci: Marxism's saviour or false prophet?', *Political Studies* 37, 282–9

Fieder, S. J., 1992, *Prehistory of the Americas*

Fieldhouse, D. K., 1982, *The Colonial Empires* (2nd edn) New York

Fisher, M., 1992, 'Feudal Europe 800–1300: communal discourse and conflictual practices', *International Organization* 46.2, 427–66

Flanagan, J. G., 1989, 'Hierarchy in simple "egalitarian" societies', *Annual Review of Anthropology* 18, 245–66

Flannery, K. V., 1968, 'Archaeological systems theory and early Mesoamerica', in B. Meggers (ed.), *Anthropological Archaeology in the Americas*, Washington, 67–87

Flannery, K. V., 1972, 'The cultural evolution of civilizations', *Annual Review of Ecology and Systematics* 3, 399–425

Flannery, K. V. and Marcus, J. (eds), 1983, *The Cloud People: Divergent Evolution of the Zapotec and Mixtec Civilizations*, New York

Fletcher, R., 1995, *The Limits of Settlement Growth*

Fligstein, N., 1990, *The Transformation of Corporate Control*, Cambridge, MA

Fligstein, N. and Freeland, R., 1995, 'Theoretical and comparative per-spectives on corporate organisations', *Annual Review of Sociology* 21, 21–43

Folz, R., 1969, *The Concept of Empire in Western Europe from the Fifth to the Fourteenth Century*, trans. by S. A. Ogilvie

Fombrun, C., 1986, 'Structural dynamics within and between organiza-tions', *Administrative Science Quarterly* 31, 403–21

Foote, P. G. and Wilson, D. M., 1970, *The Viking Achievement*, 2nd edn, New York

Ford, F. L., 1967, *Europe 1780–1830*

Forrester, J., 1971, 'Counter-intuitive behavior of social systems', *Techno-logy Review* 73, 53–68

Forrester, J., 1973, *World Dynamics*, 2nd edn, Cambridge, MA

Foss, N. J., 1994, 'Realism and evolutionary economics', *Journal of Social and Evolutionary Systems* 17.1, 21–40

Foster, J., 1993, 'Economics and the self-organization approach: Alfred Marshall revisited?', *Economic Journal* 103, 975–91

Foster, J., 1994, 'The impact of the self-organization approach on economic science: why economic theory and history need no longer be mutually exclusive domains', *Journal of Mathematical Computer Simulation* 39, 393–98

Fowler, W. R. (ed.), 1991, *The Formation of Complex Society in Southwest Mesoamerica*, Boca Raton, FL

Fox, A., 1976, *Prehistoric Maori Fortifications on the North Island of New Zealand*, Auckland

Fox, J. W., 1987, *Maya Postclassic State Formation*, Cambridge

Frank, A. G., 1990, 'A theoretical introduction to 5000 years of world system history', *Review* 13.2, 155–248

Frank, A. G., 1991, 'A plea for world system history', *Journal of World History* 2, 1–28

Frank, A. G., 1993, 'The Bronze-age world system and its cycles', *Current Anthropology* 34.4, 383–430

Frank, A. G. and Gills, B. K. (eds), 1993, *The World System: Five Hundred Years or Five Thousand?*

Frankel, B. (ed.), 1996, *Realism: Restatements and Renewal*

Freeman, C. (ed.), 1984, *Long Waves in the World Economy*, London and Dover, NH

Freeman, C., Clark, J. A. and Soete, L., 1982, *Unemployment and Technical Innovation: A Study of Long Waves and Economic Development*

Fried, M. H., 1967, *The Evolution of Political Society*, New York

Friedman, J., 1974, 'Marxism, structuralism and vulgar materialism', *Man* 9, 444–69

Friedman, J., 1994, *Cultural Identity and Global Process*

Friedman, J. and Rowlands, M. J., 1978, 'Notes towards an epigenetic model of the evolution of "civilization"', in J. Friedman and M. J. Rowlands (eds), *The Evolution of Social Systems*, 201–78

Friendly, A., 1971, *The Dreadful Day: The Battle of Manzikert, 1071*

Fukuyama, F., 1993, *The End of History and the Last Man*, London and New York

Gadamer, H. G., 1994, *Truth and Method*, 2nd edn, New York

Gaddis, J. L., 1987, 'Expanding the data base: historians, political scientists and the enrichment of security studies', *International Security* 12, 3–21

Gaddis, J. L., 1992, *The United States and the End of the Cold War*, Oxford

Gaddis, J. L., 1996, 'History, science and the study of international relations', in N. Woods (ed.), *Explaining International Relations Since 1945*, 32–48

Gaenslen, F., 1986, 'Culture and decision making in China, Japan, Russia and the United States', *World Politics* 39.1, 78–103

Galbraith, J. R., 1974, 'Organisation design: an information-processing view', *Interfaces* 4, 28–36

Galbraith, J. R., 1977, *Organization Design*, Reading, MA

Galtung, J., 1971, 'A structural theory of imperialism', *Journal of Peace Research* 8, 81–191

Gamble, C., 1993, *Timewalkers*

Gardner, K. and Lewis, D., 1996, *Anthropology, Development and the Post-Modern Challenge*

Garlake, P. S., 1973, *Great Zimbabwe*

Garlake, P. S., 1976, 'Great Zimbabwe: a reappraisal', *Proceedings of the African Congress of Prehistory and Quaternary Studies*, Addis Ababa, 221–6

Garnett, J. C., 1992, 'States, state-centric perspectives and interdependence', in J. Baylis and N. Rengger (eds), *Dilemmas of World Politics*, 61–84

Garrett, G. and Lange, P., 1995, 'Internationalization, institutions, and political change', *International Organization* 49.4, 627–55

Garzetti, A., 1974, *From Tiberius to the Antonines*

Geanakoplos, J. and Milgrom, P., 1991, 'A theory of hierarchies based on limited managerial attention', *Journal of Japanese and International Economics* 5, 205–25

Gell-Mann, M., 1994, *The Quark and the Jaguar: Adventures in the Simple and the Complex*, New York

Gellner, E., 1964, *Thought and Change*

Gellner, E., 1982, 'What is structuralisme?', in C. Renfrew, M. Rowlands and B. Seagraves (eds), *Theory and Explanation in Archaeology*, 97–124

Gellner, E. 1983, *Nations and Nationalism*

Gellner, E. 1988, *Plough, Sword and Book*

Gellner, E., 1992, *Postmodernism, Reason and Religion*

George, D. A. R., 1990, 'Chaos and complexity in economics', *Journal of Economic Surveys* 4.4, 397–414

Germain, R. (ed.), 1997, *Globalization and its Critics*

Gernet, J., 1996, *A History of Chinese Civilization*, transl. by J. R. Foster and C. Hortmann, 2nd edn

Gersick, C. J. G., 1991, 'Revolutionary change theories: a multilevel exploration of the punctuated equilibrium paradigm', *Academy of Management Review* 16.1, 10–36

Ghils, P., 1992, 'International civil society: international non-governmental organizations in the international system', *International Social Science Journal* 133, 417–29

Gibson, D. and Geselowitz, M. N., 1988 (eds), *Tribe and Polity in Late Prehistoric Europe*, New York

Giddens, A., 1984, *The Constitution of Society: An Outline of the Theory of Structuration*, Chicago

Giddens, A., 1987, 'Structuralism, post-structuralism and the production of culture', in A. Giddens and J. Turner (eds), *Social Theory Today*,

195–223

Giddens, A., 1995, *A Contemporary Critique of Historical Materialism*, 2nd edn

Gillis, P., 1992, 'International civil society: interchange, non-governmental organizations in the international system', *International Social Science Journal* 133, 417–79

Gills, B. and Palan, R. (eds), 1994, *Transcending the State-Global Divide: A Neostructuralist Agenda in International Relations*, Boulder, CO

Gilpin, R., 1981, *War and Change in World Politics*

Gilpin, R., 1987, *The Political Economy of International Relations*, Princeton, NJ

Gilpin, R., 1994, 'The cycle of great powers: has it finally been broken?', in G. Lundestad (ed.), *The Fall of Great Powers*, Oslo, 313–30

Gilpin, R., 1996, 'Economic evolution of national systems', *International Studies Quarterly* 40, 411–31

Gledhill, J., 1995, 'Introduction: the comparative analysis of social and political transitions', in J. Gledhill, B. Bender and M. T. Larsen (eds), *State and Society*, 1–29

Gleick, J., 1987, *Chaos: Making a New Science*, New York

Godelier, M., 1977, *Perspectives in Marxist Anthropology*

Goffart, W., 1980, *Barbarians and Romans AD 418–584*, Princeton, NJ

Goldfrank, W. L. (ed.), 1979, *The World System of Capitalism: Past and Present*, Beverley Hills, CA

Goldgeier, J. M. and McFaul, 1992, 'A tale of two worlds: core and periphery in the post-Cold War era', *International Organization* 46.2, 467–91

Goldstein, J. S., 1988, *Long Cycles: Prosperity and War in the Modern Age*, London and New Haven, CT

Goldstein, J. S., 1991, 'The possibility of cycles in international relations', *International Studies Quarterly* 35, 477–80

Goldstone, J. A., 1987, 'Cultural orthodoxy, risk and innovation the divergence of east and west in the early modern world', *Sociological Theory* 5, 119–35

Golte, J. W., 1995, *In Search of World Society*, University of Frankfurt, World Society Research Group

Goodman, L. D. and Burke, W., 1991, 'Creating successful organizational change', *Organizational Dynamics*, 5–17

Goody, J., 1977, *The Domestication of the Savage Mind*

Gould, S. J., 1980, 'Is a new and general theory of evolution emerging?', *Paleobiology* 6, 119–30

Gould, S. J., 1982, 'Darwinism and the expansion of evolutionary theory', *Science* 216, 380–87

Gould, S. J. 1982, 'The meaning of punctuated equilibria and its role in validating a hierarchical approach to macroevolution', in R. Milkman (ed.), *Perspectives on Evolution*, Sunderland, MA., 83–104

Gould, S. J., 1989, *Wonderful Life*, New York

Gould, S. J., 1989, 'Punctuated equilibria in fact and theory', *Journal of Social and Biological Structures* 12, 241–50

Gould, S. J. and Eldredge, N., 1977, 'Punctuated equilibria: the tempo and mode of evolution reconsidered', *Paleobiology* 3, 115–51

Gourevitch, P., 1978, 'The international system and regime formation: a critical review of Anderson and Wallerstein', *Comparative Politics* 10.3, 119–38

Grabar, A., 1966, *Byzantium from the Death of Theodosius to the Rise of Islam*

Grabher, G., 1993, *The Embedded Firm: On the Socioeconomics of Industrial Networks*

Grader, S., 1981, 'The English School of international relations: evidence and evaluation', *Review of International Studies* 14.1, 29–44

Graham-Campbell, J., 1989, *The Viking World*, 2nd edn

Granovetter, M., 1985, 'Economic action and social structure: the problem of embeddedness', *American Journal of Sociology* 91, 481–510

Gregg, S. A. (ed.), 1991, *Between Bands and States*, Carbondale, IL

Grieco, J. M., 1988, 'Anarchy and the limits of cooperation: a realist critique of the newest liberal internationalism', *International Organization* 42.3, 485–507

Griffiths, M., 1992, *Realism, Idealism and International Relations: A Reinterpretation*

Grohaugh, K. and Kaufmann, G. (eds), 1988, *Innovation: A Cross-Disciplinary Perspective*

Guelke, L., 1974, 'An idealist alternative in human geography', *Annals of the Association of American Geographers* 64, 193–202

Guelke, L., 1982, *Historical Understanding in Geography: An Idealist Approach*

Gulic, E. V., 1967, *Europe's Classical Balance of Power*, 2nd edn, New York

Gunnell, J. G., 1995, 'Realizing theory: the philosophy of science revisited', *Journal of Politics* 57.4, 923–40

Gurney, O. R., 1990, *The Hittites*, rev. 2nd edn

Haas, E. B., 1990, *When Knowledge is Power: Three Models of Change in International Organization*, Berkeley, CA

Haas, E. B., 1990, 'Reason and change in international affairs: justifying a hypothesis', *Journal of International Affairs*, 209–40

Haas, J., 1982, *The Evolution of the Prehistoric State*, New York

Haas, J. (ed.), 1990, *The Anthropology of War*

Haas, J., Pozorski, S. and Pozorski, T. (eds), 1987, *The Origins and Development of the Andean State*

Haas, M., 1970, 'International subsystems: stability and polarity', *American Political Science Review* 64.1, 93–103

Haas, P. M., 1989, 'Do regimes matter: epistemic communities and Mediterranean pollution control', *International Organization* 43, 377–404

Haas, P. M., 1992, 'Epistemic communities and international policy coordination', *International Organization* 46, 1–35

Hagerstrand, T., 1976, *Innovation as a Spatial Process*, Chicago

Hall, J. A., 1985, *Powers and Liberties*

Hall, J. A. (ed), 1986, *States in History*

Hall, J. A., 1996, *International Orders: An Historical Sociology of State, Regime, Class and Nation*

Hall, P., 1988, 'The intellectual history of long waves', in M. Young and T. Schuller (eds), *The Rhythms of Society*, 37–52

Hall, R. B. and Kratochwil, F. V., 1993, 'Medieval tales: neorealist "science" and the abuse of history', *International Organization* 47.3, 479–500

Hallam, E. M., 1980, *Capetian France 987–1328*

Halliday, F., 1994, *Rethinking International Relations*

Halliday, F., 1995, 'International relations and its discontents', *International Affairs* 71.4, 733–46

Hallinan, M. T., 1996, 'The sociological study of social change', *American Sociological Review* 62, 1–11.

Hamilton, G. G. and Biggart, N. W., 1988, 'Market, Culture, and authority: a comparative analysis of management and organization in the Far East', *American Journal of Sociology* 94 (Supplement) S52–94

Hammond, G. and Shaw, B. P., 1995, 'Conflict, the rise of nations, and the decay of states: the transformation of the international system?', *Journal of Conflict Studies* 15.1, 5–29

Hampden-Turner, C. and Trompenaars, F., 1993, *The Seven Cultures of Capitalism*, New York

Hannerz, U., 1992, *Cultural Complexity: Studies in the Social Organization of Meaning*, New York

Hansenclever, A., Mayer, P. and Rittberger, V., 1996, 'Interests, power, knowledge: the study of international regimes', *Mershon International Studies Review* 40.2, 177–228

Harris, A. L., 1996, 'Long term perspectives in international relations theory, the United States and the end of the Cold War', *Contemporary Political Studies* 1, 13–20

Harris, M., 1979, *Cultural Materialism*

Harris, M., 1991, *Cultural Anthropology*, 3rd edn, New York

Harris, M., 1994, 'Cultural materialism is alive and well and won't go away until something better comes along', in R. Borofsky (ed.), *Assessing Cultural Anthropology*, New York, 62–75

Harris, W. V., 1979, *War and Imperialism in Republican Rome*

Hart, P., 1982, 'The size and growth of firms', *Economica* 29, 29–39

Harvey, D., 1982, *The Limits to Capital*

Harvey, D., 1984, 'On the history and present condition of geography: an historical materialist manifesto', *Professional Geographer* 36, 1–11

Harvey, D., 1989, *The Condition of Postmodernity: An Enquiry into the Origins of Cultural Change*

Haselgrove, C., 1995, 'Late Iron Age society in Britain and north-east

Europe: structural transformation or superficial change?', in B. Arnold and D. B. Gibson (eds), *Celtic Chiefdom, Celtic State*, 81–7

Hastrup, K. (ed.), 1992, *Other Histories*

Hauser, J., Jessop, B. and Nielsen, K. (eds), 1995, *Strategic Choice and Path-Dependency in Post-Socialism*

Hay, C., 1994, 'Crisis and the discursive unification of the state', *Contemporary Political Studies 1994*, 236–55

Hay, D., 1989, *Europe in the Fourteenth and Fifteenth Centuries*, 2nd edn

Hayden, B. and Gargett, R., 1990, 'Big man, big heart? A mesoamerican view of the emergence of complex society', *Ancient Mesoamerica* 1, 3–20

Headrick, D. R., 1981, *The Tools of Empire*

Hearder, H., 1966, *Europe in the Nineteenth Century 1830–1880*

Hebinck, P. 1990, *The Agrarian Structure in Kenya: State, Farmers and Commodity Relations*, Sarbrucken

Hedeager, L., 1992, *Iron Age Societies*

Held, D., 1989, *Political Theory and the Modern State*

Held, D., 1989, 'The decline of the nation-state', in S. Hall and M. Jacques (eds), *New Times*, 191–224

Held, D., 1995, *Democracy and the Global Order*

Helm, J. (ed.), 1968, *Essay on the Problem of the Tribe*, Seattle

Hempel, C. G., 1959, 'The function of general laws in history', in P. Gardiner (ed.) *Theories of History*, New York, 344–56

Herper, M., 1985, 'The state and public bureaucracies: a comparative and historical perspective', *Comparative Studies in Society and History* 27, 86–110

Herrin, J., 1987, *The Formation of Christendom*

Hill, C., 1996, 'World opinion and the empire of circumstance', *International Affairs* 72.1, 109–31

Himmelfarb, G. 1987, *The New History and the Old*, Cambridge, MA

Hinkle, R. C., 1976, 'Durkheim's evolutionary conception of social change', *Sociological Quarterly* 17, 336–46

Hirsch, F., 1976, *Social Limits to Growth*, Cambridge, MA

Hirst, P. and Thompson, G., 1992, 'The problem of "globalization": international economic relations, national economic management and the formation of trading blocs', *Economy and Society* 21, 357–96

Hobden, S., 1995, 'Geopolitical space or civilizations? the international system in the work of Michael Mann', *International Relations* 12.6, 77–102

Hodge, M. G. and Smith, M. E. (eds), 1993, *Economies and Polities of the Aztec Realm*, Albany, NY

Hodges, R., 1982, *Dark Age Economics*

Hodges, R., 1989, *The Anglo-Saxon Achievement*

Hodges, R. and Whitehouse, D., 1983, *Mohammed, Charlemagne and the Origins of Europe*

Hodgson, G. M., 1991, 'Socio-political disruption and economic development', in G. M. Hodgson and F. Screpanti (eds), *Rethinking Economics: Markets, Technology and Evolutionary Economis*, 153–71

Hodgson, G. M., 1993, *Economics and Evolution: Bringing Life Back into Economics*

Hodgson, G. M., 1996, 'An evolutionary theory of long-term economic growth', *International Studies Quarterly* 40, 391–410

Hofbauer, J. and Sigmund, K., 1988, *The Theory of Evolution and Dynamical Systems*, Cambridge

Hoffman, M., 1987, 'Critical theory and the inter-paradigm debate', *Millennium* 16.2, 231–50

Hofstede, G., 1991, *Cultures and Organisations: Software of the Mind*

Holden, A. V. (ed.), 1986, *Chaos*, Princeton

Holland, J. H., 1995, *Hidden Order. How Adaptation Builds Complexity*, New York

Holland, R. F., 1985, *European Decolonization 1918–1981: An Introductory Survey*

Holling, C. S., 1987, 'Simplifying the complex: the paradigms of ecological function and structure', *European Journal of Operational Research* 30, 139–46

Hollis, M. 1996, 'The last post?', in S. Smith, K. Booth and M. Zalewski (eds), *International Theory: Positivism and Beyond*, 301–8

Hollis, M. and Lukes, S. (eds), 1982, *Relativism and Rationality*

Hollis, M. and Smith, S., 1990, *Explaining and Understanding International Relations*

Hollis, M. and Smith, S., 1991, 'Beware of gurus: structure and action in international relations', *Review of International Studies* 17.4, 393–410

Hollis, M. and Smith, S., 1992, 'Structure and agency: further comment', *Review of International Studies* 18.2, 187–8

Hollis, M. and Smith, S., 1994, 'Two stories about structure and agency', *Review of International Studies* 20.3, 241–51

Hollis, M. and Smith, S., 1996, 'A response: why epistemology matters in international theory', *Review of International Studies* 22, 111–16

Hollist, W. L. and Rosenau, J. N., 1981, 'World systems debates', Special Issue of *International Studies Quarterly* 25.1, 5–17

Holloway, R. R., 1994, *The Archaeology of Early Rome and Latium*

Holsti, O. R., Siverson, R. M. and George, A. L. (eds), 1980, *Change in the International System* Boulder, CO

Holt, I., 1994, 'The permanent crisis of a divided mankind: contemporary crisis of the nation state in historical perspective', *Political Studies* 42, 166–235

Hopf, T., 1993, 'Geting the end of the Cold War wrong', *International Security* 18, 202–15

Hopkins, T. K., and Wallerstein, I., 1979, 'Cyclical rhythms and secular trends of the capitalist world economy', *Review* 2, 483–500

Hopkins, T. K. and Wallerstein, I. (eds), 1980, *Processes of the World System*, Beverley Hills, CA

Horgan, J., 1995, 'From complexity to perplexity', *Scientific American* June, 74–9

Hourani, A., Khoury, P. S. and Wilson, M. C. (eds), 1993, *The Modern Middle East*

Houston, R. A. B. and Whyte, I. D. (eds), 1989, *Scottish Society 1500–1800*

Howard, M. C., 1993, *Contemporary Cultural Anthropology* 4th edn, New York

Hrbek, I. (ed.), 1992, *General History of Africa. Vol. III Africa from the Seventh to the Eleventh Century*

Huang, Y., 1994, 'Information, bureaucracy and economic reform in China and the Soviet Union', *World Politics* 47, 102–34

Huber, G. P., 1984, 'The nature and design of post-industrial organizations', *Management Science* 30, 928–51

Hucker, C. O., 1995, *China's Imperial Past*

Hughes, B., 1993, *International Futures*, Boulder, CO

Huizenga, F. D., 1995, 'Regime analysis: a rule-based method for studying institutions', *Administration and Society* 27.3, 361–78

Huntington, P. R., 1996, *The Clash of Civilizations and the Remaking of World Order*, New York

Huntington, S. P., 1993, 'The clash of civlizations', *Foreign Affairs* 72, 22–49

Hurrell, A., 1993, 'International society and the study of regimes: a reflective approach', in V. Rittberger (ed.), *Regime Theory and International Relations*, pp. 49–72

Hyam, R., 1975, *Britain's Imperial Century 1815–1914*

Hymer, S. and Pashigian, P., 1962, 'Firm size and rate of growth', *Journal of Political Economy* 70, 536–69

Iliffe, J., 1995, *Africans*

Inalcik, H., 1973, *The Ottoman Empire: The Classical Age 1300–1600*, New York

Ingold, T., 1986, *Evolution and Social Life*

Ingold, T., Riches, D. and Woodburn, J. (eds), 1991, *Hunters and Gatherers*

Innis, H., 1950, *Empire and Communications*, Oxford

Jabri, V. and Chan, S., 1996, 'The ontologist always rings twice: two more stories about structure and agency in reply to Hollis and Smith', *Review of International Studies* 22, 107–10

Jackman, R. W., 1989, 'The politics of economic growth: once again', *Journal of Politics* 51, 646–61

James, A., 1993, 'System or society?', *Review of International Studies* 19.3, 269–88

James, E., 1992, *The Origins of France*

Jenkins, K., 1995, *On 'What is History?'*

Jenkins, R., 1966, *Byzantium: The Imperial Centuries AD 600–1071*

Jennings, F. (ed.), 1985, *The History and Culture of Iroquois Diplomacy*, Syracuse, NY

Jervis, R., 1978, 'Cooperation under the security dilemma', *World Politics* 30, 167–214

Jessop, B., 1990, *State Theory*

Johnson, A. W. and Earle, T., 1987, *The Evolution of Human Societies*, Stanford

Johnson, G. A., 1978, 'Information sources and the development of decision-making organisations', in C. L. Redman *et al.* (eds), *Social Archaeology: Beyond Subsistence and Dating*, New York, 87–112

Johnson, G. A., 1982, 'Organizational structure and scalar stress', in C. Renfrew, M. Rowlands and B. A. Segraves (eds), *Theory and Explanation in Archaeology*, New York, 389–421

Johnston, R. J., 1993, 'The rise and decline of the corporate-welfare state: a comparative analysis in global context', in P. J. Taylor (ed.), *Political Geography at the End of the Twentieth Century*

Johnston, R. J. (ed.), 1993, *The Challenge for Geography*

Joll, J., 1990, *Europe since 1870*, 4th edn

Jones, A. H. M., 1964, *The Late Roman Empire 284–602*, 2 vols.

Jones, A. H. M. 1970, *Augustus*

Jones, E. L., 1988, *Growth Recurring: Economic Change in World History*

Jones, G., 1984, *A History of the Vikings*, 2nd edn

Jones, G. D. and Kautz, R. R., 1981, *The Transition to Statehood in the New World*

Jones, G. I., 1966, 'Chiefly succession in Basutoland', in J. Goody (ed.), *Succession to High Office*, 57–81

Jones, P., 1991, *Groups, Beliefs and Identities*

Jones, R. E., 1981, 'The English School of international relations: a suitable case for closure', *Review of International Studies* 7.1, 1–13

Jones, R. J. B., 1991, *Anti-Statism and Critical Theories in International Relations*

Jones, R. J. B., 1995, *Globalization and Interdependence in the International Political Economy*

Jones, R. J. B., 1996, 'Construction and constraint in the promotion of change in the principles of international conduct', in B. Holden (ed.), *The Ethical Dimensions of Global Change*, 23–39

Joyce, P. 1991, 'History and post-modernism', *Past and Present*, 133, 204–9

Joynt, C. B. and Rescher, N. 1961, 'The problem of uniqueness in history', *History and Theory* 1, 150–62

Juma, A. M., 1996, 'The Swahili and the Mediterranean worlds: pottery of the Late Roman period in Zanzibar', *Antiquity* 70, 148–54

Kann, R. A., 1974, *A History of the Habsburg Empire 1526–1918*, Berkeley

Katzenstein, P. J., 1975, 'International interdependence: some long-term trends and recent changes', *International Organization* 29, 1021–34

Kauffman, S. A., 1988, 'The evolution of economic webs', in P. W. Anderson *et al.* (eds), *The Economy as an Evolving Complex System*, Reading, MA, 125–46

Kauffman, S. A., 1991, 'Antichaos and adaptation', *Scientific American* August, 78–84

Kauffman, S. A., 1993, *The Origins of Order: Self-organization and Selection in Evolution*, Oxford and New York

Kauffman, S. A., 1995, *At Home in the Universe: The Search for Laws of Complexity*

Keatinge, R. W., 1988, *Peruvian Prehistory*

Kedourie, E., 1992, *Politics in the Middle East*

Keeley, L. H., 1988, 'Hunter-gatherer complexity and "population pressure": a cross-cultural analysis', *Journal of Anthropological Archaeology* 7, 373–411

Keesing, R. M., 1990, *Cultural Anthropology*, 2nd edn

Kegley, C. W., 1993, 'The neoidealist moment in international studies? realist myths and new international realities', *International Studies Quarterly*, 131–46

Kegley, C. W., 1994, 'How did the Cold War die: principles for an autopsy', *Mershon International Studies Review* 38.1, 11–42

Kegley, C. W. (ed.), 1995, *Controversies in International Relations Theory*, New York

Kegley, C. W. and Wittkopf, E. R., 1995, *World Politics: Trend and Transformation*, 5th edn, New York

Keightley, D. N., 1983, *The Origins of Chinese Civilization*, Berkeley, CA

Kelly, C. 1991, 'History and post-modernism', *Past and Present*, 133, 209–13

Kemp, B., 1991, *Ancient Egypt*

Kennedy, P., 1989, *The Rise and Fall of the Great Powers*

Kennedy, P., 1993, *Preparing for the Twenty-first Century*, New York

Kent, S. (ed.), 1996, *Cultural Diversity among Twentieth Century Foragers*

Keohane, R., 1984, *After Hegemony*, Princeton

Keohane, R. (ed.), 1986, *Neo-Realism and Its Critics*, New York

Keohane, R. O. and Nye, J. (eds), 1977, *Power and Interdependence*, Boston, MA

Keohane, R. O. and Nye, J., 1987, 'Power and interdependence revisited', *International Organization* 41.4, 725–53

Kern, S., 1983, *The Culture of Time and Space 1880–1918*

Khalil, E. L. and Boulding, K. E. (eds), 1996, *Evolution, Order and Complexity*

Kiel, L. D. and Elliot, E. (eds), 1995, *Chaos Theory in the Social Sciences*, Ann Arbor, MI

Killick, T. (ed.), 1995, *The Flexible Economy*

King, A. (ed.), 1991, *Culture, Globalization and the World System*, Binghampton, NY

King, A., 1992, *Roman Gaul and Germany*

Kirch, P. V., 1989, *The Evolution of Polynesian Chiefdoms*

Kissinger, H., 1964, *A World Restored*, New York

Klatzky, S. R., 1970, 'Relationship of organizational size to complexity and coordination', *Administrative Science Quarterly* 15, 428–48

Klegg, S., 1981, 'Organization and control', *Administrative Science Quarterly* 26, 545–62

Klegg, S. and Dunkerley, D., 1980, *Organization, Class and Control*

Knapp, A. B., 1988, *The History and Culture of Ancient Western Asia and Egypt*, Chicago

Knoke, D., 1990, *Political Networks*

Knutsen, T. L., 1992, *A History of International Relations Theory*

Koslowski, R. and Kratochwil, F. V., 1994, 'Understanding change in international politics: the Soviet empire's demise and the international system', *International Organization* 48.2, 215–47

Kosse, K., 1990, 'Group size and social complexity: thresholds in the long-term memory', *Journal of Anthropological Archaeology* 9, 275–303

Kosse, K., 1994, 'The evolution of large, complex groups: a hypothesis', *Journal of Anthropological Archaeology* 13, 35–50

Kowalewski, S. A., 1990, 'The evolution of complexity in the valley of Oaxaca', *Annual Review of Anthropology* 19, 39–58

Koyama, S. and Thomas, D. H. (eds), 1981, *Affluent Foragers*, Osaka

Krasner, S. D., 1982, 'Structural causes and regime consequences: regimes as intervening variables', *International Organization* 36, 185–205

Krasner, S. D. (ed.), 1983, *International Regimes*, Ithaca

Krasner, S. D., 1984, 'Approaches to the state: alternative conceptions and historical dynamics', *Comparative Politics* 16.2, 223–46

Krasner, S. D., 1991, 'Global communications and national power: life on the Pareto frontier', *World Politics* 43, 336–66

Kratochwil, F., 1986, 'Of systems, boundaries and territoriality: an enquiry into the formation of the state system', *World Politics* 39.1, 27–52

Kratochwil, F., 1989, *Rules, Norms and Decisions*

Kratochwil, F., 1993, 'The embarrassment of changes: neo-realism as the science of realpolitik without politics', *Review of International Studies* 19.1, 63–80

Kratochwil, F. and Mansfield, E. D. (eds), 1994, *International Organisation: A Reader*, New York

Kristiansen, K., 1991, 'Chiefdoms, states and systems of social evolution', in T. Earle (ed.), *Chiefdom: Power, Economy, and Ideology*, Cambridge, 16–43

Kristiansen, K. and Jensen, J., 1994, *Europe in the First Millennium BC*

Kroll, J. A., 1993, 'The complexity of interdependence', *International Studies Quarterly* 37, 321–47

Kuhn, T., 1962, *The Structure of Scientific Revolutions*, Chicago

Kumar, M., 1985, 'Growth, acquisition activity and firm size: evidence from the United Kingdom', *Journal of Industrial Economics* 33, 327–38

Kupchan, C. A., 1994, *The Vulnerability of Empire*, Ithaca and London

Kuper, A., 1983, *Anthropology and Anthropologists*

Kuran, T., 1989, 'Sparks and prairie fires: a theory of unanticipated political revolution', *Public Choice* 61, 41–74

la Porte, T. R. (ed.), 1975, *Organized Social Complexity: Challenge to Politics and Policy*, Princeton, NJ

Lake, D. *et al.*, 1996, 'Choice and action' *Journal of Evolutionary Economics* 6, 43–76

Langlois, J. D., 1981, *China Under Mongol Rule*, Princeton

Lapid, Y., 1989, 'The third debate: on the prospects of international theory in a post-positivist era', *International Studies Quarterly* 33, 235–54

Lapid, Y. and Kratochwil, F. (eds), 1996, *The Return of Culture and Identity in IR Theory*, Boulder, Colo.

Laserson, M. H., 1988, 'Organizational growth of small firms: an outcome of markets and hierarchies', *American Sociological Review* 53, 330–42

Lauer, R. H., 1982, *Perspectives on Social Change*, 3rd edn, Boston, MA

Laurent, A., 1978, 'Managerial subordinacy: a neglected aspect of organizational hierarchy', *Academy of Management Review* 3, 220–30

Lawless, R. I., 1980, *The Middle East in the Twentieth Century*

Lawrence, P. and Lorsch, J., 1967, 'Differentiation and integration in complex organizations', *Administrative Science Quarterly* 12, 1–47

Layne, C., 1993, 'The unipolar illusion: why new great powers will rise', *International Security* 17.4, 3–51

Layne, C., 1994, 'Kant or cant: the myth of democratic peace', *International Security* 19, 10–11

Lazlo, E., 1991, *The Age of Bifurcation: Understanding the Changing World*, Philadelphia

Lazonick, W., 1991, *Business Organization and the Myth of the Market Economy*

Lazonick, W. and West, J., 1995, 'Organizational integration and competitive advantage: explaining strategy and performance in American industry', *Industrial and Corporate Change* 4.1, 229

Leacock, E. and Lee, R. (eds), 1982, *Politics and History in Band Societies*

Leaver, R., 1994, 'International political economy and the changing world order: evolution or involution?', in R. Stubbs and G. D. Underhill (eds), *Political Economy and the Changing Global Order*, 130–41

Lebow, R. N., 1994, 'The long peace, the end of the Cold War, and the failure of realism', *International Organization* 48.2, 249–77

Lechte, J. (ed.), 1994, *Fifty Key Contemporary Thinkers: From Structuralism to Postmodernism*, 95–119 and 231–51

Lee, R. B., 1979, *The !Kung San*

Lee, R. B., 1984, *The Dobe !Kung*, New York

Lee, R. B. and De Vore, I. (eds), 1968, *Man the Hunter*, Chicago

Lees, S. H. and Bates, D. G., 1990, 'The ecology of cumulative change', in E. F. Moran (ed.), *The Ecosystem Approach in Anthropology*, 247–77

Levinthal, D., 1990, 'Organizational adaptation and environmental selection: interrelated processes of change', *Organization Science* 2, 140–5

Levy, J. S., 1985, 'Theories of general war', *World Politics* 37.3, 344–74

Levy, M. A., Young, O. R. and Zurn, M., 1995, 'The study of international relations', *European Journal of International Relations* 1.3, 267–330

Lewin, R., 1992, *Complexity: Life at the Edge of Chaos*, New York

Lewis, B., 1958, *The Arabs in History*, 4th edn

Lewis, B., 1968, *The Emergence of Modern Turkey*, 2nd edn.

Lewis, J. P., 1991, 'Some consequences of giantism: the case of India', *World Politics* 43, 367–89

Lewis, M. E., 1990, *Sanctioned Violence in Early China*

Lieshaut, R., 1996, *Between Anarchy and Hierarchy*

Linklater, A., 1990, *Beyond Realism and Marxism: Critical Theory and International Relations*

Linklater, A., 1992, 'The question of the next stage in international relations theory: a critical-theoretical point of view', *Millennium* 21.1, 77–98

Linklater, A., 1995, 'Neo-realism in theory and practice', in K. Booth and S. Smith (eds), *International Relations Theory Today*, 241–62

Lintott, A., 1993, *Imperium Romanum*

Lipschutz, R. D., 1992, 'Reconstructing world politics: the emergence of global civil society', *Millennium* 21, 389–420

Little, R., 1985, 'The systems approach', in S. Smith (ed.), *International Relations: British and American Approaches*, Oxford, 70–91

Little, R., 1991, 'International relations and the methodological turn', *Political Studies* 39, 463–78

Little, R., 1994, 'International relations and large-scale historical change', in A. J. R. Groom and M. Light (eds), *Contemporary International Relations: A Guide to Theory*, 9–26

Little, R., 1995, 'International relations and the triumph of capitalism', in K. Booth and S. Smith (eds), *International Relations Theory Today*, 62–89

Little, R., 1995, 'Neorealism and the English School: a methodological, ontological and theoretical reassessment', *European Journal of International Relations* 1.1, 9–34

Lloyd, B. B., 1972, *Perception and Cognition: A Cross-cultural Perspective*

Lloyd, C., 1993, *The Structures of History*

Lock, P., 1995, *The Franks in the Aegean 1204–1500*

Lockwood, D., 1964, 'Social integration and system integration', in G. K. Zollschan and H. W. Hirsch (eds), *Explorations in Social Change*, Boston, MA, 244–57

Long, N. and Long, A. (eds), 1992, *Battlefields of Knowledge: The Interlocking of Theory and Practice in Social Research and Development*

Lopez, L. A., 1988, 'Informal exchange networks informal systems: a theoretical model', *American Anthropologist* 90.1, 42–55

Loye, D. and Eisler, R., 1987, 'Chaos and transformation: implications of nonequilibrium theory for social science and society', *Behavioral Science* 32, 53–65

Luhmann, N., 1982, *The Differentiation of Society*, New York

Lui, L., 1996, 'Settlement patterns, chiefdom variability, and the development of early states in North China', *Journal of Anthropological Archaeology* 15, 237–88.

Lundestad, G. (ed.), 1994, *The Fall of Great Powers*, Oslo and Oxford

Lynn, J. A., 1996, 'The evolution of army style in the modern West 800–2000', *The International History Review* 18.3, 505–545

Macadam, D., McCarthy, J. D. and Zald, M. (eds), 1996, *Comparative Perspectives on Social Movements*

MacFarlane, A., 1978, *The Origins of English Individualism*

Mackerras, C., Taneja, P. and Young, G., 1994, *China Since 1978*, Melbourne

MacMullen, R., 1976, *Roman Government's Response to Crisis AD 235–337*

Maisels, C. K., 1990, *The Emergence of Civilization*

Mamatey, V. S. 1978, *Rise of the Habsburg Empire 1526–1815*, 2nd edn, New York

Mandel, E., 1995, *Long Waves of Capitalist Development*, 2nd rev edn

Mandel, E. and Wallerstein, I. (eds), 1992, *New Findings in Long Waves Research*, New York

Mango, C., 1980, *Byzantium: The Empire of the New Rome*

Mann, M., 1986, *The Sources of Social Power. Vol. 1: A History of Power from the Beginning to AD 1760*

Mann, M., 1988, *States, War and Capitalism: Studies in Political Sociology*

Mann, M., 1993, 'Nation states in Europe and other continents: diversifying developing, not dying', *Proceedings of the American Academy of Arts and Sciences* 122.3, 115–40

Mann, M., Giddens, A. and Wallerstein, I. 1989, 'Comments on Paul Kennedy's *Rise and Fall of the Great Powers*', *British Journal of Sociology* 40.2, 328–40

Mansbach, R. W., Ferguson, Y. H. and Lampert, D. E., 1976, *The Web of World Politics: Nonstate Actors in the Global System*, Englewood Cliffs, NJ

Marquardt, W. H., 1988, 'Politics and production among the Calusa of south Florida', in T. Ingold, D. Riches and J. Woodburn (eds), *Hunters and Gatherers I: History, Evolution and Social Change*, 161–88

Mascher, H. D. G., 1991, 'The emergence of cultural complexity on the northern Northwest Coast', *Antiquity* 65, 924–34

Mason, J. W., 1985, *The Dissolution of the Austro-Hungarian Empire 1867–1918*

Mastanduno, M., Lake, D. A. and Ikenberry, G. J., 1989, 'Toward a realist theory of state action', *International Studies Quarterly* 33, 457–74

Matson, R. G. and Coupland, G., 1995, *Prehistory of the Northwest Coast*,

New York

Maybury-Lewis, D., 1974, *Akwe-Shavante Society*

Mayer, H. E., 1972, *The Crusades*, trans. by J. Gillingham

Mayhew, B., 1972, 'System size and structural differentiation of military organisations; testing a harmonic series model of the divison of labor', *American Journal of Sociology* 77, 750–765

Mayhew, B., 1973, 'System size and ruling elites', *American Sociological Review* 78, 468–475

Mayhew, B. and Levinger, R. L., 1976, 'On the emergence of oligarchy in human interaction', *American Journal of Sociology* 81, 1017–49

Mayhew, B. and Levinger, R. L., 1976, 'Size and density of interaction in human aggregates', *American Journal of Sociology* 82, 86–110

Maylam, P., 1986, *A History of the African People of South Africa*, New York

McAfee, R. P. and McMillan, J., 1995, 'Organizational diseconomies of scale', *Journal of Economics and Management Strategy* 4.3, 399–426

McCarnoy, M., 1984, *The State and Political Theory*, Princeton

McCarthy, P. and Jones, E. (eds), 1996, *Disintegration or Transformation?*

McClelland, D. C., 1961, *The Achieving Society*, New York

McGrew, A., 1992, 'A global society', in S. Hall, D. Held and T. McGrew (eds), *Modernity and its Futures*, 62–113

McGrew, T. G. and Lewis, P. G., 1992, *Global Politics*

McKay, D. and Scott, H. M., 1983, *The Rise of the Great Powers 1648–1815*

McKibbin, W. J. and Sachs, J., 1991, *Global Linkages: Macro-economic Interdependence and Cooperation in the World Economy*, Washington

McNeill, W. H., 1963, *The Rise of the West: A History of the Human Community*, Chicago

McNeill, W. H., 1974, *The Shape of European History*

McNeill, W. H., 1979, *Plagues and Peoples*, Harmondsworth

McNeill, W. H., 1984, *The Pursuit of Power*, Chicago

McNeill, W. H., 1986, *Poly-Ethnicity and National Unity in World History*, Toronto

McNeill, W. H., 1986, *Mythistory and other Essays*, Chicago

McNeill, W. H., 1990, 'The rise of the West after twenty-five years', *Journal of World History*, 1, 1–2

McNeill, W. H., 1991, *A World History*, Chicago

McNeill, W. H., 1992, *The Global Condition*, Princeton

McNeill, W. H., 1993, *A History of the Human Community*, 4th edn, Englewood Cliffs, NJ

McPherson, M. J., Popielarz, P. A. and Drobnic, S., 1992, 'Social networks and organizational dynamics', *American Sociological Review* 57, 153–70

Meadows, D. H., Meadows, D. L. and Randers, J., 1992, *Beyond the Limits*

Mearsheimer, J., 1990, 'Back to the future: instability in Europe after the Cold War', *International Security* 15.1, 5–56

Megarry, T., 1995, *Society in Prehistory*

Megarry, T. (ed.), 1996, *From the Caves to Capital* New York

Meier, R. L., 1972, 'Communications stress', *Annual Review of Ecology and Systematics* 3, 289–314

Melucci, A., 1989, *Nomads and the Present: Social Movements and Individual Needs in Contemporary Society*

Melucci, A., 1996, *Challenging Codes: Collective Action in the Information Age*

Menard, C., 1994, 'Organizations as coordinating devices', *Metroeconomica* 45.3, 224–47

Mendels, F. F., 1972, 'Proto-industrialization: the first phase of the industrialization process', *Journal of Economic History* 32, 241–61

Mennell, S., 1989, 'Bringing the very long term back in', in J. Goudsblom, E. L. Jones and S. Mennell, *Human History and Social Process*, 1–10

Millar, F., 1994, *The Roman Near East 31 BC-AD 337*, Cambridge, MA

Miller, G. 1992, *Managerial Dilemmas: The Political Economy of Hierarchy*

Millon, R., 1988, 'The last years of Teotihuacan dominance', in N. Yoffee and G. Cowgill (eds), *The Collapse of Ancient States and Civilizations*, Tucson, 102–64

Milner, H., 1991, 'The assumption of anarchy in international relations theory: a critique', *Review of International Studies* 17.1, 67–86

Miner, A. S., 1990, 'Structural evolution through idiosyncratic jobs the potential for unplanned learning', *Organization Science 1, 195–210*

Modelski, G., 1962, 'Comparative international systems', *World Politics* 14, 662–674

Modelski, G., 1978, 'Long cycles of global politics and the nation state', *Comparative Studies in Society and History* 20, 214–38

Modelski, G. (ed.), 1987, *Exploring Long Cycles*, Boulder, CO

Modelski, G., 1987, *Long Cycles in World Politics*, London and Seattle

Modelski, G., 1996, 'Evolutionary paradigm for global politics', *International Studies Quarterly* 40, 321–42

Modelski, G. and Thompson, W., 1988, *Seapower in Global Politics 1494–1994*

Modelski, G. and Thompson, W. R., 1996, *Leading Sectors and World Powers: The Co-Evolution of Global Economics and Politics*, Columbia, Calif.

Mohrman, A., *et al.* (eds), 1989, *Large-Scale Organizational Change*, San Francisco

Moise, E. E., 1994, *Modern China*

Mokhtar, G. (ed.), 1981, *General History of Africa. Vol. II: Ancient Civilizations*, Paris

Montague, A. (ed.), 1980, *Sociobiology Examined*

Moore, B., 1966, *Social Origins of Dictatorship and Democracy*

Moore, D. B. and Schmitz, G. G. (eds), 1994, *Debating Development Discourse: Institutional and Popular Perspectives*

Moore, P. and Thomas, H., 1988, *The Anatomy of Decisions*, 2nd edn

Moran, E. F. (ed.), 1990, *The Ecosystem Approach in Anthropology*, Ann Arbor, MI

Morera, E., 1990, *Gramsci's Historicism*

Morgan, D., 1986, *The Mongols*

Morin, P., 1995, *Community Ecology*

Morrow, J. D., 1988, 'Social choice and system structure in world politics', *World Politics* 41.1, 75–97

Mote, F. F. and Twitchett, D. (eds) 1988, *The Cambridge History of China Vol. VII: Ming China 1368–1644*

Motyl, A. J., 1992, 'From imperial decay to imperial collapse: the fall of the Soviet Empire in comparative perspective', in R. L. Rudolph and D. F. Good (eds), *The Hapsburg Empire and the Soviet Union*, New York, 15–43

Moul, W. D., 1973, 'The level of analysis problem revisited', *Canadian Journal of Political Science* 61.1, 494–513

Mowat, R. C., 1991, *Decline and Renewal*

Mowlana, H., 1985, *International Flow of Information: A Global Report and Analysis*, Paris

Mowlana, H., 1986, *Global Information and World Communication: New Frontiers in International Relations*

Mowlana, H., 1997, *Global Information and World Communication*

Moyr, J., 1990, 'Punctuated equilibria and technological progress', *American Economic Review* 80.2, 350–54

Moyr, J., 1991, 'Evolutionary biology, technical change and economic history', *Bulletin of Economic Research* 43.2, 127–49

Mulgan, G., 1995, 'The simple truth about complexity', *Times Higher Education Supplement* 22 December, 16

Mundy, J. H., 1973, *Europe in the High Middle Ages 1150–1309*

Narroll, R., 1956, 'A preliminary index of social development', *American Anthropologist* 58, 687–715

Nelson, B. A., 1995, 'Complexity, hierarchy and scale: a controlled comparison between Chaco Canyon, New Mexico and La Quemada, Zacatecas', *American Antiquity* 60.4, 596–618

Nelson, R. R. and Winter, S., 1982, *An Evolutionary Theory of Economic Change*

Nelson, S. M. (ed.), 1995, *Archaeology of Northeast China*

Neufeld, M., 1993, 'Interpretation and the science of international relations', *Review of International Studies* 19, 39–62

Nicholis, G. and Prigogine, I., 1989, *Exploring Complexity*, New York

Nicholson, M., 1989, *Formal Theories in International Relations*

Nicholson, M., 1996, *Causes and Consequences in International Relations: A Conceptual Study*, London and New York

Nicholson, M., 1996, 'The continued significance of positivism', in S. Smith, K. Booth and M. Zalewski (eds), *International Theory: Positivism and Beyond*, 128–45

Nicholson, M. and Bennett, P., 1994, 'The epistemology of international relations', in A. J. R. Groom and M. Light (eds), *Contemporary International Relations: A Guide to Theory*, 197–205

Niemira, M. P. and Klein, P. A. 1994, *Financial and Economic Cycles*

O'Hear, A. (ed.), 1995, *Karl Popper: Philosophy and Problems*

O'Kelly, M. J., 1989, *Early Ireland*

Oates, J., 1996, 'A prehistoric communication revolution' *Cambridge Archaeological Journal* 6.1, 165–76

Oberg, K. 1955, 'Types of social structure among the lowland tribes of south and central America', *American Anthropologist* 57, 472

Odner, K., 1992, *The Varanger Saami*, Oslo

OECD, 1992, *Globalization of Industrial Activities*

Ogilvie, S. and Cerman, M. (eds), 1996, *European Proto-industrialization*

Ohmae, K., 1990, *The Borderless World*

Olson, M., 1971, 'Rapid growth as a destabilizing force', in J. C. Davis (ed.), *When Men Revolt and Why*, New York, 215–27

Olson, M., 1982, *The Rise and Decline of Nations*, New Haven, CT

Olson, W. C. and Groom, A. J. R., 1991, *International Relations Then and Now*

Onuf, N., 1989, *World of Our Making: Rules and Rule in Social Theory and International Relations*, Columbia, SC

Onuf, N., 1995, 'Levels', *European Journal of International Relations* 1.1, 35–58

Organski, A. F. K., 1968, *World Politics*, 2nd edn, New York

Organski, A. F. K. and Kugler, J., 1980, *The War Ledger*, Chicago

Ormerod, P., 1994, *The Death of Economics*

Osborne, R., 1996, *Greece in the Making: 1200–479 BC*

Overdale, R., 1992, *The Middle East since 1914*

Owen, R., 1992, *State, Power and Politics in the Making of the Modern Middle East*

Palat, R. A. (ed.), 1993, *Pacific Asia and the Future of the World System*, Westport

Palmer, A. P., 1992, *The Decline and Fall of the Ottoman Empire*

Pareto, V., 1916, *The Mind and Society*

Parker, A. J., 1987, 'Trade within the Empire and beyond the frontiers', in J. Wacher (ed.), 1987, *The Roman World*, 2 vols., vol. II, 635–57

Parker-Pearson, M., 1984, 'Economic and ideological change: cyclical growth in the pre-state societies of Jutland', in D. Miller and C. Tilley (eds), *Ideology, Power and Prehistory*, 69–92

Parsons, T., 1951, *The Social System*, New York

Parsons, T., 1964, 'Evolutionary universals in society', *American Sociological Review* 29, 339–57

Parsons, T., 1966, *Societies: Evolutionary and Comparative Perspectives*, Englewood Cliffs, NJ

Parsons, T., 1967, *Sociological Theory and Modern Society*, New York

Parsons, T., 1977, *The Evolution of Societies*, Englewood Cliffs, NJ

Parsons, T. and Smelser, N. J., 1956, *Economy and Society: A Study in the Integration of Economic and Social Theory*

Patomaki, H., 1991, 'Concepts of "Action", "structure", and "power" in critical social realism: a positive and reconstructive critique', *Journal for the Theory of Social Behaviour* 21.2, 221–50

Pattee, H. H. (ed.), 1973, *Hierarchy Theory: The Challenge of Complex Systems*, New York

Patterson, N. T., 1995, 'Clans are not primordial: pre-Viking Irish society and the modelling of pre-Roman societies in northern Europe', in B. Arnold and D. B. Gibson (eds), *Celtic Chiefdom, Celtic State*, Cambridge, 129–136

Pauketat, T., 1994 *The Ascent of Chiefs: Cahokia and Mississippian Politics in North America*, Tuscalosa

Perkins, D. and Syrquin, M., 1989, 'Large countries: the influence of size', in H. Chenery and T. M. Srinivasan (eds), *Handbook of Development Economics*, vol. 2, Amsterdam, 1691–753

Perrow, C., 1986, *Complex Organizations: A Critical Essay*, 3rd edn

Phillips, J. R. S., 1988, *The Medieval Expansion of Europe*

Phillips, W. and Rimkunas, R., 1978, 'The concept of crisis in international politics', *Journal of Peace Research* 15, 259–72

Phillipson, D. W., 1993, *African Archaeology*, 2nd edn

Pierson, P., 1993, 'When effect becomes cause: policy feedback and political change', *World Politics* 45, 595–628

Piliavin, J. A. and Charng, H-W., 1990, 'Altruism: a review of recent research', *Annual Review of Sociology* 16, 27–65

Pipes, R., 1995, 'Misinterpreting the end of the Cold War', *Foreign Affairs* 74.1, 154–60

Platt, C., 1979, *The Atlas of Medieval Man*

Polanyi, K., 1957, *The Great Transformation*, rev. edn. Boston

Polanyi, K., 1963, 'Ports of trade in early societies', *Journal of Economic History* 23, 30–45

Polanyi, K., Arensburg, C. and Pearson, H. W., (eds), 1957, *Trade and Markets in the Early Empires*, Glencoe, IL

Pomper, P., 1996, 'Historians and individual agency', *History and Theory* 35.3, 281–308

Popper, K. R., 1961, *The Poverty of Historicism*, 3rd edn

Popper, K. R., 1963, *Conjectures and Refutations*

Popper, K. R., 1972, *Objective Knowledge: an Evolutionary Approach*

Porras, J. and Robertson, P., 1992, 'Organizational development: theory, practice and research', in M. Dunnette and L. Hough (eds), *Handbook of Industrial and Organizational Psychology*, 2nd edn, Vol. 3, Palo Alto, CA, 719–822

Porras, J. and Silvers, R., 1991, 'Organizational development and transformation', *Annual Review of Psychology* 42, 51–78

Porter, R. and Teich, M. (eds), 1986, *Revolution in History*

Possehl, G. L. (ed.), 1993, *Harrapan Civilization*

Postgate, N., 1994, *Early Mesopotamia*

Postgate, N., Wang, T. and Wilkinson, T., 1995, 'The evidence for early writing: utilitarian or ceremonial?, *Antiquity* 69, 459–80

Potter, G. R. (ed.), 1961, *The Renaissance 1493–1520*

Pounds, N. J. G., 1979, *An Historical Geography of Europe 1500–1840*

Pounds, N. J. G., 1994, *An Economic History of Medieval Europe*, 2nd edn

Powell, A. (ed.), 1995, *The Greek World*

Powell, R., 1994, 'Anarchy in international relations theory: the neorealist-neoliberal debate', *International Organization* 48.2, 313–44

Prawer, J., 1972, *The Latin Kingdom of Jerusalem*

Prechel, H., 1994, 'Economic crisis and the centralization of control', *American Sociological Review* 59, 723–45

Pred, A., 1977, 'The choreography of existence: comments on Hagerstrand's time-geography', *Economic Geography* 53, 207–21

Pred, A., 1984, 'Place as historically contingent process: structuration and the time-geography of becoming places', *Annals of the Association of American Geographers* 74, 279–97

Pred, A., 1990, *Making Histories and Constructing Geographies*, Boulder, CO

Price, R., 1994, 'Interpretation and disciplinary orthodoxy in international relations', *Review of International Studies* 20, 201–4

Price, T. D. and Brown, J. A., (eds), 1985, *Prehistoric Hunter-Gatherers: The Emergence of Cultural Complexity*, New York

Price, T. D. and Feinman, G. M., 1995 (eds), *The Foundations of Social Inequality*, New York

Prigogine, I. and Stengers, I., 1986, *Order out of Chaos*, Toronto

Pugh, D. S. *et al.*, 1968, 'Dimensions of organization structure', *Administrative Science Quarterly* 13, 65–105

Quilter, J., 1991, 'Late Preceramic Peru', *Journal of World Prehistory* 5, 387–438

Radner, R., 1992, 'Hierarchy, the economics of managing', *Journal of Economic Literature* 30.3, 1382–1415

Rasler, K. and Thompson, W. R., 1991, *Global War and State-Making Processes*

Rawson, J. (ed.), 1997, *Mysteries of Ancient China*

Ray, J. L., 1989, 'The abolition of slavery and the end of international war', *International Organization* 43, 405–44

Ray, J. L. and Russett, B., 1996, 'The future as arbiter of theoretical controversies: predictions, expectations and the end of the Cold War', *British Journal of Political Science* 26, 441–70

Redmond, E. M., 1994, *Tribal and Chiefly War in South America*

Redmond, E. M. and Spencer, C. S., 1994, 'Pre-Columbian chiefdoms', *National Geographic Research and Exploration* 10, 422–39

Rees, A. and Rees, B., 1961, *Celtic Heritage*, 120–21

Reijnders, J. P. G., 1990, *Long Waves in Economic Development*

Reimann, B. C., 1973, 'On the dimensions of bureaucratic structure: an empirical reappraisal', *Administrative Science Quarterly* 18, 462–76

Renfrew, A. C., 1972, *The Emergence of Civilization*

Renfrew, A. C., 1973, *Before Civilization*

Renfrew, A. C., 1986, 'Introduction: peer polity interaction and socio-political change', in C. Renfrew and J. F. Cherry (eds), *Peer Polity Interaction and Socio-Political Change*, 1–18

Renfrew, C. and Bahn, P., 1996, *Archaeology. Theories, Methods and Practice*, 2nd edn

Renfrew, C. and Cherry, J. F. (eds), 1986, *Peer Polity Interaction and Socio-Political Change*

Renfrew, C. and Shennan, S. (eds), 1982, *Ranking, Resource and Exchange*, Cambridge

Rengger, N. J., 1988, 'Going critical? A response to Hoffman', *Millennium*, 17.1, 81–89

Rengger, N. J., 1992, 'No time like the present: postmodernism and political theory', *Political Studies*, 40.3, 561–70

Rengger, N. J., 1995, *Political Theory, Modernity and Post-modernity*

Rengger, N. J., 1996, 'Clio's cave and the claims of "substantive social theory" in world politics', *Review of International Studies* 22, 213–31

Rengger, N. J., 1996, *Duties Beyond Orders*

Rengger, N. and Hoffman, M., 1992, 'Modernity, post-modernism and international relations', in J. Doherty, E. Graham and M. Malek (eds), *Post-modernism and the Social Sciences*, 127–46

Reynolds, S., 1994, *Fiefs and Vassals*

Richards, D. S., 1973, *Islamic History 950–1150*

Richards, J., 1996, *The Mughal Empire*

Richardson, J., 1994, 'History strikes back: the state of international relations theory', *Australian Journal of Political Science* 29.1, 179–84

Richter, D. K. and Merrell, J. N. (eds), 1987, *The Iroquois and their Neighbours 1600–1800*, Syracuse, NY

Risse-Kappen, T., 1995, *Bringing Transnational Relations Back In*

Rittberger, V. (ed.), 1993, *Regime Theory and International Relations*

Roberts, J., 1967, *Europe 1880–1945*

Robertson, R., 1987, 'Globalization theory and civilizational analysis', *Comparative Civilizations Review* 17, 20–30

Robertson, R., 1992, *Globalization: Social Theory and Global Culture*

Roesdahl, E., 1991, *The Vikings*

Rosecrance, R. N., 1986, 'Long cycle theory and international relations', *International Organization* 41.2, 283–302

Rosecrance, R. N., 1991, *The Rise of the Trading State: Commerce and Conquest in the Modern World*, New York

Rosen, R., 1979, 'Morphogenesis in biological and social systems', in A. C. Renfrew and K. Cooke (eds), *Transformations*, New York, 91–111

Rosenau, J. N., 1981, *The Study of Political Adaptation*

Rosenau, J. N., 1986, 'Before cooperation: hegemons, regimes and habit-driven actors in world politics', *International Organization* 40, 879–94

Rosenau, J. N., 1989, 'The state in an era of cascading politics: wavering concept, widening competence, withering Collosus or weathering change?', in J. A. Caporaso (ed.), *The Elusive State*, Newbury Park, CA, 17–48

Rosenau, J. N., 1990, *Turbulence in World Politics: A Theory of Change and Continuity*, Princeton

Rosenau, J. N., 1992, 'Governance, order and change in world politics', in J. N. Rosenau and E-O. Czempiel (eds), *Governance Without Government: Order and Change in World Politics*, 1–29

Rosenau, J. N., 1995, 'Governance in the twenty-first century', *Global Governance* 1.1, 13–43

Rosenau, J. N., 1995, 'Signals, signposts and symptoms: interpreting change and anomalies in world politics', *European Journal of International Relations*, 1.1, 113–22

Rosenau, J. N., 1996, 'Powerful tendencies, startling discrepancies and elusive dynamics: the challenge of studying world politics in a turbulent era', *Australian Journal of International Affairs* 50.1, 23–30

Rosenau, J. N. and Tromp, H. (eds), 1989, *Interdependence and Conflict in World Politics*, Brookfield, VT

Rosenau, P. M., 1990, 'Internal logic, external absurdity: postmodernism in political science', *Paradigms* 4.1, 39–57

Rosenau, P. M., 1992, *Post-Modernism and the Social Sciences*, Princeton, NJ

Rosenberg, J., 1994, *The Empire of Civil Society*

Rosenberg, J., 1994, 'The International imagination: international relations theory and classic social analysis', *Millennium* 23, 85–108

Rosenberg, M., 1994, 'Pattern, process and hierarchy in the evolution of culture', *Journal of Anthropological Archaeology* 13, 307–40

Rosenberg, N. and Frischtak, C., 1984, 'Technological innovation and long waves', *Cambridge Journal of Economics* 8, 7–24

Roosevelt, A. C., 1987, 'Chiefdoms in the Amazon and Oronoco', in R. D. Drennan and C. A. Uribe (eds), 1987, *Chiefdoms in the Americas*, Latham, MA, 133–85

Rostow, W. W., 1960, *The Process of Economic Growth*, 2nd edn

Rostow, W. W., 1963, *The Economics of Take-off into Sustained Growth*, London

Rostow, W. W., 1971, *The Stages of Economic Growth: A Non-Communist Manifesto*, 2nd edn

Rostow, W. W., 1971, *Politics and the Stages of Growth*

Rostow, W. W., 1978, *The World Economy: History and Prospect*

Rostow, W. W., 1979, *Getting From Here to There*

Rostow, W. W., 1980, *Why the Poor Get Richer and the Rich Slow Down: Essays in the Marshallian Long Period*

Rostow, W. W., 1987, *Rich Countries and Poor Countries: Reflections on the*

Past, Lessons for the Future, London and Boulder, Colo.

Rostow, W. W., 1990, *Theorists of Economic Growth from David Hume to the Present: With a Perspective on the Next Century*, Oxford

Rowlands, M., Larsen, M. and Kristiansen, K. (eds), 1987, *Centre and Periphery in the Ancient World*

Royce, C. C., 1887, 'The Cherokee nation of Indians', in J. W. Powell (ed.), *Fifth Annual Report of the Bureau of Ethnology 1883–1884*, Washington

Roymans, N., 1990, *Tribal Societies in Northern Gaul*, Amsterdam

Ruggie, J. G., 1982, 'International regimes, transactions and change: embedded liberalism in the post war economic order', *International Organization* 36.2, 379–415

Ruggie, J. G., 1983, 'Continuity and transformation in the world polity: toward a neorealist synthesis', *World Politics* 35.2, 261–85

Ruggie, J. G., 1997, *International Transformations.*

Runciman, S., 1965, *The Fall of Constantinople 1453*

Ruse, M., 1989, 'Is the theory of punctuated equilibria a new paradigm?', *Journal of Social and Biological Structures* 12, 195–212

Saggs, H. W. F., 1995, *Babylonians*

Sah, R. and Stiglitz, J. E., 1986, 'The architecture of economic systems: hierarchies and polyarchies', *American Economic Review* 76.4, 716–27

Sahlins, M. D., 1958, *Social Stratification in Polynesia*, Seattle

Sahlins, M. D., 1963, 'Poor man, rich man, big man, chief: political types in Melanesia and Polynesia', *Comparative Studies in Society and History* 5, 285–303

Sahlins, M. D., 1977, *The Use and Abuse of Biology*

Sanderson, S. K., 1995, *Social Transformations*, Cambridge, MA and Oxford

Sanderson, S. K. (ed.), 1995, *Civilizations and World-Systems: Two Approaches to the Study of World-Historical Change*, Walnut-Creek, CA

Sawyer, P., 1978, *From Roman Britain to Norman England*

Sayer, A., 1984, *Method in Social Science*

Scammell, G. V., 1981, *The World Encompassed*

Scammell, G. V., 1989, *The First Imperial Age (1400–1715)*

Schein, E. H., 1990, 'Organizational culture', *American Psychologist* 45, 109–119

Schele, L. and Friedel, D., 1990, *A Forest of Kings: The Untold Story of the Ancient Maya*, New York

Schelling, C., 1978, *Micromotives and Macrobehavior*, New York

Schlicht, E., 1990, 'Social psychology: a review article', *Journal of Institutional and Theoretical Economics* 146.2, 355–62

Schneider, B. (ed.), 1990, *Organizational Climate and Culture*, San Francisco

Scholte, J. A., 1993, 'From power politics to social change: an alternative focus for international studies', *Review of International Studies* 19.1, 3–22

Scholte, J. A., 1993, *International Relations of Social Change*

Schroeder, P. W., 1994, 'Historical reality vs neo-realist theory', *International Security* 19.1, 108–48

Schroeder, P. W., 1996, *The Transformation of European Politics 1763–1848*

Schumpeter, J. A., 1935, 'The analysis of economic change', *Review of Economics and Statistics* 17.4, 2–10

Schumpeter, J. A., 1939, *Business Cycles*, New York

Schwartz, S. B. (ed.), 1995, *Implicit Understanding*

Scott, A., 1982, *The Dynamics of Interdependence*

Scott, A. J. and Storper, M. (eds), 1986, *Production, Work, Territory: The Geographical Anatomy of Industrial Capitalism*, Boston, MA

Scott, R. W., 1975, 'Organizational structure', *Annual Review of Sociology* 1, 1–20

Scullard, A., 1982, *From the Gracchi to Nero*

Scullard, H. H., 1991, *A History of the Roman World 753 to 146 BC*

Serra, R. and Zaharini, G., 1990, *Complex Systems and Cognitive Processes*, Berlin

Service, E. R., 1971, *Primitive Social Organization: An Evolutionary Perspective*, 2nd edn, New York

Service, E. R., 1975, *The Origins of the State and Civilization*, New York

Shaban, M. A., 1971, *The Abbasid Revolution*

Sharer, R. J., 1994, *The Ancient Maya*

Shaw, M., 1992, 'Global society and global responsibility: the theoretical, historical and political limits of international society', *Millennium* 21.3, 421–34

Shaw, M., 1994, *Global Society and International Relations*

Shaw, S. J. (with E. K. Shaw), 1976–7, *History of the Ottoman Empire and Modern Turkey*, 2 vols

Sheehan, M., 1996, *The Balance of Power*

Shinnie, M., 1965, *Ancient African Kingdoms*

Shu, C-Y. and Linduf, K., 1988, *Western Chou Civilization*, New Haven, CT

Sillitoe, A., 1996, *Key Issues in Historical and Comparative Sociology*

Sillitoe, P., 1978, 'Bigmen and war in New Guinea', *Man* 13, 252–71

Silverberg, G., Dosi, G. and Orsenigo, L., 1988, 'Innovation, diversity and diffusion: a self-organising model', *Economic Journal* 98, 1032–55

Silverman, H., 1996, 'The formative period on the south coast of Peru: a critical review', *Journal of World Prehistory* 10.2, 95–146

Simmons, A., 1987, 'Theories of international regimes', *International Organization* 41, 491–517

Simon, G., 1996, 'The end of the Soviet Union: causes and relational contexts', *Aussenpolitik* 47.1, 9–21

Simon, H. A., 1962, 'The architecture of complexity', *Proceedings of the American Philosophical Society* 106, 467–82

Simon, H. A., 1973, 'The organization of complex systems', in H. H. Pattee (ed.), *Hierarchy Theory: the Challenge of Complex Systems*, New York, 3–27

Singer, J. D., 1961, 'The level-of-analysis problem in international relations', in K. Knorr and S. Verba (eds), *The International System: Theoretical Essays*, Princeton, NJ

Skinner, G. W., 1977, 'Cities and the hierarchy of local systems', in G. W. Skinner (ed.), *The City in Late Imperial China*, Stanford, 276–351

Skinner, Q. (ed.), 1985, *The Return of Grand Theory in the Human Sciences*

Sklair, L., 1991, *Sociology and the Global System*

Skocpol, T., 1979, *States and Social Revolutions: A Comparative Analysis of France, Russia and China*

Skocpol, T., 1984, 'Sociology's historical imagination' in T. Skocpol (ed.), *Vision and Method in Historical Sociology*, Cambridge and New York, 1–21

Skocpol, T. (ed.), 1984, *Vision and Method in Historical Sociology*

Skocpol, T., 1994, *Social Revolution in the Modern World*

Smail, R. C., 1956, *The Crusaders in Syria and the Holy Land*

Smelser, N. J., 1959, *Social Change in the Industrial Revolution*, Chicago

Smelser, N. J., 1968, *Essays in Sociological Explanation*, Englewood Cliffs, NJ

Smircich, L., 1983, 'Concepts of culture in organizational analysis', *Administrative Science Quarterly* 28, 339–358

Smith, A. D., 1990, 'Towards a global culture?', *Theory, Culture and Society* 7, 171–93

Smith, A. D., 1995, *Nations and Nationalism in a Global Era*

Smith, A. K., 1991, *Creating a World Economy: Merchant Capital, Colonialism and World Trade 1400–1825*, Boulder, CO

Smith, D. 1991, *The Rise of Historical Sociology*

Smith, H., 1994, 'Marxism and international relations theory', in A. J. R. Groom and M. Light (eds), *Contemporary International Relations: A Guide to Theory*, 142–55

Smith, H., 1996, 'The silence of the academics: international social theory, historical materialism and political values', *Review of International Studies* 22.2, 191–212

Smith, M. E., 1987, 'Archaeology and the Aztec economy: the social scientific use of archaeological data', *Social Science History* 11, 237–59

Smith, M. E., 1987, 'The expansion of the Aztec Empire: a case study in the correlation of diachronic archaeological and ethnohistorical data', *American Antiquity* 52, 37–54

Smith, M. E., 1996, *The Aztecs*

Smith, N. and Dennis, W., 1987, 'The restructuring of geographical scale: coalescence and fragmentation of the northern core region', *Economic Geography* 63, 160–82

Smith, P. J., 1993, *Scipio Africanus and Rome's Invasion of Africa*, Gieben

Smith, S., 1988, 'Paradigm dominance in international relations: with development of international relations as a social science', *Millennium* 16.2, 189–206

Smith, S., 1994, 'Rearranging the deckchairs on the ship called modernity: Rosenberg, epistemology and emancipation', *Millennium* 23.2, 395–405

Smith, S., 1995, 'The self-images of a discipline: a genealogy of international relations theory', in K. Booth and S. Smith, *International Relations Theory Today*, 1–37

Smith, S., 1996, 'Positivism and beyond', in S. Smith, K. Booth and M. Zalewski (eds), *International Theory: Positivism and Beyond*, 1–44

Smith, S. J., 1981, 'Humanistic method in contemporary social geography', *Area* 13, 293–8

Smith, S. J., 1984, 'Practicing humanistic geography', *Annals of the Association of American Geographers* 74, 353–74

Snooks, G., 1996, *The Dynamic Society*

Snow, D. R., 1996, *The Iroquois*

Soja, E. W., 1989, *Postmodern Geographies: The Re-assertion of Space in Critical Theory*

Solnick, S. L., 1996, 'The breakdown of hierarchies in the Soviet Union and China: a neo-institutional perspective', *World Politics* 48, 209–38

Solomou, S., 1987, *Phases of Economic Growth 1850–1973: Kondratieff Waves and Kuznets Swings*

Solow, B. L., 1991, *Slavery and the Rise of the Atlantic System*

Songqiao, Z., 1994, *Geography of China*, New York

Sorokin, P., 1957, *Social and Cultural Dynamics*, 2nd ed, Boston

Spencer, A. J., 1993, *Early Egypt: The Rise of Civilisation in the Nile Valley*

Spencer, C. S., 1987, 'Rethinking the chiefdom', in R. D. Drennan and C. A. Uribe (eds), 1987, *Chiefdoms in the Americas*, Latham, MA, 1–9

Spencer, C. S. and Redmond, E. M., 1992, 'Prehistoric chiefdoms of the western Venezuelan Llanos', *World Archaeology* 24, 134–57

Spencer, H., 1874, *The Study of Sociology*, New York

Spiro, P. J., 1995, 'New global communities: non-governmental organisations in international decision-making institutions', in B. Roberts (ed.), *Order and Disorder After the Cold War*, Cambridge, MA, 251–62

Spivey, N. and Stoddart, S., 1994, *Etruscan Italy*

Spratt, D. A., 1989, 'Innovation theory made plain', in S. E. van der Leeuw and R. Torrence (eds), *The Process of Innovation*, 245–57

Spruyt, H., 1994, *The Sovereign State and its Competitors* Princeton, NJ

Spruyt, H., 1994, 'Institutional selection in international relations: state anarchy as order', *International Organization* 48.4, 527–57

Spyby, T., 1995, *Globalization and World Society*

Stalling, B. (ed.), 1995, *Global Change, Regional Response: The New International Context of Development*

Stanford, M., 1994, *A Companion to the Study of History*

Starbuck, W. H., 1983 'Organizations as action generators', *American*

Sociological Review 48, 91–102

Stearns, P. N., 1993, *The Industrial Revolution in World History*

Stein, G. and Rothman, M. S. (eds), *Chiefdoms and Early States in the Near East: The Organizational Dynamics of Complexity*, Madison, WI

Stinchcombe, A. L., 1990, *Information and Organizations*, Berkeley, CA

Stokes, R. G., 1975, 'Afrikaner Calvinism and economic action: the Weberian thesis in South Africa', *American Journal of Sociology* 81, 62–81

Strange, S., 1986, *Casino Capitalism*

Strange, S., 1988, *States and Markets*

Strange, S., 1990, 'Finance, information and power', *Review of International Studies* 16.3, 259–74

Strange, S., 1996, *The Retreat of the State*

Stratos, A. N., 1968–75, *Byzantium in the Seventh Century*, 3 vols, Amsterdam

Strong, D., 1991, 'Global patterns of decolonization 1500–1987', *International Studies Quarterly* 35, 429–45

Sullivan, R. J., 1990, 'The revolution of ideas: widespread patenting and invention during the English Industrial Revolution', *Journal of Economic History* 50, 349–62

Sutton, R. I. and Kahn, R. L., 1987, 'Prediction, understanding and control as antidotes to organizational stress', in J. W. Lorsch (ed.), *Handbook of Organizational Behavior*, Englewood Cliffs, NJ, 272–85

Syme, R., 1939, *The Roman Revolution*

Symons, D., 1989, 'A critique of Darwinian anthropology', *Ethology and Sociobiology* 10, 131–44

Taagepera, R., 1968, 'Growth curves of empires', *General Systems* 13, 171–5

Taagepera, R., 1978, 'Size and duration of empires: systematics of size', *Social Science Research* 7, 108–27

Taagepera, R., 1978, 'Size and duration of empires: growth-decline curves, 3000 to 600 BC', *Social Science Research* 7, 180–96

Tainter, J. A., 1988, *The Collapse of Complex Societies*

Tallman, I. and Gray, L. N., 1990, 'Choices, decisions and problem solving', *Theory and Research in Organizational Theory*, 161–94

Taylor, M., 1989, 'Structure, culture and action in the explanation of social change', *Politics and Society* 17.2, 115–62

Taylor, P., 1993, *International Organisation in the Modern World*

Taylor, P. J., 1989, *Political Geography*, 2nd edn

Taylor, P. J. (ed.), 1993, *Political Geography at the End of the Twentieth Century: A Global Analysis*

Taylor, P. J., 1994, 'The state as container: territoriality in the modern world', *Progress in Human Geography* 18, 151–62

Thomas, N., 1989, *Out of Time: History and Evolution in Anthropological Discourse*

Thompson, E. A., 1948, *A History of Attila and the Huns*

Thompson, G. *et al.*, 1991, *Markets, Hierarchies and Networks. The Coordina-*

tion of Social Life

Thompson, R. C., 1994, *The Pacific Basin Since 1945*

Thompson, W. R. (ed.), 1983, *Contending Approaches to World System Analysis*, Beverley Hills, CA

Thompson, W. R., 1986, 'Polarity, the long cycle and global power warfare', *Journal of Conflict Resolution* 30.4, 587–615

Thompson, W. R., 1988, *On Global War: Historical-Structural Approaches to World Politics*, Columbia, CA

Thompson, W. R., 1992, 'Dehio, long cycles and the geohistorical context of structural transition', *World Politics* 45, 127–52

Thompson, W. R. and Vescera, L., 1992, 'Growth waves, systemic openness, and protectionism', *International Organization* 46.2, 493–532

Thomson, J. E., 1994, *Merceneries, Pirates, and Sovereigns: State-building and Extra-territorial Violence in Early Modern Europe*, Princeton, NJ

Thorelli, H. B., 1986, 'Networks: between markets and hierarchies', *Strategic Management Journal* 7, 37–51

Thrift, N., 1989, 'New times and spaces? The perils of transition models', *Environment and Planning D: Society and Space* 7, 127–30

Thrift, N. and Pred, A., 1981, 'Time geography: a new beginning', *Progress in Human Geography* 5, 277–86

Tilly, C., 1984, *Big Structures, Large Processes, Huge Comparisons*, New York

Tirole, J., 1986, 'Hierarchies and bureaucracies', *Journal of Law, Economics and Organization* 2.3, 181–214

Todd, M., 1992, *The Early Germans*

Tonn, B. E. and Feldman, D., 1996, 'Non-spatial government' *Futures* 27.1, 11–36

Torstendahl, R., 1992, *State Theory and State History*

Tracy, J. D. (ed.), 1990, *The Rise of Merchant Empires: Long-distance Trade in the Early Modern World 1350–1750*

Tracy, J. D., 1991, *The Political Economy of Merchant Empires*

Trigger, B., 1993, *Ancient Civilizations: Ancient Egypt in Context*, Cairo

Trigger, B. G. (ed.), 1978, *Handbook of North American Indians*, Washington, DC

Trigger, B. G., Kemp, B. J., O'Connor, D. and Lloyd, A. B., 1983, *Ancient Egypt: A Social History*

Tsetskhladze, G. R. and de Angelis, F. (eds), 1988, *The Archaeology of Greek Colonisation*

Taljapurkar, S., 1990, *Population Dynamics in Variable Environments*, New York

Twitchett, D. (ed.), 1979, *The Cambridge History of China Vol. 3: Sui and T'ang China, 589–906*

Twitchett, D. and Lowe, E. (eds), 1986, *The Cambridge History of China Vol. 1: Qin and Han*

United Nations Development Programme/World Futures Studies Federation, 1986, *Reclaiming the Future*

Upham, S., 1990, 'Analog or digital?: toward a generic framework for explaining the development of emergent political systems', in S. Upham (ed.), *The Evolution of Political Systems*, 87–115

Upham, S. (ed.), 1990, *The Evolution of Political Systems: Sociopolitics in Small-scale Sedentary Societies*

Urry, J., 1981, *The Anatomy of Capitalist Societies*

Urwick, L. F., 1956, 'The manager's span of control', *Harvard Business Review* 34, 39–47

Urwin, D. W., 1968, *Western Europe Since 1945*

Uzzi, B., 1996, 'The sources and consequences of embeddedness for the economic performance of organizations: the network effect', *American Sociological Review* 61, 674–98

van Beskell, M. A. *et al.* (eds), 1986, *Approaches to 'Big Man' Systems*

van der Leeuw, S. E., 1981, 'Information flows, flow structures and the explanation of change in human institutions', in S. E. van der Leeuw (ed.), *Archaeological Approaches to the Study of Complexity*, Amsterdam, 230–312

van der Leeuw, S. E., 1987, 'Revolutions revisited', in L. Manzanilla (ed.), *Studies in Neolithic and Urban Revolutions*, 217–43

van der Leeuw, S. E., 1993, 'Decision-making in the Roman Empire during the Republic', in P. Brun, S. E. van der Leeuw and C. R. Whittaker (eds), *Frontiers d'empire*, 65–93

van der Leeuw, S. E. and McGlade, J., 1993, 'Information, coherence et dynamiques urbaines', in B. Lepetit and D. Pumain (eds), *Temporalités Urbaines*, Paris, 195–242

van Lave, T., 1987, *The World Revolution of Westernization: The Twentieth Century, a Global Perspective*

Vansina, J., 1990, *Paths in the Rainforest*, Madison WI

Vasquez, J. A., 1995, 'The post-positivist debate: restructuring scientific enquiry and international relations theory after enlightenments fall', in K. Booth and S. Smith, *International Relations Theory Today*, 217–40

Viotti, P. R. and Kauppi, M. V., 1993, *International Relations Theory. Realism, Pluralism and Globalism*, 2nd edn, New York

von Krogh, G. and Roos, J. (eds), 1996, *Managing Knowledge*

Vrba, E. S. and Eldredge, N., 1984 'Individuals, hierarchies and processes: toward a more complete evolutionary theory', *Palaeobiology* 10, 146–71

Wacher, J. (ed.), 1987, *The Roman World*

Waddington, C. H., 1974, 'A catastrophe theory of evolution', *Annals of the New York Academy of Sciences*, 231

Waddington, C. H., 1977, *Tools for Thought*

Waever, O., 1992, 'International society: theoretical promises unfulfilled?', *Cooperation and Conflict* 27, 97–128

Wakeman, F., 1985, *The Great Enterprise*, Berkeley, CA

Waldrop, H. M., 1992, *Complexity: The Emerging Science at the Edge of Order and Chaos*, New York

Waley, D., 1985, *Later Medieval Europe*

Walker, R. B. J., 1987, 'Realism, change and international political theory', *International Studies Quarterly* 31.1, 65–86

Walker, R. B. J., 1989, 'History and structure in the theory of international relations', *Millennium* 18.2, 163–83

Walker, R. B. J., 1993, *Inside/Outside: International Relations as Political Theory*

Walker, R. B. J., 1995, 'International relations and the concept of the political', in K. Booth and S. Smith, *International Relations Theory Today*, 306–27

Waller, T., 1988, 'The concept of habit in economic analysis', *Economic Issues* 22, 113–26

Wallerstein, I., 1974–88, *The Modern World System*, 3 vols., New York

Wallerstein, I., 1979, *The Capitalist World Economy*

Wallerstein, I., 1983, *Historical Capitalism*

Wallerstein, I., 1984, *The Politics of the World Economy*

Wallerstein, I., 1991, *Capitalist Civilization*, Binghampton, NY

Wallerstein, I., 1991, *Geopolitics and Geoculture*

Wallerstein, I., 1991, *Unthinking Social Science: The Limits of Nineteenth-Century Paradigms*

Wallerstein, I., 1992, *The Time Space of World-Systems Analysis*, Binghampton, NY

Wallerstein, I., 1993, 'World system versus world-systems: a critique', in A. G. Frank and B. K. Gills (eds), *The World System, Five Hundred Years or Five Thousand?*, 292–6

Wallerstein, I., 1996, 'The inter-state structure of the modern world-system', in S. Smith, K. Booth and M. Zalewski (eds), *International Theory: Positivism and Beyond*, 87–107

Walsham, G., 1993, *Interpreting Information Systems in Organisations*, New York

Waltz, K. N., 1959, *Man, the State and War*, New York

Waltz, K. N., 1979, *Theory of International Politics*, Reading, MA

Waltz, K. N., 1993, 'The emerging structure of international politics', *International Security* 18.2, 44–79

Waltzer, M., 1994, *Thick and Thin: Moral Argument at Home and Abroad*, Notre Dame

Ward, B., 1989, 'Telecommunications and the globalization of financial services', *Professional Geographer* 41.3, 257–71

Ware, R. B., 1996, 'Set theory, self-consciousness and the state', *Contemporary Political Studies*, 3, 1638–49

Watson, A., 1987, 'Hedly Bull, state systems, and international studies', *Review of International Studies* 13, 147–53

Watson, A., 1990, 'Systems of states', *Review of International Studies* 16, 99–110

Watson, A., 1992, *The Evolution of International Society*

Weaver, M. P., 1993, *The Aztecs, Maya, and their Predecessors*, New York

Wedgewood, C. V., 1964, *The Thirty Years War*, 2nd edn

Weenig, M. W. H. and Midden, C. J. H., 1991, 'Communication network influences on information diffusion and persuasion', *Journal of Personality and Social Psychology* 61, 734–42

Weick, K. E., 1985, 'Sources of order in underorganized systems: themes in recent organizational theory', in Y. S. Lincoln (ed.), *Organizational Theory and Inquiry*, Beverley Hills, CA, 103–36

Weisbuch, G., 1990, *Complex Systems: An Introduction to Automata Networks*, Reading, MA

Weiss, L. and Hobson, J. M., 1995, *States and Economic Development: A Comparative Historical Analysis*

Wellman, B. and Berkowitz, S. D. (eds), 1988, *Social Structures*

Wendt, A., 1987, 'The agent-structure problem in international relations theory', *International Organization* 41.3, 335–70

Wenke, R. J., 1990, *Patterns in Prehistory*, 3rd edn

Werner, D., 1981, 'Are some people more equal than others? status inequality among the Mekranoti Indians of Central Brazil', *Journal of Anthropological Research* 37, 360–73

Westcott, J. H. (ed.), 1986, *Predictability in Science and Society*

Westhoff, F. H., Yarbrough, B. V. and Yarbrough, R. M., 1996, 'Complexity, organization, and Stuart Kauffman's *The Origins of Order*', *Journal of Economic Behaviour and Organization* 29, 1–25

White, H., 1991, 'Comparative economic organization', *Administrative Science Quarterly* 36, 269–96

White, H., 1992, *Identity and control*, Princeton, NJ

White, L. A., 1949, *The Science of Culture*, New York

White, L. A., 1959, *The Evolution of Culture*, New York

Whitley, R., 1994, *The Social Structuring of Forms of Economic Organization: Firms and Markets in Comparative Perspective*

Wickham, C., 1981, *Early Medieval Italy*

Widmer, R. J., 1988, *The Evolution of the Calusa: A Nonagricultural Chiefdom on the Southwest Coast of Florida*

Wight, M., 1977, *Systems of States*

Wight, M., 1978, *Power Politics*

Wight, M., 1991, *International Theory: The Three Traditions*

Wilkinson, D., 1987, 'Central civlization', *Comparative Civilizations Review* 22, 31–59

Wilkinson, D., 1992, 'Cities, civilizations and oikumenes I', *Comparative Civilizations Review* 27, 51–87

Wilkinson, D., 1993, 'Cities, civilizations and oikumenes II', *Comparative Civilizations Review* 28, 41–72

Wilkinson, D., 1993, 'Civilizations, cores, world economies, and oikumenes', in A. G. Frank and B. K. Gills (eds), *The World System: Five Hundred Years or Five Thousand?*, 221–246

Williams, P. and Black, S., 1994, 'Transnational threats: drug trafficking and weapons proliferation', *Contemporary Security Policy* 15, 127–51

Williamson, O. E., 1967, 'Hierarchical control and optimum firm-size',

Journal of Political Economy 75, 123–38

Williamson, O. E. (ed.), 1995, *Organization Theory*, 2nd edn

Wilson, C., 1976, *The Transformation of Europe 1558–1648*

Wilson, E. O., 1975, *Sociobiology: The New Synthesis*, Cambridge, MA

Wilson, E. O., 1978, *On Human Nature*, Cambridge, MA

Wilson, P., 1989, 'The English School of international relations: a reply to Sheila Grader', *Review of International Studies* 15.1, 49–58

Wirsing, R., 1973, 'Political power and information: a cross–cultural study', *American Anthropologist* 75, 147–78

Witt, U., 1993, *Evolutionary Economics*

Wittek, P., 1938, *The Rise of the Ottoman Empire*

Wohlforth, W. C., 1995, 'Realism and the end of the Cold War', *International Security* 19, 91–129

Wolf, E. R., 1982, *Europe and the People Without History*, Berkeley and Los Angeles

Wood, I., 1994, *The Merovingian Kingdoms 450–751*

Woods, N., 1996, 'The uses of theory in the study of international relations', in N. Woods (ed.), 1996, *Explaining International Relations Since 1945*, New York, 9–31

Woolf, G., 1990, 'World-systems analysis and the Roman Empire', *Journal of Roman Archaeology* 3, 44–58

Woosang, K., 1992, 'Power transitions and great power war from Westphalia to Waterloo', *World Politics* 45, 153–72

Worden, N. 1994, *The Making of Modern South Africa*

Worsley, P., 1990, 'Models of the modern world system', *Theory, Culture and Society* 7.2–3, 83–96

Wright, H., 1984, 'Prestate political formations', in T. Earle (ed.), *On the Evolution of Complex Societies*, Malibu, 41–77

Wright, L. E. and White, C. D., 1996, 'Human biology in the Classic Maya collapse: evidence from palaeopathology and palaeodiet', *Journal of World Prehistory* 10.2, 147–98

Wriston, W. B., 1992, *The Twilight of Sovereignty: How the Information Revolution is Transforming our World*, New York

Yates, F. E., 1987, *Self-organizing Systems*, New York

Yesner, D., 1980, 'Maritime hunter-gatherers: ecology and prehistory', *Current Anthropology* 21, 727–50

Yodzis, P., 1989, *Introduction to Theoretical Ecology*, New York

Yorke, B., 1990, *Kings and Kingdoms of Early Anglo-Saxon England*

Young, O., 1978, 'Anarchy and social choice: reflections on the international polity', *World Politics* 30, 241–63

Young, O., 1986, 'International regimes: toward a new theory of institutions', *World Politics* 39, 115–7

Young, O., 1991, 'Political leadership and regime formation: on the development of institutions in international society', *International Organization* 43.5, 281–308

Young, R., 1990, *White Mythologies: Writing History and the West*

Yurdusev, A. N., 1993, 'Level of analysis and unit of analysis: a case for distinction', *Millennium* 22.1, 77–88

Zacher, M. W., 1992, 'The decaying pillars of the Westphalian temple: implications for international order and governance', in J. N. Rosenau and E-O. Czempiel (eds), *Governance Without Government: Order and Change in World Politics*, 58–101

Zacher, M. W. and Matthew, R. A., 1995, 'Liberal international theory: common threads, divergent strands', in C. Kegley (ed.), *Controversies in International Relations Theory*, 107–150

Zacher, M. W. and Sutton, B. A., 1995, *Governing Global Networks*

Zeeman, E. C., 1974, 'On the unstable behavior of stock exchanges', *Journal of Mathematical Economics* 1, 39–49

Zeeman, E. C., 1976, 'Catastrophe theory', *Scientific American* 234, 65–83

Zeeman, E. C., 1980, 'Catastrophe models in administration', *Association for Institutional Research: Annual Forum Proceedings* 3, 9–24

Zeeman, E. C., 1982, 'Decision making and evolution', in C. Renfrew, M. J. Rowlands and B. A. Segraves (eds), *Theory and Explanation in Archaeology*, New York and London, 315–46

Zey, M. (ed.), 1992, *Decision Making*, Newbury Park, CA

Zhongshu, W., 1982, *Han Civilization*

Zinnes, D. A. and Gillespie, J. V., 1976, *Mathematical Models in International Relations*, New York

Zolberg, A. R., 1981, 'Origins of the modern world-system: a missing link', *World Politics* 33.2, 253–81

Zucker, L. G., 1991, 'The role of institutionalization in cultural persistence', in W. W. Powell and P. J. Di Maggio (eds), *The New Institutionalism in Organizational Analysis*, Chicago, 83–107

Zuiderhout, R. W. L., 1990, 'Chaos and the dynamics of self-organization', *Human Systems Management* 9, 225–38

Zukin, S. and Di Maggio, P., 1990, *Structures of Capital: The Social Organization of the Economy*

Zysman, J., 1994, 'How institutions create historically rooted trajectories of growth', *Industrial and Corporate Change* 3, 243–83

Index

References to figures are shown in italics.